A PORTRAIT OF CROATIA

Croatia forms a meeting point between the Mediterranean and central Europe, and between the Alps and the Pannonian Plain. Its relatively small territory is made up of a wide variety of landscapes. A stun⸺ ⸺autiful country, it is slowly re-emerging from the ⸺ ⸺ of conflict and regaining its role as a popula⸺

Croatia seceded from the Federal Socialist Repub⸺ of Yugoslavia in following the first elections since World II. However, the bruta conflict that quickly followed had disastrous effects on the economy and led to the damage and destruction of many historic monuments and treasures. The United Nations administered disputed territories until 1995, and the last region, Eastern Slavonia, was returned to Croatian administration only in January 1998.

The resolution of the conflict recreated a country which had lost its autonomy long ago in 1102, when Croatian nobles handed the vacant crown to King Koloman. Under Koloman, Croatia became part of Hungary and remained so

⸺tional flag of Croatia

years, until 1918. ⸺ end of World War I, ⸺roatia declared independence but, under pressure from greater powers, agreed to become part of the kingdom of Yugoslavia. From the ruins of the Habsburg empire emerged Yugoslavia: a new state of Serbs, Croatians and Slovenes.

Few people live in the steep mountainous areas and as a result the forests of this region, among the most beautiful in southern Europe, are unspoilt. The coast and larger islands are more densely populated and the income from tourism is important to many. The political upheavals of the last decade of the 20th century have caused a shifting of the population and many Serbs have moved away.

Fruit seller on a boat in the port of Mali Lošinj

◁ People strolling along Krešimirova ulica in the busy centre of Split

Fisherman mending his nets in the port of Fažana

POPULATION

According to a census carried out in early 2000 (complete statistics are not yet available), Croatia has a population of 4,535,054, of which 4,381,352 are resident. Compared with the census of 1991 there has been a 5.2 per cent fall in the population and a 7 per cent decrease in those resident. These figures, a reflection of the upheavals of the 1990s, reduce the numbers to 1968 levels. Two different factors were responsible for these changes. Firstly, the departure of about 400,000 Serbians (partially offset by the return of Croatians resident in other parts of former Yugoslavia), and secondly, the emigration of many young people in search of work in other countries in Europe, America or Australia.

The tragic events of the 1990s have also altered the distribution of the population, emptying villages and concentrating populations in large urban centres. Changes to the size of many towns and cities, the result of enlarging their territorial boundaries, make detailed analysis difficult, particularly with regard to Zagreb, Rijeka, Split, Osijek and Zadar, where the population appears to have nearly doubled.

Woman in the typical costume of Konavle

ECONOMY

Manufacturing industries are concentrated in the larger cities and employ 20 per cent of the population. The service industry is being overhauled and provides employment for an increasing number of workers, mainly in the tourist sector, which has recovered after a decade of crisis: 7 per cent of the population is employed in this area. Demand for fresh fish to supply the tourist resorts means that the fishing industry has revived and mussel farming has also expanded, in particular along the Limski Channel and around Ston. The privatization of much agricultural land, and the introduction of modern machinery and the rationalization of crops, have reduced the number of farm workers. However, the production of fruit and wine grapes has recovered, and overall quality is improving.

The urgent need to rebuild public and privately-owned buildings damaged during the recent conflict and the increasing need for tourist facilities keeps the numbers employed in the building trade high: 7 per cent of the work force. However, in spite of an improved standard of living for most of the population, unemployment is still high. Croatia hopes to resolve most of its employment problems by joining the European Union, and by providing land, energy and labour at competitive costs. The building of a modern road network with the construction of new motorways, the modernization of the railways and plans to improve the ports will also help to alleviate high unemployment levels.

TRADITIONS AND CUSTOMS

Since the rebirth of the Croatian state, all kinds of traditional festivals have reappeared. These festivals, ceremonies or games commemorate historical, religious and military events. Some festivals are expressions of primitive or ancient faith, and mix Christianity with ancient pagan rites, others are linked to the religious calendar. Traditional costumes and jewellery, carefully preserved by the older generation, are worn on these occasions. The materials may sometimes be new but the designs stay faithfully traditional.

Other expressions of popular culture are the rites linked to the rhythms of farming: harvesting, bringing flocks down from the mountains, felling trees. The Feast of St Blaise, the patron saint of Dubrovnik, is magnificent. People from local and surrounding parishes gather, dressed in splendid costumes and displaying ancient banners in honour of the saint. Even the communists were unable to suppress this tradition. Another spectacular festivity is the Olympics of Ancient Sports in Brođanci, when young people parade in gold-embroidered costumes, followed by groups of musicians. Other important events are the Festival of the Bumbari in Vodnjan with its donkey race, the

One of many religious events in Split

Folk Festival in Đakovo and the Moreška and Kumpanija festivals in Korčula, commemorating battles against the Ottoman Turks.

LANGUAGE

The attempt to fuse the Croatian and Serbian languages lasted more than a century, but in 1991 the official language of Croatia became Croatian, and this is now part of the constitution. The language has always been a fundamental part of Croatian identity, even under foreign domination. The people continue to use three basic dialects, štokavski in southern and eastern Croatia, čakavski in Istria and parts of Dalmatia, and kajkavski in Zagreb and the north. A dialect similar to Venetian is spoken along the coast.

RELIGION

Religious feeling has always been important to Croatians. Religion was relegated to a secondary role during the communist period but the great sanctuaries are once again centres of spirituality. In the 1991 census, almost 90 per cent declared they were Christian (77 per cent Catholic, 11 per cent Orthodox), with a Muslim minority, mostly Bosnians, and a Protestant minority, mostly Hungarians. The Orthodox community has shrunk due to the fall in the number of Serbians.

The lively centre of Split, a popular meeting place

The Landscape and Wildlife of Croatia

A wide variety of landscapes can be found in Croatia, from wild uninhabited craggy gorges to steep river valleys and a stunningly beautiful indented coastline stretching into the lower Adriatic, dotted with hundreds of islands. A plateau stretches from the Istrian peninsula towards Gorski Kotar and ends in the hilly vine-growing region of Zagorje. The geological formations produced by the porous limestone terrain called karst are found in Gorski Kotar and continue to nearby Istria and the Velebit mountains, where the combination of wind, rain and rock has created strange shapes called *kukovi*. Nicknames and legends have been created by folklore for these rock formations, and for the thousands of rocky islands off the coast, remnants of an ancient mountain chain.

Seagull perched on a rocky outcrop near the island of Pag

MOUNTAINS

Mountains form 40 per cent of Croatia and rise to nearly 2,000 m (6,560 ft) high. The higher land is given over to sheep farming and the breeding of livestock. The forests are mixed, with pine, fir, chestnut and beech, depending on altitude and microclimate. The wildlife includes bears, wolves, wild boar, lynxes, badgers, foxes, roebucks and chamois. Forestry management aims to control deforestation.

The forests *are a precious resource in Croatia. Thick vegetation covers more than 30 per cent of the country.*

The chamois *was thought to have disappeared from Croatia but there are now a dozen or so animals originating from Slovenia.*

THE PLAIN

The plain is bordered by wide rivers which also define Croatia's borders for much of their length. The vast Pannonian Plain is the breadbasket of Croatia. Maize, wheat, soya and tobacco are grown here and at the fringes are vine-covered hills. At one time there were forests here, dominated by the Slavonian oak, much sought-after in Europe for the quality of its wood. A few isolated remnants of these forests can still be seen.

The oak of Slavonia, *famous since ancient times, was used to build most of the ships in the Venetian and Dubrovnik fleets, because of its extraordinary strength.*

The Croatian plain *is one of the most fertile areas in Europe. Some agricultural produce is exported.*

NATIONAL PARKS

Croatia began protecting wildlife areas of particular importance in 1949 by setting up the Plitvice Lakes National Park on the Lika plateau. A few years later, the Risnjak National Park was founded north of Rijeka, followed by the Krka National Park north of Šibenik. The Paklenica National Park, at the heart of the Velebit mountain chain, dates from 1959. In 1978 it was declared a world biosphere reserve by UNESCO and later included in the World Heritage List. It is home to over 2,400 species of plant. There are four national parks in the Adriatic: the Mljet National Park, founded in 1949, the Kornati National Park (1980), the Brijuni National Park (1983) and the new North Velebit National Park. There are also nature reserves, oases, biotopes (environments characterized by particular conditions) and two marshes: Kopački Rit and Lonjsko Polje. This conservation policy has been richly rewarded as these reserves form some of the country's greatest tourist attractions.

Risnjak National Park with its thick forests of fir and beech

THE COAST

The coast's appearance is determined by the extent of its exposure to the fierce, northeast bora wind. Mediterranean flora flourishes on the sheltered side, with olives, lemon trees and vines. Low-growing vines are cultivated along the central part of the coast and on some of the islands, sheltered from the wind by stone walls. Two common plants along the coast and on the islands are lavender, particularly on Hvar, and broom.

The marine life *is extraordinarily varied, with a wide range of species including sea-horses.*

Broom *is a common sight in Croatia. In spring, it bears bright yellow flowers.*

LAKES AND RIVERS

The lakes of Croatia are not large, but some are truly spectacular, as for example those of Plitvice and those formed by the River Krka. The rivers are another of Croatia's valuable resources. The Danube, Drava, Sava, Kupa and Mura are all navigable and form international transport routes (although traffic is currently partly interrupted). The rivers abound with a variety of fish and are a big attraction for fishing enthusiasts.

Waterlilies *are in flower in late spring, particularly in Lonjsko Polje and Kopački Rit.*

Storks *live near the rivers as well as in protected nature reserves in Croatia. The wetlands make an ideal habitat for the rare black stork.*

Art and Artists in Croatia

For centuries Croatian art has combined elements from eastern and western Europe. The coast was ruled by Venice for 400 years, and between the Middle Ages and the 17th century, Croatia was in regular contact with the other side of the Adriatic. Italian artists came to the islands to work, and the Dalmatians crossed the sea and brought Romanesque, Gothic and Renaissance styles back to their country. After the expulsion of the Turks at the end of the 17th century, many churches were rebuilt in the Baroque style, and acquired rich ornamentation. The 20th century saw the advent of Naive painting, an important artistic trend, and sculptor Ivan Meštrović was confirmed as Croatia's most famous contemporary artist *(see p157).*

Maria Banac, **sculpture by Ivan Meštrović**

SCULPTURE

The art of sculpture in Croatia has ancient origins and may have been inspired by the local stone, used to construct some of the most important Roman monuments in Pula and Split, which became models for future generations of Adriatic sculptors.

Sculpture and stone carving reached the height of expression with the Romanesque style. Dating from this time are the cathedral doors of Trogir and Split, the rose windows of Zadar and Rab, the capitals in the cloisters in Dubrovnik and Zadar, and much church statuary. The technical skills of the Renaissance period are documented in Šibenik cathedral, with masterpieces by Juraj Dalmatinac, Nikola Firentinac and Andrija Aleši.

The stonemasons should also be remembered, particularly those of Korčula. Decades of skilled work went into Korčula cathedral and the masons' work can be seen in hundreds of other towns and cities in Croatia.

Sculpture again reached a peak in the 20th century with Ivan Meštrović, the chief figure in a group of great artists which included Antun Augustinčić.

ANDREA BUVINA

All that is known of this sculptor is that he was born

Wooden panel by Andrea Buvina in Split cathedral

in Split and lived in the 13th century. The great door of the cathedral of his native city is testament to his skill. This masterpiece from 1214 consists of 28 wooden panels depicting the life of Christ, and uses simple lines allied to a wealth of detail.

MASTER RADOVAN

The sculptor Master Radovan was of Dalmatian origin and lived in the 13th century. His name appears on the door of

The door of the cathedral of Trogir by Master Radovan

the cathedral in Trogir, which he started in about 1240 and which was later completed by other artists. This complex masterpiece has columns, arches, sculpted relief figures and rich decoration. It is possible to discern scenes from the life of Christ such as the Annunciation, the Flight to Egypt, and the Martyrdom on Golgotha, while other sculptures represent the months of the year. The artist's expressive skill is revealed in the figures of Adam and Eve in particular.

JURAJ DALMATINAC

Juraj Dalmatinac, also known as Giorgio Orsini, was an ambassador for Dalmatian art, which was greatly influenced by Venice. The artist was born in Zadar in about 1400 and died in 1475. He was active in Dalmatia and in Italy as a sculptor and an architect.

Face by Dalmatinac in the cathedral of Šibenik

The cathedral of St James in Šibenik *(see pp108–9)*, to which he contributed, is regarded as one of the masterpieces of the Croatian Renaissance. Dalmatinac sculpted the faces in the upper part of the base of the apses and also the statues of Adam and Eve at either side of the Door of Lions.

ARTISTS

Painting in Croatia cannot boast a history equal to that of sculpture since it was only after contact with the Venetian school at the end of the 16th century that Croatian painting emerged in Istria and Dalmatia. The monasteries and cathedrals commissioned Venetian masters to make altarpieces and in emulating these models the great artists of Dubrovnik developed.

In the late 17th–18th centuries, the Baroque style predominated in inland Croatia in architecture as well as art. Baroque originated in German-speaking areas and inspired local artists; the Austrian artist Ivan Ranger *(see p206)* was a key figure. Interest in religious paintings then dwindled, and in the 19th century, young artists were inspired by pan-European culture. In the 1930s and 40s Naive Art developed.

Polyptych by Lovro Dobričević in the church of St Mary of Dance

VINCENT OD KASTAV

One of the most expressive cycles of frescoes in Istria bears the signature of this Istrian painter, Vincent od Kastav (Vincenzo da Castua), who lived in the 15th century. The frescoes are hidden away in the small church of St Mary (Sv. Marija na Škriljinah) in Beram. The brightly coloured frescoes, on the side walls and the inside façade, were painted in about 1471 with assistants and have a primitive but vigorous style. The *Life of Christ and the Virgin* has figures of saints; the best-known work is the *Dance of Death,* where Death, holding a scythe, punishes sinners, here represented by all the most powerful

Dance of Death **by Vincent od Kastav**

people on earth (from the pope to lords of the manor).

LOVRO DOBRIČEVIĆ

Little is known of Lovro Marinov Dobričević (Lorenzo De Boninis), pupil of Paolo Veneziano, who lived in the 15th century and is regarded as one of the most significant exponents of the Dubrovnik school. Two of his great works are in Dubrovnik: the *Baptism of Christ* (c.1448) is in the Dominican Museum and the polyptych *Virgin, Christ and the Saints Julian and Nicholas* (1465) is in the church of St Mary of Dance (Sv. Marije na Dančama).

JULIJE KLOVI

Julije Klovi (Giulio Clovio) was one of the most famous Renaissance miniaturists. A native of Croatia (he was born in Grižane in 1498), his most significant works are found outside the country. The painter developed his craft in Venice, and was then summoned to work in Rome, Mantua, Perugia and numerous monasteries. He died in Rome in 1578.

Miniature by Klovi

THE HLEBINE SCHOOL

Krsto Hegedušić (1901–75), Expressionist painter and later a Naive artist, founded a group of artists called Zemlja ("Earth"). He encouraged the work of two amateur painters from the village of Hlebine, near Koprivnica: Ivan Generalić and Franjo Mraz, who depicted their local world on glass and canvas in fresh, vivid style. Together with Mirko Virius they founded the Hlebine school which flourished from 1930 to the beginning of World War

Woodcutters **by Generalić, Museum of Naive Art, Zagreb**

II. Many other painters, including Ivan Večenaj, Dragan Gaži, Franjo Filipović and Josip Generalić, followed their ideas, concentrating on depicting the lives of outcasts, the poor, and working folk. The Hlebine school became a world-wide phenomenon with the 1952 Venice Biennale and exhibitions in Brazil and Brussels. Naive works are on show at the Hlebine Gallery in Koprivnica and the Museum of Naive Art in Zagreb.

Architecture in Croatia

Croatian architecture, like its art, has also been influenced by Croatia's position in Europe. Secular and religious buildings display a fusion of elements from nearby Italy and Germany and other forms originating in the Byzantine or Slavic worlds. This blending of influences was first noticeable in the time of the Romans and still continues today. Some styles became particularly important: for example the impressive cathedrals of the Adriatic coast, the legacy of many centuries of Venetian rule. In inland Croatia Baroque architecture prevails, characterized by exuberant decoration and expansive forms.

The Byzantine basilica of Euphrasius in Poreč

PRE-ROMANESQUE AND ROMANESQUE

True Croatian architecture begins with pre-Romanesque and dates back to the time of Duke Branimir (879–92), who created the first state of Croatia. Contact with the Byzantine world influenced the look of religious buildings in Istria and Dalmatia but some decorative elements reveal the first signs of Romanesque: small churches with irregular ground-plans appear in areas inhabited by Croatian tribes. The founding of Šibenik (1066) saw the first Romanesque buildings, introduced by the Cistercians. The style spread and remained popular until the end of the 16th century, and three-aisle cathedrals with apses were built as well as monasteries with cloisters, public buildings, town halls and loggias.

The façade consists of vertical and horizontal lines: the upper order is decorated with blind arcades and rose windows.

Romanesque rose window

The arched main door, richly decorated

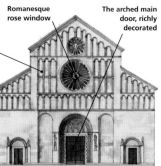

The cathedral of St Anastasia in Zadar (see p94), *founded in the 9th century but rebuilt in the 12th–13th, shows the links between Croatian and Italian Romanesque, particularly in the façade, similar to churches found in Pisa and Lucca in Italy.*

The church of the Holy Cross in Nin (see p100), *one of the most interesting examples of pre-Romanesque, and also Croatia's first cathedral, was built in the 9th century. It has a Greek cross ground-plan with three apses. It is positioned to ensure that the sun's rays fall in pre-planned positions on the floor and act as a clock.*

GOTHIC

The Gothic style, more than any other in Croatia, is lasting evidence of the long rule of the Venetians along the Istrian and Dalmatian coasts. It developed following the Venetian conquest of the Adriatic coast (1420) and is a fundamental expression of the close contact that was established. Venetian Gothic not only influenced the design of Dalmatian and Istrian churches but also mansions in Pula, Rab, Pag, Zadar, Šibenik and Split.

The door with an ogival arch is decorated with thin spiral columns and has two lions on the corbel.

Rose window

Façade of the Town Hall in Split

The cathedral of St Mark in Korčula (see p132) *is of Romanesque origins – the bell tower is evidence of this. The façade shows similarities with churches in Puglia in southern Italy. Gothic elements include the pointed arches over the entrance door, which was the work of Bonino of Milan.*

RENAISSANCE

The Renaissance style was only able to develop in those parts of the country which did not fall under Turkish rule. The most important architects and artists of the time were Juraj Dalmatinac *(see p20)*, Nikola Firentinac and Andrija Aleši, who worked mainly along the Adriatic coast. They were all involved in the construction of churches and public buildings. The cathedral of St James in Šibenik *(see pp108–9)* became a model for the churches of St Stephen in Hvar, St Mary in Zadar and St Saviour in Dubrovnik. Renaissance buildings also appeared in the north of Croatia, both in the form of private residences (Varaždin and Čakovec) and castles (Trakošćan and Veliki Tabor).

The second storey, with windows and a statue of the city's patron saint, St Blaise, in the centre, was a later addition.

The windows in Venetian Gothic symbolize the ties between Dubrovnik and Venice.

Sponza Palace in Dubrovnik (see p144) *has both Gothic and Renaissance elements, a reflection of the time it took to build. It was begun in 1312 (the beautiful Gothic windows on the first floor date from this period) and remodelled in 1516–22, when the Renaissance arcaded loggia on the ground floor was added.*

BAROQUE

This was the style that characterized the legitimization of Christian worship in Croatia after the expulsion of the Turks at the end of the 17th century. The signs of Ottoman rule were eradicated and architects, mainly of German extraction, constructed public and private buildings, enriching them with ornate decorations equal to those of the churches, castles and sanctuaries. The most notable examples of the Baroque style can be found in Varaždin, Požega, Osijek, Križevci, Ludbreg and Krapina.

Vojković-Oršić Palace, *now home of the Croatian Historical Museum* (see p158), *is one of many fine Baroque buildings in Zagreb. The façade and interior have the sumptuous decorations of the time with elegant columns, scalloped windows and a decorated tympanum.*

MODERNISM

By the 19th century Zagreb had become the centre of political and cultural life in Croatia, which gave it a prominent role as leader in the architectural field. Much experimentation took place in the following century in the capital, inspired first by the Viennese Secession style and later by Modernism. The church of St Blaise and Villa Krauss are interesting examples of the latter style.

The Neo-Renaissance Mimara Museum in Zagreb

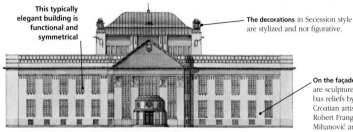

This typically elegant building is functional and symmetrical

The decorations in Secession style are stylized and not figurative.

On the façade are sculptures and bas reliefs by the Croatian artists Robert Frangeš-Mihanović and Rudolf Valdec.

The former National and University Library *in the centre of Marulić Square in Zagreb was designed by a local architect, Rudolf Lubinsky. It is regarded as the most significant work in the Secession style in Croatia.*

CROATIA THROUGH THE YEAR

The upheavals of the decade from 1991–2000 inevitably affected the calendar of events which characterizes the cultural life of Croatia. However, concerts, theatre seasons and sporting events have now largely been resumed along with religious festivals and events linked to local traditions. The different stages in the agricultural year, such as the grape

Typical costume of Pag

harvest, the threshing, fishing or hunting seasons, are also marked. In addition, every town celebrates its patron saint's day and the "town's day", which is linked to episodes in the town's history. Zagreb offers a rich calendar of cultural events all through the year, while the festivals in the towns and villages along the coast are generally held during the summer season.

SPRING

The arrival of spring in Croatia coincides with a series of important dates in the religious calendar. Spring brings warmer weather and also sees the beginning of a series of festivals and events which continue throughout the summer. Catholic churches are especially busy around Easter time, with its associated rituals.

Procession during Holy Week on the island of Korčula

MARCH

Holy Week *(Easter)*. On Korčula Easter is celebrated with processions of brotherhoods performing mystery plays and singing.

APRIL

Sonnet Day of Hanibal Lucić, Hvar *(mid-Apr)*. Poetry reading dedicated to the

great 16th-century local poet. European and Croatian poets participate.
Musical Biennial of Zagreb *(second half of Apr)*. Festival of modern music.
St George's Day, Senj *(23 Apr)*.
St Vincent's Day, Korčula *(28 Apr)*. The Kumpanija dance which commemorates an ancient battle between enemy armies is performed. At the finale local girls in costume dance in a circle.

MAY

Regatta Rovinj–Pesaro–Rovinj, Rovinj.
Meeting of Puppet Theatres, Osijek *(early May)*. Performances of professional and amateur puppet theatre companies.
Tournament of Rab *(9 May)*. Parade of costumed riders with crossbows.
Festival of the Small Theatre, Rijeka *(first half of May)*. Groups from all over Europe participate.
Josip Štolcer Slavenski Memorial, Čakovec *(first half of May)*. Musical festival dedicated to the great 20th-century Croatian composer.
Festival of Croatian Tambour Music, Osijek *(mid-May)*. Festival of ancient music with period instruments, including the tambour.
International Choir Competition, Zadar *(end May)*. Groups from all over Europe participate.

Festival of Amateur Film and Video, Požega *(end May)*. Screenings of short amateur films and videos.

SUMMER

As this is the season when most tourists visit Croatia, particularly Istria and Dalmatia, this is also the period when the calendar of events is busiest. There are festivals dedicated to music, theatre and dance, as well as many traditional festivals. The folk festivals held throughout the summer are particularly colourful events.

JUNE

Pula Opera Festival, Pula *(all summer)*. Opera season in the Roman amphitheatre.
Festival of the Harmony of Dalmatia, Omiš. Celebration of ancient and traditional folk songs and music.
Brodsko Kolo, Slavonski Brod *(mid-Jun)*. Displays of folk dancing in costume, shows and exhibitions of regional produce.

The festival of Brodsko Kolo, Slavonski Brod

AVERAGE DAILY HOURS OF SUNSHINE

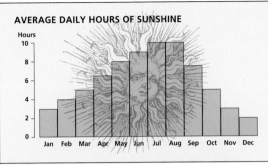

Hours: 10, 8, 6, 4, 2, 0

Jan Feb Mar Apr May Jun Jul Aug Sep Oct Nov Dec

Sunshine
The Dalmatian coast is one of the sunniest parts of Europe, and the island of Hvar holds the record with its 2,700 hours of sun a year. The summers along the coast are hot and dry, while the inland areas have a continental climate with hot summers and cold winters.

Đjakovski Vezovi, a folklore and embroidery festival in Đakovo

International Youth Festival of Music, Grožnjan *(mid-Jun–mid-Sep)*. Young artists from every country participate, not just musicians.

Summer Festival, Hvar *(second half of Jun–end Sep)*. Music, theatre, folklore and dancing.

Summer of Margherita, Bakar *(last week of Jun)*. Concerts and performances in the čakavski dialect.

International Children's Festival, Šibenik *(end Jun–beginning Jul)*. Festival dedicated to the creativity of the very young. Music, dance, theatre and film.

JULY

Labin Summer Festival, Labin *(Jul–Aug)*. Classical concerts, folk music.

Concerts in the Basilica of Euphrasius, Poreč *(Jul–mid Sep)*. Performances of church and secular music given by Croatian and European musicians.

Dance Week, Zagreb *(beginning Jul)*. International festival of dance, movement and mime, organized in collaboration with European associations.

Tournament of Rab *(20 Jul)*. A re-enactment of a tournament with riders in costume and crossbow contests. The tournament is also held in May.

Music Festival, Zadar *(beginning Jul–beginning Aug)*. Church, theatre and instrumental music.

Đakovski Vezovi, Đakovo *(first week of Jul)*. Folklore displays and exhibition of local embroidery.

Festival of Satire, Zagreb *(first half of Jul)*. International festival celebrating the satirical.

Osor Music Festival, Osor *(mid-Jul–mid-Aug)*. Chamber music.

Split Summer *(mid-Jul–mid-Aug)*. A programme of opera, concerts, dance, theatre and performances of the first plays written in the Croatian language.

International Festival of Theatre, Pula *(mid-Jul–mid-Aug)*. Multimedia festival with the participation of other European groups.

Dubrovnik Summer Festival, Dubrovnik *(mid-Jul–end Aug)*. The oldest international festival in Croatia: music, theatre, folklore, ballet, with performers from many countries.

Krk Summer Festival, Krk *(mid-Jul–end Aug)*. Music and prose, concerts, ballet, performances by young artists and folklore.

St Theodore's Day, Korčula *(27 Jul)*. The Moreška, a dance re-enacting a battle between Christians and Muslims.

International Tennis Tournament, Umag *(end Jul)*.

Pag Carnival, Pag *(last day of Jul)*. Traditional dancing, *kolo*, and various shows with the local people in traditional costumes.

International Folklore Festival, Zagreb *(end Jul)*. Croatian music and dance with international guests.

The Moreška dance, St Theodore's Day, Korčula

AVERAGE MONTHLY RAINFALL

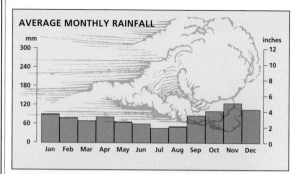

mm		inches
300		12
240		10
180		8
120		6
60		4
		2
0		0

Jan Feb Mar Apr May Jun Jul Aug Sep Oct Nov Dec

Rainfall
Rain is sparse along the coast, particularly in summer, when there is often the threat of drought. However, in the mountains, rain and snow are plentiful. In northeastern parts of the country there may be summer thunderstorms. Winter brings snow.

Costumed jousters on horseback during the folk festival, Sinj

AUTUMN

Visiting Croatia in this season means there are fewer crowds, even along the busy Adriatic coast. However this season also offers an unexpectedly rich and varied calendar of events. Many of the events are cultural but there are also several festivals celebrating wine and food – offering an ideal opportunity to discover some of the local produce of this country.

AUGUST

Summer Carnival, Novi Vinodolski *(Aug)*.
Festival of the Bumbari, Vodnjan *(Aug)*. "Bumbari" is what the local people call themselves. A folk festival in costume with an unusual donkey race and the preparation of *crostoli*, cakes of Venetian origin.
Olympics of Ancient Sports, Brodanci *(Aug)*. Folk festival with traditional costumes and musicians playing in the streets.
Mediterranean Symposium of Sculpture, Labin *(Aug–Sep)*. A meeting place for artists from all over the world since the 1960s.
Baljanska Noć, Bale *(first Sun in Aug)*. Festival of the city.
Trka na prstenac, Barban *(first Sun in Aug)*. Jousting tournament, dating back as far as 1696.

Sinjska Alka, Sinj *(beginning Aug)*. Folklore festival commemorating victory over the Turks, with jousting competitions for horse riders. Parades, dancing, folk music and displays of regional produce.
St Roch's Day, Žrnovo and Postrana (on Korčula) *(16 Aug)*. Events include the Mostra, a traditional sword dance. At one time the festivities ended with the sacrifice of an ox.

Festival of Vinkovačke Jeseni, Vinkovci

SEPTEMBER

International Doll Festival, Zagreb *(beginning Sep)*.
Vinkovačke Jeseni, Vinkovci *(Sep–Oct)*. Festival of music and folk traditions. Parades in costume.
Rovinj Art Programme, Rovinj *(second half of Sep)*. Multimedia festival with the participation of international artists.
Baroque Evenings in Varaždin, Varaždin cathedral *(second half of Sep–first half of Oct)*. Festival of Baroque music with the participation of top Croatian and European musicians.
Grape Festival, Buje *(last Sun in Sep)*.
Festival of New Cinema, Dubrovnik *(end Sep–beginning Oct)*. The presentation of new films and videos by amateur filmmakers.
Lace Exhibition, Lepoglava *(Sep)*.

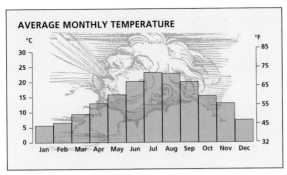

AVERAGE MONTHLY TEMPERATURE

°C / °F — Jan Feb Mar Apr May Jun Jul Aug Sep Oct Nov Dec

Temperature
The climate in Croatia is typically Mediterranean along the coast, with mild winters and hot, dry summers. Inland the climate is continental with hot summers and cold winters. The mountainous areas have an alpine climate.

Exhibition of traditional hand-made lace, still made according to ancient methods.

OCTOBER

Dora Pejačević Memorial, Našice *(Oct)*. Music festival commemorating this composer, with concerts, performances by artists and competitions.
Bela Nedeja, Kastav *(first Sun in Oct)*. Wine festival.
Maronada, Lovran *(first Sun in Oct)*. Chestnut festival.
Triennial of Ceramics, Zagreb *(mid-Oct–mid-Nov)*. Ceramics festival.

NOVEMBER

International Music Festival, Pula *(first half of Nov)*. Musicians from all over the world come to participate in this music festival.

The Town's Day, Lipik *(4 Nov)*. Traditional festival celebrating the town.

WINTER

The cold makes itself felt throughout Croatia, with the temperatures in Zagreb and Slavonia dropping well below freezing point and the cold bora wind sweeping across Istria and Dalmatia. But Croatians still love to go out and enjoy themselves and attend cultural events.

DECEMBER

The Town's Day, Osijek *(2 Dec)*. Celebration of Osijek's main feast day with music and dancing.

JANUARY

International Competition for Young Pianists, Osijek *(second half of Jan)*. For young musicians under 21.

FEBRUARY

Shrovetide Sezona, Kraljevica. Traditional masked ball.
Carnival of Rijeka, Rijeka. Colourful parade in elaborate costumes.
Carnival of the Riviera, Opatija.
International Competition for Young Violinists, Zagreb *(first half of Feb)*. For violinists under 30.
Carnival, Lastovo.
Feast of St Blaise, Dubrovnik *(2 Feb)*. Processions celebrating town's saint.

Costume at the Carnival of Lastovo

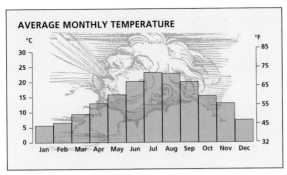

A Baroque music ensemble playing in the cathedral, Varaždin

CROATIAN HOLIDAYS

New Year's Day 1 Jan
Epiphany 6 Jan
Easter Sunday and Monday Mar or Apr
Labour Day 1 May
Anti-Fascist Victory Day 22 Jun
Statehood Day 25 July
Victory and National Thanksgiving Day 5 Aug
Assumption Day 15 Aug
Independence Day 8 October
All Saints' Day 1 Nov
Christmas 25 Dec
Boxing Day 26 Dec

THE HISTORY OF CROATIA

*S*ituated between eastern and western Europe, Croatia has long been a land of passage but also a point of contact between different worlds and cultures. Diverse events and cultural influences have all contributed to the country's history. Croatia is particularly proud of its close ties to the West; for more than a century, parts of the country struggled to free themselves from harsh Turkish domination. The history of Croatia goes back almost as far as man's first appearance on earth.

PREHISTORY

Early in the 19th century ancient human remains were found at Krapina in the north of Croatia. Dating from the Neanderthal period, "Krapina man" places human presence in Croatia in the middle-Palaeolithic. Other traces of prehistoric cultures have been found in Croatia. The richest site is probably Vučedol, near Vukovar, where the Neolithic "Vučedol Dove" *(see p188)* was found.

Clay vase found in Vučedol, 2800–2500 BC

THE ILLYRIANS

Around 1200 BC, tribes of Indo-European origin settled on the Pannonian Plain, the larger islands and along the coast. The tribes had different names (Istrians, Liburnians, Dalmatians, Japods) depending on where they settled, but the area was known under one name, Illyria. They traded amber and had dealings with other Mediterranean people and northern European traders. Traces of ancient walls on some hilltops confirm their presence.

THE CELTS

In the 4th century BC, the Celts began to search for new lands when Gaul became over-populated. Some tribes followed the River Danube to the present-day Bohemia, some went as far as the Greek border. In the same period the Greeks founded fortified colonies on some Dalmatian islands including Vis and Hvar and in the area of Trogir and Salona. Greek historians claim the Celts fought against Alexander the Great in 335 BC on the southern banks of the Danube. A century later, they attacked Delphi and on their return stopped at the Paludes Volcae, an area between the rivers Sava, Drava and Danube. These people were called Scordisci and mixed with the Illyrians. The Celts and Illyrians were defeated by the Romans in the 2nd century BC. After a number of rebellions, some people were expelled, but those remaining adopted Roman customs and gave Rome no fewer than six Emperors.

TIMELINE

50,000–30,000 BC Homo sapiens neanderthalensis lives at Krapina

Krapina man, dating from the middle-Palaeolithic

1200 BC Illyrian settlement in the Balkans

279 BC Celts, now settled in the Balkans, defeat the Greeks

6500 BC   3500 BC   500 BC

6000–2500 BC Neolithic: sites of Danilo, Hvar, Butmir

2200-1800 BC Aeneolithic: sites of Lasinje and Vučedol

Bronze cap 7th–6th centuries BC

390 BC Dionysius the Elder of Syracuse captures the island of Vis and founds an administrative post

◁ St Paul and St Blaise, patron saint of Dubrovnik, in a triptych by Nikola Božidarević

THE ROMAN CONQUEST

The Romans conquered Croatia at different times and in different ways. First, they wanted to put an end to attacks on their merchant ships, which were falling into the hands of the Liburnians or the Dalmatians, so they subdued the coastal towns by landing Roman legions transported by the fleet. The first battle took place in 229 BC, when Teuta, the queen of the Illyrians, put to death a Roman ambassador who had tried to persuade her to put an end to the acts of piracy. Roman revenge was fierce and the towns of Epidaurum, Lissa and Pharos were attacked, conquered and forced to pay taxes to Rome. However, despite promises to the contrary, acts of piracy continued and Rome decided to deploy its legions based in Aquileia, east of Venice, a fortified town founded in 181 BC.

Symbol of the Roman Empire, Sisak

The legions succeeded in subduing Istria, a process completed by 177 BC. Twenty years later Publius Scipio Nasica inflicted the first defeat on the Dalmatians at Delminium and again on the Dalmatians and the Japods who inhabited the area of the delta of the River Neretva. In 107 BC the Romans defeated the Scordisci and the Illyrians and conquered the town of Segestica (Sisak). In 87 BC another war broke out between the Romans and the Illyrians which lasted for three years and was won by the Romans. In 48 BC the Illyrians sided with Pompey in the fight against Caesar, providing ships and men. Pompey's defeat also at first appeared to be the decisive defeat of the Illyrians. However, many Illyrians, still determined to fight, fled to inland forests not occupied by the Romans. A few decades later, in 6 AD, the Illyrian people staged their greatest united rebellion yet, under the command of Batone. The first battles were won by the Illyrians who soon began to march towards Italy. After three further years of war, the Romans managed to get the better of Batone's exhausted, famished army, thanks to better military organization.

Over the years that followed, Caesar Augustus made the Balkans part of the Roman Empire. After a military campaign waged by Tiberius and completed in AD 12, the Illyrian defences were dismantled and cities were founded, linked by roads wide enough for marching armies. The inhabitants became Roman citizens and were allowed to stand for public office. No fewer than seven Roman emperors were of Illyrian origin, including Septimius Severus, Aurelian, Claudius II, Probus, Diocletian, Valens and Valentinian.

ROMAN ROADS

The roads were the first great public works built by the Romans. They allowed them to move legions

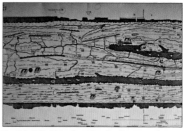

The Tabula Peutingeriana showing Roman roads

TIMELINE

229 BC The Roman army destroys Illyrian forts, subdues the Greek colonies of Lissa and Pharos and forces Illyrians to pay taxes

107 BC Decisive Roman victory over the Scordisci who are driven from the region; Rome owes the victory to Quintus Minucius Rufus

300 BC   **200 BC**   **100 BC**

177 BC The Roman fleet is attacked by Istrians; Rome sends an army which defeats them and drives them out

One of the many Roman fragments from the city of Sisak

119 BC The Dalmatian Lucius Metellus defeats the Scordisci and Dalmatian tribes near Segestica (Sisak); Romans settle in Salona and begin work on the Via Gabina from Salona to Andretium

quickly and in fact the Roman road network remained the principal means of communication in this part of the Balkans for many centuries.

Two important arteries led from Aquileia: one towards the Istrian peninsula to Pula, the other in the direction of Aemona (Ljubljana). The main communication link in Dalmatia began in Aenona (Nin), went on to Zadar and continued, connecting Scardona (Skradin), Tragurium (Trogir), Salona, Narona, Epidaurum (Cavtat) and finally Catarum (Kotor). Other roads branched off inland from this coastal road: the busiest was that from Salona which went towards present-day Bosnia, through Klis and Sinj, near the town of Aequum (Čitluk). Another road followed the river Narenta (Neretva) to Sirmium, the present-day Sremska Mitrovica, which would become one of the capitals of the Roman Empire.

Pula in Roman times, in an engraving from 1819

The inland roads were no less important: these followed the rivers Sava, Drava and the Danube. In the centre of Pannonia, one town which grew in importance was Siscia (Sisak), from which roads led towards Andautonia (Šćitarjevo), Mursa (Osijek), Cuccium (Ilok), Marsonia (Vinkovci) and the thermal spas of Aquae Salissae (Daruvar), Aquae Valissae (Lipik) and Aquae Iasae (Varaždinske Toplice), which were used by the emperors.

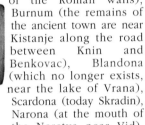

Relief in the Baths in Varaždinske Toplice

FOUNDING OF TOWNS

The Romans initially founded the Istrian towns of Poreč, Rovinj and Pula, which became a place of great importance in the 2nd century. Later the existing Illyrian towns on the main islands and along the coast were turned into Roman towns. The main towns were Senia (Senj), Aenona (Nin), Jadar (Zadar), Delminium (now a village east of Salona with few remains), Promona (a village near Makarska, with parts of the Roman walls), Burnum (the remains of the ancient town are near Kistanje along the road between Knin and Benkovac), Blandona (which no longer exists, near the lake of Vrana), Scardona (today Skradin), Narona (at the mouth of the Neretva near Vid), Tragurium (Trogir) and lastly, Salona (near Split). The towns had walls, forums, triumphal arches and aqueducts, the remains of which can often still be seen. The best-preserved aqueduct, built to serve Salona, was extended by Diocletian as far as Split and is, for the most part, still in use.

The principal Roman monuments remaining today in Croatia are in Pula, with its magnificent Roman amphitheatre *(see pp62–63)*, and in Split, site of the extraordinary Palace of Diocletian *(see pp120–121)*.

AD 6–9 Augustus conquers all of Pannonia and begins construction of forts along the rivers; later the region becomes part of the Roman Empire with the name Provincia Pannoniae

A statue of Emperor Augustus

271 Aurelian defines the border of the Empire as the Danube, unable to defeat the Dacians who live along the river

AD 1   100   200

AD 12 Final defeat of the Illyrians. In Rome Tiberius celebrates his triumph with a solemn procession, at the front of which is Batone, chief of the rebels, now a prisoner

284 Diocletian becomes emperor; some years later work begins on the palace in Split, to which he retires in 304

Aerial view of the Roman ruins of the ancient city of Salona, destroyed in 614

THE BARBARIAN INVASIONS AND THE CRISIS OF THE ROMAN EMPIRE

In 378, after a century of relative peace, the Goths invaded Pannonia and then turned towards Italy. From that time, and for the entire 5th century, the Balkans were attacked by the Huns, Vandals, Visigoths and Longobards which finally caused the fall of the Roman empire in 476.

THE AVARS AND SLAVS IN THE BALKANS

The beginning of the 6th century saw invasion by the Avars, who were followed by other Slavic tribes. Those Roman inhabitants who did not manage to flee to the mountains or the islands were captured and sold as slaves. In 582 the Avars conquered and destroyed Sirmium (Sremska Mitrovica), one of the ancient capitals of the Roman Empire. Later they also subdued other nomadic tribes and organized a powerful army to

conquer Constantinople, but they were defeated by the Byzantines. Some of the troops returned to the Asiatic steppes, while others settled between the Danube and Tisza rivers, leaving the field clear for the Slavs who occupied Moravia and Bohemia to push southwards and towards the Adriatic, conquering all the Roman cities and destroying Salona (614). The Slavs settled in the countryside or in what remained of the sacked cities. These people cultivated the land and bred livestock and formed extended family groups (*zadruge*) with a *župan* at the head of each.

THE BULGARS AND THE BYZANTINE RECONQUEST

The Slavs' expansion to the south was halted by the Bulgars, a people of Turkish origin, who settled along the final stretch of the Danube. After the fall of the Western Empire, Byzantium attempted to reconquer

TIMELINE

Roman bust recovered from ancient Mursa

	380 With the Edict of Thessalonica, Theodosius the Great divides the Roman Empire in four parts		**476** The Ostrogoths of Odoacer depose Romulus Augustulus, the last Roman emperor
300	**400**		**500**
	378 Ostrogoths conquer and destroy Mursa (Osijek)	**437** Dalmatia comes under the rule of Constantinople; the Huns invade and conquer Pannonia	**500** The Slavs occupy Pannonia, which would become Slavonia

the Balkans and inflicted various defeats on the Slavs, while at the same time trying to make them part of the empire. The Byzantine fleet was able to move the army rapidly and in this way Greece, part of Macedonia and the Dalmatian islands and cities were retaken. Inland areas remained in Slav possession.

Foundations of one of the churches in Biskupija

THE CROATS

At the beginning of the 7th century, perhaps summoned by the Byzantine emperor Heraclius, the Croats, a Slavic people possibly from what is now Iran, settled in upper Pannonia and Dalmatia, mixing with the native Roman people or refugees from the interior. In the inland regions, in the 8th and 9th centuries, the Croats set up territorial bases, while the coastal cities and the islands were governed by Byzantine officials with a fleet based in Zadar. In the 9th century, the Croats established a fledgling state in a hilly area now called Biskupija on the Dalmatian plateau, far from the Byzantine-controlled coast and away from central Croatia, subject to the Franks. Several churches were built here and the small settlement was named Pet Krikvah Polje. Recent archaeological digs have unearthed the foundations of religious buildings. The finds are now in Split and Knin.

Dalmatia. The area was divided into counties which were entrusted to loyal nobles or bishops. The Aquileian patriarch assumed particular importance for these lands when, in the 9th century, he sent monks and priests from Byzantium to spread the gospel and convert the Croats to Christianity. Among the priests were Cyril and Methodius, who devised Glagolitic script to spread the word in a language intelligible to the Slavs *(see pp34–5)*.

THE FIRST CROATIAN TOWNS

During the 8th and early 9th centuries, the first Croatian towns were built next to the Byzantine-governed towns. Many (Dubrovnik, Zadar, Split and Trogir) were inhabited by people of mainly Roman origin. Biograd was founded near Zadar, and the town of Knin was repopulated by Croats under Prince Višeslav. Later, the town of Šibenik was founded. In Pannonia, the Roman town of Siscia (now Sisak) and the town of Mursa (Osijek) were revived by Prince Voinomir.

The baptismal font of Prince Višeslav, found near Nin

THE FRANKS

Towards the end of the 8th century, the Franks led by Charlemagne succeeded in conquering what is now northern Croatia, Bohemia, Istria, Slovenia and part of

---

614 The Slavs and Avars conquer and destroy Salona; the Roman population seeks refuge in Split and the nearby islands

From 820 Croats found the cities of Biograd, Šibenik and Knin; Sinj and Osijek revive

| 600 | 700 | 800 |

Early 7th century The Croats settle in upper Pannonia and Dalmatia

799 Charlemagne defeats and subdues Croats in Laurana (Lovran); beginning of Croats' conversion to Christianity. Their cultural centre is in Aenona (Nin); first writing in Croat appears

Bust of Charlemagne (742–814)

Cyril and Methodius

The two key figures in the process of converting the Slav population to Christianity were the brothers Cyril (827–69) and Methodius (815–85). They were the sons of a Byzantine army officer and were born in Thessalonica, where they learnt several languages, including Slavic. The city, at that time Byzantine territory, was one of the most cosmopolitan in the Mediterranean. Initially, the two brothers took up different careers, but both eventually became monks. In 863 Emperor Michael III of Byzantium sent the two brothers to Moravia to spread the Slavonic (rather than Latin) liturgy among the people. The two men devised the Glagolitic alphabet to represent the Slav tongue, and translated religious texts. Croatian priests, especially along the coast, adopted Glagolitic and texts survive in a number of places. Glagolitic was a forerunner of Cyrillic script, named after Cyril.

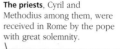

The priests, Cyril and Methodius among them, were received in Rome by the pope with great solemnity.

Methodius *followed an administrative and military career, later entering a monastery. In 869 he was invited to Prague as the Archbishop of Moravia and Pannonia and the papal delegate to the Slav population. Here he undertook evangelical work, and completed the translation of the Bible into Slavonic.*

The Glagolitic alphabet *is composed of 40 letters, arranged in a sequence based on the Greek alphabet. Extra signs were added to represent particular sounds in the Slavic language, which are not found in Greek.*

Methodius and his brother presented the pope with the relics of St Clement, the third Roman pope, who had died in the Crimea in the year 102.

The Croat population's acceptance *of Christianity soon became evident in the country's artworks and crafts. The working of stone and gold was already a traditional craft, but was now used for sacred objects. A primitive representation of the figure of Christ can be seen in this small cross from Zadar, dating from the 9th century.*

The use of Glagolitic script spread among the Slavonic clergy. Although banned from Roman-controlled territories, it was used for centuries in more far-flung monasteries.

Cyril and Methodius became patron saints of mainland Europe in 1979. Many churches, centres of religious studies, university institutions and libraries, including that of Bulgaria, are dedicated to Cyril, often with Methodius.

Cyril, whose real name was Constantine (he changed his name in Rome when he became a monk), dedicated himself to humanist studies. He was a teacher of philosophy and later responsible for the Library of Byzantium, becoming famous for his work. He died in Rome in 869.

CYRIL AND METHODIUS IN ROME

In 867, the two brothers were invited to Rome by Pope Hadrian II. Convinced by their cause, the pope approved the use of Slavonic language in liturgy. After his return to Moravia, Methodius had to face the hostility of the Aquileia patriarch and the Archbishop of Salzburg who wanted to reserve the Slavs' conversion to Christianity for priests of German origin. Methodius was arrested, tortured and only freed 15 months later after intervention by Pope John VIII.

TIMELINE

863 King Ratoslav invites Cyril and Methodius to Moravia to help convert the local population to Christianity	**869** Cyril, sick, retires to a monastery in Rome where he dies shortly after. Methodius is nominated Archbishop of Pannonia and Moravia and the papal delegate to the Slav population. Methodius moves to Prague		**893** Glagolitic is altered, introducing Greek characters: the new Cyrillic alphabet spreads among Serbs, Macedonians and Russians.
860	**870**	**880**	**890**
866 Cyril and Methodius translate the Gospel and sacred texts into Slavonic and devise Glagolitic script. Slavonic liturgy is introduced to Bohemia	**867** Cyril and Methodius are invited to Rome by Pope Hadrian II, who agrees to the use of Slavonic in liturgy	*Mosaic on the tomb of Cyril*	**885** Pope Stephen V forbids the use of the Slavonic language in liturgy

THE HUNGARIANS

The situation in the Balkans seemed stable enough towards the end of the 9th century. However, Hungarians from the Urals came to Europe and, under the leadership of King Arpad, settled along the middle stretches of the Danube and in the valleys of Transylvania, forcing out the Slavs and other tribes. They carried out military raids in Italy and Austria but were defeated in 955 by Emperor Otto II at Lechenfeld, on the plain near Ljubljana, and were forced to retreat to what are today the borders of Hungary and Transylvania. This Hungarian invasion was the last great invasion of the first millennium.

Monument to the first Croat king, Tomislav

THE KINGDOM OF THE CROATS

In the meantime, in 845, under Prince Trpimir, the Croats obtained a tacit autonomy from the Franks and formed a state which also controlled part of Dalmatia. This was recognized by the pope while Duke Branimir (879–92) was its leader. Prince Tomislav was crowned king in 925 and his death, in 928, was followed by years of anarchy until King Petar Krešimir IV (1058–74) came to power and united Croatia. Krešimir also conquered the

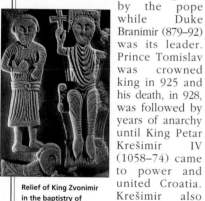

Relief of King Zvonimir in the baptistry of St John in Split

islands of Dalmatia. In 1054, with the schism of the Roman and Byzantine churches, Croatia sided with Rome. After the death of Petar Krešimir IV, his successor Zvonimir, who had married the sister of the Hungarian king Ladislaus, was crowned king by Pope Gregory VII and declared himself subject to Rome. The Croat nobles refused to accept this and killed Zvonimir in 1089.

THE UNION WITH HUNGARY

Claiming the right of succession, Koloman (1102–1116), the Hungarian king, came to power after Ladislaus. He conquered Croatia and was crowned king of Dalmatia and Croatia. In 1102 an agreement united the two states under one dynasty. A Croatian parliament (Sabor) was set up, to be ruled by a royally appointed Ban (governor), and the state was divided into counties governed by Croatian and Hungarian nobles. In the following century, to deal with the Tartar raids, King Bela IV reorganized the state into two parts (Croatia and Slavonia), each ruled by a Ban. New cities were founded and some were granted the privileges of a free city.

THE ROYAL FREE CITIES

These cities, defended by walls, moats and towers, were built mainly in Pannonia and the northern counties. Varaždin, founded at this time, became one of the area's busiest trading centres and, for a long period, the seat of the Sabor. The cities which emerged from the ruins

TIMELINE

896 Hungarians settle between the Tisza and the Danube	**901** Prince Tomislav defeats the Hungarians and forces them beyond the Sava. He obtains from Byzantium the authority to administer the cities of Dalmatia	**956** Branimir, prince of Croatia, rebels against the Byzantines. He obtains the title of king of Croatia with the pope's blessing

850	900	950	1000

899 Hungarians enter the Balkans and destroy the cities of the Croats, who seek refuge in Dalmatia	**930** The Byzantines renew the union with the coastal towns and cities who pay taxes to the emperor **925** Tomislav becomes king of the Croats with the pope's blessing	**1000** Venice's first armed naval expedition against pirates near mouth of Neretva river; towns on islands and coast of Istria and Dalmatia declare allegiance to Venice

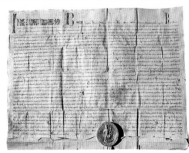

The Golden Bull of 1242 declaring Zagreb (Gradec) a Free Royal City

Croatia, was enlarged and given a fort, as were Klis, Knin and Sinj in Dalmatia. Several noble families were also given the task of building and manning forts, as was the case with the Bribir counts, who moved to Zrin (taking the name of Zrinski). This intense programme strengthened a state which was threatened on many sides: after the danger of the Tartars had passed, threat of a Turkish invasion loomed.

of old Roman towns were fortified: as in Križevci, proclaimed a royal city in 1252, Koprivnica, declared a free town in 1356, and Ludbreg, which became a free town in 1320 and played an important role in the region's defences. The lower stretch of the Drava was strengthened, with a rebuilt Sisak and, further south, a new Slavonski Brod. Zagreb became a free royal city and seat of the Sabor in 1242; Vukovar became a free town in 1231. Thanks to tax advantages and non-subjection to feudal lords, these towns grew in importance and began to attract foreign merchants and artisans.

THE DEFENCES
King Bela IV built forts in strategic positions which were directly dependent on royal power or granted to the great feudal lords. Impressive ruins remain of these forts, including the famous one of Ružica near Orahovica in Slavonia. Samobor, in central

The taking of Zadar by the Venetians depicted by Andrea Vicentino

VENICE, ISTRIA AND DALMATIA
The Adriatic coast fared differently; its fate was linked to that of Venice. Much of Istria belonged to the Aquileian patriarchate, which held civil and ecclesiastical jurisdiction. From the year 1000, many coastal towns had agreements of mutual assistance with Venice, which had a powerful fleet for defence against attacks by pirates. Venice needed the Istrian cities, which often had fortified ports, for mooring their merchant fleets which plied the Croatian coast on their expeditions to the East. In the 13th century, some cities asked to come under Venetian rule for defence reasons, a process which in most cases took place peacefully. In Zadar, however, two warring factions forced Venice to employ crusaders on their way to the Holy Land to subdue the city (1202). In 1204 Zadar surrendered, and a year later Venice also conquered Istria and the city of Dubrovnik.

1058 King Krešimir enlarges his kingdom by uniting Croatia and conquering the Dalmatian islands

1102 The Hungarian king, Koloman, successor to Ladislaus, is crowned king of Croatia and Dalmatia

Royal coin of Slavonia from 1200

1202 To repay the debt to Venice the crusaders undertake to conquer Zadar which falls after long resistance

1050	1100	1150	1200

1091 Ladislaus, king of Hungary, brother of Zvonimir's widow, unites Croatia and the Hungarian kingdom

1242 With the Golden Bull the king of Hungary, Andrew II, guarantees the rights of the Croatian nobility, surrendering some of his power to the aristocracy

1075 Zvonimir is crowned king of Croatia by Pope Gregory VII

THE REPUBLIC OF RAGUSA

The story of the city of Dubrovnik, for a long time known as Ragusa, takes up an entire chapter in Croatia's history. The city was founded by exiles from Epidaurum which had been destroyed by the

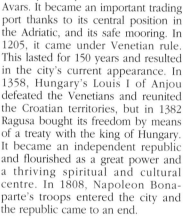

The Republic of Ragusa in a contemporary illustration

Avars. It became an important trading port thanks to its central position in the Adriatic, and its safe mooring. In 1205, it came under Venetian rule. This lasted for 150 years and resulted in the city's current appearance. In 1358, Hungary's Louis I of Anjou defeated the Venetians and reunited the Croatian territories, but in 1382 Ragusa bought its freedom by means of a treaty with the king of Hungary. It became an independent republic and flourished as a great power and a thriving spiritual and cultural centre. In 1808, Napoleon Bonaparte's troops entered the city and the republic came to an end.

TURKISH DOMINATION

The Kingdom of Hungary went through a long period of dynastic crisis when the house of Arpad died out after the death of Andrew III in 1301. There were numerous contenders for the crown, provoking fierce battles until 1308 when Charles Robert of Anjou, of the Neapolitan royal family, came to the throne. Under the Angevin dynasty, with Matthias Corvinus (1458–90), the Hungarian-Croatian kingdom enjoyed long periods of prosperity, competing with Venice for possession of the coast and Adriatic islands. However,

a Turkish invasion was imminent and after the battle of Kosovo Polje in 1389, the Turks conquered nearby Bosnia and part of Serbia. In 1463, the Sultan Mohammed II began to invade Croatia from Bosnia. The Croatian army was defeated in 1493 at the battle of Krbavsko Polje. In the Battle of Mohács, on 29 August 1526, the Hungarian king, Louis II, died without heirs, leaving the way clear for the Turks of Suleyman II the Magnificent to conquer almost all of Croatia and much of Hungary.

Ottoman army in the Battle of Mohács

TIMELINE

Silver coin commemorating the Battle of Mohács

1301–08 The Arpad dynasty dies out with the death of Andrew III. After lengthy controversy, Charles Robert of Anjou comes to the throne

1527 The kingdom of Hungary and Croatia passes to the Habsburgs

1526 King Louis II dies in the Battle of Mohács against the Turks

1300	1350	1400	1450	1500

1409 After a costly war against Sigismund of Habsburg, Ladislaus of Anjou becomes king of Hungary and Croatia. He sells Dalmatia to Venice

1493 Croatian troops are defeated at Krbavsko Polje by Jacub, a Pasha of Bosnia

1520 Marko Marulić writes *Judita*, the first work written in Croat

View of Osijek at the time of liberation from the Turks in 1687

VENICE AND THE PURCHASE OF DALMATIA

The wars with Venice over coastal Dalmatia continued until 1409 when Ladislaus of Anjou, the King of Naples, renounced all rights over Dalmatia and sold it for 100,000 gold ducats to Venice. The towns and islands stayed under Venetian rule from 1409 until 1797, when Venice surrendered to Napoleon. As well as the territories purchased by Venice, other towns wanted to become Venetian possessions. They were given a great deal of autonomy by Venice, whose principal interest was in the security of the ports and their defence, building the ramparts which today characterize these towns. During the wars of the early 18th century, Venice conquered the whole of Dalmatia, except for Dubrovnik, then an independent republic, and a small stretch of coast, extending its borders to the Velebit passes, which still separate Croatia from Bosnia-Herzegovina today.

Fran Krsto Frankopan, beheaded in 1671

TIES WITH THE HABSBURGS

In 1527, Croatian and Hungarian nobles granted what remained of the kingdom to Archduke Ferdinand of Habsburg, who then concentrated all power in the court, depriving the nobility of control of the cities and border areas. In 1578, he established the Military Frontier *(Vojna Krajina)* which was administered by the military governor of Vienna. This was to serve as a buffer zone against the advancing Turks. To populate this frontier, Serb, Morlach and Bosnian refugees were brought in and integrated with the military garrisons. For some decades there was a truce, then the Turkish offensive against Vienna resumed, but the Turks were pushed back, first in 1664 and again in 1683. The slow retreat of the "infidels" from Croatia began at this point. Croatia was liberated ten years later, while Bosnia remained under the Turks. The liberated areas became border lands and remained so until 1881. Vienna's heavy taxation and centralized rule caused discontent, but a plan to detach Croatia from Hungary and Vienna, in 1670 by some of Croatia's most influential families (including the Frankopans and Zrinskis) *(see p177)*, resulted in the beheading of Ban Petar Zrinski and Fran Krsto Frankopan and the other two rebel leaders in 1671, halting any attempt at revolt.

1566 Suleyman II besieges Siget, which, led by Nikola Zrinski, resists for five weeks	**1670** Attempted revolt by the Croatian princes Petar Zrinski and Krsto Frankopan against Leopold of Austria	**1718** Treaty of Passarowitz (Požarevac): Turkey loses Serbia and part of inland Dalmatia
1573 Peasant revolt in Zagorje, against nobles and emperor, put down with much bloodshed		

1550	1600	1650	1700	1750

Nikola Zrinski, Ban of Croatia

1592 The Turks capture Bihać and extend the borders to the river Kupa, which still separates Bosnia from Croatia

1688 Pope Innocent XI promotes Holy League against Turks; the battle of Petervaradino brings Turkish defeat and liberation of all of Croatia

1683 Siege of Vienna by the Turks; Austria wins and reconquers Buda and Pannonia

Drawing showing the Congress of Vienna

THE KINGDOM OF THE ILLYRIAN PROVINCES

The Napoleonic wars also affected Croatia, where the Kingdom of Illyrian Provinces was established in 1809, governed by the French marshal, Marmont. This relatively short period (five years) saw the introduction of important economic and legal reforms which left a deep impression on Croatian culture. With the mood of growing nationalism in Europe, people felt inspired to rebuild a united state. However, at the Congress of Vienna (1815), Croatia supported the expansionist aspirations of Austria, which annexed all the Istrian and Dalmatian territories which had belonged to Venice, and the Republic of Dubrovnik.

THE ILLYRIAN MOVEMENT

Croatian aspirations were apparent in movements which also influenced and politicized the newly emerging working class, a product of early industrialization. The origins of this nationalist trend can be dated to the 1834 writings of Ljudevit Gaj (1809–72),

Ban Josip Jelačić, a Croatian national hero

known as "the Illyrian". Moving against this trend, however, was the expansion of Hungary, which tried to extend its influence in frontier zones by imposing the use of the Magyar language in administrative affairs and schools. In the former Venetian territories on the other hand, a pro-Italian nationalism, with ideas of unification, was spreading among the middle classes in the Dalmatian and Istrian cities. The Austrian government opposed all these movements and continued to govern without compromise. Indeed, they tried to introduce the teaching of German in schools. Any possible unification of Croatian territories was blocked by maintaining the *Krajina*, the military border, and by customs barriers between the various areas. Major public works, the expansion of the ports of Rijeka and Pula, which became a base for the Austrian fleet, and a renewed road network were all made to promote Austrian interests.

FROM THE REVOLT OF 1848 TO AUSTRO-HUNGARIAN REIGN

After 1847, when the Sabor (parliament) of Zagreb managed to proclaim Croatian as the official language and abolished feudalism, the revolt of the Hungarian people and the hopes aroused by the Italian revolution in 1848 also involved Croatian political movements. The failure to understand the Hungarian rebels and ambiguous Austrian policy forced the Ban, Josip Jelačić, into war against Hungary, now ruled by

TIMELINE

1809 Napoleon Bonaparte founds kingdom of Illyrian Provinces

Napoleon Bonaparte

1830 Ljudevit Gaj publishes *Essential Rules of Croatian-Slavic Spelling*, introducing to the script the signs missing from the Latin alphabet

Ljudevit Gaj, head of the Croatian national revival

| 1800 | 1810 | 1820 | 1830 | 1840 | 1850 |

1815 Treaty of Vienna: Austria is allotted all the territories of the Republic of Venice

1832 Janko Drašković publishes *Dissertation* against Hungarian and Austrian supremacy, introduces idea of Illyria as the "mother" of Croats

1847 The Illyrian Movement gains majority in Croatian Parliament and proclaims Croat the official language

1848–50 Hungarian uprising against Austria: Vienna abolishes local autonomy, dissolves the Sabor and makes German the official language

rebels. The Austrian monarchy was saved but then became, if anything, even more keen on centralization. In 1867, Franz Joseph, the Austrian emperor, modified the structure of the state and established the Austro-Hungarian empire. Hungary was granted autonomy and a corridor to the sea. Rijeka and the hinterland became part of the Magyar state. However, under pressure from the Sabor, in 1868 the Austrian emperor granted Croatia the status of "a nation with territory within the Austro-Hungarian Empire", and Zagreb became its cultural and political centre. In 1863 the bishop of Đakovo, Josip Juraj Strossmayer, founded the Croatian Academy of the Arts and Sciences and the University (1874), the first in the Balkans.

Political contention continued to develop along different lines. Some people dreamed of a confederation

Bishop Josip Juraj Strossmayer, founder of the University of Zagreb

of states within the Habsburg monarchy, others felt that the moment had come to unite the Slav peoples in one state, and lastly, others felt it was time for Croatian independence.

Tension increased in 1878 when Bosnia and Herzegovina came under Austrian rule, sparking reaction from the Kingdom of Serbia, which had been established in 1862 after the expulsion of the Turks. The Serbian ruling classes aspired to unify the southern Slavs and intended to extend their territories towards Dalmatia and Slavonia, which they regarded as Serbian land. In the last decade of the 19th century a political battle developed in Dalmatia and Istria. It formed between a movement supported by the bourgeoisie in the cities formerly under Venetian rule which pushed for autonomy, and other groups which aimed at a union with Serbia. Austria, which as always took advantage of these internal controversies, did not concede any form of autonomy.

WORLD WAR I
In 1914, with the assassination of Archduke Franz Ferdinand in Sarajevo, World War I broke out which caused the dissolution of the Habsburg Empire. Croatians paid dearly for their involvement in the war, as did many other countries, but finally the Croatian population was able to free itself from foreign rule.

Flag of the Hungarian-Croatian Imperial regiment

1860 Austrian emperor reinstates the Sabor

1885 Vienna dissolves the *Krajine* and those areas become part of the Croatian state again

1904 Antun and Stjepan Radić found the People's Peasant Party

1914 Assassination in Sarajevo and World War I begins

| 1860 | 1870 | 1880 | 1890 | 1900 | 1910 |

1868 Birth of United Kingdom of Croatia and Slovenia supported by Emperor Franz Joseph

Emperor Franz Joseph

1908 Austria annexes Bosnia and Herzegovina

1912 Slavko Cuvaj proclaimed Ban of Croatia, dissolves the Sabor and abolishes the Constitution

Assassination of King Alexander in Marseilles (1934)

FROM THE STATE OF SLOVENES, CROATS AND SERBS TO THE KINGDOM OF YUGOSLAVIA

Croatia proclaimed independence in 1918, but a few months later agreed to be part of a state formed by Slovenes and Serbs under the Serbian dynasty of Karađorđević. The Treaty of Rapallo (1920) allotted Istria, Zadar, the islands of Cres, Lošinj, Lastovo and Palagruža to Italy, followed in 1924 by Rijeka. The discontent of Croatians led many citizens to join the People's Peasant Party, led by Stjepan Radić until he was shot and fatally wounded in parliament in Belgrade in 1928. The revolts which broke out in Croatia were repressed and in 1929 King Alexander abolished the constitution and then

Tito with his wife and son in a photo from 1927

established the Kingdom of Yugoslavia. The assassination of the king in Marseilles (1934) by the Ustaše (Croatian fascists), led by Ante Pavelić, increased tension and in an attempt to suppress the uprising and placate the discontented, in 1939 the government of Belgrade established the Banovina of Croatia within the Kingdom of Yugoslavia. However, a few days later World War II began.

WORLD WAR II

Initially, Yugoslavia supported the Axis, but a military revolt removed the king of Yugoslavia, and the country was then invaded by Nazi troops. A kingdom of Croatia was established, which was to be governed by Aimone of Savoy, but in reality it was an independent state led by Pavelić. Italy took control of the islands and cities of the Dalmatian coast. Resistance gained ground in all of Yugoslavia led by the Communist Party and its chief, Marshal Tito: from 1941 to 1945 Croatia was bloodied by war and internal conflicts which caused hundreds of thousands of deaths.

MARSHAL TITO

At the end of the war the state of Yugoslavia was reunited, and regained land granted to Italy after World War I (see p49), as well as the area of Prekomurje and a part of Baranja, which were both Hungarian at the time.

In 1948, the break between the Yugoslav Communist Party and the Soviet Union led Marshal

TIMELINE

1919 Treaty of Paris: a country of Slovenes, Croats and Serbs is created, which later becomes the kingdom of Yugoslavia	**1932** Civil war breaks out in Yugoslavia **1934** King Alexander is killed in Marseilles; his cousin Paul takes power	**1948** Yugoslavia breaks away from Soviet influence and begins policy of non-alignment
1920	**1930**	**1940**	**1950**	**1960**

1929 King Alexander Karađorđević proclaims a dictatorship. Croat Ante Pavelić founds terrorist organization of Ustaše to fight the Serbs

1939–41 World War II: Yugoslavia is conquered and divided, and Croatia nominally becomes a kingdom under Aimone of Savoy

1947–48 Exodus of nearly all the Italians from Istria and Dalmatia

1945 The Yugoslav Federal state is founded

Tito to employ a policy of mediation and neutrality between the opposing international factions of the Cold War. Tito held together the country's various ethnic groups with great difficulty and these ties showed signs of strain after he died in 1980. The reform of the constitution, aimed at weakening Serbia's dominance over the other states, did not alter the resentment of the Croats and Slovenes who sought support for opposition to the regime in religion and nationalism.

Stipe Mesić, elected president in 2000 and 2005

THE DISSOLUTION OF THE SOCIALIST REPUBLIC OF YUGOSLAVIA

The fall of the Berlin Wall (November 1989) and the break-up of the Soviet Union at the end of 1991 convinced the governments of Slovenia, Croatia (under its first president, Franjo Tudjman) and Macedonia that they should dissolve federal ties and proclaim independence, after a referendum which was won by a wide margin by the secessionists (May 1991). However, a Serb faction, supported by the Yugoslav People's Army (JNA) from Belgrade, stirred up rebellion and war broke out. In Slovenia the war lasted only six days, but the battle in Croatia was prolonged. Under the pretext of defending the Serbs, parts of Slavonia and Baranja were occupied by the JNA, and in Krajina the Serbian Republic of Krajina was created with Knin as its capital. A fifth of Croatia fell to Serb soldiers, and the city of Dubrovnik was held under a seven-month siege.

THE INDEPENDENT STATE OF CROATIA

Five years later the land occupied by the Serbs was liberated by the Croatian army and the Erdut Agreement (1995) sanctioned re-unification, although the disputed territories (Slavonia and Krajina) were overseen by the UN until 1998.

Croatia joined the World Trade Organization and elections held in December 2000 voted in a coalition of democratic parties. As a result steps were taken for Croatia's entry into the European Union. In March 2002, the Italian bank, UniCredito, bought the important Croatian bank, the Zagrebačka Bank, bringing it into the European circuit. However, in 2005, after failing to hand over an indicted general, Croatia was accused of not co-operating fully with the international war crimes tribunal at the Hague and negotiations for entry to the EU stalled. Soon after, the general was captured and talks resumed. Croatia was given EU applicant status with possible entry to the European Union by 2010.

Bombed houses in Vukovar during the war of 1991–95

CROATIA
AREA BY AREA

Croatia at a Glance

Croatia is a fascinating country with great ethnic, historical and architectural diversity as well as varied topography. The north had close ties with the former Austrian empire, and the bell towers alongside 19th-century Baroque churches and buildings have a Viennese look. The eastern side marks the start of the Hungarian plain with broad rivers and houses with overhanging roofs. The Adriatic coast is quite different, with its indented coastline fringed with lovely islands. The coastal cities reflect the centuries-old Venetian culture with churches, monasteries, palaces and forts testifying to the brilliance of the late Middle Ages and the greatness of the Renaissance period.

St Mark's Square
(pp154–5), *with its Gothic church of the same name, is the heart of the Gornji Grad district in Zagreb and the city's oldest square.*

ZAGREB
(pp148–65)

ISTRIA AND
THE KVARNER AREA
(pp48–87)

CENTRAL CROATIA
(pp166–79)

Basilica of Euphrasius
in Poreč (pp54–5) has marvellous mosaics, some of the best preserved examples of Byzantine art in Croatia.

**Amphitheatre,
Pula (pp62–63)**

**Plitvice Lakes
National Park**
(pp86–7) *is one of nature's natural wonders with 16 lakes surrounded by woods. The cascading waterfalls create an impressive display of light and colour.*

DALMATIA
(pp88–147)

Kornati National Park
(pp98–9) *is made up of over 150 islands with underwater caves and sheltered coves. The park covers an area of about 300 sq km (115 sq miles) and is surrounded by clear seas. These wooded, rocky islands present an unforgettable sight.*

*ADRIATIC
SEA*

◁ **Typical cultivated landscape in the north of Croatia**

Zagorje (pp200–1), west of Varaždin, towards the border with Slovenia, is a fascinating area with vine-covered hills, thermal spa towns and castles.

0 kilometres 50

0 miles 50

THE NORTHERN COUNTIES (pp198–215)

Kopački Rit Park (pp194–5) is an oasis of great ornithological interest. In spring and summer the Danube overflows, transforming this area into a large lake attracting more than 200 bird species.

SLAVONIA AND BARANJA (pp180–97)

Lonjsko Polje Nature Park (p176)

The Tvrđa in Osijek (pp192–3), the fortified nucleus of the city, has 18th-century military buildings. Initially Roman, then Hungarian, Turkish and lastly Austrian, the city retains traces of most of these diverse cultures.

The Palace of Diocletian in Split (pp120–1) was built by Emperor Diocletian at the end of the 3rd century. The city of Split grew up in and around it. Almost in its original state, it is the largest Roman building in the Adriatic.

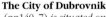

The City of Dubrovnik (pp140–7) is situated on the coast. It is surrounded by fortifications begun in the early 10th century and enlarged over the years.

ISTRIA AND THE KVARNER AREA

The Istrian peninsula, nestling at the northern end of the Adriatic Sea, and the islands that tumble down the Kvarner gulf are some of the most sought-after holiday destinations in Europe. The coast is spectacular and the towns and cities are fascinating. Three National Parks: the Brijuni Islands, the Plitvice Lakes and Risnjak preserve the natural charm of the area.

Until 1000 BC, the region was inhabited by Illyrians. From 42 BC Istria became part of the Roman empire, when the Province of Dalmatia was founded. Cities were built along the coast and on the islands, and many traces of Roman presence remain. Pula has a well-preserved amphitheatre dating back to the 1st century, the sixth largest arena of its kind in the world.

Mosaic in the Basilica of Euphrasius in Poreč

With the fall of the western Roman empire, much of the eastern Adriatic coast came under the control of Byzantium. The intricate, well-preserved golden mosaics of the 6th-century basilica of St Euphrasius in Poreč survive from that time.

In 1420 the area came under Venetian rule, a situation which was to last until 1797, when Napoleon dissolved the Venetian Republic. Nearly 400 years of Venetian rule are recorded by 15th-century open air loggias, elegant bell towers and buildings with Venetian-Gothic windows, built by wealthy merchants.

With the Treaty of Vienna in 1815, Austria-Hungary extended its domain to include Venetian lands. Rijeka developed into an industrial port under Austro-Hungarian rule and is still today a hub for Croatian shipping. Close by in Opatija the Habsburgs built elegant villas and planted lush gardens for their winter holidays.

In 1918 Istria briefly became part of the new kingdom of Serbs, Croats and Slovenes, which subsequently became Yugoslavia in 1928.

Many Istrian towns have two official names, an Italian and a Croatian, a legacy from 1920, when Istria was given to Italy as a reward for having joined the Allies in World War I. During World War II, the region became a stronghold for Italian partisans. After 1945, most of Istria was given back to Yugoslavia.

The Roman amphitheatre at Pula, one of the best preserved Roman theatres in the world

◁ View of the shoreline, Rab

Exploring Istria and the Kvarner Area

Istria is a triangular peninsula, traditionally divided into three areas. White Istria is a central plateau of karst or limestone with sparse areas of oak, pine and ash trees; grey Istria consists of a strip of eroded limestone with rich soil, used for vines and olive trees; and red Istria is a plateau furrowed by the rivers Mirna and Rasa, farmed for cereals and vegetables. The most popular destinations in Istria are Poreč, Rovinj, Pula and the Brijuni National Park. The Kvarner area includes the city of Rijeka and the coastline as far as Jablanac. Woods cover the northern hinterland, with the Risnjak National Park to the north, and the Plitvice Lakes National Park to the southeast. The islands of Krk, Cres, Lošinj and Rab are delightful places to explore. Many of the towns on the coast have an Italianate appearance.

The cathedral of St Mary the Great on the island of Rab

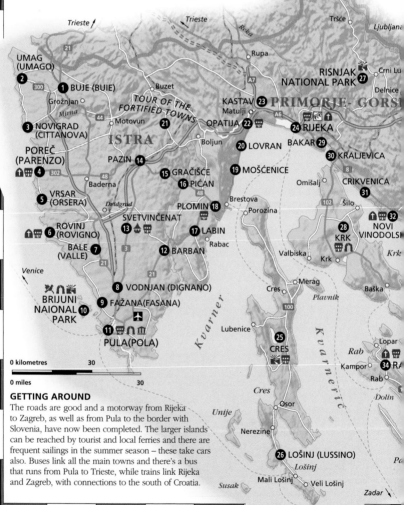

GETTING AROUND

The roads are good and a motorway from Rijeka to Zagreb, as well as from Pula to the border with Slovenia, have now been completed. The larger islands can be reached by tourist and local ferries and there are frequent sailings in the summer season – these take cars also. Buses link all the main towns and there's a bus that runs from Pula to Trieste, while trains link Rijeka and Zagreb, with connections to the south of Croatia.

For additional map symbols *see back flap*

SIGHTS AT A GLANCE

LOCATOR MAP

KEY

══	Two lane motorway, toll-free
━━	Major road
╌╌╌	Minor road
═ ═	Motorway under construction
▭▭▭	Main railway
━━	County border
━━	International border
---	Ferry route
△	Summit

The rocky coastline near Rovinj

SEE ALSO

Façade of the church of St Servelus, Buje

Buje (Buie) ❶

Map A2. 🏛 *3,200.*
✈ *Pula, 70 km (43 miles) S.*
🚌 *from Pula, Rijeka, Kopar, Trieste.*
ℹ *Istarska 2, (052) 773 353.*
🎭 *Nights of Kanegra (Aug);*
Grape festival (Sep).
www.tzg-buje.hr

On an isolated hill, among flourishing vineyards, stands Buje, the ancient Roman settlement of Bullea. Formerly a Frankish feudal village, in 1102 it became part of the Patriarchate of Aquileia and in 1410 the town came under Venetian rule.

The town still retains the outline of the ancient walled castle and has kept its original medieval layout, with narrow alleys and lanes leading to the main square. The church of **St Servelus** (Sv. Servul) and its Aquileian bell tower stand here. The church was built in the 16th century over the remains of a Roman temple, of which a few columns and pieces survive.

Inside the church are wooden statues from the 14th and 15th centuries (*Madonna with Child* and *St Barbara*), sculptures representing St Servelus and St Sebastian (1737) by Giovanni Marchiori, and an organ by Gaetano Callido (1725–1813).

A 15th-century Venetian Gothic palace and a 16th-century loggia with a frescoed façade also face the square.

Outside the walls is the church of **St Mary** (Sv. Marija), erected in the 15th

century: a wooden statue of the Virgin and a *Pietà* are from the same period. Some of the paintings of biblical scenes are by Gasparo della Vecchia (early 18th century).

The **Civic Museum** houses an interesting collection of handicrafts and pieces made by local craftsmen.

🏛 **Civic Museum**
Trg Josipa Broza Tita 6. **Tel** (052) 772 023. ⏱ *Jun–Sep: 4–8pm Mon, Wed, Fri; 9am–1pm Tue, Thu, Sat; Oct–May:by appt.*

Environs
Perched on a hilltop, 8 km (5 miles) south-east of Buje, is the medieval town of **Grožnjan** (Grisignana).

In 1358 the Venetians bought the town from Baron Reiffenberg and since that time it has been the administrative and military centre of the surrounding area. A tower, some parts of the walls and two doors are all that remain of the old town.

Within the walls are a 16th-century loggia, in the main square, and the Baroque church of St Vitus and St Modest. The church has splendid altars and a marble choir.

After World War II, the inhabitants, nearly all of them Italian, abandoned the town. In 1965, however, it was declared a "City of Artists". Contemporary artists work and exhibit their art in the

various local galleries and workshops. In summer the town plays host to concerts and international musical events (*see p24–5*).

Umag (Umago) ❷

Map A2. 🏛 *4,900.* ✈ *Pula, 83 km (51 miles).* 🚌 *Kolodvorska ulica, (052) 741 817.* ℹ *Trgovačka 2, (052) 741 363.* 🎭 *Feast of St Pilgrim (last Sun in May); International tennis tournament (end Jul); concerts in summer.*
www.istra.com/umag

This town is located on a narrow peninsula which frames a small bay. It was founded by the Romans and given the name of Umacus. In 1268, it became an important port when it passed into Venetian hands. Later, in the 14th century, a wall and towers were built, some of which remain.

The town still has many 15th- and 16th-century stone houses, some with ornate Gothic windows.

On the left outer wall of the 18th-century church of **St Mary** (Sv. Marija) is a relief

15th-century polyptych, church of St Mary, Umag

of St Pilgrim and the fortified town of Umag, and inside the church is a 15th-century Venetian-school polyptych.

Today Umag is a busy seaside resort with numerous hotels. It has become known for its well-equipped sports centres and major tennis tournaments are held here.

View of the ancient wall and port of Umag

Boats in the harbour at Poreč

Novigrad (Cittanova) ❸

Map A2. 🏠 2,500. ✈ Pula, 60 km (37 miles). 🚉 Pazin, 41 km (25 miles). 🚌 (052) 757 660. 🛈 Porporella 1, (052) 757 075, (052) 758 011. 🎷 Jazz music festival (Aug), Patron saint's day, St Pelagius (last weekend Aug).

Originally a Greek colony and later a Roman one called Aemonia, Novigrad stands at the mouth of the River Mirna. In the Byzantine period (6th century) when it was enlarged, it was called "New Town" (Neopolis). From the early Middle Ages until 1831 it was an episcopal seat. In 1277 it passed into Venetian hands and oak from Motovun Forest was shipped to Venetian dockyards.

In the 13th century the town was walled for defence, but it was unable to withstand a Turkish attack in 1687 and the town was partially destroyed along with many works of art.

Evidence of the Venetian period can be seen on the façades of the houses in the narrow lanes which lead to the main square (Trg Slobode). An 18th-century loggia stands here. Of the early Christian basilica of **St Pelagius** (Sv. Pelagij), rebuilt in the 16th century, only the Romanesque crypt from the 11th-century remains. In the present-day Baroque church are paintings from the Venetian school of the 18th century. Evidence of the Roman and medieval periods can be seen in the museum housed in the Urizzi Palace.

Poreč (Parenzo) ❹

Map A2. 🏠 7,600. ✈ Pula, 53 km (33 miles). 🚉 Pazin, 32 km (20 miles). 🚌 Ulica K Hoguesa 2, (052) 432 153. 🛈 **Local:** Zagrebačka 9, (052) 451 458; **Regional:** Pionirska 1, (052) 452 797. 🎷 Season of classical music (at St Euphrasius) and jazz festival (both Jul–Aug) . www.istra.com/porec

Poreč was a Roman town (Colonia Julia Parentium) which, after centuries of splendour, was sacked by the Goths and fell into decline. In 539 it was conquered by the Byzantines, who founded a bishopric around the year 800. The town then became part of the kingdom of the Franks, who gave it to the Patriarchate of Aquileia. In 1267 it was the first Istrian town to choose Venetian rule, and the town acquired a Venetian look as palaces, squares and religious buildings were built.

In 1354 it was destroyed by the Genoese and later, plague, pirates and a long war greatly reduced the population. During Austrian domination it became the seat of the Istrian Diet (parliament) and an important shipyard.

The old centre shelters on a narrow peninsula protected by rocks and the island of St Nicholas. Despite being a popular base for visitors to Istria, the old town has

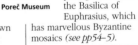

Archaeological exhibit in the Poreč Museum

remained intact and Poreč invariably wins an annual award for "best-kept town".

The layout is based on the original Roman network, with a main road (Decumanus) and another main road at right angles (Cardo). The main monuments of the town line these roads.

Along the Decumanus stand many Gothic houses. At the easternmost point is the Baroque Sinčić Palace (17th century), which houses the **Poreč Museum** (Zavičajni Muzej Poreštine). It is dedicated to Roman and early Christian archaeology; an ethnographic section illustrates daily life in the Poreč region. Nearby in St Maurus Street (Sv. Mauro) is the House of Two Saints, all that is left of the abbey of St Cassius (12th century), with two Romanesque figures on the façade. To the west, the Decumanus leads to Trg Marafor, once the site of the forum, with houses from the 12th and 13th centuries and the remains of a pre-Roman temple.

North of the square is the church of **St Francis** (Sv. Frane, 12th–14th centuries), altered in the Baroque period. To the east is the parish house with an ornate Romanesque façade. From here there is a passage that leads to the Basilica of Euphrasius, which has marvellous Byzantine mosaics (see pp54–5).

🏛 **Poreč Museum**
Sinčić Palace, Dekumanska 9.
Tel (052) 431 585. ☐ Jun–Sep: 10am–1pm, 6–9pm daily; Oct–May: by appt. 📷 🎫

A typical trefoil window in Venetian Gothic style, Poreč

Poreč: Basilica of Euphrasius
Eufrazijeva Bazilika

A mosaic in the apse

This 6th-century church, a Byzantine masterpiece, is decorated with splendid mosaics on a gold background. The basilica of Euphrasius was built for Bishop Euphrasius between 539 and 553, by enlarging the existing 4th-century Oratory of St Maurus Martyr. Some of the original floor mosaics still survive. Over the centuries the building has undergone numerous alterations. In December 1997 the basilica was added to the UNESCO World Heritage List. Classical concerts are held in the church from May to September.

★ Ciborium
Dominating the presbytery is a beautiful 13th-century ciborium, supported by four marble columns. The canopy is decorated with mosaics.

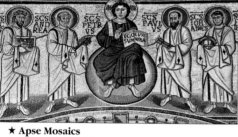

★ Apse Mosaics
Mosaics from the 6th century cover the apse. On the triumphal arch are Christ and the Apostles (above), on the vault, the Virgin enthroned with Child and two Angels, to the left St Maurus, Bishop Euphrasius with a model of the basilica, and Deacon Claud with his son.

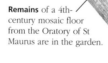

Remains of a 4th-century mosaic floor from the Oratory of St Maurus are in the garden.

Sacristy and the Votive Chapel
Past the sacristy's left wall is a triple-apsed chapel with a mosaic floor from the 6th century. Here lie the remains of the saints Maurus and Eleuterius.

For hotels and restaurants in this region see pp222–6 and pp240–42

STAR FEATURES

★ Apse Mosaics

★ Ciborium

Interior
The entrance leads to a large basilica with a central nave and two side aisles. The 18 Greek marble columns have carved capitals featuring animals, some of Byzantine origin and others Romanesque. All bear the monogram of Euphrasius.

VISITORS' CHECKLIST

Eufrazijeva. **Tel** *(052) 451 711.*
◻ Jun–Aug: 9am–7pm daily; Apr–May, Sep–Nov: 10am–2pm.

Baptistry
This octagonal building dates from the 6th century. In the centre is a baptismal font and there are also fragments of mosaics; to the rear rises a 16th-century bell tower.

The Bishop's Residence, a triple-aisled building dating from the 6th century, now houses several paintings by Antonio da Bassano, a polyptych by Antonio Vivarini and a painting by Palma il Giovane.

Atrium
This has a roughly square portico with two columns on each side. Tombstones and a variety of archaeological finds dating from the medieval period are displayed in this area.

The church of St Anthony in
Vrsar, built in the 15th century

Vrsar (Orsera) ❺

Map A3. 🏘 *1,700.* ✈ *Pula, 41 km
(25 miles).* 🚌 *Pazin, 42 km (26
miles).* ℹ *Rade Končara 46, (052)
441 187.* 🎭 *International sculpture
exhibition, Montraker quarry
(summer); classical music concerts
(summer).* **www**.*istra.com/vrsar*

The remains of a villa,
a quarry and the foundations
of an early Christian building
all provide evidence that
Romans once settled here. In
documents preceding 1000
AD, this village is mentioned
as the feudal territory of the
bishop of Poreč, who owned
a fortified summer residence
here. Until 1172 it remained
under the protection of the
bishop and then came under
Venetian rule.

The town had an outer wall
and towers which have now
almost disappeared except for
the Sea Gate. Near the gate is
the church of **St Mary** (Sv.
Marija) from the 10th century,
one of the most important
Romanesque monuments in
Istria. Inside are frescoes
which are among the oldest
in the region and a mosaic
floor with floral motifs.

The town is dominated by
the 18th-century **Vergotini
Castle**, built by restructuring
the bishop's former residence.
Near the only remaining gate
in the medieval wall is the
small church of **St Anthony**,
built in the 15th century with
an open portico.

Environs

Just outside Vrsar lies
Koversada, Europe's largest
naturist resort.

To the south of Vrsar,
towards Rovinj, is the **Limski

Channel**, now a marine
reserve. The channel is 9 km
(5 miles) long, and 600 m
(1,970 ft) wide with steep
sides, perforated by limestone
caves which have been lived
in from time to time since the
Neolithic Age. In the early
11th century, one of the caves
was the home of the hermit
St Romualdo, who founded
the monastery of St Michael
near Klostar.

Many of the restaurants in
the area offer the oysters and
mussels farmed in the channel.

Fishermen on the Limski Channel

Rovinj (Rovigno) ❻

Map A3. 🏘 *13,000.* ✈ *Pula, 49
km (30 miles).* 🚌 *Pula.* ⛴ *Trg na
Lokvi, (052) 811 514, 811 453.*
ℹ *Obala P Budicina 12, (052) 811
566.* 🎭 *Grisia, International art
exhibition (2nd Sun Aug); Patron St
Euphemia's day (16 Sep).*
www.*istra.com/rovinj*

Rovinj was originally an
island port built by the
Romans. In 1763, Rovinj was
joined to the coast by filling
in the channel dividing the
island from the mainland,
creating a peninsula.

Initially ruled by the
Byzantines and the Franks,
from 1283 until 1797 the town
was under Venetian control.

Traces of a wall dating back
to the Middle Ages can still
be seen.

In the square in front of the
pier is Balbi's Arch (1680), an
ancient city gate, as well as a
late-Renaissance clock tower.
A loggia from 1680 is now the
Civic Museum, housing 18th-
century art from the Venetian
school and works by modern
Croatian artists.

In the roads branching off
the square are Baroque and
Renaissance buildings. The
backs of many of these face
the sea. The **cathedral**,
dedicated to St Euphemia
(Sv. Eufemije) dominates the
town. Originating in early
Christian times, it was rebuilt
in 1736. The saint's remains
are preserved in a Roman
sarcophagus in the apse on
the right of the three-aisle
church. The adjacent bell
tower is 61 m (200 ft) high,
and was modelled on that
of San Marco in Venice. It
is crowned by a copper
statue of St Euphemia.

In the east of the city is the
13th-century **Baptistry of the
Holy Trinity** (Sv. Trojstvo).

Along the waterfront is the
Institute of Marine Biology. It
was founded in the late 19th
century and has an aquarium.
Nearby, Red Island (Crveni
otok), is in fact two islands
linked by an embankment.

South of the town is Zlatni
Rt, a park planted with
cedars, pines and cypresses,
with well laid-out trails.

🏛 **Civic Museum**
Trg M Tita 11. **Tel** (052) 816 720,
830 650. ◻ summer: 9am–12pm,
7–10pm Mon–Sat; winter:
9am–1pm Sun, Tue–Fri.

The port of Rovinj, dominated by the cathedral

For hotels and restaurants in this region see pp222–6 and pp240–42

The church of St Elizabeth inside the walls of Bale

Bale (Valle) ❼

Map A3. 🏛 900. ✈ Pula, 28 km (17 miles). 🚊 Pula, 25 km (15 miles). 🚌 Trg palih Boraca. ℹ Trg palih Boraca 3, (052) 824 270, (052) 824 303. 🎭 Night of Bale, Baljanska Noć (first Sun in Aug); Castrum Vallis, art exhibition (Jul & Aug).

On a hill of limestone, the Illyrians constructed a fort which dominated the surrounding countryside. The Romans also built a *castrum* (Castrum Vallis) on the same site, which was renovated when the place became a feudal estate of the Patriarchate of Aquileia. During Venetian rule, which began in 1332, the town grew in size and acquired its present layout of an elliptical wall with towers enclosing two parallel rows of houses. Interesting buildings include the Gothic-Venetian Magistrates' Court with coats of arms on the portico, the loggia, and the Gothic-Renaissance **Castle** dating from the 15th century, a residence for the Soardo Bembo family. Under one of the two side towers is a gate leading to the old town.

The church of **St Elizabeth** (Sv. Elizabete), of Romanesque origins, was reconstructed in the 16th century and again in the 19th. The church contains a splendid Romanesque crucifix, a sarcophagus, a polyptych and a crypt with a marble Renaissance altar.

There are two other churches in the town. One dates from the 14th century and is dedicated to St Anthony; the other, dedicated to the Holy Spirit, was built in the 15th century.

Vodnjan (Dignano) ❽

Map A3. 🏛 3,700. ✈ Pula, 11 km (7 miles). 🚊 Ulica Željeznička, (052) 511 538. ℹ Narodni trg 3, (052) 511 700, 511 672. 🎭 Bumbari, a festival in costume based on the name given to the town's inhabitants (Aug).

The town of Vodnjan stands on a hill among vineyards and olive groves. At one time it was an Illyrian fort and later, a Roman military post known as Vicus Atinianus. From 1331 until 1797 the town was under Venetian rule.

The old part of town still has various buildings in Venetian-Gothic style, including the Bettica Palace and the 18th-century church of **St Blaise** (Sv. Blaž). In the church are some splendid statues and about 20 paintings from the 17th to 19th centuries, as well as a *Last Supper* by G Contarini (1598) and an *Encounter of Saints* attributed to Palma il Vecchio.

Seven rooms of the church are given over to religious art (730 pieces): vestments, china and silver reliquaries, statues and paintings, and a fine polyptych by Paolo Veneziano from 1351 (*Portrait of the Blessed Leon Bembo*). There are also six mummies of saints, which have survived miraculously without being embalmed. The most revered is that of St Nicolosia.

🔒 **St Blaise**
Trg Zagreb. **Tel** (052) 511 420.
🕐 9am–7pm daily. **Collection of Religious Art Tel** (052) 511 420.
🕐 Jun–Sep: 9am–7pm daily; Oct–May by appt.

Fažana (Fasana) ❾

Map A3. 🏛 2,800. ✈ Pula, 8 km (5 miles). 🚊 Vodnjan, 5 km (3 miles). 🚢 to the Brijuni Islands. ℹ Riva 2, (052) 383 727. **www**.fazana.hr

This small town is known mainly as the embarkation point for the islands of the Brijuni National Park *(see pp58–9)*. Its ancient name, Vasianum, derives from the production of oil and wine amphorae during the Roman period. Facing the sea is the church of **SS Cosmas and Damian** (Sv. Kuzma i Damjan), which was founded in the 11th century and has undergone various reconstructions. Inside is a painting by Jurai Ventura of *The Last Supper* (1578) and in the sacristy are remains of frescoes by Italian artists from Friuli dating from the 15th–16th centuries.

To the side of the church is a seven-storey bell tower with an octagonal spire. The church of **Our Lady of Carmel** from the late 14th century has Gothic frescoes by unknown artists and a 17th-century loggia. Nearby is the church of **St Elys** from the 6th century, with a stone doorway and blind-arch windows, which preserves its Byzantine appearance from the 8th–9th centuries.

Thanks to the growth in numbers of visitors heading for the Brijuni Islands, the town has grown and new facilities have been built.

The façade of the church of SS Cosmas and Damian in Fažana

Brijuni National Park ⑩
Nacionalni Park Brijuni

The Brijuni Archipelago is made up of 14 islands and was declared a national park in 1983. The two largest islands have been inhabited since the Palaeolithic era. In Roman times there were aristocratic villas and later religious communities. The islands were abandoned in 1332 because of malaria, but people returned in the following century to work the stone quarries. In the late 19th century, the islands were bought by the Tyrolean industrialist Paul Kupelwieser. After World War II they were used as a summer residence by Marshal Tito, and were visited by heads of state. Visitors are only allowed on the two main islands, Veli Brijun and Mali Brijun.

The Fort of Mali Brijun is situated on the second largest island in the archipelago. The Austro-Hungarian fort was built at the end of the 19th century.

SV. MARKO

GAZ

OKRUGLJAK

MALI BRIJUN
LESSER BRIJUN

SUPIN

SUPINIĆ

Barban

Aerial View of the Brijuni Islands
The islands are covered with lush vegetation, much of it undisturbed by human habitation.

GALIJA

GRUNJ

KRASNICA

Safari Park
Tito introduced many species of exotic animal, including zebra. Many were gifts from visiting heads of state.

VRSAR

Native Animals
Numerous indigenous animals also live freely in the park: fallow deer, moufflon, roedeer, hares, peacocks and about 200 species of wild bird.

KEY

═══ Minor road

🚢 Ferry

🚆 Electric train

ℹ Tourist information

⋔ Archaeological site

Ancient Trees

Hundreds of different plant species from all over the world were planted on Brijun. Many of the trees, like this ancient olive, are now fully mature and are regarded as living monuments.

Roman Villa

Excavations have unearthed the foundations of a Roman villa, its calidarium *(hot room) and a* frigidarium *(cold room). A large room where the family met for banquets and ceremonies is decorated with mosaics.*

The museum, opened in 1955, contains cultural and archaeological finds from the island.

In the area around Brijuni harbour hotels and a golf course have been built.

VELI BRIJUN
GREATER BRIJUN

Brijuni

MADONA

Rt Ploče

Peneda

| 0 metres | 800 |
| 0 yards | 800 |

The Tegetthoff Fortress is a ruined Austrian defence system which was built in the 19th century.

The White Villa (Bijela Vila) dates from the Venetian period. It was restored in 1721. This was Tito's summer residence and was used for receptions and political meetings.

Byzantine Castle

On the western coast, in the gulf of Dobrika, are the ruins of a complex of buildings dating from the Byzantine era (539–778), with towers and walls for defence.

Pula (Pola)

Pula is well-known for its magnificent monuments from the Roman era, when it was a colony known as Pietas Julia. It became an episcopal seat in 425 and still has the foundations of some 5th-century religious buildings. It was destroyed by the Ostrogoths, but flourished again when it became the main base for the Byzantine fleet in the 6th and 7th centuries: the cathedral and church of St Mary of Formosa date from this time. In 1334 it came under Venetian rule, but by mid-17th century the population had declined to 300. Revitalized in 1856 when Austria made it the base for its fleet, it is still one of the most important naval bases in Croatia. Today, Pula is a university town and, with Pazin *(see pp64–5)*, the administrative centre of Istria.

Vase, Archaeological Museum

The cathedral's interior, a combination of styles and periods

Arch of the Sergii, 1st century BC

Arch of the Sergii
Slavoluk obitelji Sergijevaca
Ulica Sergijevaca.
The arch was erected in the 1st century BC on the orders of Salvia Postuma Sergia, to honour three brothers who held important positions in the Roman Empire. The arch is small with fluted columns, a winged victory and Corinthian capitals. Its frieze has a bas-relief depicting a chariot pulled by horses.
Next door is a bar named Uliks ("Ulysses"), in memory of James Joyce, who lived here for six months in 1904.

Church of St Mary of Formosa
Kapela Marije Formoze
Maksimilijanova ulica. ☐ to public.
A small Byzantine church, built on a Greek cross plan, this was once a chapel, part of the large Basilica of St Mary of Formosa. Inside are remains of mosaics from the 6th century.

Church of St Francis
Sv. Frane
Ulica Sv. Frane. ☐ *Jun–Sep: 10am–1pm, 4–8pm; for mass.*
Built at the same time as the adjacent monastery in the late 13th century, this white stone church has a fine doorway with a Gothic rose window. The interior is a single nave with three apses; on the main altar is a splendid wooden 15th-century polyptych by the Emilian school. Various exhibits from the Imperial Roman era can be seen in the monastery cloisters.

Temple of Romae and Augustus
Augustov hram
Forum. **Tel** *(052) 218 603.*
☐ *Jun–Sep: 8am–9pm Mon–Fri, 9am–3pm Sat & Sun; Oct–May: by appt.*
Built in the 1st century AD, this temple stands in the square which was once the site of the Roman forum. It is a splendid example of Roman

Temple of Romae and Augustus, a jewel of Roman architecture

architecture, built on simple lines, with six plain columns and beautiful carved capitals.

Cathedral
Katedrala
Obala Maršala Tita. ☐ *Jun–Sep: 10am–1pm, 4–8pm; Sep–May: for mass.*
The cathedral, dedicated to the Blessed Virgin Mary, was founded in the 6th century after Pula became an episcopal seat. It was enlarged in the 10th century, but its present appearance dates from the 17th century. However, parts of the walls, some of the capitals and the windows are from the original building. On the right is a doorway from 1456, while the bell tower, built by 1707, contains stone blocks from the amphitheatre.

Church of St Nicholas
Sv. Nikola
Castropola. ☐ *by appt.*
ℹ *(052) 212 987 (Tourist office).*
This church dates from the 6th century but was partially rebuilt in the 10th century. Towards the end of the 15th century it was assigned to the Orthodox community. Inside are some fine icons from the 15th and 16th centuries.

Castle and Historical Museum of Istria
Povijesni Muzej Istre
Kaštel. **Tel** *(052) 211 740.*
☐ *Jun–Sep: 8am–9pm daily; Oct–May: 9am–5pm daily.*
This star-shaped castle with four bastions houses the Historical Museum of Istria

and was built by the Venetians in the 14th century on the ruins of the Roman Capitol in the city centre. The walls linking the four towers offer splendid views over the city. Nearby are the remains of a 2nd-century theatre.

🏛 Archaeological Museum of Istria
Arheološki Muzej Istre
Carrarina 3. *Tel* (052) 218 603. ☐
Jun–Sep: 8am–9pm daily; Oct–May: 8.30am–4.30pm Mon–Sat. ✎

The Archaeological Museum is housed in the former German school, within a park which is reached from the Twin Gate. On display are finds from Pula and the surrounding area, with collections from the Prehistoric era to the Middle Ages. On the

Headless Statue, Archaeological Museum

ground floor are architectural remains, mosaics, altars and other exhibits from antiquity to medieval times.

The rooms on the first floor contain exhibits from the Neolithic to the Roman era. Three rooms on the second floor are dedicated to Roman antiquity (including a headless female statue found at Nesactium, near Pula). Two rooms have exhibits from the late-Classical to medieval periods. Of particular interest are pieces from Slavic tombs dating from the 7th to 12th centuries.

�n Twin Gate
Dvojna vrata
Carrarina.
The gate, from the 2nd–3rd centuries, has two arches with an ornate frieze. Nearby are parts of the wall which once encircled the city.

VISITORS' CHECKLIST

Map A3. 🏠 62,500. ✈ 8 km (5 miles), (052) 530 111.
🚢 (052) 211 878.
🚉 (052) 541 982. 🚌 Sijanska Cesta 4, (052) 500 012. ℹ
Tourist office, Forum 3, (052) 212 987. 🎭 Pula Opera, Pula Amphitheatre (summer), Croatian Film Festival (summer).
www.pulainfo.hr

�n Gate of Hercules
Herculova vrata
Carrarina.
South of the Archaeological Museum stands the single-arched Gate of Hercules. Built in the 1st century BC, it is the oldest and best preserved Roman monument in the city. At the top of the arch is a carving of the head of Hercules with a club.

�n Amphitheatre
See pp62–3.

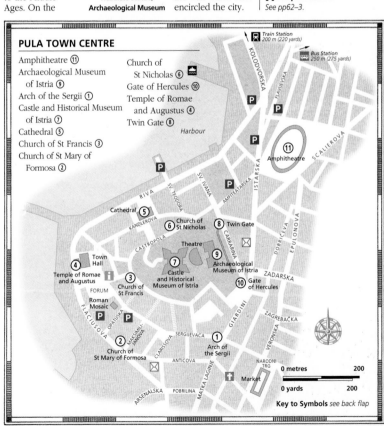

PULA TOWN CENTRE

Amphitheatre ⑪
Archaeological Museum of Istria ⑨
Arch of the Sergii ①
Castle and Historical Museum of Istria ⑦
Cathedral ⑤
Church of St Francis ③
Church of St Mary of Formosa ②
Church of St Nicholas ⑥
Gate of Hercules ⑩
Temple of Romae and Augustus ④
Twin Gate ⑧

Train Station 200 m (220 yards)
Bus Station 250 m (275 yards)

KOLODVORSKA
FLAVIJEVSKA
Harbour
⑪ Amphitheatre
SCALIEROVA
ISTARSKA
SV. IVANA
SV. TEODORA
RIVA
AMFITEATARSKA
Cathedral ⑤
KANDLEROVA
⑥ Church of St Nicholas
⑧ Twin Gate
CARRARINA
DOBRIĆEVA
EPULONOVA
CASTROPOLA
Theatre
⑨ Archaeological Museum of Istria
ZADARSKA
④ Town Hall
⑦ Castle and Historical Museum of Istria
⑩ Gate of Hercules
Temple of Romae and Augustus
③ Church of St Francis
FORUM
Roman Mosaic
FLACIUSOVA
OPATIJSKA
GIARDINI
ZAGREBAČKA
MAKSIMILIJANOVA
KLARISSOVA
SERGIJEVACA
① Arch of the Sergii
VENERSKA
② Church of St Mary of Formosa
ANTICOVA
NARODNI TRG
ARSENALSKA
POBRILINA
MATKA LAGINJE
Market

0 metres   200
0 yards   200
Key to Symbols *see back flap*

Pula Amphitheatre
Amfiteatar

The elliptical arena in Pula is one of the six largest Roman amphitheatres existing today. Originally a small amphitheatre built here by Claudius, it was enlarged by Vespasian in AD 79 for gladiator fights. The amphitheatre could hold 23,000 spectators and had about 20 entrances. It remained intact until the 15th century when some of the stone was used to construct the castle and other buildings in the city. It was restored, first by the French governor of the Illyrian provinces, General Marmont, and again more recently when it was adapted for musical events. It can seat 5,000 spectators and is a venue for concerts ranging from opera to rock as well as for an annual film festival.

View of the amphitheatre today

Four Towers
The roofs of the towers were designed to collect the scented water that was sprayed onto the stalls. It is also thought that there was a structure capable of supporting large awnings as protection from the sun and rain.

Amphitheatre Wall
The well-preserved external wall of the amphitheatre has three floors on the side facing the sea, and two on the opposite side, because it was constructed on an incline. At its highest point, the external wall measures 29.40 m (96 ft).

For hotels and restaurants in this region see pp222–6 and pp240–42

Interior of the Amphitheatre
When first built, the broad tiers could seat an audience of 23,000 people. Shows of every kind were performed, including naval battles. Today, during the summer season, operas, ballets and plays are put on here.

The various corridors which led to the seats allowed spectators to find their places efficiently.

RECONSTRUCTION
The main floor of the arena, 67.75 m (222 ft) long and 41.05 m (135 ft) wide, was originally framed by iron railings to separate spectators from the performance. Between the tiers of seats and the railings there was a space, 3m (10 ft) wide, reserved for staff. Along the main axis, under the arena, were underground corridors which were used by the gladiators and cages for animals. The animals were kept here before being sent into the stadium.

Today the southwest tower is one of the entrances.

Underground Area
Many archaeological finds from the amphitheatre and other Roman buildings are kept in the underground passages, where there were once cages and prisons.

Arches
The first two floors have 72 arches, the third has 64 large rectangular openings. The arches lit the internal corridors which enabled spectators to move from one sector of the amphitheatre to another.

Barban  ⑫

Map B3. ∰ *250.* ⊠ *Pula, 28 km (17 miles).* ⛴ *Pula.* ⛴ *from Pula.*
⛪ **Regional:** *Pionirska 1, Poreč, (052) 452 797.* ⚑ *Trka na prstenac, Tournament of the Ring (Aug).*

A free town in the late Middle Ages, in 1334 Barban came under the rule of the county of Pazin, and from 1420 until 1797 it was part of Venetian territory. It was granted to the Loredan family in 1535, and many buildings acquired their current Venetian look. The town still has some medieval fortifications which now incorporate several Renaissance buildings.

The church of **St Nicholas** (Sv. Nikola) faces the square, which is reached through the Great Gate (Vela Vrata). The church has five marble Gothic altars and many Venetian paintings (16th–18th centuries), one attributed to the Italian artist Padovanino.

In the same square is the Loredan Palace from 1606 and, towards the Small Gate (Mala Vrata), the Town Hall dating from 1555 with a loggia and a clock tower.

Outside the Great Gate is the 14th-century church of **St Anthony** (Sv. Antun), with some frescoes from the 15th century. In 1970, the Tournament of the Ring was revived and costumed lancers on horses participate in this traditional annual event.

🏛 **St Nicholas**
***Tel** (052) 567 173.* ⃝ *by appt.*

Svetvinčenat ⑬

Map A3. ∰ *300.* ⛴ *Pazin.* ⛴ *from Pula.* ⛪ **Local:** *Svetvinčenat 96, (052) 560 005.* **Regional:** *Pionirska 1, Poreč, (052) 452 797.*

This walled village was built in the 10th century on a small hill around a much restructured fort. The main square is one of the most beautiful in Istria. Many of the main buildings in the village are found here, including the 15th-century church of the **Annunciation** which contains two paintings by Palma il Giovane and an *Annunciation* by the artist Giuseppe Salviati.

Church of the Annunciation, Svetvinčenat

The **Castle** dates from the 13th century and is one of the best preserved in the region. It belonged to the Venetian families of Castropola, the Morosini and the Grimani. In 1589, the Grimani commissioned the architect Scamozzi to convert one of the square towers into a residence for the Venetian governors, the other into a prison. High walls connecting the other two round towers enclose a large internal courtyard. This is reached through the citadel's only gate, which at one time had a drawbridge. The town's coat of arms and that of the Grimani family can also be seen here.

The town's name derives from the Romanesque church and cemetery of **St Vincent** (Sv. Vinčenat), whose walls were frescoed by an unknown 15th-century artist.

🏛 **St Vincent**
*Cemetery. **Tel** (052) 560 004.* ⃝ *by appt.*

Environs

About 10 km (6 miles) away are the ruins of **Dvidgrad** (Duecastelli), an atmospheric, abandoned walled village, surrounded by lush vegetation.

Around 1000 AD, two castles were built on neighbouring hills and were later enclosed by an oval wall. A village of 200 inhabitants grew up inside the wall around the basilica of St Sophia, built between the 11th and 12th centuries. Although attacked and burnt by the Genoese in the 14th century during the war with Venice, the village soon recovered. In the 17th century, sacking by the Uskoks *(see p81)* and a malaria epidemic depopulated the village. It has not been inhabited since then.

Reconstruction of a room in the Ethnographic Museum, Pazin

Pazin ⑭

Map B2. ∰ *5,300.*
⛴ *(052) 624 310.* 🚌 *(052) 624 437.* ⛪ *Franine i Jurine 14, (052) 622 460.* **www**.istra.com/pazin

The town of Pazin originated in the 9th century as a fort and stands on a cliff 130 m (426 ft) high. One side of the cliff falls away to an abyss called Fojba which is 100 m (328 ft) deep and about 20 m (65 ft) wide, and is said to have inspired Dante's description of the Gateway to Hell in *Inferno*.

In the 14th century, Pazin passed into the hands of the

The imposing, overgrown ruins of Dvidgrad

For hotels and restaurants in this region see pp222–6 and pp240–42

Habsburgs, who granted it to the Montecuccoli family as a reward for their services in the war against the Turks. The family maintained ownership of the castle after the end of the feudal regime.

The castle's present layout dates from the 16th century, when the wings were joined and a large tower was added. The tower is reached through a doorway in the façade made in 1786. Since 1955 it has housed the **Ethnographic Museum of Istria** (Etnografski muzej). In 1996 the **Civic Museum** was set up, with weaponry and finds from the castle on display.

The church of **St Francis** (Sv. Frane) and its 15th-century monastery were cultural centres for the area. The first schools to be set up in inland Istria were built here.

🏛 **Ethnographic Museum of Istria and Civic Museum**
Castle, Trg Istarskog razvoda 1.
Tel *(052) 622 220.* ⬜ *May–Oct: 9am–6pm Mon–Sat, 9am–3pm Sun; Nov–Apr: 9am–4pm Mon–Sat.* 📷

Gračišće ⑮

Map B2. 🚶 *350.* 🚉 *Pazin, 7 km (4 miles).* 🚌 *Labin.* ℹ *Aldo Negri 20, Labin, (052) 855 560.*

The small village of Gračišće stands on a hill among woods and vineyards. At one time this was a strong military garrison, which stood on the borders of the Venetian Republic and the Habsburg empire. The town has some interesting buildings, such as the 15th-century **Salamon Palace** in Venetian-Gothic style and, to the side, the **Bishop's Chapel**, also in Venetian Gothic style, where the bishop of Pićan spent the summer.

The church of **St Mary** (Sv. Marije) was consecrated in 1425 and has a characteristic barrel vault and several frescoes. The Romanesque church of **St Euphemia** (Sv. Fumija) was rebuilt in the 16th century and still has a wooden crucifix from the 14th century. The loggia near the main gate dates from 1549.

The picturesque town of Pićan, once a bishop's see

Pićan ⑯

Map B2. 🚶 *316.* 🚉 *Pazin, 17 km (10 miles).* ℹ *Aldo Negri 20, Labin, (052) 855 560.*

Known as Petena under the Romans, Pićan stands on a hilltop 350m (1,150 ft) high. It was a bishop's see from the 5th century to 1788, and has some intriguing medieval buildings. Inside the medieval walls is a cathedral dedicated to St Nicephorus, built in the 14th century, and rebuilt in the early 18th century after an earthquake. The story of the Christian martyr Nicephorus, whose remains were brought to Pićan by horse, are shown in a painting by Valentin Metzinger (1699–1759) in the cathedral. The Romanesque church of St Michael (Sv. Mihovil) in the cemetery has early 15th-century frescoes.

Labin ⑰

Map B3. 🚶 *320.* 🚌 *Rudarska ulica 5, (052) 855 022.* ℹ *Aldo Negri 20, (052) 855 560, 851 486.* 🎵 *Classical music concerts (summer).*

The old part of Labin is made up of the medieval part inside the walls, and the part from the Venetian period around Tito Square (Titov Trg). Here stand the 19th-century Town Hall, a 17th-century bastion, a loggia (1550) and the St Flora gate (1587) with a Lion of St Mark.

In the square called Stari Trg is the Gothic **Church of the Blessed Mary's Birth** (Rodjenje Marijino), built in the late 14th century but frequently renovated. A rose window decorates the façade

and inside are works by Venetian artists of the 16th and 17th centuries, including a painting by Palma il Giovane.

In the same square are the Magistrates' Court (1555), Scampicchio Palace (16th century) and the early 18th-century Baroque Lazzarini Palace, now the **Town Museum** with Roman and medieval finds, and a lifelike reconstruction of a coal mine. Labin was Croatia's most important coal mining town until the mines were closed down in 1999. In 1921, in opposition to rising Fascism in Italy, 2,000 coalminers set up the Labin Republic, a socialist mini-state that barely lasted a month.

🏛 **Town Museum**
Trg 1 Maja 6. ***Tel*** *(052) 852 477.*
⬜ *Jun–Sep: 10am–1pm, 5–7pm Mon–Sat; Oct–May: 7am–3pm Mon–Fri.*

Environs
About 4 km (2 miles) from Labin lies the popular seaside resort of Rabac.

Stepped road and ancient buildings, Labin

Detail of the altar in the church of
St George the Younger, Plomin

Plomin ⑱

Map B3. ![icon] *140.* ![icon] *Pula, 72 km
(45 miles).* ![icon] *Rijeka, 40 km (25
miles).* ![icon] *Aldo Negri 20, Labin; (052)
855 560;* **Regional:** *Pionirska 1,
Poreč, (052) 452 797.*

An ancient fortified town
once stood here on the
site of the Roman town
Flanona, which was destroyed
by the Avars in the 6th
century. It was rebuilt after
1000 AD and took on its
present look in the 13th
century after it had become
Venetian territory. Plomin,
built on a sheer cliff 180 m
(590 ft) above the bay of
the same name, was once
densely populated.

   Houses take up nearly all
the space inside the walls
(from the 13th–14th centuries
and only partially preserved).
Worn, narrow roads climb
towards the centre, where the
13th-century Romanesque
church of **St George the
Elder** (Sv. Jurai Stari) stands.
Inside is a tablet in Glagolitic
script *(see p35)* from between
the 11th and 12th centuries,
one of the oldest Croatian
Glagolitic documents in Istria.

   The church of **St George
the Younger** (Sv. Jurai) also
contains treasures of artistic
merit. The church was
consecrated in 1474, but was
greatly altered in the 18th
century. There are two
Renaissance altars in carved,
painted wood and a rich
church treasury. Two frescoes
by Robert, a German painter,
were found on the wall
during restoration work.

Mošćenice ⑲

Map B2. ![icon] *330.* ![icon] *Rijeka, 53 km
(33 miles), on the island of Krk.* ![icon]
Rijeka. ![icon] *Aleja Slatina, Mošćenička
Draga, (051) 737 533.*

This small village was founded
by the Liburnians on a small
hilltop. The structure of the
medieval town is still evident,
with houses pressed against
the walls, narrow streets, small
alleys and courtyards. There
are lovely views over the
Kvarner Gulf from the village.

   In the main square is the
church of **St Andrew** (Sv.
Andrije), a building of
medieval origin which
was rebuilt in the
Baroque style in the
17th century. Inside are
some statues by the
Paduan sculptor
Jacopo Contieri,
which adorn the
beautiful 16th-
century choir. The
tall bell tower
dominates the town.
Just outside the walls
are the small church of
St Sebastian from the
16th century, and the
17th-century church
of St Bartholomew.

   The history of the
area is documented
in the **Ethnographic
Museum** Etnografski
Muzej).

Statue by Contieri,
church of St
Andrew, Mošćenice

🏛 **Ethnographic Museum**
Tel *(051) 737 551.*

Environs
A series of steps leads down
to Mošćenička Draga (2 km/1
mile), where there is a large
pebble beach.

Lovran ⑳

Map B2. ![icon] *3,640.* ![icon] *Rijeka, 35 km (22 miles).* ![icon]
Rijeka, 35 km (22 miles). ![icon] *Rijeka, 35
km (22 miles).* ![icon] *Šetalište Maršala
Tita 63, (051) 291 740.* ![icon] *Festival of
St George (23 Apr); Marunada,
chestnut festival (first Sun in Oct).*
www.tz-lovran.hr

The modern part of Lovran
(whose name derives from
the laurel trees which are
common in the area) is built
on the slopes of the Gorica
hill and extends along the
coast until it meets the long
seafront at Opatija *(see p67).*
The old part of the town
stands on a small peninsula
along the coast. The
houses in the ancient
fortified town lean
against the enclosing
walls, of which very
few parts remain: just
a tower and the
Stubiza Gate. In the
main square, as well
as a medieval tower
there are several houses
with Venetian Gothic
façades and the church
of **St George** (Sv.
Jurai), built in the
14th century and
rebuilt in the
Baroque period,
along with a
Romanesque bell
tower. Inside the
church, on the vault and the
arch of the apse are some late
Gothic frescoes (1470–79)
representing the life of Christ
and several saints. A building
with a figure of St George
stands in the main square.

   Along the coastal
promenade which extends

Old mill at the Ethnographic Museum, Mošćenice

The Villa Angiolina in Opatija, surrounded by a splendid park

between Lovran and Ika stand several beautiful early 20th-century Secessionist villas *(see p23)*, surrounded by lush gardens.

⚑ St George
Tel (051) 291 611. ⬭ *by appt.*

Tour of the Fortified Towns ㉑

See pp68–9.

Opatija ㉒

Map B2. 🏛 *9,000.* ✈ *Rijeka, 25 km (15 miles), island of Krk.* 🚌 *Rijeka.* 🚢 *Rijeka.* ⓘ **Local:** *Nazarova 3, (051) 271 710;* **Regional:** *Nikole Tesle 2, (051) 272 909, 272 988.* 🎭 *Karneval na Opatijskoj Rivijeri (Carnival); International regatta (May); Gastrofest (Mar).* **www**.opatija.hr

The tourist resort of Opatija takes its name from a 14th-century Benedictine abbey, around which a village was built. On the site of the monastery now stands the church of St James (Sv. Jakov), built in 1506 and enlarged in 1937.

Tourist interest began to grow in around 1845 when a nobleman from Rijeka, Iginio Scarpa, built the grand **Villa Angiolina** here. The villa is surrounded by a large park and became the first hotel.

A few years later the Austrian Empress Maria Anna stayed here and her visit was immediately followed by visits from other court dignitaries. More luxury hotels and villas were then built and the small town became a fashionable turn-of-the-century resort. Tourism in Opatija was given a boost by the construction of the railway line which linked Austria with Rijeka, with a tram line to Opatija.

The Emperor Franz Joseph also built a villa here, where he used to stay for long periods in the winter, so as to enjoy the mild climate of the area. Today the coast is still lined with luxury late 19th-century hotels and villas surrounded by parks and gardens. It is no longer the height of fashion, although older visitors are drawn by its comparative tranquillity.

Kastav ㉓

Map B2. 🏛 *930.* ✈ *Rijeka, 20 km (12 miles), island of Krk.* 🚌 *Rijeka, 11 km (7 miles).* 🚢 *Rijeka, 11 km (7 miles).* ⓘ *Kastav 43, (051) 691 425.* 🎭 *Bela Nedeja, wine festival (first Sun in Oct).*

On a hill a short distance from Rijeka is the town of Kastav, which originated in the early Middle Ages. The castle was the residence of the local lord of the manor until the 16th century, and later the home of the Austrian governor. In Lovkine square stand the 17th-century church of St Helen of the Cross (Sv. Jelena Krizarica), the church of St Anthony of the Desert (15th century), and a loggia from 1571, restored in 1815. By the water trough a plaque recalls the drowning in 1666 of Captain Morello, guilty of imposing excessive taxes.

The harbour at Opatija, once a great favourite with the Habsburg royals

Tour of the Fortified Towns ㉑

Message box for denunciations

The villages and towns of Istria were all fortified. The first people to build walls were the Istri (Illyrian tribes), who put up defences on the hilltops where they settled. There are 136 such fortified towns in Istria. Many were abandoned, but evidence in some shows continuous occupation from 1000 BC up to the present day. The walls were reinforced in Roman times and rebuilt in the late Middle Ages, then enlarged when the towns came under Austrian or Venetian rule. Documents written in the ancient Glagolitic script can be seen on a detour.

Hum ③
This small village is protected by an oval wall, reinforced by the Venetians. The church of St Jerome has splendid 12th-century Byzantine frescoes.

Buzet ④
An Illyrian fort and a Roman fortification (Pinguentum), Buzet belonged to the Venetians from 1420 onwards. They rebuilt the town wall with a Large Gate (1457) and a Small Gate. Today Buzet is known for its truffles.

Istarske Toplice

Livade

Račice

↓ *PAZIN*

Draguč ⑤
Medieval walls form the backs of the houses in this village. Ramparts were built by the Venetians after 1420. The 14th-century church of St Roch has a series of frescoes, including a Journey of the Magi.

KEY

▬▬▬	Tour route
▪ ▪ ▪	Trail of the Glagolitics
▭ ▭ ▭	Other roads
🛈	Tourist information
※	Viewpoint

Motovun ⑥
This medieval town stands on a hill dominating the valley. The old town is still encircled by an original 13th–14th-century wall. Later, a second wall was built around the suburbs. An internal gate, under a 15th-century tower, leads from the Lower Town to the Upper Town.

Roč ②

The wall around Roč was built by the Patriarchate of Aquileia in the 14th century. Towers were added in the 1500s. Roč was an important centre for Glagolitic writing and in the 1200s the alphabet was carved on a wall in the church of St Anthony Abbot. The Romanesque church of St Roch contains two fresco cycles.

TIPS FOR WALKERS

Departure point: Boljun.
Distance: 77 km (48 miles) one way. *Stopping-off points:* **Motovun** Restaurant Mcotic, (052) 681 758; **Hum** Humska Konoba, (052) 660 005 (restaurant); **Buzet** Gostiona Most, (052) 662 867 (restaurant). ▮ **Buzet** Trg Fontana, (052) 662 343. **Poreč** Head office for Istria, Pionirska 1, Poreč, (052) 452 797.

0 kilometres 3

0 miles 3

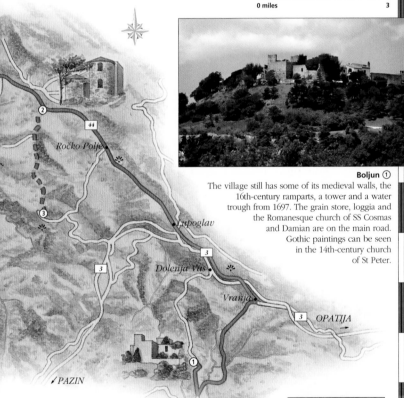

Boljun ①

The village still has some of its medieval walls, the 16th-century ramparts, a tower and a water trough from 1697. The grain store, loggia and the Romanesque church of SS Cosmas and Damian are on the main road. Gothic paintings can be seen in the 14th-century church of St Peter.

Ročko Polje

Lupoglav

Dolenja Vas

Vranja

OPATIJA

PAZIN

THE TRAIL OF GLAGOLITIC DOCUMENTS

The "Trail of the Glagolitics" (Aleja Glagoljaša) winds between Roč and Hum. It is 7 km (4 miles) long and was created from 1977 to 1985 to commemorate this ancient Croatian script. Along the way are 11 significant Glagolitic documents recalling events and people who contributed to the spread of the writing, invented in the 11th century by the saints Cyril and Methodius to translate the scriptures *(see pp34–5)* into Slavonic.

Glagolitic document in stone on the trail to Roč

Rijeka ㉔

Founded by the Liburnians and conquered by the Celts, this town became a Roman city called Tarsatica. Over the centuries it frequently changed hands, and finally came under the rule of the Habsburgs. In 1719, to develop its maritime role, Ferdinand of Habsburg declared Rijeka a free town. The city became part of the kingdom of Hungary in 1769 and its economic importance continued to grow. Together with shipyards and industry, Rijeka is one of Croatia's main ports and a key rail and road junction. In February and March each year, Rijeka hosts Croatia's largest carnival celebrations.

Local handicraft
(see p252)

The Korzo, a pedestrian avenue with 19th-century buildings

Exploring Rijeka

Over recent decades, the city has expanded, somewhat chaotically, along the coast and into the surrounding hills. However, its Central European atmosphere is still preserved in the majestic 19th-century buildings along the Korzo and the Riva, two broad avenues south of the Old Town (Stari Grad), built on land reclaimed from the sea. The Korzo is the heart of the city, lined with cafés, bars, restaurants and shops.

🔒 Church of the Capuchins
Kapucinska crkva
Kapucinske stube 5. *Tel (051) 335 233.* ◯ *7am–noon, 4–7.45pm.*
North of Žabica Square (Trg Žabica) is the Capuchin Church, built between 1904 and 1929. The church is also known as the Madonna of Lourdes, because it was built on the 50th anniversary of the miracle of Lourdes.

🔒 Church of St Nicholas
Sv. Nikola
Ulica Ivana Zajca. *Tel (051) 335 399.* ◯ *8.30am–noon Tue–Sun.*
The church of St Nicholas, built by the Orthodox community in 1790, contains fine icons from Vojvodina in Serbia.

🕍 Civic Tower
Gradski Toranj
About halfway along the Korzo is the Civic Tower. The tower is the result of alterations made to the gate of the Old Town from the 15th century. It was erected in the 18th century and the clock *(Pod Uriloj)* was also added. In 1890 the dome was built. An imposing building, it is decorated with coats of arms, including those of the city and the Habsburgs, and busts of the emperors Leopold I and Charles VI.

Detail of the Civic Tower

🕍 Town Hall
Municipij
Trg Riječke Rezolucije.
In 1883, the 14th-century Augustinian monastery was turned into the Town Hall. It takes up three sides of the square and is today the office of the University Rector.

♫ Roman Arch
Stara Vrata
Trg Ivana Koblera.
In an alley leading from the north side of the square are the remains of a Roman arch, which was probably a gate to the city. It is a simple stone structure. Nearby, excavations have unearthed the foundations of a perimeter wall from the Roman period.

🔒 Church of the Assumption
Crkva Uznesenja Blažene Djevice Marije
Pavla Rittera Vitezovića 3. *Tel (051) 214 177.* ◯ *7am–noon, 4–7pm.*
The Church of the Assumption, once a cathedral, preserves little of its original 13th-century aspect. It was renovated in the Baroque style in 1695 and altered in 1726 with Rococo details, and a 16th-century rose window was inserted. Inside, the altars, some paintings and the chancel are from the Baroque period. The bell tower bears the date of its construction (1377); the upper part is in Gothic style.

🔒 Cathedral of St Vitus
Katedrala Sv. Vida
Trg Grivica. ◯ *7am–noon, 5–8pm.*
The church of St Vitus, patron saint of the city, is now the cathedral. This large Baroque church was built between 1638 and 1742 by the Jesuits. Baroque altars, and a Gothic crucifix from the 13th century, adorn the interior.

🏛 Maritime and Historical Museum of Coastal Croatia
Pomorski i Povijesni Muzej Hrvatskog Primorja
Muzejski trg 1/1. *Tel (051) 553 666.* ◯ *9am–6pm Tue–Fri, 9am–1pm Sat.* 🎟 *(students free).*
This is the oldest museum in Rijeka, founded in 1876, but

Gothic crucifix in the cathedral of St Vitus

since 1955 housed in the Governor's Palace built in 1896. The history of navigation is told through the collections of model ships, weapons and seafaring equipment from the 17th and 18th centuries. There are also rich archaeological collections from prehistory to the Middle Ages, displays of prints, furniture, paintings and an ethnographic collection.

🏛 Our Lady of Trsat
Gospa Trsatska
Frankopanski trg. *Tel (051) 492 900.*
⬜ *daily.*

On the opposite bank of the Rječina river, above the centre of Rijeka, is Trsat. At the top of the 561 steps from Tito Square (Trg Titov) is the Sanctuary of Our Lady of Trsat. The church and Franciscan monastery were built in 1453 by Martin Frankopan on the site of a 12th-century church. It was in this church, from 1291 to 1294, that parts of the Holy House of Mary of Nazareth were preserved before being transferred to

The altar of Our Lady of Trsat, with the painting of the Virgin

Loreto in Italy. To compensate the local people for this loss, in 1367 Pope Urban V donated to them a *Virgin with Child*, painted by St Luke, which now stands on the main altar.

The sanctuary was visited by soldiers and sailors who left votive gifts, now kept in a chapel next to the cloisters. The church was remodelled in 1864 but retained the triumphal arch, the marble altar which sits underneath the painting of the Virgin, and many tombs of the Frankopan family.

VISITORS' CHECKLIST

Map B2. 🏘 *168,000.* ✈ *Krk, (051) 842 040.* 🚌 *Krešimirova ulica, (051) 211 111.* 🚆 *Trg Žabice 1, (060) 302 010.* ⛴ *Riva, (051) 212 696; Adriatic: Verdijeva 6, (051) 214 300; Jadrolinija Riva 16, (051) 211 444.* 🛈 *Korzo 33, (051) 335 882.* 🎭 *Rijeka's Summer Nights arts festival (Jun–Jul), Rijeka carnival (Feb).*

🏛 Trsat Castle
Gradina Trsat
Ulica Zrinskog. *Tel (051) 217 714.*
⬜ *summer: 8am–8pm; winter: 9am–5pm.* 🎫 💻 🎵

The Sanctuary of Our Lady leads to a castle built by the Romans to defend Tarsatica, parts of which still survive. In the 13th century, Trsat was owned by the Frankopans, who built another castle on the same site. In the 19th century it was bought and renovated by an Austrian general, Laval Nugent, who lived and was buried here. There are fine views from the site over the Kvarner gulf.

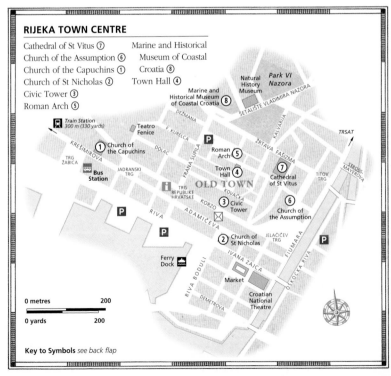

RIJEKA TOWN CENTRE

Cathedral of St Vitus ⑦
Church of the Assumption ⑥
Church of the Capuchins ①
Church of St Nicholas ②
Civic Tower ③
Roman Arch ⑤
Marine and Historical Museum of Coastal Croatia ⑧
Town Hall ④

Natural History Museum
Park VI Nazora
ŠETALIŠTE VLADIMIRA NAZORA
KALVARIJA
ŽRTAVA FAŠIZMA
TRSAT
STROSS-MAYEROVA

Train Station 300 m (330 yards)
Teatro Fenice
F. KURELCA
DEŽMANA
Marine and Historical Museum of Coastal Croatia ⑧
KREŠIMIROVA
TRG ŽABICA
① Church of the Capuchins
DOLAC
JADRANSKI TRG
Bus Station
FRANA SUPILA
Roman Arch ⑤
Town Hall ④
Cathedral of St Vitus ⑦
TITOV TRG
TRG REPUBLIKE HRVATSKE
OLD TOWN
KOVAČKA
③ Civic Tower
⑥ Church of the Assumption
P
RIVA
ADAMIĆEVA
KORZO
② Church of St Nicholas
JELAČIĆEV TRG
FIUMARA
P
Ferry Dock
RIVA BODULI
IVANA ZAJCA
OSROČKA RIVA
Market
DEMETROVA
Croatian National Theatre

0 metres   200
0 yards   200

Key to Symbols *see back flap*

Cres

The narrow island of Cres is 65 km (40 miles) long. In the north, a colony of native griffon vultures, protected by law since 1986, nests on a plateau swept by the dry, cold bora wind. The south is milder and olives and vines are grown. A single road travels from the north of Cres to the south of Lošinj, linking the islands by a bridge. Tourism focuses on just a few villages such as Cres, Osor, Martinšćica and Valun.

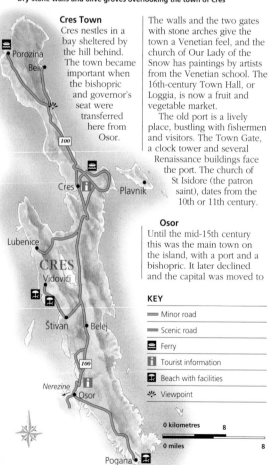

Dry-stone walls and olive groves overlooking the town of Cres

Cres Town
Cres nestles in a bay sheltered by the hill behind. The town became important when the bishopric and governor's seat were transferred here from Osor.

The walls and the two gates with stone arches give the town a Venetian feel, and the church of Our Lady of the Snow has paintings by artists from the Venetian school. The 16th-century Town Hall, or Loggia, is now a fruit and vegetable market.

The old port is a lively place, bustling with fishermen and visitors. The Town Gate, a clock tower and several Renaissance buildings face the port. The church of St Isidore (the patron saint), dates from the 10th or 11th century.

Osor
Until the mid-15th century this was the main town on the island, with a port and a bishopric. It later declined and the capital was moved to

Cres. Today the entire town is a museum, with Bronze Age remains and some splendid monuments, making it a centre of great artistic interest.

The beautiful 5th-century cathedral of the Assumption was renovated in 1497 and is built of honey-coloured stone. The façade has an arched tympanum above a doorway with a relief of the Virgin Mary. Inside the church there is a painting of SS Nicholas and Gaudentius on the altar.

The Archaeological Museum (Arheološki muzej) occupies the Town Hall and has stone inscriptions and interesting finds from the Illyrian and Roman periods, and the early Middle Ages. The façade of the Bishop's Palace (second half of the 15th century) bears coats of arms of the bishops and nobles of the island and the interior is richly decorated. Some walls, foundations and mosaics are all that remain of the cathedral of St Peter. Nearby are two Romanesque churches dedicated to St Plato and St Catherine.

🏛 Archaeological Museum
Arheološki musej
Town Hall, Palazzo Petrić.
Tel (051) 571 127. for restoration. Contact Tourist Office for information.

KEY

▬▬	Minor road
▬▬	Scenic road
🚢	Ferry
ℹ	Tourist information
🏖	Beach with facilities
🌿	Viewpoint

0 kilometres   8

0 miles   8

Door of the Gothic church of Our Lady of the Snow, Cres

Map labels: Porozina, Beli, Cres, Plavnik, Lubenice, CRES, Vidovići, Štivan, Belej, Nerezine, Osor, Pogana

Lošinj (Lussino)

The island of Lošinj has a mild climate and sub-tropical vegetation with maritime pines, palms, oleanders and citrus trees. The main town, Mali Lošinj, was founded in the 6th century, when 12 Croat families landed here. The most famous beach is at Čikat bay, southwest of Mali Lošinj. It is 30 km (19 miles) long and a popular place for water sports.

Interior of the church of St Anthony Abbot, Veli Lošinj

Mali Lošinj
This pretty town, which, like Cres, belonged to Venice for many centuries, has many buildings from the 18th and 19th centuries, when maritime activity was at its height. The oldest part of the town lies around the 18th-century church of St Mary. Large hotel complexes just outside the town cater for package holidaymakers at this popular and bustling resort.

Veli Lošinj
Quieter than Mali Lošinj, this is a lovely town with villas hidden among the lush vegetation. The church of St Anthony Abbot is from the 15th century but was rebuilt at a later date. It has a rich store of paintings, including examples by Bartolomeo Vivarini (1430–90), Bernardo Strozzi (1581–1644) and Francesco Hayez (1791–1882). The Baroque style is much in evidence on the seven altars.

There is a splendid view of the town and the coastline from the 16th-century tower of the Uskoks (*see p81*).

Environs
The island of **Susak** is renowned for its unusual geology: a 10-m (33-ft) layer of sand covering a calcareous platform. Vines grow well on this soil and all the islanders have vineyards; their wealth is measured by the number of vines they own. The vines, grown on terraces and protected by cane wind-breaks, are further sheltered by dry-stone walls which are typical of the islands and the coastline of the upper Adriatic. The picturesque, brightly coloured women's costumes are famous. They are made by the islanders during the winter months and shown off at festivals.

The island of **Ilovik**, south of Lošinj, covers an area of nearly 6 sq km (2.3 sq miles) and is home of about 350 people, most of whom live in the village of Sv. Petar on the northeast coast. Vines, olives, fruit and flowers grow well in this mild climate. Nearby is the uninhabited island of Sv. Petar, where there are the ruins of a Venetian fortress and a Benedictine Abbey with a church and monastery. Prehistoric and Roman finds (mosaics, coins and other objects) have been discovered on Susak and Ilovik.

Unije is the largest of the lesser islands. It is hilly with little vegetation and a steep rocky coast on the western side, but there is a more accessible coast on the eastern side. The village is built around the church of St Andrew and its bell tower can be seen from a distance. The islanders tend to make their living from market gardening or fishing.

KEY

	Minor road
	Path
	Ferry
	Airport
	Tourist information
	Beach with facilities
	Viewpoint

Overlooking the fishing harbour of Mali Lošinj

Risnjak National Park: The Leska Trail ㉗
Nacionali Park Risnjak

The vast Gorski Kotor plateau, which separates Croatia from Slovenia, begins north of Rijeka. Part of the area has been declared a national park in order to protect the forests and natural environment and the ecological balance of the area. The park, set up in 1953, originally covered an area of 34 sq km (13 sq miles), but it is now double that size, most of it made up of forests and grasslands with many karst (limestone) features. The climatic conditions, caused by the territory's particular exposure and altitude, are very varied and about 20 different plant communities have been identified. The Leska trail was set up in 1995 to inform visitors about various aspects of this area.

☐ Park area

☐ The Leska trail

Silver Fir Forest ⑧
The silver fir, in great demand for boat building, has disappeared from many woods in Croatia; here it mingles with beech trees.

Chasm ⑦
Cold air from the chasm and the damp subsoil of this rocky fissure make the flora of great interest: plants which normally only grow at the higher altitudes of the park can be found here.

Feed Troughs ⑥
Feed troughs are set up here in winter to provide food for all the animals in the park.

Hranilište

⑥

⑤

685

⑧

⑦

Osmatračnica
⑨
Klada

690

Gmajna

MARKOV
BRLOG

686

Observatory ⑨
From this viewing platform the behaviour of animals such as bears, foxes, lynxes, martens and wild cats can be observed in the woods. There are also many birds, both non-migratory and birds of passage. Towards evening at certain times of the year, eagles, hawks and crows can also be seen.

707

⑫

⑩

Leska

⑪

Cultivating the Countryside ⑩
Only one house is inhabited in the village of Leska. It is used from spring to autumn by farmers, who come to grow potatoes, peas and beans on specially built terraces.

Tree Trunks ⑫
Fungi thrive in the cracks of old tree trunks providing a source of food for insects too.

Springs ⑪
Water flows under the layers of impervious rock and springs are created where the water emerges.

Beech and Fir Forests ⑤
The trail goes through woods of fir and beech trees; many of the trees are very large. The undergrowth consists of hazelnut, bilberry and elder bushes.

Mountain Meadows ④
The areas which were deforested for agriculture or grazing land for animals are now mountain meadows. In late spring they explode with the varied colours of heather, purple moor grass, fescue and other grasses.

Conservation of Trees ①
The protection of the older, larger plant species was one of the reasons the reserve was set up. Within the park are examples of enormous ancient beech, silver and spruce fir trees, and also some rarer trees, such as the mountain elm and maple.

0 metres   200
0 yards   200

CRNI LUG

Storm Damage ②
When strong winds blow down old or sick trees, they are left where they fall as they provide suitable growing conditions for microorganisms such as fungi.

Karst Sinkholes ③
A karst sinkhole is a funnel-shaped hollow in the land. This feature is caused by water erosion of the rock and is characteristic of limestone areas.

KEY

▬ Pedestrian trail

= Other roads

Krk 28

Part of the Frankopan castle

This is the largest of the Adriatic islands, with an area of 409 sq km (158 sq miles). A bridge links the island to the mainland, built to provide good connections to the island's international airport. Along the eastern coast the island looks almost ghostly, its white rocks swept by the bora wind. Inland and on the more protected western coast, there is rich, lush vegetation.

VISITORS' CHECKLIST

Map B3. 🏠 *16,500.* 🛬 *(051) 842 040.* **Krk** 🚢 *(051) 863 170.* 🛈 *Trg Sv. Kvirina 1, (051) 221 359; Krk Vela Placa 1, (051) 222 583.* **Baška** 🚢 *(051) 856 821.* 🛈 *Kralja Zvonimira 114, (051) 856 544.* **Omišalj** 🛈 *Ribarska Obala 10, (051) 846 243.*

The crystal-clear waters surrounding the island of Krk

Krk was first inhabited by the Liburnians, followed by the Romans, who founded Curicum (the present-day Krk) and Fulfinum (now Omišalj). Traces of walls, baths and villas with floor mosaics still remain.

In the 6th century it came under Croatian rule and after the Frankish and Byzantine occupation it became part of the possessions of Venice. It was then granted to Dujmo, founder of the Frankopan family, and from 1480 to 1797 it was directly ruled by Venice.

Krk was a centre for Glagolitic script and the Baška Tablet, now in the Croatian Academy of Arts and Sciences in Zagreb, was found on the island.

Krk Town

The town of Krk developed in the Middle Ages on the site of the Roman town of Curicum. The wall and three Venetian city gates are still visible: the City Gate with a guard tower called Kamplin, the Sea Gate (Pisana) and the Upper Gate. Facing the main square are Renaissance-era buildings and in the area of the Roman baths is the

cathedral of **Our Lady of the Assumption,** dating from the 1100s but modified since. The three-aisle church has a façade of light-coloured stone. Inside are four paintings (1706) by Cristoforo Tasca, and a wooden Baroque pulpit.

The treasury is in the adjacent Romanesque church of **St Quirinus** which houses the **Diocesan Museum**. This contains works from the cathedral and other churches on the island, including the silver Frankopan altarpiece depicting the *Virgin Mary in Glory* and a polyptych (1350) by Paolo Veneziano.

Behind the cathedral stands the Frankopan castle with four square towers from 1191, and a round tower from the Venetian period. Inside the walls are churches dedicated to Our Lady of Health and St Francis. The latter has an engraved wooden pulpit.

Omišalj

Omišalj lies on a headland near the site of Roman Fulfinum. The village (Castrum Musculum in the Middle Ages) was enclosed by walls, some of which

KEY

🟰	Major road
🟰	Minor road
▬	Scenic route
🚢	Ferry
🛬	Airport
🛈	Tourist information
🏖	Beach with facilities

Kraljevica
Omišalj
Rudine
Njivice
Klimno
102
Šilo
Porat
Glavotok
Šepići
Kozarin • Vrbnik
KRK
Krk
Valbiska
Košljun • Punat
102
Jurandvor
Baška
Stara Baška

0 kilometres _____ 8
0 miles _____ 8

◁ **Red-tiled roofs of the town of Krk**

survive. Narrow streets lead up to a square with a 17th-century Venetian loggia, the church of St Helen with reproductions of Glagolitic script, and the Romanesque church of St Mary (13th century) with a dome, bell tower and 16th-century choir, and a 15th-century triptych by Jacobello del Fiore.

Glagolitic inscription and rose window, St Mary, Omišalj

Baška

Stara Baška (Old Baška) is opposite Omišalj. Baška (New Baška) is on the coast and is a popular tourist resort with a beautiful beach, 2 km (1 mile) long, and clear sea. The church of the Holy Trinity (1772) stands in a small square; inside is a fine *Last Supper* by Palma il Giovane.

Behind Baška, around a castle destroyed in the 11th century, is Starigrad, with the Romanesque church of St John, rebuilt in 1723.

In the church of St Lucy in Jurandvor, a short distance from Baška, is a copy of the Baška Tablet (the original is in Zagreb), the oldest document in Croatia written in Glagolitic script.

Košljun

Since 1447 a Franciscan monastery has stood on this small island. In the cloisters are stone inscriptions from the Roman and medieval eras and the library has over 20,000 Glagolitic documents. In the church is a polyptych by Girolamo di Santacroce (1535) and a *Last Judgment* by Ughetto. The treasury and many sacred objects are in the church of St Bernard.

Bakar ㉙

Map B2.
🏚 *1,900.* 🚌 *(051) 761 214.*
ℹ️ *Primorje 39, (051) 761 411.*
🎭 *Daisy Summer, concerts and shows in the čakavski dialect (last week Jun).*

The demolition of a refinery and a coke plant has brought visitors back to this village, which was once a popular destination for people attracted to the landscape of the area and curious about the phenomena of the fresh-water springs. These springs originate in underground sources and flow out to the coast.

The **Frankopan Castle** and surrounding fishing village are also worth a visit. The village stands on the site of the Roman Volcera. From the 15th century until 1778 it belonged to the Frankopans who, in 1530, built a triangular-shaped castle. It is still well-preserved with high windows which were salvaged when it was transformed into a palace for the Šubić-Zrinski family who lived in the property after the Frankopans.

The parish church has a painting of the *Holy Trinity* by Girolamo da Santacroce and a Crucifix from the 14th century. Evidence of the past is preserved in the **Civic Museum** which has many tombstones and sculptures dating from the Roman and early Middle Ages. Bakar keeps its naval traditions alive thanks to the prestigious Maritime Academy, which was founded in 1849.

The internal courtyard in the Frankopan castle, Kraljevica

Kraljevica ㉚

Map B2. 🏚 *4,600.* 🚂 *Rijeka.*
🚌 *(051) 282 078.* ℹ️ *Rovina bb, (051) 282 078.* 🎭 *Shrovetide Sezona, traditional masked ball (carnival).*

A well-known tourist resort on the mainland, Kraljevica is linked to the island of Krk by a long bridge which also connects with Rijeka airport (on Krk). In the old town (Stari Grad) is a castle, built in the 16th century by the family of the counts of Šubić-Zrinski. The castle walls also shelter the small church of St Nicholas.

A village inhabited by families from the fortress of Hreljin developed around the castle. In the new district (Novi Grad), on a small promontory above the sea, is a castle built by the Frankopan family in 1650 in the late-Renaissance style. It has a square ground-plan with four round towers. It was turned into a magnificent palace in the middle of the 18th century.

In 1728, the Austrian emperor Charles VI began to create a sizeable port here, at the end of a road that went from Karlovac to the sea.

The Frankopan castle in Bakar, dominating the village

For hotels and restaurants in this region see pp222–6 and pp240–42

Crikvenica ③

Map B2. 5,800.
Rijeka, 16 km (10 miles), island of Krk. Nike Veljačića 3, (051) 781 333. Trg Stjepana Radića 1, (051) 241 867. Trade fair of Croatian products (5–12 Jul); Town festival (Aug). **www**.tzg-crikvenica.com

A Roman staging post called Ad Turres existed here at one time, with a port for trading in timber. In 1412 Nikola Frankopan (whose name derives from the noble Roman family of the Frangipani) built a castle here. It was later donated to the Pauline order, who set up a church, monastery and school. In the 16th century a wall and a round tower were built and, in 1659, the church was enlarged by adding a nave. The town, now a popular tourist resort, takes its name from the monastery. At the beginning of the 19th century, the Pauline order was dissolved and in 1893 the ancient monastery was turned into the Hotel Kastel (see p222).

The town has a long gravel beach and is one of the most popular tourist resorts along this stretch of coast. Thanks to its position, protected from the winds by the Velebit mountains, it enjoys a mild climate with dry summers and warm winters.

The altar in the church of SS Philip and James, Novi Vinodolski

Novi Vinodolski ③

Map B3. 3,800. Rijeka, 28 km (17 miles), island of Krk. Rijeka, 49 km (30 miles). Ulica Kralja Tomislava 6, (051) 244 306. Patron saints' day, Philip and James (May); Novi Vinodolski summer carnival (Aug).

The old town, built on a hill overlooking the Vinodol valley, holds an important place in Croatian history. On 6 January 1288, in the castle built by the Frankopan dukes, the Vinodol Codex, one of the oldest legislative Croatian texts in Glagolitic script (see pp34–5), was produced. The document is now in the National Library in Zagreb. It was signed by the representatives of nine communes, and established rules for the ownership and use of local land.

Costume in the castle of Novi Vinodolski

In 1988, the 700th anniversary of the Vinodol Codex, a fountain created by the sculptor Dorijan Sokolić was placed in the central square of Novi. The fountain bears the names of the places which participated in drawing up the laws.

The town is also remembered for the stratagem used by Bishop Kristofor to save the troops defeated by the Turks: the horses' shoes were put on backwards so as to foil their pursuers. Having reached the safety of Vinodol Castle, the bishop gave thanks by rebuilding the church of **SS Philip and James** (Sveti Filip i Jakov). He was buried here in 1499. The church, decorated in the 17th century in the Baroque style, has a magnificent altar from that period. The side altar has a Gothic Virgin Mary from the 15th century.

The 13th-century **Frankopan Castle**, recently restored, is now a museum, with exhibits from the Roman and medieval periods and a rich, varied collection of traditional folk costumes.

Senj ③

Map C3.
6,000. Rijeka, 52 km (32 miles). Ulica Kralja Zvonimira 8, (053) 881 235. Stara cesta 2, (053) 881 068. Feast of St George (23 Apr). **www**.lickosenjska.com/senj www.tz-senj.hr

The cold wind known as the bora of Senj blows through a pass in the Velebit chain of mountains, making the town the chilliest place in the Adriatic. People have long been aware of it, yet despite this notoriety, Senj has always been inhabited, first by the Illyrians, then by the Romans who created a port at Senia.

Gate of the former Pauline monastery, now a hotel, in Crikvenica

For hotels and restaurants in this region see pp222–6 and pp240–42

THE USKOKS

In 1526, shortly before the Battle of Mohács, numbers of Christians from the hinterland fled to the safer coastal cities to escape the Turks. The refugees were called "Uskoks" (fugitives), and their main desire was to fight those who had taken their land. Initially they were organized by Venice around the fortress of Klis, from which they attacked the Turk-occupied land. In 1537 the Turkish government made a treaty of non-belligerence with Venice on condition that the Uskoks were removed from Klis. Some Uskoks went to Primosten, but the main nucleus settled in Senj, under the rule of the Habsburgs, who encouraged them to procure fast boats in order to plunder the heavy Turkish ships. When Austria also slowed down operations against the Turks, the Uskoks took up piracy and started sacking coastal towns. At the end of the war between Venice and the Ottoman empire in 1617, the emperor was forced to remove the Uskoks from the coast and they and their families were transported to the west of Zagreb, to the Žumberak mountains.

Relief in the Museum of the Uskoks, Senj

This soon became a bishopric and an important trading port for the transport of timber. After 1000 AD it was granted to the Templar Knights. It then passed to the Frankopans, and finally came under the direct rule of the King of Hungary. As

Nehaj Castle, dominating the town of Senj

defence against the Turks, the Habsburgs established the first station of the Military Frontier (*Vojna Krajina*) here. This stronghold had a powerful outer wall which is now only partially preserved.

After the Battle of Mohács in 1526, many Uskoks from Sinj and Klis came to Senj, and were co-opted by the local Austrian governor in the fight against the Turks. Their presence is recorded in **Nehaj Castle**, a fortress built on a square plan, constructed in 1553–8 by the Uskok captain, Ivan Lenković, on a hill a short distance from the town. It was positioned so as to sight approaching ships. The well laid-out **Museum of the Uskoks** is on the first floor of the fort, and has an excellent view over the bay.

In the southern part of the wide bay is the main square, called Cilnica. Facing the square is the Frankopan palace, built in 1340 and altered in the 19th century. There are also large salt warehouses, and, further in, the **Cathedral of St Mary**

(Sv. Marija), built in the 13th century and altered in the Baroque period. It has tombstones with Renaissance reliefs and Baroque works, including an altar decorated with four marble statues.

A short distance from the square is the Vukasović Palace which houses the **Civic Museum** (Gradski Muzej Senj), a museum of local history. The palace was once the residence of an Uskok captain. Flanking the roads of the town and in the Small Square (Mala Placa), also known as Campuzia, are Renaissance buildings such as

the Town Hall with its splendid loggia. Nearby is the Leonova Kula tower, dedicated to Pope Leo X, and the small, pretty church of St Mary. Senj is the departure point for ferries to Baška (on the island of Krk) and the island of Rab.

Environs

The small village of **Jablanac** lies 37 km (23 miles) south of Senj. This bustling place is also a departure point for ferries to the island of Rab, and a good starting point for visiting the Velebit massif.

Jablanac is worth an unhurried visit so as to enjoy the well-preserved town, the harbour houses and the numerous archaeological finds scattered over the area. Jablanac was a county seat and its representatives met in the medieval castle. The castle was built by the Ban (governor) Stjepan Subić, as was the church and its cemetery, both known from documents from 1251. The castle is now in ruins.

Jablanac, south of Senj, departure point for the island of Rab

Rab

A window in the Prince's Palace in Rab town

The island of Rab lies parallel to the Velebit massif, creating a channel which was much dreaded by sailors because it forms a tunnel for the cold, dry bora wind which makes this part of the coast rocky and barren. The opposite, western side of the island is protected from the wind and the climate is mild. Here the landscape is much greener and maquis alternates with woods of pine, oak and holm oak. The Romans knew the island by the name of Arba, or Scadurna, and, after its conquest, built a settlement on the site of the present-day town of Rab. This island is a popular holiday destination with its sandy beaches, rocky coves and mild climate.

Rab Town

The main town, Rab, which gives its name to the island, became a bishopric in the early Christian period and was inhabited by Slavic people in the 6th century. After it had been conquered by the Franks, it was administered by Venice and a treaty of mutual defence was agreed upon which lasted until 1000 AD. Rab was at times under the rule of the Hungarian kings until 1409, when it became Venetian territory. Venice ruled the island until 1797.

View of Rab with its four bell towers

The town, famous for its four bell towers which make it look like a ship with four masts, has some lovely Venetian architecture. Along the three main streets are fine aristocratic buildings with Romanesque doorways, such as the Nimira, Tudorin, Kukulić, Galzigna and Cassio Palaces. The ancient medieval

The Sea Gate, one of the ways into the town of Rab

walls around the Old Town (Kalbanat) on the southern point of the peninsula were destroyed, and in the 15th century a wall was built which also enclosed the New Town, called Varos. Part of this wall is well-preserved, particularly the stretch facing the bay of St Euphemia.

🏛 Loggia

Ulica Sdreanja, Rab.
Where the main road, Ulica Sdreanja, widens out, there is a beautiful Venetian loggia, built in 1506 in Renaissance style, and a granary *(fondak)*. To the left is the Sea Gate (Morska Vrata), a tower from the 14th century. Through the gate is the town square.

🏛 Prince's Palace
Knežev Dvor

Trg Municipium Arba, Rab. **Tel** *(051) 724 064.* ☐ *call for opening times.*
The port and the town square are the heart of Rab, and this is also where the Prince's Palace was built in the 13th century in the Romanesque style. It was later enlarged in the Gothic style and then rebuilt in the Renaissance style. It has Venetian Gothic

windows and Renaissance mullioned windows. In the courtyard are some Roman and medieval remains.

🔒 Monastery and Church of St Andrew
Sv. Andrija

Ulica Ivana Rabljanina, Rab.
This small Romanesque church is annexed to a Benedictine convent founded in 1118. The bell tower, the oldest in Rab, is from the following century. The belfry has trefoil windows.

🔒 Cathedral of St Mary the Great
Katedrala Sv. Marija Velika

Ulica Ivana Rabljanina, Rab.
This splendid Romanesque building was consecrated by Pope Alexander III in 1177. The façade has alternating layers of pink and white stone and above the portal is a sculpted *Deposition* by Petar Trogiranin dating from 1514. The three-aisle interior, divided by columns, has a beautiful baptismal font made by the same sculptor in 1497, and a polyptych by Paolo Veneziano (1350) on the altar.

In the presbytery is a splendid altar canopy with marble columns and on the main altar, surrounded by an ornate wooden choir, is a reliquary from the 12th century with the remains of St Christopher.

The 13th-century bell tower stands 70 m (230 ft) away from the cathedral. It is the tallest of all the bell towers on the island.

The bell tower of the Cathedral of St Mary the Great

For hotels and restaurants in this region see pp222–6 and pp240–42

⛪ Chapel of St Anthony of Padua

Sv. Antun

Ulica Ribara, Rab.

The small church of St Anthony, dating from 1675, is a good example of religious Baroque architecture. Inside is a marble inlaid altar and a 17th-century painting from the Venetian school.

⛪ Franciscan Convent of St Anthony Abbot

Sv. Antun Opat

Rab. **Tel** (051) 724 064. ☐ call for opening times.

The church and convent of St Anthony Abbot stand behind the cathedral at the end of the promontory. This convent, built for a closed order of nuns, was founded in 1497 by the noblewoman Magdalena Budrišić.

⛪ Church of St Francis

Sv. Frane

Parco Komrcar, Rab.

The church dates from 1491 and stands to the north of the town in Komrcar Park. It is a blend of Gothic and Renaissance and has an original façade with three sculpted shells.

The altar in the Renaissance church of St Justine in Rab

⛪ Convent and Church of St Justine

Sv. Justine

Gornja Ulica, Rab. ◑ temporarily for reconstruction.

The convent and church were consecrated in 1578, and were intended for nuns from non-noble families. The bell tower with its onion dome dates from 1672. The church now houses a Museum of Holy Art, with the crucifix of King Koloman from 1112, and the reliquary of St Christopher (12th century), protector of

VISITORS' CHECKLIST

Map B3. 🚣 9,200. **Rab** ⛴ from Rijeka, Senj, Pag, Zadar; (051) 724 122. ⛴ Mali Palid. (051) 724 189. ℹ Trg Municipium Arba 8, (051) 724 064. 🎭 musical evenings, Church of the Holy Cross (Jun–Sep); Tournament of Rab, (9 May, 7 Jul). **www**.tzg-rab.hr

the town. Also on display are paintings and panels, including a polyptych by Paolo Veneziano (1350), Gospels and illuminated books in Glagolitic script.

Kampor

Kampor lies at the end of a long bay (Kamporska Draga) and has preserved its stone houses and terraces of olives and vines. Many private holiday houses have sprung up around the village.

The Franciscan convent of St Euphemia, with a small adjacent Romanesque church, is near the church of St Bernard. The church contains two panels by Bartolomeo and Antonio Vivarini, a Byzantine panel (14th century) and other works. In the cloister there are various tombs and the sarcophagus of Magdalena Budrišić, the noblewoman who founded the convent of St Anthony Abbot in Rab.

Lopar

The village of Lopar is at the end of a rocky peninsula. It is a popular spot thanks to the sandy beaches fringed by pinewoods and the leisure facilities on offer (tennis, football and mini-golf).

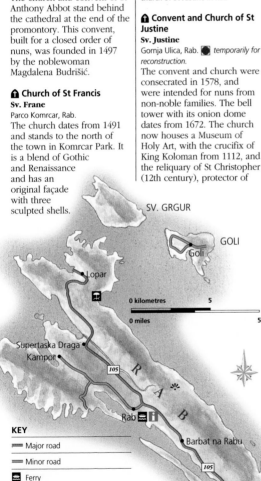

SV. GRGUR

GOLI

Goli

Lopar

0 kilometres 5

0 miles 5

Supertaska Draga

Kampor

105

R A B

Rab

Barbat na Rabu

105

DOLIN

Pudarica

Mišnjak

KEY

▬ Major road

▬ Minor road

⛴ Ferry

ℹ Tourist information

🏖 Beach with facilities

☆ Viewpoint

Polyptych by the Vivarini, church of St Bernard, Kampor

One of the spectacular waterfalls at the Plitvice Lakes ▷

Plitvice Lakes National Park ㉟
Nacionalni Park Plitvička Jezera

The Plitvice Lakes National Park, located in the heart of Croatia, was founded in 1949. This area of 300 sq km (115 sq miles), covered in lakes and forest, has been part of the UNESCO World Heritage list since 1979. It is particularly known for its spectacular waterfalls. There are 16 lakes within the park and visitors can move around by following the paths along the shores or by using footbridges. Electric buses take people to the starting points of the trails and to the hotels in the park. The largest lake can be toured by electric boat. There are no towns or villages in the reserve, only hotels.

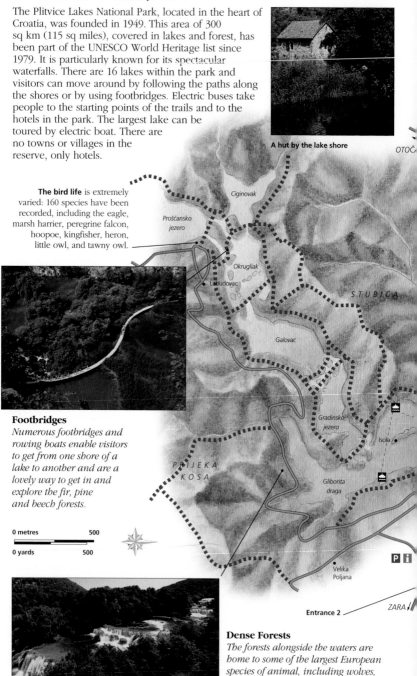

A hut by the lake shore

OTOČ

The bird life is extremely varied: 160 species have been recorded, including the eagle, marsh harrier, peregrine falcon, hoopoe, kingfisher, heron, little owl, and tawny owl.

Ciginovak

Proščansko jezero

Okrugliak

Labudovac

STUBICA

Galovac

Gradinsko jezero

Isola

PLJEKA KOSA

Gliborita draga

Footbridges
Numerous footbridges and rowing boats enable visitors to get from one shore of a lake to another and are a lovely way to get in and explore the fir, pine and beech forests.

0 metres   500
0 yards   500

Velika Poljana

P H

Entrance 2

ZARA

Dense Forests
The forests alongside the waters are home to some of the largest European species of animal, including wolves, lynxes, foxes, wild boar, roebucks, wild cats, otters and badgers.

Flora
The park flora is very varied, from waterlilies on the lakes to forests of gigantic trees. There is also a rich undergrowth of shrubs, a source of food for wildlife.

Waterfalls
It is possible to follow signposted routes and walk behind the waterfalls to watch the rushing waters as they cascade from the lake above.

The park vehicles, electric buses, take visitors around the area on special routes.

KEY

▬	Major road
▬	Route for park vehicles
▪▪	Footpath
---	Boat route
⛴	Electric boat
🛈	Tourist information
🅿	Parking

View of the River Korana
Along the banks of the River Korana, into which the lakes drain, are a few shepherds' huts and several sawmills which are run on hydraulic power. The river flows between steep cliffs in a spectacular natural landscape.

DALMATIA

almatia is the most visited region of Croatia. Although tourism collapsed in the 1990s because of the war, visitors are again flocking to the rocky coastline and sandy beaches, the deserted islands and the splendid cities of this Adriatic region. As a consequence of relationships and trade with Italy, an Adriatic culture developed here which has given Dalmatia an Italianate feel.

In the 1st century BC, after two centuries of war, the Romans managed to conquer the Dalmatian and Liburnian tribes and integrate them into their system. For over three centuries the region enjoyed a period of prosperity which was eventually brought to an end by the arrival of peoples from Asia, including the Slavs in the 7th century.

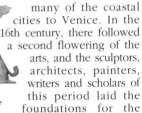

The Lion of St Mark on the Land Gate in Zadar

In 915, after a long period of wars and unrest, the first Croatian kings founded a new state, blessed by papal authority. New public and religious buildings, walls and town halls were built, the arts began to flourish, and trading with the Italian coast increased. This was a period of great cultural vitality, which survived the collapse of the Croatian state and its integration into the Kingdom of Hungary in the 12th century. In 1409, after a long series of conflicts, the Hungarian king sold the islands and

many of the coastal cities to Venice. In the 16th century, there followed a second flowering of the arts, and the sculptors, architects, painters, writers and scholars of this period laid the foundations for the future development of Croatian culture, art and literature.

In late spring, when the Jadranska Magistrala coast road has yet to be invaded by heavy summer traffic, this must be one of the loveliest parts of Europe. From Karlobag the road winds along the edge of the Velebit mountain chain and the Dalmatian and the Biokovo plateaux. Seawards is the long, lunar-surfaced island of Pag and further along are the islands around Zadar, those around Split, and finally the lovely island of Mljet, set in an azure sea. Behind are hillsides covered in vineyards and maquis vegetation, dominated by the bright yellow flowers of broom.

View of the city of Šibenik with the white dome of the Cathedral of St James

◁ Lavender flowering on the island of Hvar

Exploring Dalmatia

To the north is Zadar, with its exceptional monuments, and the islands of the Zadar archipelago, the southern part of which is designated the Kornati National Park. The road travels on to Šibenik, with its perfectly preserved old town centre and splendid cathedral, and Trogir, an architectural jewel. The ruins of the Roman town of Salona are just outside the city of Split, which developed within the Palace of Emperor Diocletian. The coastal road turns inland to cross the delta of the Neretva and reaches Ston, a point of access to the peninsula of Pelješac. Finally, on a rocky spur stands the medieval city of Dubrovnik, now a UNESCO World Heritage Site.

Bell tower of the cathedral, Zadar

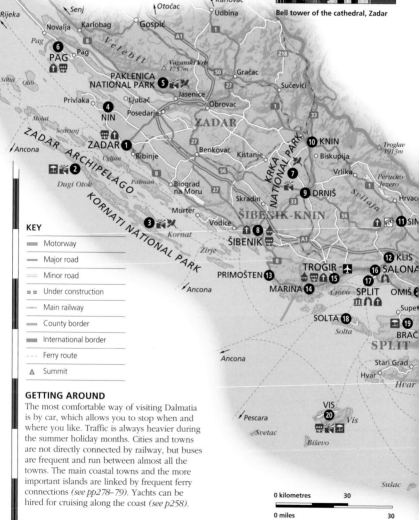

KEY

▬▬	Motorway
▬▬	Major road
▭▭▭	Minor road
▬ ▬	Under construction
▬▬	Main railway
▬▬	County border
▬▬	International border
- - -	Ferry route
△	Summit

GETTING AROUND

The most comfortable way of visiting Dalmatia is by car, which allows you to stop when and where you like. Traffic is always heavier during the summer holiday months. Cities and towns are not directly connected by railway, but buses are frequent and run between almost all the towns. The main coastal towns and the more important islands are linked by frequent ferry connections (see pp278–79). Yachts can be hired for cruising along the coast (see p258).

The imposing 15th-century Minčeta Tower in Dubrovnik

HUNGARY
SLOVENIA
ZAGREB
BOSNIA-HERZEGOVINA
ADRIATIC SEA

LOCATOR MAP

SIGHTS AT A GLANCE

Badija 30
Brač 19
Cavtat 35
Drniš 9
Dubrovnik pp140–47 33
Elaphite Islands 34
Gradac 24
Hvar pp126–7 21
Klis 12
Knin 10
Konavle 36
Korčula pp132–34 29
Kornati National Park pp98–9 3
Krka National Park pp104–5 7
Lastovo 31
Makarska 23
Marina 14
Mljet National Park pp136–7 32
Narona 26
Neum 27
Nin 4
Omiš 22
Opuzen 25
Pag pp102–3 6
Paklenica National Park 5
Pelješac Peninsula 28
Primošten 13
Salona pp116–17 16
Šibenik pp106–9 8
Sinj 11
Šolta 18
Split pp118–23 17
Trogir pp112–15 15
Vis 20
Zadar pp92–95 1
Zadar Archipelago pp96–7 2

The island of Dugi Otok, in the Zadar Archipelago

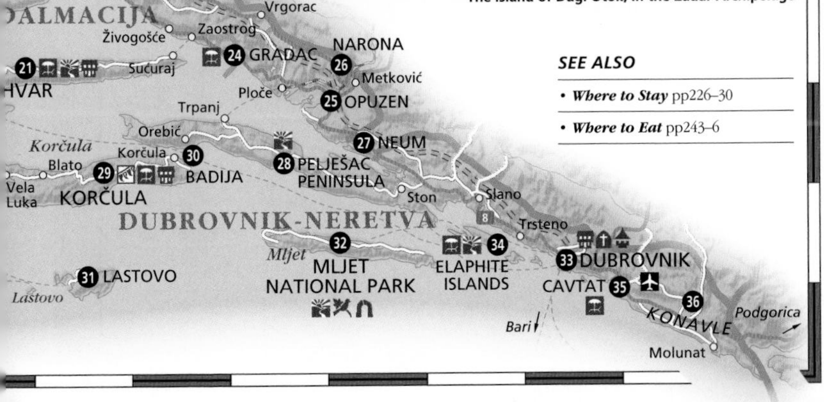
Livno
220
39
60
Imotski
Mostar
62
Cista Provo
Biokovo
Brač
8
23 MAKARSKA
DALMACIJA
Vrgorac
Živogošće
Zaostrog
24 GRADAC
NARONA
26
21
Sućuraj
HVAR
Metković
Ploče
25 OPUZEN
Trpanj
Orebić
27 NEUM
Korčula
Korčula
30
Blato
28 PELJEŠAC PENINSULA
29
BADIJA
Vela Luka
KORČULA
Ston
Slano
DUBROVNIK-NERETVA
8
Trsteno
32
Mljet
34
33 DUBROVNIK
31 LASTOVO
MLJET NATIONAL PARK
ELAPHITE ISLANDS
CAVTAT 35
Lastovo
36
KONAVLE
Podgorica
Bari
Molunat

SEE ALSO

• ***Where to Stay*** pp226–30
• ***Where to Eat*** pp243–6

Zadar ❶

Originally Illyrians inhabited this narrow peninsula, but its present layout dates back to Roman rule, when the straight roads and forum were built. It became an important *municipium*, and a port for the trading of timber and wine. In the Middle Ages it was the main base for the Byzantine fleet. Venice and the king of Hungary fought over Zadar in the 12th–13th centuries but in 1409, King Ladislaus of Hungary sold his Dalmatian islands and cities to Venice for 100,000 ducats. Zadar became Zara and enjoyed a spell of prosperity; churches and palaces were built. After World War I, Zadar was ceded to Italy by the Treaty of Rapallo, but many Italians left after the forming of Yugoslavia in 1947. Zadar was repeatedly bombed during World War II and suffered considerable damage.

The Sea Gate, rebuilt from a Roman arch

The medieval tower, Bablja Kula, with part of the ancient wall

✠ Land Gate and Walls
Kopnena Vrata

The Land Gate was built in 1543 by the great Veronese architect Michele Sanmicheli as the entrance to the city. The gate has a large central aperture and two smaller openings at the sides, divided by four white stone pilasters supporting four half-columns.

Above the main gate is a relief of St Chrysogonus on horseback and the lion of St Mark, symbol of Venetian rule. Beyond the gate are a few remains of the ancient walls, the former Venetian arsenal, and Liberation Square (Trg Zoranića) with a Roman column in the centre.

On one side of the square stands the medieval tower of Bablja Kula. At the base of the tower are five fountains (Trg Pet Bunara), which once supplied water to the city of Zadar.

⛪ Church of St Simeon
Sv. Šime

Trg Šime Budinića. **Tel** (023) 211 705. ⭕ before mass.
Originally constructed in Romanesque style, the church was rebuilt after 1632 to house the remains of the saint, which are kept in a silver reliquary. This impressive work is nearly 2 m (6 ft) long and was made between 1377 and 1380 by Francesco da Milano and bears reliefs showing scenes of St Simeon's life.

Among the other works, of note is an altarpiece depicting the *Virgin and Saints*, the work of a Venetian artist. It was covered with silver leaf by a local goldsmith in 1546.

✠ People's Square
Narodni trg

Heart of the medieval city, the site of political debate and the business district, the square is still the centre of public life today. The Town Hall, which was built in 1938, faces the square, as does the Renaissance City Loggia (Gradska loža) built by Michele Sanmicheli in 1565 as the city courts. It is now used for exhibitions.

Nearby, the 16th-century Town Guard Palace, with a clock tower dating from 1798, houses the Ethnographic Museum, with collections of costumes and objects from the entire county.

✠ Sea Gate
Vrata Sv. Krševana

This complex construction is the result of rebuilding work carried out by Michele Sanmicheli in 1573 on a Roman arch dedicated to the Sergi family. On the seaward side is the lion of St Mark and a memorial stone recalling the Battle of Lepanto (1571). On the inner side of the gate is a stone commemorating Pope Alexander III's visit in 1177.

⛪ Church of St Chrysogonus
Sv. Krševan

Poljana Pape Aleksandra III.
⭕ during the concert season.
Prior to AD 1000 a church and monastery were built by Benedictines on the site of the Roman market. While the church, rebuilt in 1175, has survived with few alterations, the monastery was destroyed in World War II. At the height of the monastery's splendour it possessed a rich library and a *scriptorium*, famous for its transcribed and illuminated

The apse of the church of St Chrysogonus

works. The three-aisle church, divided by columns (salvaged from a previous building), has a simple Romanesque appearance, except for the Baroque main altar with statues of Zadar's four patron saints: Chrysogonus, Zoilus, Simeon and Anastasia. The apse is the best-preserved part, with some 13th-century frescoes and a Romanesque crucifix on the altar.

🏛 Archaeological Museum
Arheološki Muzej
Trg opatice Čike 1. **Tel** (023) 250 516. ◯ summer: 9am–1pm, 5–8pm Mon–Fri, 9–1pm Sat, 5–8pm Sun; winter: 10am–1pm, 4.30–6.30pm Mon–Fri, 9am–1pm Sat. 🎫 by appt. ⛔

The Archaeological Museum is housed in a new building near the old Roman Forum. The collections date from prehistory to recent times and come from the entire Zadar area and the islands. Of particular interest is glass from the Roman period and the early Christian and medieval liturgical objects.

The beautiful Renaissance façade of the church of St Mary

🔒 Church of St Mary and Museum of Sacred Art
Sv. Marija i Zlato i Srebro Zadra
Zeleni trg. **Tel** (023) 250 496. ◯ summer: 10am–12.30pm, 6–8pm Mon–Sat, 10am–12.30pm Sun; winter: 10am–12.30pm, 5–6.30pm Mon–Sat. 🎫 📷 🚫 ⛔

On one side of the square called Zeleni trg stand a tall, Romanesque bell

Sculpture, Museum of Sacred Art

tower, built for King Koloman in 1105, and the church of St Mary. The church, built in 1066, has undergone various alterations and now has a Renaissance façade. The three-aisle interior has a large women's gallery; the stucco-work is from 1744. The monastery next door is now the Museum of Sacred Art: on the ground floor are gold pieces; on the upper floor are paintings and statues, including a polyptych by Vittore Carpaccio (1487).

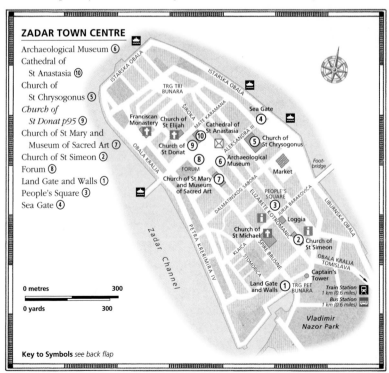

ZADAR TOWN CENTRE

Archaeological Museum ⑥
Cathedral of St Anastasia ⑩
Church of St Chrysogonus ⑤
Church of St Donat p95 ⑨
Church of St Mary and Museum of Sacred Art ⑦
Church of St Simeon ②
Forum ⑧
Land Gate and Walls ①
People's Square ③
Sea Gate ④

0 metres 300
0 yards 300

Key to Symbols see back flap

Forum

The main square of the ancient Roman city of Jadar was built between the 1st and 3rd centuries. The Forum, 90 m (295 ft) long and 45 m (147 ft) wide, was bordered on three sides by porticoes with marble columns. In the present square, Zeleni trg, are the foundations of public buildings, including a meeting hall, some of the original paving, several *tabernae* (rectangular-shaped trading areas) and a Corinthian column on the western side.

Rose window, St Anastasia

The right-hand altar inside the Cathedral of St Anastasia

Cathedral of St Anastasia

Katedrala Sv. Stošije
Forum. **Tel** (023) 251 708.
🕙 8am–1pm, 5–6.30pm daily.

The magnificent cathedral of St Anastasia also stands on the site of the Forum. It was founded by the Byzantines in the 9th century and rebuilt in the Romanesque style in the 12–13th centuries. It has a rectangular ground-plan with a large semicircular apse.

The harmonious façade with three doors, completed in 1324, is divided in half horizontally with the upper part characterized by arches and columns and two splendid rose windows. The main window is Romanesque and the other is Gothic.

Statues adorn the outside of the central door; above are five orders of small columns culminating at the top in a semicircle and enclosing a rectangular stone door carved with festoons; above is a relief of the *Annunciation*.

The three-aisle interior is divided by two rows of columns and pilasters which support the high arcades. At the sides of the raised presbytery are engraved wooden choir stalls, the work of the Venetian Matteo Moronzoni (early 15th century). The ciborium with four Corinthian columns is decorated with different motifs (1332). Underneath is a small sarcophagus containing the remains of St Anastasia, dating from the 9th century.

The altars are mostly Baroque; on one there is a lovely painting by Palma il Giovane. In the right-hand nave is an imposing Baroque altar dedicated to the Holy Sacrament; just beyond is the hexagonal baptistry. The bell tower, which stands to one side of the cathedral, was begun in 1452. It was eventually completed in the 19th century by the British architect Thomas G Jackson.

The Romanesque façade of the Cathedral of St Anastasia

PLAN OF THE CATHEDRAL OF ST ANASTASIA

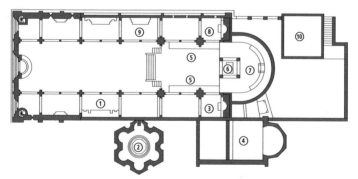

KEY

① Altar of the Holy Sacrament
② Baptistry
③ Roman pilaster
④ Sacristy
⑤ Choir stalls
⑥ Main altar and ciborium
⑦ Bishop's chair
⑧ Chapel of St Anastasia
⑨ Souls of Purgatory altar
⑩ Bell tower

0 metres   15
0 yards   15

Zadar: Church of St Donat
Sv. Donat

The Church of the Holy Trinity, which later took the name of its founder Bishop Donat, is one of the finest examples of Byzantine architecture in Dalmatia. It was built in the early 9th century on the paving stones of the former Roman Forum and has a circular ground-plan with three circular apses. Inside is a women's gallery which goes all the way around the church and creates an upper storey. St Donat has not been used as a church since 1797, but because of the good acoustics, concerts are often held here.

VISITORS' CHECKLIST

Forum. 🏢 (023) 250 516.
⏰ summer: 9am–11pm; winter: 9am–3pm. 🌐

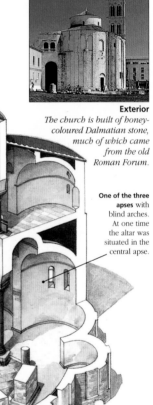

Dome
The cylindrical-conical dome rises in the centre of the church to a height of 27 m (88 ft).

Exterior
The church is built of honey-coloured Dalmatian stone, much of which came from the old Roman Forum.

One of the three apses with blind arches. At one time the altar was situated in the central apse.

The Women's Gallery
The interior of the church has a matroneum, or women's gallery, supported by six pilasters and two Roman columns which border the circular nave and divide the structure into two floors.

The internal walls are completely bare. Probably the original decorations, frescoes or mosaics, have been lost.

Roman Fragments
Stones from the Roman Forum were used for the paving; other Roman material is visible in the walls, entrance and gallery.

Zadar Archipelago  ❷

Crucifix in SS Cosmas and Damian, Pašman

The Zadar Archipelago is made up of more than 300 islands surrounded by crystal-clear waters. The larger islands are covered in Mediterranean scrub and olive trees. The archipelago is what remains of a mountain chain which once ran parallel to the Velebit mountains, but which is now almost submerged. Only about a dozen of the islands are inhabited, and the small communities live by fishing, farming and rearing animals. There are a few hotels on the larger islands closer to Zadar, and private accommodation can be found on all the others. Daily ferry services link Zadar with the main islands.

Dugi Otok, the largest island in the Zadar archipelago

Dugi Otok

Covering an area of 124 sq km (48 sq miles), this is the largest island in the archipelago. The inhabitants live in about ten villages. Fishing and farming takes place in the northern part of the island and on the flatter areas of the island, while the southern, hillier terrain is given over to sheep farming. The western coast is steep and desolate but beaches and bays punctuate the eastern coast.

Proximity to Zadar means that since Roman times it has been a popular place for the city nobles to build holiday villas. In the Renaissance period more summer residences were built here, particularly in **Sali**. This is the largest town and port on the island and there are some houses in the flamboyant Gothic style. The Renaissance church of St Mary of the Assumption has some paintings from the same period by Juraj Čulinović.

The fishing village of Božava, at the northernmost point, is also a popular yacht marina. It has a small church, dedicated to St Nicholas, which dates from the 10th century. Inside the church a sculpture depicts Arab saints.

The long bay of Telašćica, to the south, is a natural harbour and was once used by the Venetian fleet. One side ends in a sheer cliff and the other in thick pine woods. This area is being reforested after a disastrous fire in 1995. The southern part of the island is part of the Kornati National Park (see pp98–9).

Ugljan

This lush, green island is 22 km (13 miles) long and covers an area of 50 sq km (19 sq miles). It has a population of 7,600 and the small villages lie along the eastern coast of the island. In the main village, Ugljan, is the Franciscan monastery of St Jerome, built in the 15th century. It has a pretty cloister and the library contains numerous works written in Glagolitic script.

A more newly built village is **Preko**, where the wealthier citizens of Zadar own villas. There are also hotels, camping sites and rooms in private houses. The village is dominated by the large Venetian fortress of St Michael which stands on a hill 265 m (869 ft) high. A bridge links the island to Pašman.

View from the fortress of St Michael, Preko

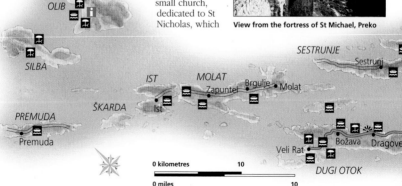

OLIB

SILBA

PREMUDA
• Premuda

SESTRUNJE
Sestrunj

IST   MOLAT   Brgulje • Molat
          Zapuntel

ŠKARDA   Ist

Božava   Dragove

Veli Rat
DUGI OTOK

0 kilometres   10

0 miles   10

The Monastery of SS Cosmas and Damian in Pašman

Pašman

This wild, unspoilt island has a population of 3,500, who live in villages on the coast facing the mainland. There are fewer tourists than on Ugljan. The western side is given over to vineyards, while the eastern part has thick maquis right down to the coastline, where there are also some pebble beaches.

South of **Pašman**, a fishing village and the main centre on the island, is **Tkon**, an embarkation point for ferries. On Mount Čokovac, north of Tkon, is the Benedictine **Monastery of SS Cosmas and Damian** (Sv. Kuzma i Damjan). Built in 1125, it became a centre of Glagolitic culture and has a well-stocked library with Glagolitic texts. In the 15th century the church and monastery were rebuilt in the Gothic style when they were taken over by the Franciscan order. The church (14th–15th century) has some good sculptures, including a painted crucifix.

Premuda

This island covers an area of 9 sq km (3 sq miles) and has fewer than 100 inhabitants, all of whom live in the village of Premuda. It is the most isolated of the islands in the archipelago. There are no hotels but visitors can find rooms in private houses.

In Italy, the island is remembered for a naval battle between Italy and Austria which took place on 10 June 1918 during World War I.

The island has beautiful beaches and thick pine woods, and as there are no private cars it is also very peaceful. There are several weekly connections to Zadar.

Molat

The three villages on Molat support several hundred people, who depend on fishing and farming. There are two ports, Zapuntel, the main ferry port, and Brgulje, which is used when the main port is inaccessible.

For centuries the island belonged to Venice, which fostered the establishment of a community of monks and local people, who set about re-establishing the woods which had disappeared with over-exploitation. Over the last decade an intense reforestation programme has been under way.

The church of St Andrew is all that remains of the monastery. There are no hotels on the island but accommodation can be found in private houses in Molat, Zapuntel and Brgulje. There are many coves along the low, jagged coastline.

VISITORS' CHECKLIST

Map B–C4. Harbour master's office: (023) 254 888; Jadrolinija: (023) 254 800.
Zadar Sv. Leopolda Mandića 1, (023) 315 107.
www.zadar.hr
Dugi Otok Obala L. Lorinija, Sali, (023) 377 094.
www.dugiotok.hr
Ugljan Preko, (023) 288 011.
www.ugljan.hr

Olib

About 700 people live here in the village of Olib, where buildings include several 16th-century houses and a tower. The church of St Anastasia is from the same period and was once part of a monastery. In the parsonage are manuscripts and sacred books written in Glagolitic, as well as many stone remains, which confirm the presence of a community here in Roman times. The sea is delightful, and rocky cliffs alternate with coves and sandy beaches. Rooms can be found in private houses.

Goat on the peaceful island of Olib

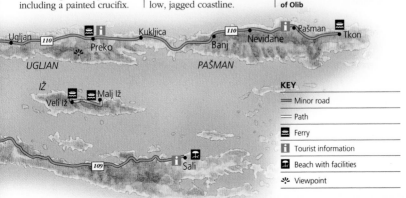

Ugljan · Preko · Kukljica · Banj · Nevidane · Pašman · Tkon

UGLJAN · PAŠMAN

IŽ · Veli Iž · Malj Iž

Sali

KEY

═══	Minor road
══	Path
🚢	Ferry
ℹ	Tourist information
🏖	Beach with facilities
⚘	Viewpoint

Kornati National Park ❸
Nacionalni Park Kornati

In 1980 the southern part of the Zadar Archipelago was declared a national park. The name Kornati derives from the name of the main island in the group, Kornat. The park was set up to protect the waters, to allow all kinds of marine life to flourish, and to stop people building on the islands. The park is 36 km (22 miles) in length and 6 km (4 miles) wide and is made up of 147 islands of white stone. Nearly all the islands are uninhabited and have little or no vegetation. The islands are surrounded by clear blue sea, with jagged coastlines, hidden coves and underwater caves.

One of the few houses on the Kornati Islands

Exploring Kornati National Park

The Kornati Islands were the peaks of a mountain chain about 20,000 years ago. When this area was part of the Roman empire, the main islands were holiday resorts, popular with the prosperous inhabitants of Zadar. Beautiful Roman villas with mosaic floors as well as fishponds and baths were built.

During the long period under Venetian rule the islands, which were then covered with rich vegetation, were used as a base for the Venetian fleet. At present the Kornati Islands belong to the inhabitants of Murter, to the east, who bought them around the end of the 19th century to use as grazing for sheep and goats.

The islands are bare and arid and are characterized by steep cliffs, stony ground and sinkholes typical of a karst (limestone) landscape. Sheep farming has impoverished the flora of these islands. In fact, the vegetation disappeared when the shepherds of Murter cut down the trees and burnt the scrub in order to grow grass for their livestock, which were left here to graze freely from spring to autumn. Dry-stone walls were built between the plots of land to form pens for the animals.

On some of the islands near the coast there are small cottages. Each has a stable at the side with an outdoor hearth for making cheese. Many also have a small jetty.

The Kornati Islands have become a popular destination for scuba divers and sailors. The marine life is varied with around 350 plant species and 300 animals. To conserve this diversity, fishing is prohibited throughout the entire Kornati National Park.

Besides dozens of rocky outcrops, the islands of Kornat, Levrnaka, Piškera, Lavsa, Kasela, Mana and Katina make up the park, as well as the southern part of Dugi Otok (see p96), with the bay of Telašćica the only wooded area. The best way to visit is by sailing boat, and there are organized day trips from Murter and Zadar.

Aerial view of the Kornati Islands

DUGI OTOK
• Sali

Mala Proversa

Telašćica   KATINA

SVRŠATA

KORNAT

Lučica

• Vrulje

MANA

PIŠKER

KEY

— Path

— Borders of the park

⛴ Ferry

🏖 Beach with facilities

❊ Viewpoint

0 kilometres   10

0 miles   10

The steep chalk cliffs on the island of Kornat

warehouse for fish and a tower for the tax collector. The houses and tower are now almost all in ruins. However, the church from 1560 is still standing.

Kornat
The island of Kornat is the largest island in the park. There is a small medieval church dedicated to the Virgin Mary here. There is also a look-out tower with the Venetian name of Toreta dating from the 6th century, an example of Byzantine military architecture. Near the old village of Vrulje, the main village in the archipelago, is **Vela Ploča**, where there is a spectacular chalk cliff leaning at a 40-degree angle over the sea, measuring 200 m (656 ft) long and 150 m (492 ft) high.

Mala Proversa
At Mala Proversa, the straits which divide Dugi Otok from the island of **Katina**, it is possible to see some interesting Roman remains: the ruins of a villa, a fishpond and a huge tank for water, which was distributed to the villa's rooms. The few mosaics found here are now in the Archaeological Museum in Zadar *(see p93).*

Lavsa
This island with its pretty bays and coves is a popular tourist destination. The ruins of a partly submerged wall are all that remain of an ancient Roman salt works.

Piškera
There are also traces of Roman presence in Piškera. Once there was a village here with about 50 houses, a

Svršata
On the small island of Svršata there are two walls that go down to the sea and continue into the water, where they join up with another wall. It is thought that this square tank was a Roman construction for keeping fish fresh.

Mana
The island of Mana is famous for its semicircular cliffs. Spray from the waves breaking on the cliffs can reach up to a height of 40 m (131 ft). On top of the cliffs are the ruins of a Greek-style fishing village, built for the film *The Raging Sea* in 1961.

THE KORNATI ISLANDS BY BOAT
The archipelago of the Kornati Islands is a real paradise for sailors. These are beautiful, mysterious islands where the only sounds are those of the sea and the wind. There is only one small port, Piškera, which is open from May to September; electricity and fresh water are rationed. The natural beauty of the area makes sailing here unforgettable.

A typical island of white rock, bare of vegetation

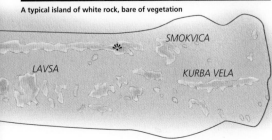

SMOKVICA

LAVSA

KURBA VELA

Kornati National Park, a paradise for sailing

Nin ❹

Map C4. 🏠 *1,700.* 🚆 *Zadar, 24 km (15 miles).* 🚌 *Zadar, 36 km (22 miles).* 🚌 *Zadar, 36 km (22 miles).* ℹ️ *Trg hrvatskih branitelja 1, (023) 264 280.*

Founded by the Liburnians, the town was important in Roman times, when it was called Aenona. It later became one of the first permanent Croat settlements. The use of Glagolitic script spread from here when it became a Bishop's see in the 9th century. It was the centre of a long controversy between the local Church and the Pope over the use of the Croatian language in liturgy.

Malaria and the difficulty of defending the town caused it to be abandoned once again, and the bishopric was abolished in the 12th century. The few remaining monuments date from this glorious period (9th–12th centuries): the churches of the Holy Cross, St Anselm and St Ambrose. The cathedral of St Anselm, where the kings of Croatia were crowned, no longer exists.

Inside the town walls is the small 9th-century church of the **Holy Cross** (Sv. Križ), one of the finest examples of pre-Romanesque churches in typical Croatian style *(see p22)*. The name of its founder, the prefect Gladeslaus, is engraved on the lintel. The church's small size, harmony and beauty encapsulate the spirituality of the era.

Nearby is the 18th-century church of **St Anselm** (Sv. Anselm). It has a rich treasury

The small Romanesque church of St Mary in Ljubač, near Nin

with silver reliquaries from the 9th to 15th centuries. Near the church stands a large statue by Ivan Meštrović of Bishop Gregory of Nin, promoter of Glagolitic script. Also inside the walls is the church of **St Ambrose** (Sv. Ambroz), built in the 12th century in the Romanesque style with Gothic additions.

At the end of the main road, Zadraska ulica, is a small Archaeological Museum with prehistoric, Roman and medieval remains.

> 🔒 **Church of the Holy Cross, of St Anselm and of St Ambrose**
> ℹ️ (023) 264 160, 264 162 (Archaeological Museum).
> 🕐 by appt.

Statue of Gregory of Nin, by Ivan Meštrović

Environs
A short way southwest of Nin stands the church of St Nicholas (Sv. Nikola) in Prahulje. This unusual building, constructed on an Illyrian tumulus, has a dome with an octagonal watch tower from the 16th century on top of it, added during the Turkish invasion. Dating from the 9th century, the church is built on a trefoil plan and once held inscriptions and tombs of

members of the court of Princes Višeslav and Branimir, now in the archaeological museum in Zadar. The church is a well-preserved example of primitive Croatian art.

Ljubač is 13 km (8 miles) northeast of Nin and the site of some ruins: the wall, central buildings and towers of the medieval Castrum Ljubae, built by the Templar Knights. It fell into ruin after the order was dissolved. Still standing is the 12th-century Romanesque church of **St Mary**, noted for its three semicircular apses. Near the village is the small church of St John from the Middle Ages.

> 🔒 **Church of St Nicholas**
> **Tel** (023) 264 160. 🕐 by appt.

The church of St Nicholas in Prahulje, not far from Nin

The salt works on Pag, of Roman origin, still in use today

A LAND OF SALT WORKS
Salt trading was a very lucrative business in the Middle Ages. Three areas were suitable for its production in the upper Adriatic: the mouth of the River Dragonja, today the border between Slovenia and Croatia, the bay of Pag, and the lowlands around Nin. The salt works of Pag, of Roman origin, which were protected by two ranges of hills, were the largest and most profitable, unlike those of Nin. The possession of these salt flats, still profitable today, has been the cause of various wars ever since.

Paklenica National Park ❺

Nacionalni Park Paklenica

Map C4. 🛈 *Starigrad Paklenica,*
(023) 369 202, 369 155.
⬛ *8am–4pm daily.* 📷
www.paklenica.hr

Situated in the imposing
Velebit massif, Paklenica
National Park was founded
in 1949. The entrance is east
of Starigrad Paklenica, on
the Magistrala coastal road
(E65), halfway between
Karlobag and Zadar.

The park covers an area of
36 sq km (14 sq miles), and is
formed by two gorges, Velika
Paklenica (Big Paklenica)
and Mala Paklenica (Small
Paklenica), which cut into the
limestone mountains. The
gorges were eroded by two
rivers and parts of the canyon
walls are more than 400 m
(1,312 ft) high.

The rock faces are pierced
by numerous caves, but they
are not easily accessible. Only
the Manita cave can be
visited, accompanied by a
guide. The bare rock faces of
Velika Paklenica are popular
with rock climbers.

High up, majestic birds of
prey make their nests, in an
ideal habitat for breeding.
Golden eagles, vultures,
hawks, and especially
peregrine falcons can be seen
here. In the forests there are
bears, wild boar, foxes,

Lilies in the Botanical Garden in Paklenica National Park

roebucks and hares. A path
in the valley penetrates far
into the interior of the park
to a cliff edge where there
is a magnificent view of
the wooded Vaganski Vrh
mountain, the highest in
the Velebit chain.

The **Velebit** mountain chain
is nearly 150 km (93 miles)
long. The terrain is
karst (limestone)
with many sink
holes and
plateaux separated
by deep fissures.
In 1978 UNESCO
listed Velebit as a
biological reserve for
humanity with the aim
of protecting this wild
environment, with its 2,700
plant species and numerous
colonies of large birds of
prey. The *kukovi* – strange,
impressive rock formations
sculpted by wind and water
– are also protected.

**One of many birds of
prey in the park**

The park is also home to
an interesting **Botanical
Garden** (Botanički Vrt),
founded in 1966 on the
slopes of Mount Zavisan at an
altitude of 1,576 m (5,169 ft).

Near Gradac are the
Cerovac caves, discovered in
1912 during the construction
of a railway line. They are
dedicated to Turkalj, the
engineer who discovered
them. The two large caves
are called Upper
Grotto, 1,250 m
(4,100 ft) long,
and Lower
Grotto, 2,500 m
(8,200 ft) long.
The caves have
typical karst
(limestone) formations with
stalactites and stalagmites,
small lakes and waterfalls.

A good starting point for
visiting the caves and the
botanical garden is the
bridge of Maslenica.

One of the paths leading into Paklenica National Park

Pag ❻

The island of Pag is 63 km (39 miles) long and has two mountain chains running parallel to the coast: at the southern end cliffs frame a deep bay with numerous inlets. The island was inhabited in the Neolithic Age, and was occupied by the Liburnians in around 1200 BC. When Dalmatia was conquered by Publius Cornelius Scipio in the 1st century AD, the Romans built the town of Cissa and the fortified port of Navalia here. In the Imperial period, villas were built and some mosaic floors and an aqueduct still survive. The Slavs settled in Pag in the 6th century and became sheep farmers. After 1000 AD Zadar and Venice fought over the island to gain control of the salt pans *(see p100)*. When Cissa was destroyed by the inhabitants of Zadar, the islanders chose a new location for a village, Stari Grad, which was fortified by the Venetians in 1192.

Sheep grazing on Pag

in maquis, olive groves and aromatic herbs, particularly sage. As well as the production of olive oil and a distinctive wine called Žutica, sheep farming is one of the main occupations on the island. Pag is famous for its sheep's cheese *(paški sir)*, which has a distinctive taste thanks to the aromatic herbs in the grazing. The cheeses are coated with olive oil, and undergo lengthy maturation.

The dry, barren east-facing coast, swept by the bora wind

Exploring Pag

The island, connected by a bridge to the Magistrala coast road (E65) at its eastern tip, just beyond Dinjiška, is dry and barren, with only a few areas cultivated with vines and olive trees. The coastline facing the mainland, rocky and jagged and white in colour, is exposed to the bora wind and bears little vegetation. The typical dry-stone walls were built to protect the land from the wind and to separate the flocks of sheep belonging to different farmers. The southwest coast is a little flatter with some small beaches. Here the land is covered

Pag Town

The small main island town occupies a sheltered bay facing the mainland. It was granted the status of a free town by King Bela IV in 1244, but rivalry with Zadar brought about its destruction. The walls, the castle, a monastery and the church of St Mary in the old town are in ruins. In 1409, Pag came definitively under the rule of Venice.

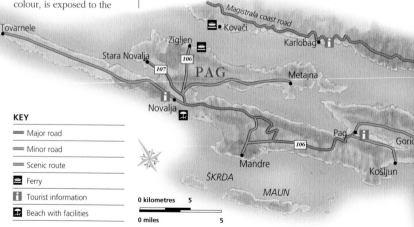

KEY

━━ Major road

━━ Minor road

━━ Scenic route

🚢 Ferry

ℹ Tourist information

🏖 Beach with facilities

0 kilometres 5

0 miles 5

LACE, SYMBOL OF THE TRADITIONS OF PAG

Typical Pag lace

Pag is renowned for its clean waters and its delicious sheep's cheese, but it is also well-known for its lace. For centuries this lace has been created by the patient hands of the women of the island who, in warm weather, sit by their doorsteps intent on creating this intricate lace. Made using a special stitch, the lace is used to decorate blouses, bedlinen, altar cloths and table centrepieces. Some decades ago a school was established here to train new lacemakers. A collection of antique lace was left to the school by former lacemakers and the examples are used as models. Lace is sold here and some of the rooms are set up as a museum.

VISITORS' CHECKLIST

Map C4. 🕴 8,000. 🚢 Prizna-Žigljen. **Pag** 🛈 Ulica od spitala, (023) 611 301. 🎭 Lace exhibition (summer); Carnival of Pag, traditional kolo dance and traditional costumes (31 Jul). **www**.pag-tourism.hr **Novalja** 🛈 (053) 661 404. **www**.tz-novalja.hr **Karlobag** 🛈 dr. Tuđmana 2, (053) 694 251. **www**.tz-karlobag.hr

The Duke's Palace in the main square, Pag

In 1443 the Venetian rulers, with the assistance of local nobles, entrusted the design of a new town to the famous architect Juraj Dalmatinac (Giorgio Orsini). It took several decades to build what is now the present-day Pag.

Venetian rule brought a long period of peace and prosperity, bolstered by the income from the productive salt works. Between the 15th and 18th centuries, important public buildings and a parish church, locally called the cathedral, were built.

The town has preserved its original structure with two main roads intersecting in the main square, and minor roads running parallel.

The high walls with eight towers and four gates were demolished at the end of the 19th century, but some traces (a gate and two bastions) still remain. The 15th-century Duke's Palace (Kneževa Palaća), which has been altered, and the unfinished Bishop's Palace by Juraj Dalmatinac face the main square.

A monument to Dalmatinac by Ivan Meštrović and the church of **St Mary of the Assumption** (1443–1448) stand in the same square. The church is a blend of Romanesque and Gothic, with three aisles divided by white stone columns with carved capitals. The façade has a rose window and there is a lunette above the door. Numerous works of art are preserved here, including a wooden 12th-century crucifix, a *Virgin of the Rosary* by Giovanni Battista Pittoni, an organ, and a treasury.

Novalja

Located at the beginning of the narrow peninsula of Lun, Novalja is the second town on the island. It makes its living entirely by tourism, thanks to its level beach. In the centre of the town are the remains of an early Christian basilica and a pre-Romanesque church dating from the 9th–10th centuries.

A new ferry service connects the island to the mainland, running from Novalja to Prizna.

Environs

Boat excursions to Pag leave from **Karlobag** on the mainland. Karlobag lies in a pretty bay and takes its name from the fortress that the Archduke of Austria, Charles Augustus of Habsburg, built in 1579 on the site of a village destroyed by the Turks.

The fortress lost its importance after the Turkish threat had passed and was abandoned. Its attractive stones were then used to build the houses in the village. Still visible are some of the massive walls and the remains of a monastery, which once had a famous library and a church.

Kraljevica Zadar

106

Dinjiška

Kraljevica Zadar

Vlašići

108

Povljana

The harsh but fascinating landscape, characteristic of the island of Pag

Krka National Park ❼
Nacionalni Park Krka

The park covers an area of 142 sq km (55 sq miles) and was established in 1985 to protect the middle and lower stretches of the River Krka, which flows into the bay of Šibenik. The source of the river is near Knin, and the river begins its journey of 75 km (47 miles) inside a canyon on the limestone plateau behind Šibenik. It finally spills over into the spectacular Roški Slap and Skradinski Buk waterfalls, forming a series of lakes and rapids surrounded by vegetation. The bird life in the park is very varied.

Monastery of Visovac
In the middle of the lake is the monastery of Visovac. It was founded by Franciscans in 1445 who were joined by Franciscans from Bosnia in 1576. They brought books, illuminated manuscripts and sacred vestments with them.

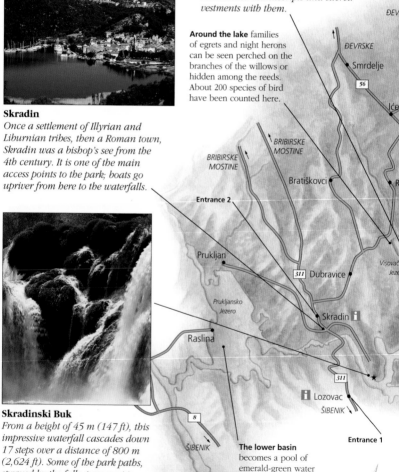

Skradin
Once a settlement of Illyrian and Liburnian tribes, then a Roman town, Skradin was a bishop's see from the 4th century. It is one of the main access points to the park; boats go upriver from here to the waterfalls.

Around the lake families of egrets and night herons can be seen perched on the branches of the willows or hidden among the reeds. About 200 species of bird have been counted here.

ĐEVRS

ĐEVRSKE

Smrdelje

56

Ićev

BRIBIRSKE MOSTINE

BRIBIRSKE MOSTINE

Bratiškovci

Ru

Entrance 2

Prukljan

311 Dubravice

Visovačko Jezero

Prukljansko Jezero

Skradin ℹ

Raslina

311

ℹ Lozovac

ŠIBENIK

Entrance 1

Skradinski Buk
From a height of 45 m (147 ft), this impressive waterfall cascades down 17 steps over a distance of 800 m (2,624 ft). Some of the park paths, sprayed by the falls, pass next to what is one of the most spectacular natural displays in Croatia.

8

ŠIBENIK

The lower basin becomes a pool of emerald-green water in the summer and is an attractive place to sunbathe or picnic.

Roški Slap

Here the river widens and deepens within the forest before finally cascading from between the trees, producing waterfalls over 25 m (82 ft).

VISITORS' CHECKLIST

Map C–D4. **Park** ![i] *Trg Ivana Pavla II br 5, Šibenik, (022) 201 777.* **www**.npkrka.hr
⬤ *summer: 8am–8pm; winter: 9am–4pm. The park can be visited by car or coach entering at Lozovac or Skradin.* 📷
Monastery of Visovac: *can be visited on organized boat trips from Roški Slap.*

Krka monastery, first mentioned in 1402.

Kistanje

Nečmen

Citluk

Mratovo

Oklaj

Brljansko Jezero

GRAČAC

Knin

Vrbnik

DRNIŠ

Lake Visovac is at the heart of the park. After the waterfalls, the river flows through a narrow valley and then widens to form the lake. Some stretches of the banks are steep and others hilly with oak woods.

DRNIŠ

River Čikola

After Lake Visovac, the Krka is joined by the River Čikola and from here the river flows towards the Skradinski Buk and then on to the sea.

Širitovci

Monastery of Visovac

Drinovci

DRNIŠ

Kalik

ŠIBENIK DRNIŠ

Čikola

0 kilometres   5
0 miles   5

VISITING THE PARK

View of Krka Park

The protected area begins at the Knin valley and continues to the bridge of Šibenik. Road signs mark the entrances to the park; each has a parking area, a tourist information centre, and a ticket office. Cars can enter from Lozovac, while the Roški Slap waterfalls can be reached from Miljevci or Skradin. About 15 km (9 miles) from Burnum, other road signs indicate the entrance to the area of the Roški Slap waterfalls. Boats leave from Skradin for trips to the Skradinski Buk waterfalls and from here it is possible to take a short cruise to the Roški Slap falls, crossing the lake of Visovac and visiting the monastery on the island.

KEY

▬▬ Major road

▬▬ Minor road

▬▬ Scenic route

![i] Tourist information

★ Waterfall

Šibenik 🟤

The town is first documented in 1066 as Castrum Sebenici, when King Petar Krešimir IV described it as a triangular fortified town. In the 12th century it came under Hungarian-Croat rule. Between 1412 and 1797 it was ruled by the Venetians, and the old centre acquired grand buildings and three large forts as well as bastions on the island of St Nicholas. It was a prosperous time, the arts flourished and Šibenik became one of the liveliest cultural centres in Renaissance Croatia.

Statue of Juraj Dalmatinac

Venetian rule gave way to a brief period of French occupation until Austria took over and ruled until 1917. The recent war brought about the collapse of local industry however, and mass unemployment.

Aerial view of the Cathedral of St James

🟤 Church of St Francis
Sv. Frane
Trg Nikole Tomaszea 1. *Tel (022) 214 241.* ⬜ *by appt.*

Along the busy seafront, on the southern edge of the old town centre, once stood the monastery and church of St Francis, founded in 1229 and destroyed during a raid in 1321. Some capitals, a few statues, and parts of the arches in the cloister remain of the original structure. Towards the middle of the 15th century several new chapels were added on.

The buildings were completely rebuilt in the Baroque style around the middle of the 18th century. The church underwent complete renovation: the wooden ceiling and the sumptuous gilded carved wooden altars were remade, and every wall was decorated with paintings.

Inside, in the first chapel on the left, is a great organ from 1762, made by Petar Nakić.

The large cloister has kept its 14th-century structure and there is a library with manuscripts and liturgical material in the monastery.

🟤 Church of St Barbara
Sv. Barbara
Kralja Tomislava.

The small church of St Barbara, behind the apse of the cathedral of St James, was built around the middle of the 15th century, and conserves parts of an older building. Irregular openings make the façade unusual: the lunette on the main door has a statue of St Nicholas from the workshop of Bonino of Milan (1430). Inside is an altar made by a youthful pupil of Juraj Dalmatinac, Giovanni da Pribislao, who was obliged to match another altar which had been saved from the previous church.

The church also houses a rich and interesting collection of religious art, with paintings, sculptures and illuminated texts dating from the 14th to 16th centuries.

🏛 Count's Palace – Civic Museum
Muzej Grada Šibenika
Gradska Vrata 3. *Tel (022) 213 880.* ⬜ *summer: 10am–1pm, 6–10pm; winter: 10am–1pm, 5–7pm daily.*

This palace takes its name from the Venetian Count Niccolò Marcello who built it in the first decade of the 17th century. It was the Venetian governor's residence and is now a Civic Museum. This late-Renaissance building houses coin collections, archaeological finds from the Neolithic to Roman periods, tomb finds, early Croatian sculptures (7th–9th centuries), and a rich archive of historical documents about the town and its territory, many from the medieval period. There is a statue of the count (1609–11) on the façade next to the entrance doorway.

🟤 Cathedral of St James
Katedrala Sv. Jakova
See pp108–9.

⛪ Old Loggia
Gradska vijećnica
Trg Republike Hrvatske.

In front of the cathedral's Door of Lions stands the Old Loggia, formerly the seat of the town council, built between 1532 and 1543 to a design by Michele Sanmicheli, and restored after it was damaged during World War II.

This is a two-storey structure: the ground floor is an open portico with nine large arches, the upper floor is a loggia, with a balustrade.

The 16th-century Old Loggia, designed by Michele Sanmicheli

⛪ Foscolo Palace
Palača Fosclo
Andrije Kačića.

The Venetian governor, Leonardo Foscolo, built this palace in the Venetian Gothic style in around 1450.

The façade was decorated with Renaissance reliefs by Juraj Dalmatinac's pupils (15th century), and another relief, attributed to the master, has two putti supporting the coats of arms of the noble family, at the side of the entrance door.

View of Šibenik from the medieval Fort of St Anne

⛫ Fort of St Anne
Tvrđava Sv. Ana
ℹ️ *(022) 214 448.*
The fort is of medieval origins and the oldest defensive structure in Šibenik. It was destroyed after lightning struck the powder magazine. When it was rebuilt, account was taken of the town's altered defence needs, and the towers were omitted. Its present appearance dates from the 16th–17th centuries. Now officially renamed St Michele, it offers magnificent views over the islands.

⛫ Fort of St John
Tvrđava Sv. Ivan
ℹ️ *(022) 214 448.*
Standing on a hill 125 m (410 ft) high, the fort, originally 15th century, was rebuilt in a star shape after the town was attacked by the Turks in 1649.

⛫ Šubićevac Fort
Tvrđava Šubićevac
ℹ️ *(022) 214 448.*
The third large fort called Šubićevac, or Baron's Fort, was constructed rapidly in 1646, in the face of an imminent Turkish attack. The fort, in fact, greatly contributed to the defeat of the Turks in 1647. After a long siege, large parts of it had to be rebuilt. The present structure dates from the middle of the 17th century and a pretty garden is laid out in front of the bastions.

⛫ Fort of St Nicholas
Tvrđava Sv. Nikola
ℹ️ *(022) 214 448.*
The fort was planned by the Italian architect Gian Girolamo Sanmicheli, and

built between 1540 and 1547 on a cliff overlooking the city. It is a fine example of military architecture, both for its strength and for the beauty of the decorations above the entrance gate, in the apertures, in the rooms, and along the corridors. The fort was often used as a prison.

The Fort of St Nicholas, outside the entrance of Šibenik harbour

ŠIBENIK TOWN CENTRE

0 metres   200
0 yards   200

Key to Symbols *see back flap*

Fort of St John

Fort of St Anne ⑦

JURJA DALMATINCA
BUGOŽAICA
PROMINKA
POD TVRĐAVOM
PUT GROBLJA
KNINKA
KRALJA ZVONIMIRA
NIKOLE VADANOVA

Foscolo Palace ⑥
OBALA PALIH OMLADINACA
MIDDLE KAČIĆA
SV. LUCE

Cathedral of St James ④
Old Loggia ⑤
Church of St Chrysogonus

Count's Palace – Civic Museum ③
Church of St Barbara ②
DON KRSTE STOŠIĆA
Church of St John

Krka
KRALJA TOMISLAVA
JURJA BARAKOVIĆA
SV. N. TAVELICA
USOCKA
OBALA OSLOBOĐENJA

TRG PAVLA RUBICA I
ZLARINSKI PROLAZ

BOTIĆARE KRALJICE JELENE
Church of the Ascension

Šubićevac Fort

Theatre
POLJANA

TRG IVANA GORANA KOVAČIĆA
Perivoj Roberta Visianija

Fort of St Nicholas

Church of St Francis ①

Train Station
200m (220 yards)
Bus Station
200m (220 yards)

Šibenik: Cathedral of St James
Katedrala Sv. Jakova

It has taken Croatian and international experts several years to restore Šibenik's cathedral since its shelling in 1991. Its original construction by renowned Dalmatian and Italian artists began in 1432 and was completed in 1555. The original project was entrusted to the Venetian, Antonio Dalle Masegne, who built the lower Gothic level.

A face on the cornice of the apse

His successor, Juraj Dalmatinac (see p20), designed the upper Renaissance part, the sculptures by the doors, with Adam and Eve by the Door of Lions, the 72 faces on the outside of the apse, many of the capitals, the tomb of Juraj Šižgorić and, along with Andrija Aleši, the beautiful baptistry. On Dalmatinac's death in 1475, the work was continued by Nikola Firentinac, who built the splendid presbytery with the choir, the dome, the galleries and vaulted roof.

The Dome, a unique structure built of interlocking slabs of stone, was badly damaged in 1991.

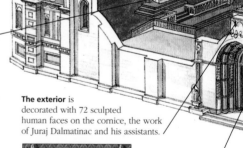

Transept
The transept is supported by a square structure; on three sides is an arch surmounted by a statue. The stones were worked in such a way that they fitted together without the need for mortar.

The exterior is decorated with 72 sculpted human faces on the cornice, the work of Juraj Dalmatinac and his assistants.

★ **Presbytery**
The finely worked stone stalls were made by Juraj Dalmatinac and Nikola Firentinac. Other sculpted reliefs adorn the upper parts.

Door of Lions
This door is named after the two stone lions which support statues of Adam and Eve. The doorway is framed by slim, finely carved columns.

STAR FEATURES

★ Baptistry

★ Presbytery

★ Baptistry
At the end of the right aisle is an impressive baptistry with many statues and reliefs sculpted by Juraj Dalmatinac, Nikola Firentinac and Andrija Aleši. The fine baptismal font is supported by three putti.

VISITORS' CHECKLIST

Trg Republike Hrvaste 1. *Tel* (022) 214 899. ☐ *daily.* ◙ ♿ ☑ *www.*sibenik.hr/vodic-eng/sibenik/kulturno_povijesna_bastina2.asp

Façade
The symmetrical façade has an arched tympanum in the centre. The taller central section has a rose window in the centre and a smaller one above on the tympanum. The façade is framed by two pilasters and has only one door.

The cathedral was built entirely in local stone and is a tribute to the great technical skill of the stone-cutters.

The Gothic doorway is decorated with groups of sculptures of saints ascending the arch, which is framed by two spires.

Interior
The three-aisle interior is divided by columns with carved capitals supporting pointed arches. The tall central nave has a frieze and women's gallery.

Drniš **9**

Map D4. 4,700.
Šibenik, 25 km (15 miles), (022)
333 699. Šibenik, (022) 212 087.
(022) 212 346.

The town of Drniš first
appears in documents
towards the end of the 15th
century, as the site of a fort
built to stop a Turkish
invasion, at the point where
the River Čikola cuts into
the valley and flows down
towards Šibenik.

In 1526 the fort was
captured and enlarged by the
Turks, who made it one of
their outposts. A village
with a mosque and baths
developed around the fort,
but during the wars between
Venice and the Ottoman
empire, from 1640 to 1650,
the fort and the village were
almost entirely destroyed by
the Venetians.

In the reconstruction that
followed the mosque was
remodelled and became the
church of St Anthony. The
minaret became the bell
tower of the church of St
Roch. Serbs populated the
town and it became part of
the Krajina territory.

Along the road from Drniš
to Šibenik, the ruins of
defence structures with high
walls and a tower can be seen.

Environs

Some 9 km (5 miles) east of
Drniš is the village of **Otavice**,

the birthplace of Ivan
Meštrović's parents. The great
sculptor *(see p157)* built a
Mausoleum here for himself
and his family. It is simply
designed in the form of a stone
cube with a shallow dome.

**Meštrović Mausoleum in Otavice,
near Drniš**

Knin **10**

Map D4.
12,000. (022) 663 722.
(022) 212 346.

A town on the main road
from Zagreb to Split,
Knin has long played an
important role in Dalmatia's
history. It occupies a strategic
position on the plateau, and
there have been defences
of some kind here since
prehistoric times. In the 10th

century, when the town was
known as Ad Tenen, the **Fort
of St Saviour** (Sveti Spas),
was built here. It was used by
reigning Croat monarchs, who
often stayed in the nearby
town of Biskupija and held
coronations here.

Early in the 11th century
Knin became a bishopric and
the residence of several
aristocratic Croatian families.
Occupied by the Turks in the
early 16th century, in 1688
Knin fell to the Venetians.

The Morlachs, in the pay of
Venice, distinguished themselves in the battle to retake
the fort by scaling the walls.
Afterwards they rebuilt the
fort and settled in the town.

In 1991, the Serbian army
used the fort when most of
the inhabitants of Croat origin
were forced out. It became a
focus for the Serb rebellion
and the Republic of the Serb
Krajina, of which Knin was
the capital, was created. In
August 1995 the territory was
returned to the Croats.

Environs

About 5 km (3 miles) away is
Biskupija, once known as the
"Field of five churches", for its
religious buildings (9th–11th
centuries) attended by the
Croat kings. King Zvonimir
was killed here by Croat nobles
who did not accept his allegi-
ance to the pope. By the main
building is a church designed
by Ivan Meštrović and
frescoed by Jozo Kljaković.

The imposing fort of St Saviour in Knin, on Mount Spas

Primošten, once an island but now linked to the mainland

Sinj ⓫

Map D5. 👥 *11,500.* 🚉 *Split.*
🚌 *Split.* ℹ️ *Vrlicka ulica 41, (021)*
826 352. 🎭 *Sinjska Alka, jousting*
tournament in costume (1st Sun Aug).

On the Cetina plateau
the Romans founded
Aequum, the present-day
Čitluk, on the road towards
Bosnia, but the unhealthy
area and malaria forced the
inhabitants to abandon the
town and move to a nearby
hill called Castrum Zyn. This
was safer and easier to defend
and they built a fort here.

At the end of the 1400s
some Franciscan monks, who
had fled from a monastery in
Rama, a Bosnian town, came
here, bringing with them an
image of the Virgin believed
to be miraculous and they
built a **Franciscan
Monastery** (Franjevacki
Samostan) and a church.

The town, by
now called
Sinj, was
captured
by the Turks in 1513
and remained in
their possession
until 1699 when it
was liberated by the
Venetians. Its strategic
position urged the
Turks to attempt
to recapture it
in 1715, but an

**Sculpture of
the jousting
tournament, Sinj**

unexpected attack
by 600 horsemen, citizens
of the town, against the
Ottoman troops prevented
its capture.

This historical event is
commemorated every year on
the first Sunday in August
with a jousting tournament
(Sinjska Alka), when expert
riders take part in a
competition to capture
a shield, the symbol of
victory. A bronze sculpture
representing the joust stands
in the public gardens.

The Franciscan church,
rebuilt at various times, is a
popular pilgrimage site. The
monastery has recently been
renovated and some of the
rooms house archaeological
finds from ancient Aequum.

🏛️ **Franciscan Monastery**
A Stepinca 1. **Tel** (021) 707 010.

Klis ⓬

Map D5. 👥 *2,300.* 🚉 *Split.* 🚌
Split. ℹ️ *Megdan ulica 57, (021) 240*
578. **www.tzo-klis.hr**

The little village of Klis is
dominated by an imposing
Fort which consists of three
concentric walls. It was
founded by the Romans on a
hill above a mountain pass
which led from the plateau
onto the plain. The
Venetians
strengthened the fort
and enlisted the
Uskoks to help fight
off the Turks, who
however finally
captured it in 1537.
The Turks enlarged the
fort, building a mosque
and a minaret and from
here they menaced
the city of Split
until 1648 when they
were driven off by
Venetian troops. The
fort was in use until
the Austrians took over. The
mosque was turned into a
church and the minaret
was demolished.

The town's restaurants are
particularly known for their
excellent spit-roasted lamb.

**The Fort of Klis, the scene of
many bloody battles**

Primošten ⓭

Map D5. 👥 *1,750.*
🚉 *Split.* 🚌 *Split (022) 338 483.*
🚢 *Marina (022) 570 068.*
ℹ️ *Rudina Biskupa J. Arnerica 2,
(022) 571 111.* 🎭 *Wine
exhibition "Babic" (Oct).*

Originally an isolated
island, Primošten is now
connected to the mainland by
a bridge and a causeway. The
name Primošten means
"brought closer by a bridge".
The island was inhabited in
prehistoric times, and was
settled by Bosnian refugees
fleeing from the Turks. Under
Venetian rule, walls were
built around the town.

The top of the town is
dominated by the church of
St George, built in the late
15th century and enlarged
around 1760. Inside is an icon
of the Virgin on a silver
panel, and a Baroque altar.

A popular resort with
pebbly beaches, Primošten is
also famous for its vineyards
(see p129) and a good red
wine called Babić.

Marina ⓮

Map D5. 👥 *900.*
ℹ️ *(021) 889 015.*

This small holiday resort lies
in a sheltered bay and has a
marina and a pretty beach.
The village has been
inhabited since the 15th
century. In 1495 the Bishop
of Trogir built a massive
tower in the port, now the
Hotel Kaštil.

The two churches in the
village, St Luke and St John,
were built in the 15th century
and restructured at various
times by the Sobota family,
the feudal lords of the village.

Trogir ⓯

Set on a small island just off the mainland, Trogir is one of the jewels of the Dalmatian coast, with many splendid monuments. The Greeks of Issa (now Vis) first settled here in 380 BC, when they founded the fortified town of Tragyrion (island of goats) which became Tragurium under the Romans in 78 AD. In the Middle Ages Trogir was protected by the Byzantine fleet, but in 1123 it was attacked and destroyed by the Saracens, and abandoned by the few surviving inhabitants. It revived again 70 years later and a period of extraordinary artistic growth ensued, first under the kings of Hungary and, from 1420, under Venetian rule. In 1997 Trogir was listed as a UNESCO World Heritage site.

The seafront of Trogir, with Kamerlengo castle in the distance

Most of the old historic centre of the town is on an island and is encircled by a wall with two gates. A bridge now joins the island to the mainland and another links it to the island of Čiovo. Tourism is important to the town: ice-cream parlours, restaurants and pizzerias line the small squares. The main public and religious monuments, and other important buildings, have been the subject of restoration for some years.

🏛 Land Gate
Kopnena Vrata
Rebuilt in the 16th century, this gate was made from a tall doorway in pale rusticated stone, with grooves which once supported a drawbridge. On the cornice above the arch stands the lion of St Mark and, above that, on a pedestal, stands a statue of the Blessed John of Trogir (Sv. Ivan Trogirski), one of the town's patron saints.

🏛 Civic Museum
Muzej Grada Trogira
Gradska vrata 4. *Tel* (021) 881 406.
◯ Jun–Sep: 9am–noon, 6–9pm, Mon–Sat; Oct–May: 7am–3pm, Mon–Sat. 📷 📸
On the other side of the Land Gate is the Baroque Garagnin Fanfogna Palace, now the Civic Museum, with 18th-century furnishings. There are archaeological collections, books, documents, drawings and antique clothes linked to the town's history.

🏛 Stafileo Palace
Palača Stafileo
Matije Gupca 20. ◯ to the public.
Stafileo Palace was built in the late 15th century. A series of five windows in Venetian Gothic style punctuates each of the two floors, the openings framed by pillars, capitals and carved arches. Around the arches are reliefs of flowers and leaves. The design is attributed to the school of Juraj Dalmatinac, who worked for many years in Trogir.

🔒 Cathedral of St Lawrence
Sv. Lovre
Trg Ivana Pavla II. *Tel* (091) 531 4754.
◯ mid May–Oct: 9am–8pm; Nov–mid May: by appt.
The cathedral stands on the site of an ancient church, destroyed by the Saracens. Construction started in 1193, but was prolonged for decades and involved dozens of artists. The three-aisle building has three semicircular apses: the central nave is higher than the side aisles from which it is divided by eight columns.

There are two entrances. The side door, known as "the count's", is very simple, and dated 1123. The other entrance is a magnificent Romanesque door under an atrium, to the right of which stands a beautiful Venetian-Gothic bell tower, built between the early 15th century and the end of the 16th century. This door was carved in around 1240 by the Dalmatian sculptor Master Radovan *(see p20)*, and is the finest expression of Romanesque sculpture to be found in Dalmatia. Two stone lions support statues of Adam and Eve either side of the door. Scenes of the different months of the year are carved on the pilasters and on the second semicircle there are images of saints.

Above the door, in the large lunette, is a relief of the Nativity and in the semicircles are episodes from the Bible. The door is enclosed under a sloping roof with a corbel at the top with a statue of St Lawrence. In the atrium is a baptistry designed by Andrija Aleši in around 1460 with a relief of the Baptism of Christ.

The intricate Romanesque door of the Cathedral of St Lawrence

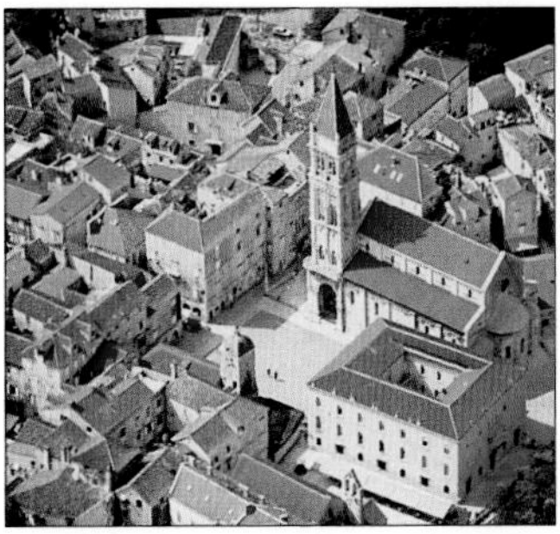

Aerial view of the square and the cathedral

The church interior contains an octagonal stone pulpit from the 13th century built and sculpted by Mauro, a choir with wooden stalls inlaid by Ivan Budislavić towards the mid-15th century, and a ciborium on the main altar with sculptures depicting the Annunciation. On the altars are paintings by Palma il Giovane and Padovanino.

Along the left aisle is the chapel of the Blessed Orsini, a masterpiece by Nikola Firentinac and Andrija Aleši made in 1468–72, with 12 statues of the apostles in shell-shaped niches and, in the centre, the sarcophagus of the Blessed Orsini, the first bishop of Trogir. The sculptures are by Nikola Firentinac, Andrija Aleši and Ivan Budislavić.

In the sacristy are paintings by Salvator Rosa and Gentile Bellini, cabinets carved by Grgur Vidov, and a Treasury with many gold pieces, reliquaries and paintings dating from the 17th-century.

The tall bell tower was built in the 14th century, but was partly destroyed during the wars early in the following century and only the ground floor remains of the original building. When Trogir became part of Venetian territory, the bell tower was rebuilt. The first floor with a balustrade by Matej Gojković (1422), is in the Venetian-Gothic style, with two narrow mullioned windows with a trefoil, surmounted by blind arches. The second level has two tall windows on each side: the north and south walls have mullioned windows with four trefoil eyes, those on the east and west walls are surmounted by fretwork grilles, with columns and capitals at the centre and corners, giving a feeling of lightness to the entire floor. Recent studies attribute this work to the Italian sculptor Lorenzo Pincino, who worked in Trogir and Dalmatia for many years, with the assistance of local craftsmen.

The third storey, from the late 16th century, was built by the sculptor Trifun Bokanić and has large arched openings.

VISITORS' CHECKLIST

Map D5. *10,500.* *Split, 30 km (18 miles).* *Split, 30 km (18 miles).* *(021) 881 405.* *Obala bana Berislavića 12, (021) 881 412.* *(021) 881 508.* **www**.trogir.hr

TROGIR TOWN CENTRE

Cathedral of St Lawrence ④
Church of St Dominic ⑪
Church of St John the Baptist ⑧
Church of St Nicholas ⑩
Čipiko Palace ⑤
Civic Museum ②
Kamerlengo Castle and St Mark's Tower ⑫
Land Gate ①
Loggia and Clock Tower ⑦
Sea Gate and Fish Market ⑨
Stafileo Palace ③
Town Hall ⑥

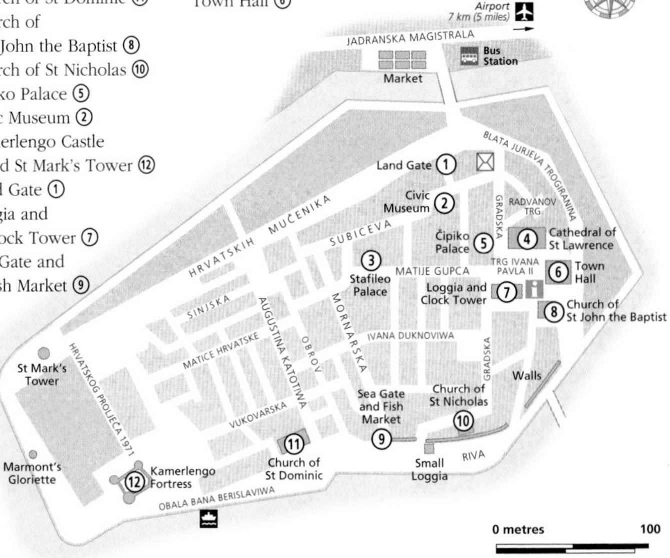

Key to Symbols *see back flap*

Exploring Trogir

A good time to visit Trogir is the late spring or early autumn, when the narrow streets, flanked by ancient stone houses, are not so busy with summer visitors, and there is space to stop and admire the ingenious architectural details that make this island so fascinating. A carved doorway, a coat of arms, or a mullioned window may decorate the façade of a building; the entrance to a courtyard may offer glimpses of scented gardens. These are all indications of a once widespread prosperity and also evidence of Trogir's cultural past, when it was an important centre for the arts. After many years of hardship and neglect, the town is now gradually being restored to its former glory.

The Clock Tower

supported by six columns with Roman capitals and dates from the 14th century. On the wall are two reliefs, one from 1471 sculpted by Nikola Firentinac *(Justice)*, and one from 1950 by Ivan Meštrović *(Ban Berislavić)*. The Clock Tower stands to the left of the Loggia. It supports a pavilion dome, salvaged in 1447 from the chapel of the oratory of St Sebastian. The saint's statue on the façade was sculpted by Nikola Firentinac.

A Renaissance well in the courtyard of Čipiko Palace

🏛 Čipiko Palace
Palača Čipiko
Gradska ulica. 🔵 *to the public, except courtyard.*
An inscription indicates 1457 as the year of completion of the beautiful Čipiko Palace, built for Trogir's most illustrious family. Over a Renaissance doorway, distinguished by its columns with capitals, is a shell decoration above a finely worked cornice.

The first floor has a mullioned window with a balustrade in light coloured stone. In the centre, two columns with capitals support pointed arches and at the ends of the window are two thin pilasters surmounted by capitals with spiral decorations. Between the arches are four sculptures of angels. Two central ones hold a scroll with the coats of arms

of the Čipiko family. The second floor lacks a balustrade, and is similar in style to the lower floor, although its decorations are less ornate.

A second door, opening on to a side street, has a complex structure. Two fluted door jambs support capitals with carved foliage decoration and a stone cornice with two sculpted lions holding a coat of arms. These are flanked by two sculptures of angels in medallions.

🏛 Town Hall
Municipija
Trg Ivana Pavla II.
On the eastern side of the square is the Town Hall. This building originates from the 15th century and has three storeys with open arches and a beautiful mullioned window with a balustrade on the upper floor, which was restored in the 19th century. Numerous coats of arms decorate the façade which has three Renaissance doors framed by projecting stone. The pretty porticoed courtyard is open to the public. However, the interior, which has been altered at various times, has nothing of significant interest.

🏛 Loggia and Clock Tower
Gradska loža
Trg Ivana Pavla II. ⬜ *daily.*
The Loggia and the Clock Tower face John Paul II Square (Trg Ivana Pavla II). The Loggia has a roof

🔒 Church of St John the Baptist
Sv. Ivan Krstitelj
🔵 *for restoration.*
This small Romanesque church, built in the 13th century, is the pantheon of the powerful Čipiko family. The church houses an **Art Gallery** (Pinacoteca) with collections of medieval illuminated manuscripts, ornaments, paintings and precious gold pieces from various churches. The collection also includes a sculpture *(Deposition)* by Nikola Firentinac, organ panels by Gentile Bellini *(St Jerome and St John the Baptist)*, two polyptychs by Blaise of Trogir and other paintings dating from the 15th–17th centuries.

The doorway of the Romanesque church of St John the Baptist

contains the tomb of Giovanni Sobota, a lawyer, attributed to Nikola Firentinac (1469), and a splendid painting by Palma il Giovane (*Circumcision of Christ*).

The Fish Market, housed in a 16th-century loggia

🏛 Sea Gate and Fish Market
Južna Vrata
Obala Bana Berislavića.
The Sea Gate was built at the end of the 16th century and has two beautiful columns made of blocks of light-coloured stone which frame the opening and support a projecting block on which stands the lion of St Mark.

Nearby is the Fish Market which is held in an open loggia with nine columns supporting the roof. It was built in 1527 and was formerly the customs house.

Ceremonial costumes made by the tailor Boris Burić Gena

BORIS BURIĆ GENA

Trogir can boast a unique present-day success story: Boris Burić Gena, a tailor who specializes in making traditional Croatian suits. His signature jackets are made without lapels and have antique-style brocade buttonholes. They are often worn in ceremonies and parades. The careful choice of fabrics, meticulous design and matching of accessories have made this talented craftsman's name. His workshop, the Buric Palace, now draws wealthy and famous clients from all over Europe.

🔒 Church of St Nicholas
Sv. Nikola
Gradska ulica 2. **Tel** *(021) 881 631.*
⭕ *summer: 8am–noon, 4–7pm daily.*
The church and Benedictine convent date from the 11th century, but were rebuilt in the 16th century. The convent rooms now house the **Zbirka Umjetnina Kairos**, an art collection which includes the *Kairos*, a relief of Greek origins (1st century BC) depicting the god of opportunity, a Gothic Crucifix, and a Romanesque statue (*The Virgin with Child*).

Relief depicting Kairos, St Nicholas

🔒 Church of St Dominic
Sv. Dominik
Obala Bana Berislavića.
⭕ *summer: 8am–noon, 4–7pm daily.*
The church and monastery of St Dominic are Romanesque-Gothic buildings constructed in the 14th century. They were renovated by Nikola Firentinac in the Renaissance style. The single-nave church

🏛 Kamerlengo Castle and St Mark's Tower
Kaštel Kamerlengo
In the southwest corner of the island stands Kamerlengo Castle, which was at one time the residence of the Venetian governor. It was built by the Venetians in about 1430, and is a four-sided structure with a hexagonal base. It faces the sea. High walls connect the three towers and the bastion. This imposing structure was once connected to St Mark's Tower (Kula svetog Marka). The large open space inside the castle is used for outdoor theatre performances and concerts in the summer.

St Mark's Tower was built by the Venetians after the construction of the castle and has the typical structure of defences built in the Renaissance period. A circular tower stands on a truncated cone base and there is a long series of embrasures on the roof. Artillery was installed on the top level in readiness to defend the strip of water that separates the island from the mainland.

What was once the parade ground, between the castle and St Mark's Tower, is now the town's sports field.

The imposing St Mark's Tower, built for defence in 1470

Salona 16

Detail of the Tusculum

The ancient town of Salona, 5 km (3 miles) from Split, is famous for its Roman ruins. The name Salona (or Salonae) derives from the salt *(sal in Latin)* works in the area. Originally an Illyrian settlement, it was then Greek, but did not become a important centre until the Romans built a town next to the Greek city. During the rule of Augustus it became a Roman colony called Martia Julia Salonae and later it was the capital of the province of Dalmatia. In the 1st century AD the Romans built an amphitheatre, theatres, temples, baths, a Forum and town walls reinforced with towers, and Salona became the richest and most populated city in the mid-Adriatic. In 614 the Avars and the Croats destroyed it and it fell into disuse. The buildings and the churches were stripped and the stone was used for new buildings.

Salona's main road

Ruins of the walls and triangular tower

Exploring Salona

At the end of the 19th century excavations began to bring to light the buried remains of this ancient settlement. The work has clearly shown that the town had two districts dating from different periods: the original, old centre *(Urbs vetus)* and a later part which dates from the Augustan era *(Urbs nova occidentalis* and *Urbs nova orientalis).* The excavations have uncovered only a part of the layout of the **Outer Walls**, which were frequently reinforced over the centuries. However, the foundations and the remains of towers with triangular or rectangular bases are visible.

A good place to begin a tour is the **Necropolis of Manastirine**, the burial area just outside the walls, north of

the city (near the parking area). In the 4th century a religious building was constructed here to house the relics of the Salonian saints, victims of Diocletian's persecution of Christians. The ruins of the necropolis and the basilica are well preserved.

From Manastirine, after the entrance, you reach the **Tusculum**, a villa built in the last century for the distinguished archaeologist Frane Bulić, to enable him to study Salona. A scholar and director of the Archaeological Museum in Split, he devoted much of his life to researching the ancient ruins of this city. The building is now a small museum.

However, the most interesting material is now in the Archaeological Museum in Split *(see p123).*

Further on is the richest area of ruins with the foundations of early Christian basilicas, baths and the Caesarea Gate. The **Baths** were built in the 1st century when the city became the capital of the province of Dalmatia. In the early Christian period the buildings were probably transformed into religious buildings: the **Bishop's Complex** in the northeastern sector of Salona comprised basilicas, a baptistry and the bishop's residence. Before Christianity became widespread, early Christian martyrs were slayed here, including St Domnius (the patron saint of Split), Venantius and Anastasius.

The foundations of two basilicas have been excavated. One is known as the **Urban Basilica**, the other, called **Honorius' Basilica**, had a Greek cross

The Necropolis of Manastirine, just outside the walls

Basilica Urbana in the Bishop's Complex

plan. This is also the site of what remains of the **Caesarea Gate:** arches flanked by two octagonal towers, showing the building techniques used by the Romans in the Imperial era.

Going west along the walls you reach the **Necropolis of Kapljuć**, another early Christian burial site, and then the imposing ruins of the **Amphitheatre**, in the eastern-most part of the city.

The amphitheatre, in brick, was probably covered in stone and stood in the newer part of the city on the northwest edge of *Urbs vetus* (Old Town) close to the walls. According to historians, the amphitheatre could seat 18,000–20,000 people. The foundations and a part of the lower tribune have been excavated and the discovery of a network of underground channels has led to the theory that simulated naval battles were held in the arena.

The amphitheatre's construction date was controversial for a long time,

but has now been established as the second half of the 2nd century AD.

From the amphi-theatre, another path leads to the **Theatre** at the edge of the old city. This was built in the first half of the 1st century AD and part of the stage and the foundations of the stalls have been excavated. Next to the theatre is the **Forum**, the political and commercial heart of the city. Unlike the Forum in Zadar *(see pp92–95)*, the paving was dismantled and only the foundations remain. In the Roman era some of the most important buildings stood around the Forum, which was begun in the 1st century AD and subsequently modified.

The best-preserved Roman construction in ancient Salona is the **Aqueduct**, built to bring water from the River

VISITORS' CHECKLIST

Map D5. 🚌 *from Split.* ℹ️ *(021) 210 048. www.solin-info.com* 🕐 *summer: 7am–7pm; winter: call to check opening times.* ♿

Jadro to the city and extended in the time of Emperor Diocletian to reach his palace in Split *(see pp120–1)*. Repair work was carried out at the end of the 19th century and the southern part of the aque-duct is still in use. Alongside the walls it is possible to see some parts of the aqueduct above the surface – more evidence of the great skills of Roman civil engineers.

From the theatre you return to the Manastirine necropolis. North of this site is the **Necropolis of Marusinac**, built outside the city around the tomb of St Anastasius. In this area a few traces of a basilica dating from the 5th century are still visible.

The Amphitheatre, of which only a part of the lower tribune remains

THE RUINS OF SALONA

Amphitheatre ⑦
Baths ③
Bishop's Complex ④
Caesarea Gate ⑤
Forum ⑨
Necropolis of Kapljuć ⑥
Necropolis of Manastirine ①
Necropolis of Marusinac ⑩
Theatre ⑧
Tusculum ②

0 metres 500

0 yards 500

Key to Symbols *see back flap*

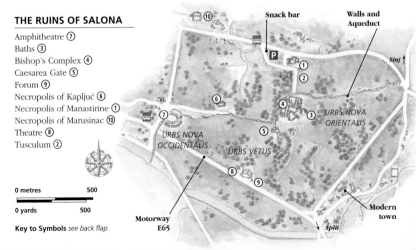

Snack bar

Walls and Aqueduct

Sinj ↑

URBS NOVA ORIENTALIS

URBS NOVA OCCIDENTALIS

URBS VETUS

Modern town

Motorway E65

Split

Split ⑰

Detail of Papalić Palace

Shipyards, factories and a busy port present the modern face of Split, which expanded unchecked after World War II. The old town centre is still full of charm however; it grew up in and around the Emperor Diocletian's vast Roman palace, one of the largest and best-preserved left from the Roman world. In 614, the palace took in refugees from Salona *(see p116–17)*, which had been razed by the Avars, and these newcomers began to use the Roman structure as housing. Among the refugees were the bishop and other religious dignitaries, who breathed new life into the bishopric of Split. After two centuries of Byzantine rule and the establishment of Croat communities, Split became part of the Venetian territories in 1409. Under the Venetians, new walls and the Gripe Fort were built and the arts flourished.

View of the port and the seafront of Split

🏛 Golden Gate
Zlatna Vrata
This was the main entrance to Diocletian's Palace *(see p120)* and was the most impressive of the gates, with towers and decorative elements above the arches. In the 11th century, the corridor between the palace and the gate was closed and turned into the church of **St Martin** (Sv. Martin). An inscription commemorates Father Dominic, the founder.

🏛 Museum of Split
Muzej Grada Splita
Papalićeva 1. *Tel (021) 344 197, 360 171.* ☐ *Jun–Sep: 9am–9pm daily; Oct–May: 9am–4pm Tue–Fri, 10am–noon Sat & Sun.* 🖼
The Gothic Papalić Palace is one of the most interesting of the 15th–16th-century buildings constructed in the abandoned parts of the Diocletian complex. It houses an exhibition with various artistic finds, paintings, 16th-century works and books illustrating the city's celebrated history from the 12th to the 18th centuries.

🏛 Peristyle
The interior courtyard of the Roman complex is a truly impressive part of the complex where the layers of centuries of building can clearly be seen. The slender columns bordering three sides rest on a high plinth and have finely worked capitals. The access to the former private quarters of Diocletian has a tall arched tympanum and relief decorations.

🔒 Baptistry of St John
Sv. Ivan Krstitelj
Tel (021) 342 589. 📷 *for restoration.*
This small, beautiful building, consecrated in the 6th century, was the Palace's Temple of Jupiter. Inside, the baptismal font incorporates a pre-Romanesque panel of King Zvonimir and other dignitaries. The statue of St John on the end wall is by Ivan Meštrović and was added before World War II. The tomb of Bishop John is from the 8th century and the one in front of it, that of Bishop Lawrence, dates from the 11th century.

Baptismal font in the Baptistry of St John, former Temple of Jupiter

🔒 Cathedral of St Domnius
Katedrala Sv. Duje
See p121.

🏛 Silver Gate and Church of St Dominic
Srebrna Vrata i Sv. Dominik
Hrvojeva ulica. **Church of St Dominic** ☐ *am.*
Near the Silver Gate there is a market, a wonderful chaos of seasonal fruit and vegetables, homemade cheeses, hams and dried herbs. Because of the open space, this also provides the best view of the Palace of Diocletian. It is still possible to distinguish the different structures of the complex, and part of the guards' corridor, on the walls, can be walked along.

In front of the gate is the Oratory of St Catherine, built in the Middle Ages. It was used by the Dominicans while they built their own monastery (1217). The oratory was almost entirely rebuilt in the 17th century and became the church of St Dominic (Sv. Dominik). Inside the church, which was enlarged in 1930, are a *Miracle in Surian* by Palma il Giovane and an *Apparition in the Temple*, attributed to his school.

🏛 Brass Gate
Brončana Vrata
Ethnographic Museum
Sevarova 1. *Tel (021) 344 164.* ☐ *9am–2pm Mon–Fri, 9am–1pm Sat.*
Although the Brass Gate is plain and faces the sea and port, it opens on to the richest façade of the palace. The upper floor had a portico

which was later enclosed to make living quarters. The vast cellars have been excavated to reveal impressive arched vaults and skilful masonry. Shops occupy some of these but other huge cellars house an exhibition about the palace and temporary local displays.

Close to the Brass Gate, on Severova, is the **Ethnographic Museum** (Etnografski Muzej), displaying an array of skilled

Dalmatian folk crafts such as silver jewellery, weapons, wooden objects and costumes.

🚪 Iron Gate
Željezna Vrata

The church of **Our Lady of the Belfry** (Gospa od Zvonika), has an early Romanesque bell tower, the city's oldest (1081), and was constructed in the outer passageway above this entrance to the Palace.

🚪 People's Square
Narodni Trg (Pjaca)

This was the centre of business and administration from the 15th century and the nobility erected prestigious buildings here. Examples are the Venetian-Gothic **Cambi Palace** and the Renaissance **Town Hall** (Obćinski Dom), built in the first half of the 15th century, with a loggia with three arches on the ground floor and a Gothic window on the upper floor.

The Renaissance Town Hall on People's Square in the centre of Split

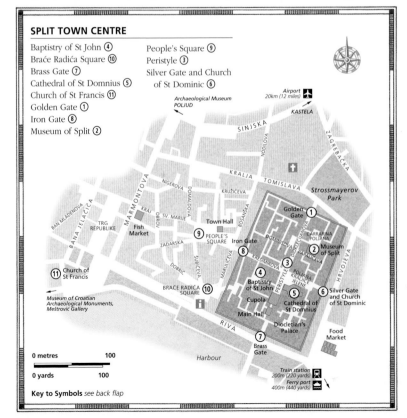

SPLIT TOWN CENTRE

Baptistry of St John ④
Braće Radića Square ⑩
Brass Gate ⑦
Cathedral of St Domnius ⑤
Church of St Francis ⑪
Golden Gate ①
Iron Gate ⑧
Museum of Split ②

People's Square ⑨
Peristyle ③
Silver Gate and Church of St Dominic ⑥

Airport
20km (12 miles)

Archaeological Museum
POLJUD

KASTELA

SINJSKA

NODILOVA

ZAGREBAČKA

KRALJA TOMISLAVA

Strossmayerov Park

NIGEROVA

DOMALDOVA

KRUŽIĆEVA

MARMONTOVA

KRAJ

OBROV

SV. MARIJE

BOSANSKA

Golden Gate ①

CARRARINA POLJANA

BAN MLADENOVA

BANA JELAČIĆA

TRG REPUBLIKE

Fish Market

Town Hall

⑨ PEOPLE'S SQUARE

Iron Gate ⑧

POKINSOVA

DIOKLECIJANOVA

PAPALIĆEVA

Museum of Split ②

ZADARSKA

KREŠIMIROVA

③

HRVOJEVA

DOBRIĆ

ŠUBIĆEVA

MARULIĆEVA

④ Baptistry of St John

PERISTYLE

POLJANA KRALJICE JELENE

⑪ Church of St Francis

BRAĆE RADIĆA SQUARE ⑩

Cupola

⑤ Cathedral of St Domnius

⑥ Silver Gate and Church of St Dominic

Museum of Croatian Archaeological Monuments, Meštrović Gallery

Main Hall

Diocletian's Palace

Food Market

RIVA

⑦ Brass Gate

Harbour

0 metres 100
0 yards 100

Train station
200m (220 yards)
Ferry port
400m (440 yards)

Key to Symbols see back flap

Palace of Diocletian

Diocletian, probably a native of Salona, became emperor in 284 and set out to reorganize the immense Roman Empire, dividing it into two parts with an Augustus at the head of one half and a Caesar at the head of the other. After governing for 20 years, Diocletian retired from public life and in 305 moved to the palace which he had commissioned from the architects Filotas and Zotikos in the bay of Split. After Diocletian's death in 313, the palace was used as administrative offices and the governor's residence. In 615, crowds of refugees from Salona found shelter here after the destruction of their city by the Avars. The richest settled in the emperor's apartments, the poorer in the towers and above the gates. The corners of the palace were marked by four square towers, and four towers along the north, east and south sides, while the side facing the sea had a loggia with arches.

Iron Gate and the Clock Tower
This is the best preserved gate: beyond is the church of Our Lady of the Belfry with a 12th-century tower next to it.

Temple of Jupiter
This had an atrium with six columns. The body of the building had a coffered vault and rested on an underground crypt. In the early Middle Ages it was turned into the Baptistry of St John.

The Temples of Venus and Cybele were circular outside and had a hexagonal ground-plan inside. A colonnaded corridor ran around the outside.

The Mausoleum of Diocletian, now the Cathedral of St Domnius

Peristyle
Near the crossroads where the Cardo and Decumanus intersected, the peristyle gave access to the sacred area. On one side were the temples of Venus and Cybele and, further back, that of Jupiter (now the Baptistry of St John); on the other side, the Mausoleum, now the cathedral.

Portrait of Diocletian
After reorganizing the empire, the emperor sought the spiritual unification of its citizens. The state religion, personified by the emperor, gained in importance, and temples were constructed bearing his image. Christians were subject to extremely violent persecution.

The Golden Gate, facing Salona, was the main entrance to the palace. This was the most imposing of the gates with two towers and many decorations.

The Silver Gate, or eastern gate, was a simpler copy of the Golden Gate.

RECONSTRUCTION OF DIOCLETIAN'S PALACE

The palace, shown here in its original form, was like a typical Roman military camp. It was 215 m (705 ft) long and 180 m (590 ft) wide and was enclosed by very thick walls, at times 28 m (92 ft) high. The four-sided stronghold was reinforced with towers on the north, east and west sides. There is a gate on each side, connected by two roads corresponding to the Roman *Cardo* and *Decumanus*.

⛪ Cathedral of St Domnius
Katedrala Sv. Duje
Kraj Sv. Duje 5. **Tel** (021) 342 589.
🕐 Jul & Aug: 8am–noon, 4–7pm daily; Sep–Jun: 10am–noon daily.

Originally Diocletian's mausoleum, the cathedral was consecrated in the 7th century when the sarcophagus containing the body of Diocletian was removed and replaced with the remains of St Domnius. It was the archbishop of Split at the time who transformed the mausoleum into a Christian church. It has remained practically unaltered since that time except for the construction of a Romanesque bell tower (12th–16th centuries) and the addition of the 13th-century choir inside.

An ancient sphinx in black granite rests at the foot of the bell tower. The entrance doorway has wooden panels from 1214, with scenes from the Gospel in floral frames. The cathedral, built on an octagonal ground-plan, has a double order of Corinthian columns, most of them the Roman originals; above these is a frieze decorated with scenes of Eros hunting, supporting medallions with portraits of Diocletian and his wife Prisca. In the second niche on the right, with frescoes dating from 1428, is the

The 13th-century hexagonal pulpit, Cathedral of St Domnius

Altar of St Domnius, the work of Bonino of Milan (1427). The wooden choir stalls in the 17th-century presbytery are an example of Romanesque carving from the beginning of the 13th century.

To the side is a chapel housing the **Altar of St Anastasius**, designed in 1448 by Juraj Dalmatinac. The niche after this was altered in the 18th century to create the Baroque chapel of St Domnius. The 13th-century hexagonal **pulpit** is supported by thin columns with carved capitals. The 14th-century building behind the cathedral houses the sacristy and the name of one of the architects, Filotas, is inscribed by the entrance. In the sacristy, now the Cathedral Museum, are many works of art, including objects in gold and silver, ancient manuscripts, medieval icons and vestments.

Of particular importance are the *Historia Saloniana* written by Archdeacon Toma in the 13th century and a 7th-century Gospel.

Detail of the Altar of St Anastasius, Cathedral

Exploring Split

As well as Diocletian's palace, Split has much in the way of historical and artistic interest to offer. In the medieval period, villages were built near the walls and when the city became a free town these settlements were linked in a more orderly fashion. The present-day Braće Radića Square and the People's Square were built, along with the Cambi Palace and the Town Hall. After 1420, construction of the external defences began and town walls were built. Between Split and Trogir, castles built for defence against the Turks still survive.

The 15th-century Marina Tower, built by the Venetians

Distant Agreements by Ivan Meštrović, Meštrović Gallery

🏛 Braće Radića Square
Trg Braće Radića

This medieval square is at the southwest corner of Diocletian's Palace. The tall **Marina Tower** (Hrvojeva Kula) is the only evidence of the imposing castle built by the Venetians in the second half of the 15th century after the final defeat of Split. Built on an octagonal ground-plan, it stands on the southern side of the square.

On the northern side is the Baroque **Milesi Palace**, which dates from the 17th century. There is also a work by Ivan Meštrović in the centre of the square: the great monument to Marko Marulić, the writer and scholar (1450–1524) who was the founder of literature in the Croatian language. The imposing bronze statue dedicated to the writer has an inscription with some verses by the poet Tin Ujević.

Monument to Marko Marulić

🛐 Church of St Francis
Sv. Frane

Trg Republike. 📞 *(021) 348 600 (Tourist office).* ⏱ *by appt.*

The church has been rebuilt in recent times but the small Romanesque-Gothic cloister, with thin columns enclosing a flower garden, is original.

The church, with mainly Baroque furnishings, has a 15th-century crucifix by Blaž Juriev Trogiranin. It also houses the tombs of the city's illustrious citizens, including that of Archdeacon Toma (the first Dalmatian historian), writer Marko Marulić and the well-known composer Ivan Lukačić.

🏛 Museum of Croatian Archaeological Monuments
Muzej Hrvatskih Arheoloških Spomenika

Šetalište Ivana Meštrovića. **Tel** *(021) 358 420, 358 455.* ⏱ *winter: 9am–3pm Tue–Sat, 10am–noon Sun; summer: 9am–3pm, 5–7pm Tue–Sat, 10am–noon Sun.* 📷 **www.mhas-split.hr**

Set up in 1975, this museum houses finds from the area around Split dating from the early Middle Ages. The collection also includes the works of early Croat sculptors, dating from 800. The stone fragments, salvaged from churches and castles, consist mainly of tombs, capitals, altar fronts, ciboria and windows. Highlights include Prince Višeslav's hexagonal baptismal font in marble, dating from the beginning of the 9th century, and the sarcophagus of Queen Jelena (10th century), discovered in the ancient Roman city of Salona.

🏛 Meštrović Gallery
Galerija Meštrović

Šetalište Ivana Meštrovića 46. **Tel** *(021) 358 450.* ⏱ *Jun–Sep: 10am–6pm Tue–Sat, 10am–3pm Sun; Oct–May: 10am–4pm Tue–Sat, 10am–2pm Sun.* 📷

The building housing this gallery was the residence of Ivan Meštrović in the early 1930s (*see p157*). The sculptor himself designed the building with two low towers at the ends and a loggia with eight columns on the façade. His sculptures, including *Distant Agreements* and *The Robes*, decorate the garden and the interior. Among statues in marble, wood and bronze are *The Contemplation*, *The Vow* and *Psyche*. Part of the building still preserves the artist's apartments.

The **Kaštelet**, further down the road at No 39, can be visited with the same ticket. This 17th-century residence belonged to the Cavagnin family and was bought by Meštrović in 1932 to set up an exhibition hall. The artist also built a small church here to exhibit a series of reliefs called *New Testament*, now replaced by a different work, the *Author of the Apocalypse*.

🏛 National Art Gallery
Galerija Umjetnina

Lovretska 11. **Tel** *(021) 480 149, 480 150.* ⏱ *winter: 9am–noon, 4–6pm Mon–Sat; summer: 9am–noon, 5–7pm Mon–Sat.*

The gallery offers a broad overview of art in Split and the rest of Dalmatia from the 16th to the 20th centuries.

The Venetian masters have a place of honour in the gallery but there are also important icons from the so-called school of Bocche di Cattaro (18th–19th centuries) and more contemporary work, including works by Ivan Meštrović and Vlaho Bukovac. Temporary exhibitions are also held here.

🏛 Archaeological Museum
Arheološki Muzej

Zrinsko Frankopanska 25. *Tel* (021) 318 720. ⏰ *winter: 9am–1pm Tue–Sat, 10am–noon Sun; summer: 9am–1pm, 4–7pm Tue–Sat, 10am–noon Sun.*

The museum was founded in 1820 and has been on its present site since 1921. It contains a considerable number of finds from the Roman, early Christian and medieval periods which are exhibited in rotation. Of great interest are the finds from Roman Salona, including sculptures, capitals, sarcophagi (those from the 4th–5th century still have pagan reliefs), jewellery, coins, small objects in glazed terracotta and ceramics. There are also finds from the Roman town of Narona (*see p130*).

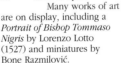

Sarcophagus, Archaeological Museum

🔒 Our Lady of Grace in Poljud
Gospa od Poljuda

Poljudsko Šetalište 17. 🛈 (021) 355 088. ⏰ *by appt.*

Towards Zrinsko-Frankopanska in the direction of the suburbs lies an area once

Polyptych by Girolamo da Santacroce, Our Lady of Grace

called the marsh (*poljud*). In the 1400s, the Franciscans built a fortified monastery here with large lateral towers, and a church with a trussed roof. A polyptych by Girolamo da Santacroce from 1549 stands on the main altar, depicting the *Virgin and Saints*: the figure holding a model of the city is St Domnius, patron saint of Split.

Many works of art are on display, including a *Portrait of Bishop Tommaso Nigris* by Lorenzo Lotto (1527) and miniatures by Bone Razmilović.

Not far from the monastery is the stadium of the famous Hajduk Split football team, built in 1979 in the suburb of Poljud and designed by Boris Magaš.

♣ Marjan Peninsula

This protected nature reserve is on the west side of town, and is reached by a winding flight of steps. On the way is the 13th-century church of St Nicholas (Sv. Nikola). A path leads out to the wooded

peninsula, from where there are fine views out to sea, with the islands of Šolta, Brač and Hvar clearly visible. You can also find the best beaches in Split in this pleasant area.

Environs:
Seven Castles (Kaštela) is the name given to a series of fortifications built by the Venetian governor and local nobles to defend the town against the Turks between the end of the 15th century and the 16th century, between Split and Trogir. The village of Kaštela grew up around the complex. Five of the original castles are still preserved, as are the fortified villas which rose from their reconstruction.

St George's Castle (Kaštel Sućurac), the summer residence of the bishop of Split, was built at the end of the 14th century and strengthened the following century by building a wall, of which some traces remain.

Abbess Castle (Kaštel Gomilica) was built on an island which is now linked to the mainland.

Vitturi Castle (Kaštel Lukšić) was transformed into a large villa, keeping only the old external structure. It was built by the Vitturi family, who donated a sculpture by Juraj Dalmatinac to the church of St Raynerius (Sv. Arnir).

Kaštel Stari has kept its original aspect; the sea-facing side looks like a palace with Gothic windows.

All that remains of the **New Castle** (Kaštel Novi) are the tower and St Roch church, built by the Čipiko family.

The stadium of the Hajduk football team, built in 1979 in the suburb of Poljud

Šolta ⑱

Map D5. 🏃 1,400. 🚢 from Split.
ℹ️ Grohote, (021) 654 151.
www.solta.hr

This long island, indented with bays and coves, covers an area of 52 sq km (20 sq miles). The economy is based on agriculture thanks to reasonably fertile soil and, over recent years, tourism has also become important. The Romans called the island Soletta and it was a holiday resort for the nobility of Salona. The ruins of many villas can be found in lovely locations on the island.

After the attack on Salona in 614, some of the refugees fled here and villages were built. Some still have small churches dating from the early Middle Ages. The island was later abandoned in favour of Split and after 1537 stayed uninhabited for over a century, due to constant Turkish raids. Near Stomorska, Grohote, Donje Selo and Nečujam, traces of defence towers can be seen.

Many people from Split have holiday homes here.

Brač ⑲

Map D5. 🏃 14,000. ✈ (021) 524 116. 🚢 to Supetar from Split. 🚌 (021) 631 122. ℹ️ Trg P Jakšića 17, (021) 630 551. **Bol** ℹ️ Uz Pjacu 4, (021) 635 638. **www**.bol.hr

The third largest island in the Adriatic at 40 km (25 miles) long and 15 km (9 miles) wide, Brač has an interesting geological structure. In some areas the ranges of limestone hills have sinkholes and are cut by deep ravines and gorges. In other areas a white, hard stone prevails. The stone has been quarried since ancient times *(see p134)* and is still much sought after as a quality building material. Extensive woods cover some parts of the island and other areas are cultivated.

Although Brač has always been inhabited, it was first subject to Salona (the rich Salonians built villas and also sought refuge here when their town was attacked by the Avars), and then to Split. Both Split and Brač came under Byzantine and then Venetian rule. Under the Venetians (1420–1797), villages were built in the interior but no defences were built to prevent the pirates and Turks landing.

Ferries from Split on the mainland dock at the old town of **Supetar**, which has some good beaches.

Bol's famous golden beach, changing with the tides

To the southwest lies the town of **Milna**, which was founded at the beginning of the 18th century and faces a sheltered bay. The exterior of the church of the Annunciation of Mary (Velika Gospa) is Baroque and the interior is decorated in the Rococo style.

Nerežišća, in the centre of the island, was for a long period the main town. The Governor's Palace, the Loggia and a pedestal with the lion of St Mark are signs of its former status.

The major attraction at **Bol**, on the southern coast, is its famous long beach (Zlatni Rat, meaning Golden Horn), a triangular spit of shingle

The town of Pučišća on the island of Brač

KEY

▬▬ Major road

▬▬ Minor road

🚢 Ferry

✈ Airport

ℹ️ Tourist information

🏖 Beach with facilities

| 0 kilometres | 10 |
| 0 miles | 10 |

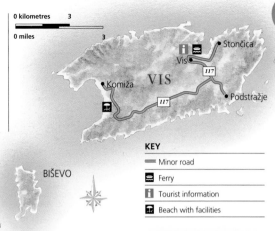

which reaches out into the sea and changes shape with the seasonal tides. It is a popular spot for windsurfing.

A Dominican monastery, founded in 1475, stands on a charming headland at the edge of the village. The beautiful church is decorated with paintings, including a *Virgin with Saints* attributed to Tintoretto. A rich treasury includes liturgical objects. From Bol you can climb up **Mount St Vitus** (Vidova Gora), a two-hour walk to one of the highest peaks in the Dalmatian islands (778 m/2,552 ft), near which a fortified monastery (Samostan Blaca) clings to rocks.

In **Selca** quarrymen can be seen at work and the Roman quarries where they extracted stone can also be visited. The blocks were loaded onto ships at the port of **Pučišća**, a charming, peaceful spot similar to **Sumartin**, further east, which was built around a monastery founded by Franciscans of Makarska in 1645. The monks brought with them a treasury and many of the paintings now preserved in the monastery.

Škrip is probably the site of the first settlement on the island and the presumed birthplace of Helen, mother of Emperor Constantine. The church and a painting by Palma il Giovane on the main altar are dedicated to Helen.

A fortified house houses **Brač Museum** and exhibits archaeological finds, evidence of mankind's ancient presence on the island.

🏛 **Brač Museum**
Škrip. 🛈 *(021) 356 706.* ⏱ *by appt.*

KEY

▬ Minor road
🚢 Ferry
🛈 Tourist information
🏖 Beach with facilities

Vis ⑳

Map D6. 👥 *4,300.* **Vis** 🚢 *(021) 711 032.* 🛈 *Šetalište Stare Isse 2, (021) 717 017.* **Komiža** 🛈 *(021) 713 455.*

Further out in the Adriatic than the other Dalmatian islands, Vis was until 1989 a military base and closed to tourism. Now gradually being rediscovered by intrepid travellers, it has a jagged coastline with beaches, and an inland mountain chain with Mount Hum reaching a height of 587 m (1,925 ft).

The island was chosen by Dionysios of Syracuse as a base for Greek domination of the Adriatic. The Greeks founded the town of Issa here. Later the island was ruled by the Romans, then Byzantines and, from 1420, the Venetians.

The island played a key role during World War II – in 1944 Marshal Tito used it as a base for co-ordinating partisan

The façade of the church of Our Lady of Spilica in Vis

military operations. The cave is still called "Tito's Cave". Crucial meetings between partisans, the Yugoslav government in exile and the Allies were also held on Vis.

The main town of **Vis** has Venetian Gothic buildings and the Renaissance church of Our Lady of Spilica (Gospa od Spilica), with a painting by Girolamo di Santacroce. In the town of **Komiža**, there is a castle built by the Venetians.

Environs
The **island of Biševo**, to the southwest of Vis, has a Blue Grotto (Modra Spilja), where, at midday, the water takes on beautiful colours. Day trips by boat to the cave depart from Komiža in the morning (contact the Tourist Office).

A monastery was built here around 1000 AD, which resisted raids by pirates and Saracens for 200 years. The ruins remain, along with a 12th-century church.

Part of the coastline near Komiža, on the island of Vis

Hvar ㉑

Art treasures, a mild climate, good beaches and fields of scented lavender make this island one of the treasures of the Adriatic. Limestone hills form the central ridge. Hvar's story begins in the 4th century BC when the Syracusans of Issa (now Vis) founded Pharos (the present-day Stari Grad) and Dimos (Hvar). Traces have been left by the Romans, the Byzantines, the Croatian sovereigns and the Venetians, who ruled from 1278 until 1797. After 1420, defences were built, and the capital was moved from Pharos to Hvar. In 1886, under Austria-Hungary, the "Hvar Hygienic Society" began to promote the town as a health resort. It is also the birthplace of a number of famous people: the painter Juraj Plančić (1900–30), and writer and art critic Tonko Marojević (b. 1941), a Croat intellectual.

Main square of Hvar, with the Cathedral of St Stephen

A peaceful bay on the island of Hvar

Hvar Town

This town is one of the most visited on the Dalmatian coast, thanks to the treasures within its walls (1278). During Venetian rule, governors and local nobles decided to make it a safe harbour for the fleets going to, or returning from, the Orient. They also transferred the bishopric and built monasteries.

Hvar has a long tradition of art and culture and one of the first theatres ever built in Europe is here. It was also the birthplace of the Renaissance poet Hanibal Lučić (c.1485–1553), and the playwright Martin Benetović (died 1607).

The town's most important buildings stand on three sides of the main square: the fourth is open to the sea. The Renaissance **Cathedral of St Stephen** (Katedrala Sv. Stjepana) has a trefoil pediment and a 17th-century bell tower standing to one side. The interior houses many works of art: *Virgin and Saints* by Palma il Giovane (1544–1628), *Pietà* by Juan Boschetus, *Virgin with Saints* by Domenico Uberti and a fine 16th-century wooden choir.

The **Clock Tower**, the **Civic Loggia** below and **Hektorović Palace** (Hektorovićeva Palača), recognizable by the beautiful Venetian-Gothic mullioned window, all date from the 15th century.

On the south side of the square is the **Arsenal**, which dates from the late 16th century. A theatre was built on the first floor in 1612, the first "public theatre" in the Balkans. People of all classes could come and see drama here, regardless of their social standing.

Outside the walls of the old town is the **Franciscan Monastery** (Franjevački Samostan) dating from 1461 and the church of **Our Lady of Charity** (Gospa od Milosti), with a relief on the façade by Nikola Firentinac. Inside are two paintings by Palma il Giovane (*St Francis receiving the Stigmata* and *St Diego*), three polyptychs by Francesco da Santacroce, a *Christ on the Cross* by Leandro da Bassano, and six scenes inspired by the

SVETI KLEMENT

PAKLENI ISLANDS

Hvar

116

Stari Grad · Vrboska

Jelsa

116

Poljica

HVAR

Zavala

ŠĆEDRO

0 kilometres   5

0 miles   5

A field of lavender on the island of Hvar

Passion of Christ by Martin Benetović. There are also many works of art in the rooms facing the cloister. The painting of the *Last Supper* in the refectory is of uncertain attribution – possibly Matteo Ingoli, Matteo Ponzone or the school of Palma il Giovane. There are splendid views from the 16th-century Španjola fort and from the Napoleon fort (1811).

The cloister of the Franciscan monastery, outside Hvar

Stari Grad
This town was originally called Pharos and was founded by the Syracusans in the 4th century BC (remains can be seen in Ciklopska ulica). Around Pod Dolom are the ruins of a Roman villa with mosaic floors. Stari Grad lies at the end of a long bay and the main sights are situated around the main square. Facing the square are the 17th-century church of **St Stephen** (Sv. Stjepan) and the

Baroque **Bianchini Palace** (Biankini Palača), the home of a **Nautical Collection**.

The heart of the town is dominated by **Kaštel Tvrdalj**, the fortified residence of Petar Hektorović which has a seawater fishpond. An Ethnographic Collection is now housed in the fort. Hektorović, a humanist poet, built the fort in around 1520. He was the author of the poem *Ribanje i ribarsko prigovaranje (Fishing and Fishermen's Conversation)* in which he vividly describes a fishing trip around the islands of Hvar, Brač and Šolta in which he took part.

The **Dominican Monastery** (Dominikanski Samostan), founded in 1482 and rebuilt and fortified after destruction by the Turks, has a rich library and a collection of paintings. In the town there is also an International School of Painting and Sculpture run by Professor Emil Tanay, for young people and postgraduates.

Kaštel Tvrdalj, Stari Grad

🔒 Dominican Monastery
Tel (021) 765 442. ☐ Jun–Sep: 10am–noon, 4–8pm; Oct–May: by appt.

Vrboska
The road leading to this small village offers a marvellous sight in June: vast fields of scented lavender.

Vrboska is home to the 16th-century church of **St Mary** (Sv. Marija), fortified in 1575 to provide shelter for villagers in the event of a siege. The Baroque church of **St Lawrence** (Sv. Lovro) has a polyptych on the main altar by Paolo Veronese (c.1570) and a *Virgin of the Rosary* by Leandro da Bassano.

Sućuraj
Lying in a sheltered bay is this village with the remains of a castle built by the Venetians in around 1630.

Environs
The **Pakleni Islands**, facing the town of Hvar, are uninhabited and mostly woodland. Their name derives from the resin *(paklina)* at one time extracted from the pines and used to waterproof boats. During the summer boat trips to the islands depart from Hvar. The nearest island, Jerolim, is given over to naturism.

The island of **Šćedro**, south of Hvar, is covered in pines and maquis. Illyrian tombs and parts of a Roman villa have been found here.

KEY

▬	Major road
▬	Minor road
⛴	Ferry
🛈	Tourist information
🏖	Beach with facilities

Boating on the river in the Cetina Valley Nature Park

Omiš ㉒

Map D5. 🏛 *6,100.* 🚌 *(021) 864
210.* 🚢 *(021) 861 025.* 🛈 *Trg
Kneza Miroslava, (021) 861 350.*
www.tz-omis.hr 🎭 *Klapa (Jul).*

In the late Middle Ages
Omiš was known as the
residence of the terrifying
corsairs who fought
fiercely against
Venetian rule from
the 12th century
until 1444, when
the town fell to
Venice. Today it is
a peaceful holiday
resort with some
light industry
along the coast,
and the starting
point for visits to the valley
of the River Cetina.

In July, the Dalamatinksa
Klapa festival attracts many
visitors who come to hear
Klapa, a kind of plainsong
traditional to Dalmatia. It is
still very popular, even
among the young.

Only a few traces of the
Roman *municipium* of
Oeneum remain but many of
the medieval defences built
by the counts of Kačić and
Bribir are still visible on a
hill, once the site of the Old
Town, or Starigrad. These
consist of the walls going
down to the River Cetina and
also the ruins of a large fort
(Fortica) with its distinctive
high tower. From the fort,
built between the 16th and
the 17th centuries, there is a
splendid view of Omiš and
the central Dalmatian islands.

**The church of St Peter in
Priko, a district of Omiš**

There are three interesting
religious buildings in the town.
One is the Renaissance
church of **St Michael** (Sv.
Mihovil) with a pointed bell
tower, originally a defensive
structure. Inside is a 16th-
century wooden altar, a large
13th-century wooden cross
and two paintings by
Matteo Ingoli of
Ravenna
(1580–1631). At
the end of the main
road is the 16th-
century **Oratory of
the Holy Spirit** (Sv.
Duh) with *Descent
of the Holy Spirit*
by Palma il
Giovane
(1544–1628).

However, the most
fascinating monument here
is in Priko, on the opposite
bank of the River Cetina. This
is the 10th-century church
of **St Peter** (Sv. Petar), one of
the most appealing pre-
Romanesque churches in
Dalmatia. It has a single nave,
a dome and remains from
the early Christian period
incorporated into the walls.

Environs
The **Cetina Valley Nature
Park**, immediately behind
Omiš, shelters a river which
flows into the artificial lake of
Peruča. The river runs out of
the lake and parallel to the
coast for some distance and
then, near Zadvarje, abruptly
turns and cascades down
before flowing into a narrow
gorge. This beautiful natural
environment, with its myriad
bird species, can be explored
on foot or by bicycle, but the
most popular way to see it is
to take one of the many boats
through the park.

Makarska ㉓

Map E5. 🏛 *14,000.* 🚌 *Ante Starčevića ulica, (021) 612 333.* 🚢 *(021)
611 977.* 🛈 *Obala Kralja Tomislava 16,
(021) 616 288.* **www**.makarska.hr

The Makarska coast extends
from Brela to Živogošće and
includes a long stretch of
shore with lush vegetation
sheltered by the Biokovo
massif. Makarska, one of
Dalmatia's most popular
mainland resorts, lies within
a bay sheltered by the
peninsula of St Peter's. The
town has ancient origins. It
was the site of the Roman
Muicurum which was
destroyed by the Goths in

The Makarska coast, with white beaches and a mountainous backdrop

THE VINEYARDS OF DALMATIA

Vines are grown all along the coast of Dalmatia, and on many of the islands. Vineyards first start appearing around Primošten, near Trogir *(see p111)*, where the good quality red wine Babić is made, and become part of the landscape along the Makarska coast. Built on stony hillsides, these vineyards are often "fortified" with low dry-stone walls, painstakingly constructed with geometrical precision by peasant farmers. Low-growing vines cultivated inside the walls are protected from the cold north winds and kept cool in the hot summer months. A monument to human toil, the result of immense patience and effort, without these walls it would not be possible to cultivate this difficult ground.

Vines protected by dry-stone walls

The beach at Gradac, the longest in the eastern Adriatic

The Franciscan monastery, Makarska, now a museum

548, and rebuilt at a later date. It belonged to the Kingdom of Croatia until 1499, when it was conquered by the Turks, for whom it was a port and trading centre until 1646, the beginning of Venetian rule.

There are two ancient monasteries in Makarska. St Philip Neri (Sv. Filipa Nerija) was built in 1757, and has medieval and Roman-era fragments in the cloister. The Franciscan monastery (Franjevački Samostan), built in 1614 on the foundations of a 15th-century monastery, houses the **Malacological Museum** (Muzej Mala-kološki), with a collection of mollusc shells.

The centre of the modern town is the square called Brother Andrjia Kačić Miošić

(1704–60), dedicated to the Dalmatian scholar and author of theological and philosophical works. Two seafront promenades extend towards the wide beaches and Kalelarga, where there are 18th-century buildings.

🏛 **Malacological Museum**
Franjevački Samostan put.
***Tel** (021) 611 256.*

Gradac ㉔

Map E5. 🏠 *1,200.*
ℹ Ulica Stjepana Radića 5,
(021) 697 511.

This town's fame and popularity are due to the fact that it has the longest beach in the eastern Adriatic. Over 6 km (4 miles) long, the beach is lined with hotels and camping sites.

In the town itself there are two large 17th-century towers while nearby, in Crkvine, the remains of a Roman staging post between Muicurum (the present-day Makarska) and Narona (see p130) have been found. Gradac gets its name from the fort (grad) built in the 17th century to defend the town against the Turks.

Environs

In **Zaostrog**, 14 km (8 miles) northwest of Gradac, is a Franciscan monastery (Franjevački Samostan) founded in the 16th century and completed a century later. The façade of the church has an inscription written in Cyrillic script. In the rooms around the beautiful cloister there is a fascinating folklore collection, an art gallery, and a library and archive where documents about the period of Turkish occupation are kept. The scholar Andrjia Kačić Miošić *(see Makarska, p128–9)* lived and died in the monastery.

Around 20 km (12 miles) from Gradac, towards Makarska, is **Živogošće**, one of the oldest settlements on the Makarska coast. Today it is a busy tourist resort, but it was once famous for a spring which flowed from the rocks.

A Franciscan monastery was founded near this spring in 1776, and its beautiful church boasts an ornate Baroque altar. The monastery is famous for its well-stocked library and archives, which are the main source for the study of the area around the Biokovo massif.

Franciscan monastery, Zaostrog

The delta of the River Neretva in Opuzen, drained and turned into fertile fields

Opuzen ㉕

Map E6. 2,800.
Metković, (020) 681 951.
Stjepana Radica ulica 3, Metković,
(020) 681 899.

At the edges of the delta of
the River Neretva, where the
road leaves the Magistrala
coast road (E65) and climbs
the river valley, stands
Opuzen. For centuries it
was fortified and has always
been considered something
of a border town.

Towards the end of
the 15th century, the
Hungarian-Croat king,
Matthias Corvinus,
built the fort of Koš
here. It was captured
by the Turks in 1490
who ruled until 1686,
when it came under
Venetian rule. There
are also traces of a
13th-century castle
built by the
Republic of
Dubrovnik and the
remains of a fort
(Fortis Opus), built by the
Venetians to defend the
border of their territories. The
town takes its name from this
fort and the ruins can be seen
on the eastern side of town.

In the entrance hall of the
former Town Hall are some
fragments discovered in the
ancient town of Narona.

**Head of Emperor
Vespasian, now in
Vid's Museum**

Narona ㉖

Map E6. Metković, (020) 681
951. Stjepana Radica ulica 3,
Metković, (020) 681 899.

The ancient Roman town of
Colonia Julia Narona was
founded by the Romans in
the 2nd century BC. It was
an important road junction
and a trading centre with the
Pannonian hinterland, and
had temples, baths, a theatre
and other buildings grouped
around the Forum. A walled
town, it was one of the first
dioceses in the Balkans
and flourished until
the 7th century when
it was occupied and
destroyed by the
Avars. It fell into
disuse afterwards.

At the beginning of
the 19th century, after
a few chance
discoveries,
the Austrian
archaeologist
Karl Patsch began
to carry out
excavations. Work continued
after World War II and
uncovered numerous finds
from pagan and Christian
temples, houses and public
works. Large parts of the area
still have to be explored, but
it is possible to get an idea of
the importance of the town
by visiting the Archaeological

Museum in **Vid**. This village
stands on much of the site
of ancient Narona, 3 km
(2 miles) from Metković. In
the museum are statues of
gods and emperors, as well as
weapons and jewels that were
found in Narona. Other finds
are in Split's Archaeological
Museum *(see p123)*.

The 16th-century church
of St Vitus (Sv. Vid) stands
just outside the town on
the site of an old church,
of which only parts of
the apse remain.

Neum ㉗

Bosnia-Herzegovina. **Map** E6.
1,200. Metković, (020) 681 951.
Stjepana Radica ulica 3, Metković,
(020) 681 899.

All the buses running along
the coastal road between
Split and Dubrovnik pass
through the 9-km (5-mile)
stretch of coast that is part of
Bosnia-Herzegovina. The
main town here is Neum, a holiday
resort and Bosnia's only
coastal town. Prices are
cheaper here than in Croatia,
and as a result it is a popular
place for Croatians to stop
off and go shopping.

Neum is a border town,
and visitors should carry
passports. There are several
hotels and tourist facilities.

Pelješac Peninsula ㉘

Map E6. 🚌 Metković, (020) 681 951. **Ston** 🚶 580.
🚌 (020) 754 026. 🛈 Pelješka Cesta, (020) 754 452. **Orebić** 🚶 1,600.
🚌 (020) 743 542. 🛈 Trg Mimbelli, (020) 713 718.

The peninsula of Pelješac juts out 65 km (40 miles) from the mainland, but it is only 7 km (4 miles) wide at its broadest point. A mountain chain forms its backbone, which peaks at Mount St Elijah (961 m/3,152 ft). The slopes and plain are covered with vineyards and fruit trees, and the shallow coastal waters are given over to oyster farming.

The peninsula was first colonized by the Greeks, then by the Romans and later by the Byzantines. From 1333 to 1808 it belonged to Dubrovnik.

The Pelješac coast, a centre for oyster farming

Ston

The town closest to the mainland, Ston was formerly called Stagnum because of its shallow waters. There have been salt pans here since the time of the Romans, who built a *castrum* on the site. It was enclosed by walls prior to 1000 AD.

The present defensive walls, still impressive above the town, were begun in the 14th century and completed in the 15th century on Dubrovnik's orders. There are more than 5 km (3 miles) of walls climbing from Veliki Ston, the main heart of the town, to St Michael's Mount and descending the opposite slope until they reach Mali Ston. The 41 towers, seven bastions and two forts make this one of the largest and most interesting defensive structures in the Adriatic. Some of the best military architects such as Michelozzo Michelozzi, Župan Bunić, Bernardino of Parma, Juraj Dalmatinac and Paskoje Miličević contributed to its design and construction. The walls are still in good condition despite being bombed in 1991 and struck by an earthquake in 1996.

The main structures are at **Veliki Ston**, which is built on an irregular pentagonal ground plan. These are currently without decoration as the works of art are being restored. The buildings include the largest fort (Veliki Kastio), the neo-Gothic church of St Blaise (Sv. Vlaho), built in 1870 to replace a cathedral from the 16th century which was destroyed by the earthquake of 1850, the Governor's Palace (Knežev Dvor), enlarged in the same century and the Bishop's Palace (1573). The **Church and Franciscan Monastery of St Nicholas** (Sv. Nikola) was built between the end of the 14th century and the 16th century.

Mali Ston, the other focus of the town, is dominated by Fort Koruna, which dates from 1447, with two arsenals and a fortified warehouse for storing salt. There are wonderful views over the island of Korčula from here.

The Franciscan monastery between Orebić and Lovište

Orebić

Towards the tip of the peninsula, Orebić is the boarding point for ferries to Korčula. The town is also worth visiting for its **Maritime Museum** (Pomorski Muzej), which illustrates the history of its inhabitants, who were the most sought-after sea captains in the Mediterranean. At the end of their careers these seamen invested in villas along the coast or in the hills.

Just outside the village, towards Lovište, stands a massive **Franciscan Monastery** (Franjevački Samostan), founded in the 15th century. In the church alongside are two reliefs: one is a *Virgin with Child* by Nikola Firentinac (1501), who was a pupil of Donatello.

🏛 **Maritime Museum**
Trg Mimbelli. *Tel* (020) 713 009.
◻ 8am–noon, 6–8pm. 🖼

Overlooking the circle of walls connecting the two parts of Ston

Korčula ㉙

Dense forests of aleppo pine, cypress and oak are found all over this island, one of the largest in the Adriatic at 47 km (29 miles) long. Mountains run the length of the island, reaching 560 m (1,837 ft) at their peak. Inhabited since prehistoric times, the Greeks named the island Korkyra Melaina (Black Corfu). After 1000 AD, it was fought over by Venice and the Croat kings and later by the Genoese and the Turks (in the 1298 naval battle between Genoa and Venice, the Genoese captured Marco Polo, said to be a native of the island). Today it is a popular holiday spot for its cliffs and sandy beaches, its villages and Korčula, its main town.

Gothic relief in All Saints' Church

VISITORS' CHECKLIST

Map E6. 🏙 *17,000.* 🚢 *from Orebić, Split and Rijeka.* **Korčula** 🚌 *(020) 711 216.* 🚢 *(020) 715 410.* 🛈 *Obala dr. Tuđmana 20, (020) 715 701, 715 867.* **www**.korcula.net ⚑ *Moreška, 9pm every Mon & Thu in summer.* **Lumbarda** 🛈 *(020) 712 005, 712 602.* **Blato** 🛈 *Ulica 31 br 2, (020) 851 850.* ⚑ *Kumpanija (28 Apr).* **Vela Luka** 🚌 *(020) 812 023.* 🛈 *Ulica 41 br 11, (020) 813 619.*

The Land Gate, main entrance to the old town of Korčula

Korčula Town

The town is perched on a peninsula, surrounded by strong 13th-century walls, reinforced with towers and bastions by the Venetians after 1420. The whole town is enchanting. The **Land Gate** (Kopnena Vrata) was fortified by a huge tower, the Revelin, which overlooked a canal dug by the Venetians to isolate the town. There are now steps in this area. Narrow streets branching off the main road are designed to lessen the impact of the bora wind.

Facing **Strossmayerov trg**, the central square, is the town's main monument: the 13th-century **Cathedral of St Mark** (Katedrala Sv. Marka), built in pale, honey-coloured stone. Most of it dates from the end of the 15th century. The skill of Korčula's sculptors and stone masons is evident in the door, where two lions guard the entrance, decorated with thin spiral columns and a lunette with the figure of St Mark, attributed to Bonino of Milan. Two further doors open onto the side aisles. On the left stands an imposing bell tower.

Inside are large columns with elaborately decorated capitals and several important sculptural works: a 15th-century holy water stoup, a font from the 17th century, and the tomb of Bishop Toma Malumbra, attributed to the workshop of Marco Andrijić,

who also made the ciborium in the presbytery in 1481. There is also a statue of St Blaise by Ivan Meštrović. The paintings include *St Mark with St Jerome and St Bartholomew* by Tintoretto. On a wall are trophies recalling the Battle of Lepanto of 1571.

Next to the cathedral, in the Bishop's Palace, now the Abbot's House, is the **Abbey Treasury** (Opatska Riznica), which is particularly known for its Dalmatian and Venetian art, including a

Impressive entrance to the Gothic Cathedral of St Mark, Korčula

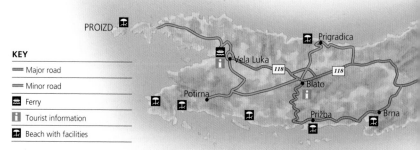

KEY

═══ Major road

──── Minor road

🚢 Ferry

🛈 Tourist information

🏖 Beach with facilities

PROIZD

Prigradica

Vela Luka

118   118

Blato

Potirna

Prižba   Brna

Korčula, the main town on the island, on an isthmus on the northeast coast

polyptych by Blaž of Trogir, two altar paintings by Pellegrino of San Daniele, a *Sacred Conversation* by Titian, a *Portrait of a Man* by Vittore Carpaccio and an *Annunciation* by Titian. A door by Bonino of Milan decorates the Gothic church of **St Peter** (Sv. Petar) to the left of the cathedral. Facing St Peter are the Gothic **Arneri Palace** and the Renaissance Gabriellis Palace (16th century). The latter has been the **Civic Museum** (Gradski Muzej) since 1957 and contains documents on Korčula's seafaring history, an interesting archaeological section covering the period from prehistoric to Roman times and other works of art, with many portraits of the local nobility.

Along the seafront is **All Saints' Church** (Svi Sveti), built in 1301 and remodelled in the Baroque style, which belongs to the oldest brotherhood on the island.

Inside is an 18th-century carved wooden *Pietà*, by the Austrian artist George Raphael Donner, and a 15th-century polyptych by Blaž of Trogir.

In the nearby quarters of the brotherhood is the **Icon Gallery** (Galerija Ikona), which is famous for its rich collection of Byzantine icons from the 13th to 15th centuries, many from Crete.

Outside the walls are the **Church and Monastery of St Nicholas** (Sv. Nikola), from the 15th century, with many paintings by Dalmatian and Italian artists.

🏛 **Abbey Treasury**
Trg Sv. Marka. 🛈 *(020) 715 701.*
⏱ *Jun–Aug: 9am–7pm; Sep–May: by appt.* 📷

🏛 **Civic Museum**
Trg Sv. Marka. **Tel** *(020) 711 420.*
⏱ *Jun–Aug: 9am–1pm, 5–7pm; Sep–May: 8am–3pm Mon–Sat.*

🏛 **Icon Gallery**
Trg Svihsvetih. 🛈 *(020) 711 306 (Tourist office).* ⏱ *Jun–Aug: 10am–1pm, 5–7pm; Sep–May: by appt.*

ANCIENT DANCES AND FESTIVALS

The Moreška and the Kumpanija are Korčula's two most noted folk festivals. Officially, the Moreška sword dance takes place in Korčula on 27 July, the patron saint's day (St Theodore). However, it is repeated on Thursdays during the summer as a tourist event. It commemorates the clash between Christians and Moors in the attempt to free a young girl kidnapped by the infidels. In Blato, the Kumpanija festival is dedicated to the patron saint, St Vincenza, and is celebrated with songs and music. At the end of the battle, girls in bright costumes appear, accompanied by pipes and drums. The festival takes place in front of the church on 28 April, but is repeated at other times in other towns on the island.

Actors performing the ancient Moreška sword dance

The sea and rocky coastline of Korčula

Lumbarda

Lumbarda is a village 6 km (4 miles) southeast of the town of Korčula and is thought to have been founded by Greeks from Vis. It was called Eraclea by the Romans. In the 16th century it became a holiday resort for the nobles of Korčula. Some inscriptions from the Greek period are now in the Archaeological Museum of Zagreb *(see pp162–3)*.

Today this village is one of the centres of production for the liqueur-like wine called Grk, which is made from vines grown in the sand. The nearby small beaches are havens of tranquillity. It is also possible to rent cottages.

Blato

In the central square of Blato, a town where the festival of the Kumpanija *(see p133)* is held every April, are an 18th-century Baroque loggia, the Renaissance **Arneri Castle**, where the Civic Museum documenting local history is being set up, and **All Saints' Church** (Svi Sveti), of medieval origin. This church was enlarged and rebuilt in the 17th century and has an altarpiece of the *Virgin with Child and Saints* on the main altar by Girolamo

di Santacroce (1540) and, in the chapel, the relics of the martyr St Vincenza, the object of veneration in the local community. The cemetery church of the **Holy Cross** and that of **St Jerome** date from the 14th century.

Vela Luka

Situated about 45 km (28 miles) west of Korčula is Vela Luka, called "the oldest and the newest town", because it was built at the beginning of the 19th century on the neolithic site of Vela Spilja. It is one of the largest towns on the island and industries coexist with attractive bays and numerous islands.

The hills surrounding the town shelter this area from the winds from the north and south. Vela Luka is also the main port on the island and there are regular ferry services to Split and Lastovo.

Lumbarda on the island of Korčula, one of the greenest in the Adriatic

THE STONE OF DALMATIA

The excellent quality of the stone in the Dalmatian islands was known to the Romans, who used it to build the monuments of Salona and Diocletian's Palace in Split. On Brač, the old Roman quarries are still visible in Pučišća. Brač stone was used for the cathedral in Šibenik *(see pp108–9)*, for which Juraj Dalmatinac devised a method of cutting the stone so that blocks interlocked without mortar. Most of the palaces and churches in Venice are also made of Dalmatian stone. Further afield, part of the White House in Washington and the Royal Palace in Stockholm were faced with stone from Brač. In Korčula, quarrying ceased long ago, and stone cutting skills have largely died out. However, the quarries on the small island of Vrnik, facing Korčula, are still active and stone from here was used in the church of St Sophia in Istanbul, the Duke's Palace in Dubrovnik and the United Nations building in New York.

The ancient Roman quarries, Brač

The Franciscan church and monastery on the island of Badija

Badija ⑩

Map E6.
🚤 taxi-boats from Korčula.

This is the largest of the small islands, 1 sq km (0.4 sq m), surrounding the island of Korčula. It takes its name from the Franciscan monastery built here in 1392 for a community of monks who had fled from Bosnia. The monastery and church were enlarged in the following century and remained the property of the religious community until 1950, when Badija became a military site, and later a holiday resort for state employees.

The church, whose furnishings have been transferred to the Civic Museum and the cathedral in Korčula, has a façade in pale-coloured stone and a large central rose window.

The cloister is a good example of Gothic architecture at its most charming, with columns and arches.

The Loggia in the main square in Lastovo, venue for festivals

Lastovo ⑪

Map E6. 👥 1,200.
🚤 from Vela Luka (Island of Korčula) and from Split. Harbour Master: (020) 805 006. ℹ (020) 801 018.

The island of Lastovo, surrounded by about 40 small islands and rocky outcrops, was a military area until a few years ago and thus closed to tourists. The island is 9 km (5 miles) long and about 6 km (4 miles) wide. Although it is mostly mountainous terrain (Mount Hum reaches a height of 417 m/1,368 ft), vines, olives and fruit are cultivated on the terraced slopes. The coast is rocky apart from the bay close to the town of Lastovo.

Traces of the long period of rule by Dubrovnik (1252–1808) are visible in the upper part of the town and in the fort, built by the French in 1819 on the site of an earlier castle destroyed by Dubrovnik in 1606.

A church from the 14th century and a 16th-century loggia stand in the main square. Religious festivals are celebrated here.

Mention of the small church of **St Blaise** (Sv. Blaho), situated at the entrance to the village, is found in 12th-century documents. Also of ancient origins, in the cemetery, is the Romanesque **Oratory of Our Lady in the Field** (Gospa od Polja) from the 15th century. Some remnants of buildings and rustic villas testify to the presence of the Romans on the island. The lack of tourism has helped to preserve the old buildings.

Religious holidays are very popular and celebrated with traditional dances with antique musical instruments. The locals wear brightly coloured traditional costumes.

Some of the many uninhabited, unspoilt islands in the sea around the island of Lastovo

Mljet National Park ❷
Nacionalni Park Mljet

The island of Mljet, called Melita by the Romans and
Meleda by the Venetians, covers an area of
98 sq km (37 sq miles). It is mountainous, with two
limestone depressions in which there are two salt-
water lakes linked by a channel. In Roman times
Mljet was the holiday resort of the wealthy of
Salona, who built villas here. Some ruins can still
be seen. In 1151, Duke Desa gave the island to the
Benedictines of Pulsano in Gargano (Italy), who
founded a monastery here. Two centuries later
Stipan, the Ban (governor) of Bosnia, gave it to
Dubrovnik, to which it belonged until 1815. In 1960
the western part was declared a national park to
save the forest of Aleppo pine and holm oak.

Roman Palatium
*Near Polače lie the ruins of a
Roman settlement named
Palatium, including the
remains of a large villa and
an early Christian basilica.*

Monastery of St Mary
*In the centre of Big Lake (Veliko Jezero)
is a small island with a 12th-century
Benedictine monastery, remodelled in
the 1500s. It was a hotel from 1961 to
1991 and is now being restored.*

Big Lake (Veliko Jezero)
*The lake covers an area of 1.45 sq km (320
acres) and reaches a depth of 46 m (150 ft).
A channel links the lake to the sea, and another
channel links it to a smaller lake, Malo Jezero.*

National Park
*The area of 31 sq km
(12 sq miles) is almost
entirely forested.
Mongooses, introduced
here at the end of the 19th
century to kill snakes, live
in the forests.*

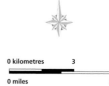

0 kilometres   3

0 miles   3

Marine Life
Dozens of species of fish, including grouper, inhabit the underwater ravines and caves along the coast. The most valued creature is the endangered monk seal, protected in these waters.

The village of Babino Polje
was founded in around the middle of the 10th century by a group of refugees from the mainland. The governor's residence was built in 1333 when the island became part of the territory of the Republic of Ragusa (now Dubrovnik).

Saplunara
Saplunara lies at the southernmost point of the island and boasts the most beautiful beach in the area. It has been declared a nature reserve for its lush vegetation.

Sobra
Babino Polje
Prožura
Okuklje
Korita
Maranovići
120

Uninhabited Islands
Nature is left undisturbed on these islands, with woods of pine, holm oak and oak going right down to the rocky shore.

KEY

▬▬	Minor road
═══	Path
──	Park border
🚢	Ferry
🛈	Tourist information
🏖	Beach with facilities

Fishing Villages
The island's ancient stone villages are inhabited mainly by farmers and fishermen. These villages and the delightful bays and coves around the island are lovely places in which to spend time.

A secluded beach on the island of Mljet ▷

Street-by-Street: Dubrovnik ㊴

Detail of the door of the Rector's Palace

Set in the limpid waters of the Adriatic, Dubrovnik had been, until war broke out in 1991, one of the top international tourist destinations of Dalmatia, renowned for the beauty of its monuments, its magnificent walls and welcoming atmosphere.

According to Emperor Constantine Porphyrogenitus it was founded by fugitives from Roman Epidaurum (now Cavtat) in the 7th century. It came under Byzantine, Venetian (1205–1358) and Hungarian rule, and attained formal independence after 1382, when it became the Republic of Ragusa. In the 15th and 16th centuries its fleet numbered over 500 ships. Artistically it flourished and its wealth was greatly influenced by the discovery of America and new trade routes. Much of the old town centre dates from the rebuilding that took place after the earthquake of 1667.

★ Rector's Palace
The highest level of city government met here. The rector lived here during his period of office, which was limited to one month.

★ Cathedral Treasury
The provenance of the objects here clearly demonstrates how the Dubrovnik merchants developed trading relations with the principal cities of the Mediterranean. The Treasury has works from the Byzantine, Middle Eastern, Apulian and Venetian schools. There are gold and enamel objects and also paintings by great artists.

KEY

--- Suggested route

LUČARICA   GUNDULIĆEVA POLJANA

PRED. DVOROM

POLJANA MARINA DRŽIĆA

KNEZA DAMJANA JUDE

View of Dubrovnik
Lovely views of Dubrovnik can be seen from the coast about 2 km (1 mile) to the south, where there is an elevated terrace. From here you can look over the entire city and its walls.

Church of St Blaise
This 16th-century church was rebuilt in the following century. At the beginning of the 18th century, it was redesigned by Marino Groppelli.

Sponza Palace
Originating in the 14th century, today the palace houses the State Archives. On the lintel is a Latin inscription: "Falsifying and cheating with the weights is forbidden. While I am weighing the goods, God is measuring me".

VISITORS' CHECKLIST

Map F6. 49,000. Čilipi, (020) 773 377. Put Republike, (060) 305 070. Harbour Master: (020) 418 988; Jadrolinija: (020) 418 000. **Local:** *Cvijete Zuzorić 1, (020) 323 887;* **Regional:** (020) 324 222. St Blaise (3 Feb); Festival of Dubrovnik (Jul & Aug).

Franciscan Monastery and the Big Fountain of Onofrio

PLACA

PRIJEKO

ZLATARSKA

SVETOG DOMINIKA

The outer city walls

★ **Dominican Monastery**
Since its foundation in 1315, the monastery has played a leading role in cultural activities in the city. Important sculptors and architects played a part in its construction.

Ploče Gate
Next to the Dominican monastery is the Ploče Gate, which leads to the port. Goods arrived from, and were sent to, every port in the Mediterranean.

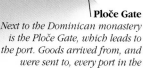

0 metres 50
0 yards 50

Fort of St John
To make the city impregnable, the governors employed the most important European architects of the time. This fortress was one of many bulwarks.

STAR SIGHTS

★ Cathedral Treasury

★ Dominican Monastery

★ Rector's Palace

Exploring Dubrovnik

From the autumn of 1991 until May 1992, Dubrovnik was the target of relentless, heavy bombing by Yugoslav troops. During this period over 2,000 bombs and guided missiles fell on Dubrovnik, damaging some of the most significant symbols of Dalmatian culture. Over half the houses and all the monuments were shelled. The war also hit the city's productivity, especially tourism, which suffered a dramatic decline for four years. Only after the Erdut Agreement of 1995 did life begin to return to normal. UNESCO and the European Union set up a special commission for the reconstruction of the city, and in a remarkably short space of time much of the damage has been repaired. Dubrovnik has now regained much of its former splendour and tourism is once again flourishing.

The solid Minčeta Tower, part of the wall defences

The splendid view from the impressive city walls

🏰 Walls

Gradske Zidine

🛈 *(020) 324 641.* ◯ *summer: 9am–7pm daily; winter: 10am–3pm. Access to the walls near the Franciscan monastery in Poljana Paška Miličevića, the large square behind Pile Gate.* 📷

A symbol of Dubrovnik, the walls offer splendid views from the guards' walkway. They were built in the 10th century, with modifications in the 13th century. They were then reinforced at various times by great architects such as Michelozzo Michelozzi, Juraj Dalmatinac and Antonio Ferramolino.

The walls and ramparts are 1,940 m (6,363 ft) long and reach a height of 25 m (82 ft) in some parts. Those facing inland are up to 6 m (20 ft) wide and strengthened by an outer wall with ten semicircular bastions. Other towers and the Fort of St John defend the part facing the Adriatic and the port. Completing the defences to the east and west of the city are two fortresses: the Revelin and the fortress of Lovrjenac.

🏰 Pile Gate

Gradska Vrata Pile

This is the main entrance to the old fortified centre. The stone bridge leading to Pile Gate is from 1537. The bridge crosses a moat which is now a garden. The gate is a strong

Pile Gate, leading to the old town

defensive structure built on different levels. In a niche above the ogival arch stands a small statue of St Blaise, the patron saint of Dubrovnik, by Ivan Meštrović. In the ramparts between the inner and outer walls is a Gothic door dating from 1460.

🏰 Minčeta Tower

Tvrđava Minčeta

This is the most visited of the walls' defensive structures. It was designed by Michelozzo Michelozzi in 1461 and completed by Juraj Dalmatinac three years later. The semicircular tower is crowned by a second tower with embrasures at the top.

🏰 Ploče Gate

Vrata od Ploča

The gate faces a small port and is preceded by the polygonal **Asimov Tower**. Dating from the 1300s, the gate is reached by an imposing stone bridge. It is a complex structure with a double defence system. A moat separates the gate and **Revelin Fort** (Tvrđava Revelin), designed in 1580 by Antonio Ferramolino. It was the last of the defences to be built. It is based on a pentagonal ground-plan and has massive walls enclosing three large rooms and a terrace. The city's art treasures were brought here for safety in times of difficulty because of the fort's strength.

🏰 Fort of St John
Tvrđa Sv. Ivana

Aquarium **Tel** (020) 427 937.
◯ Jun–Sep: 9am–7pm daily;
Oct–May: 9am–6pm Mon–Sat. 🖼
Maritime Museum Tel (020) 323
904. ◯ 9am–2pm Tue–Sun. 🖼

A chain once helped to
defend the harbour, stretching
from this fort to the island in
front and then across to the
Tower of St Luke (Kula Sv.
Luke) along the walls.

The upper areas of the fort
house the **Maritime Museum**
(Pomorski Muzej), where
the seafaring history of
Dubrovnik is told through
model ships, standards, prints,
diaries and portraits.

On the lower level is an
Aquarium (Akvarij) with an
assortment of Mediterranean
marine life, including sea
horses, symbol of the
institution. At the top is
Bokar Fort (Tvrđava Bokar), a
circular bastion built by
Michelozzo Michelozzi.

🏰 Big Fountain of Onofrio
Velika Onofrijeva Fontana

This is one of the best-known
monuments in the city. It
stands in the square which

The Big Fountain of Onofrio (1438–44)

opens out immediately after
the Pile gate. It was built in
1438–44 by the Neapolitan
architect, Onofrio de la Cava,
who was also responsible for
designing the city's water
supply system. He
decided to draw
the water from the
River Dubrovačka
for this purpose. The
imposing fountain
once had two storeys,
but the upper level
was destroyed in the
earthquake of 1667.

Tucked between
the city walls and the
Franciscan monastery
is the **Church of St
Saviour** (Sv. Spas).
The façade of the
church is an example
of Venetian-Dalmatian
Renaissance
architecture, a style
dating from after
the earthquake
of 1520.

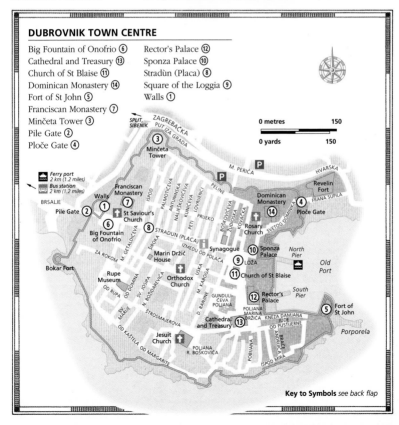

DUBROVNIK TOWN CENTRE

Big Fountain of Onofrio ⑥
Cathedral and Treasury ⑬
Church of St Blaise ⑪
Dominican Monastery ⑭
Fort of St John ⑤
Franciscan Monastery ⑦
Minčeta Tower ③
Pile Gate ②
Ploče Gate ④

Rector's Palace ⑫
Sponza Palace ⑩
Stradùn (Placa) ⑧
Square of the Loggia ⑨
Walls ①

0 metres 150
0 yards 150

SPLIT
ŠIBENIK

ZAGREBAČKA
PUT IZA GRADA

③ Minčeta
Tower

Ferry port
2 km (1.2 miles)
Bus station
2 km (1.2 miles)

BRSALJE

M. PERIĆA

HVARSKA

M. PERIĆA

PELINE

Revelin
Fort

FRANA SUPILA

Walls ①
Pile Gate ②

Franciscan
Monastery ⑦

St Saviour's
Church

ISPOD
PALMOTIĆEVA
ANTUNINSKA
NALJEŠKOVIĆEVA
KUNIĆEVA
LOVRIJENCI
PRIJEKO
PETI
BOŠKOVIĆEVA
ŽUDIOSKA
KOVAČKA

Dominican
Monastery ⑭

SVETOG DOMINIKA

Ploče Gate ④

⑥ Big Fountain
of Onofrio

⑧ STRADUN (PLACA)

ŠIROKA

IZMEĐU OD POLAČA

Rosary
Church

Synagogue

⑩ Sponza
Palace

North
Pier

ZA ROKOM
M. GETALDIĆEVA

Marin Držić
House

⑨ LOŽA

South
Pier

Old
Port

Bokar Fort

Rupe
Museum

SV. JOSIPA
N. BOŽIDAREVIĆA

Orthodox
Church

USKA
M. KABOGA

⑪ Church of St Blaise

North
Pier

OD RUPA
OD DOMINA
SV.
MARIJE

Jesuit
Church

STROSMAJEROVA

D. RANJINE
GUNDULI-
ĆEVA
POLJANA

POLJANA
MARINA
DRŽIĆA

⑫ Rector's
Palace

KNEZA DAMJANA
JUDE
OD PUSTIJERNE

Fort of ⑤
St John

OD KAŠTELA OD MARGARITE

⑬ Cathedral
and Treasury

POLJANA
R. BOŠKOVIĆA

POBIJANA

BRAĆE
ANDRIJIĆA

ISPOD MIRA

Porporela

Key to Symbols see back flap

The lovely late Romanesque cloister, Franciscan monastery

🔒 Franciscan Monastery
Franjevački Samostan
Placa 2. **Tel** (020) 321 410. ⬜ 9am–
4pm daily. **Franciscan Museum** ⬜
9am–3pm daily. 🗷 🗷
Construction of the monastery
began in 1317 and was
completed in the following
century. It was almost entirely
rebuilt after the earthquake in
1667, but the south door
(1499), in Venetian Gothic
decorated with a Pietà in the
lunette, and a 15th-century
marble pulpit escaped
damage. The cloister, which
was completely undamaged
by the earthquake, reveals
elements of the Romanesque
and the Gothic style and has
a fountain from the 15th
century in the centre.
  One side of the cloister
leads to the **Pharmacy** (Stara
Ljekarna), in use since 1317,
where alembics, mortars,
measuring apparatus and
beautifully decorated jars are
displayed on the old shelves.
  The capitular room of the
monastery houses the
Franciscan Museum (Muzej
Franjevačkog Samostana),
which brings together
religious works of art and
objects belonging to the

order. Instruments from the
pharmaceutical laboratory
are kept here and there is
a valuable library.

⛪ Stradùn (Placa)
This wide street, which
crosses the city from east to
west between two city gates,
is known as Stradùn or Placa.
It was constructed in the 12th
century by draining and filling
in the marshy channel which

separated the island of
Ragusa from the mainland.
The street was paved in 1468
and a series of stone houses
was built after the earthquake
of 1667. Today the street is
lined with busy bars and
cafés, and is a popular place
for locals and visitors to
gather in the evening.

⛪ Square of the Loggia
Loža
This square, the political and
economic heart of Dubrovnik,
is situated at the eastern end
of Stradùn and surrounded
by important buildings. Today
it is still a popular meeting
place, in particular around
Orlando's Column, which was
built by the sculptor Antonio
Ragusino (1418).
  On the eastern side of the
square is a **Clock Tower**
(Gradski Zvonik). Repair
work carried out in 1922
restored a 15th-century look
to the Clock Tower. The
nearby **Loggia of the Bell**,
with four bells, dates from
1480. The bells were rung to
call the citizens to gather
whenever danger threatened.
  Next to this stands the
Main Guard House, rebuilt in
1706 after the earthquake of
1667. It has a large Baroque
doorway, similar to a city
gate, and is enlivened on the
first floor by the Gothic
mullioned windows,
reminiscent of the earlier
building which was built in
the late 15th-century.
  The **Small
Fountain of Onofrio**
(Mala Onofrijeva
Cesma), dating from
1438, stands alongside
the Guard House.

⛪ Sponza Palace
Palača Sponza
Tel (020) 321 032.
⬜ 8am–3pm, by appt.
To the left of the
square is Sponza
Palace. Remodelled in
1516–22, it has an
elegantly sculpted
Renaissance loggia on
the ground floor and a
beautiful Venetian
Gothic three-
mullioned window
on the first floor,
evidence of its 14th–

Stradùn, the main street of Dubrovnik

century origins, and a statue of St Blaise on the upper floor. It was the Mint in the 14th century and now houses the State Archives.

🔒 Church of St Blaise
Crkva Sv. Vlaha
Loža. **Tel** (020) 411 715.
⬜ 8am–noon, 4.30–7pm daily.
St Blaise was rebuilt in the early decades of the 18th century according to a 17th-century design and contains many Baroque works of art.

On the main altar stands a statue of the patron saint, Blaise. It was produced in the 15th century in gold-plated silver, and depicts the saint holding a model of the city in the Middle Ages.

Baroque façade of the church of St Blaise

🏛 Rector's Palace
Knežev Dvor
Knežev Dvor 1. **Tel** (020) 321 437.
⬜ 9am–2pm Mon–Sat. 📷
The Rector's Palace was for centuries the political and administrative centre of the Republic of Ragusa. It housed the Upper Council, as well as the rector's quarters and rooms for diplomatic meetings and official audiences. The building was designed by Onofrio de la Cava in 1435. In 1465 the portico was added, the work of Michelozzo Michelozzi, who also sculpted the capitals. The Gothic works are by Juraj Dalmatinac.

During the Festival of Dubrovnik concerts are held in the atmospheric internal courtyard. The arches and loggias were designed by Onofrio de la Cava.

The Rector's Palace, built in the 15th century as the administrative seat

The rooms of the palace house the **Museum of Dubrovnik** (Dubrovački Muzej), which offers an overview of the city's history through furniture, paintings by Venetian and Dalmatian artists (a *Venus and Adonis* by Paris Bordon and a *Baptism of Christ* by Mihajlo Hamzić), weights and measures, including the famous "Dubrovnik arm" (a unit of measurement), and coins from 1305 to 1803.

Over 15,000 works are on display, documenting the major periods of artistic and commercial vitality in the city. There are numerous uniforms, once worn by the governors and nobles. Also of great interest are the portraits of illustrious personalities who were born or lived in Dubrovnik, whose history is told through their heraldic coats of arms and commemorative medals.

Next door is the neo-Renaissance **Town Hall** (Skupština Općine), designed by Emilio Vecchietti in 1863. It is also the home of Gradska Kavana, a restaurant, and the Civic Theatre.

🔒 Cathedral and Treasury
Velika Gospa
Kneza Damjana Jude 1.
⬜ 9am–noon, 3–8pm daily.
Cathedral Treasury Tel (020) 411 715. ⬜ 9am–noon, 3–7pm daily. 📷
The cathedral was built after the earthquake of 1667 by the Roman architects Andrea Buffalini and Paolo Andreotti. Inside are three aisles enclosed by three apses. Paintings by Italian and Dalmatian artists from the 16th–18th centuries decorate the side altars, while an *Assumption* by Titian (c.1552) dominates the main altar.

Alongside the church is the **Cathedral Treasury** (Riznica Katedrale), famous for its collection of about 200 reliquaries. It includes the arm of St Blaise which dates from the 13th century, and a Holy Cross which contains a fragment of the cross on which Jesus was said to have been crucified. The tondo *Virgin of the Chair* is thought to have been painted by Raphael himself, and is a copy of the masterpiece which is now in Florence.

The treasury also has an extraordinary collection of sacred objects in gold, including a pitcher and basin in gold and silver with decoration that illustrates the flora and fauna of the area around Dubrovnik.

The great dome of Dubrovnik's Baroque cathedral

The church of St Dominic, inside the monastery

🔒 Dominican Monastery
Dominikanski Samostan Bijeli Fratri

Sv. Dominika 4. **Tel** *(020) 321 423.*
⬜ *summer: 9am–6pm; winter: 9am–3pm.* 🖼

Building began in 1315 and it soon became clear that because of the size of the complex, the city walls would have to be enlarged. The monastery was later rebuilt after the earthquake of 1667.

A long flight of steps with a stone balustrade leads up to the church. The door, the work of Bonino of Milan, is decorated with a Romanesque statue of St Dominic. The interior has a wide single nave and, hanging from the central arch, a splendid gilded panel (*Crucifix and Symbols of the Evangelists*) by Paolo Veneziano (14th century).

The various rooms of the monastery, arranged around the Gothic cloister by Maso di Bartolomeo (15th century), house the **Dominican Museum** (Muzej Dominikanskog Samostana). It contains an extraordinary collection of works from the so-called "Dubrovnik school", including a triptych and an *Annunciation* by Niccolò Ragusino, from the 16th century, and works from the Venetian school, including *St Blaise, St Mary Magdalene, the Angel Tobias and the Purchaser* by Titian, as well as precious reliquaries and objects in gold and silver.

Environs
The island of **Lokrum**, 700 m (2,296 ft) across the water from Dubrovnik, is a nature reserve set up to protect the exotic species of plants found here.

The first people to settle on the island were the Benedictines, who founded an abbey here in 1023. This was rebuilt in the 14th century, but later destroyed by the earthquake of 1667. In 1859, Archduke Maximilian of Habsburg built a palace here and renovated the cloister which later became the Natural History Museum.

There are good views from the fort, which was built by the French in 1808. Lokrum's beauty makes it a popular tourist destination.

In **Trsteno**, 20 km (12 miles) northwest of Dubrovnik, is an Arboretum. This was begun in 1502 in the park surrounding a villa built by Ivan Gučetić. The park has the typical layout of a Renaissance garden with grottoes and ancient ruins.

There are several Renaissance summer houses around Dubrovnik, including the **Villa Stay** in Rijeka Dubrovačka. It houses the Croatian Restoration Institute, an organization devoted to the conservation and restoration of paintings.

A statue in the *Arboretum* in Trsteno

Elaphite Islands ㉞

Map F6. 🏘 *2,000.* ⛴ *from Dubrovnik.* 🛈 *Dubrovnik regional tourist office (020) 324 222.*

Lying to the north of Dubrovnik, the Elaphite islands (Elafitski otoci) can be reached from Dubrovnik by motorboat. There are several daily crossings. The islands were described by the natural historian Pliny the Elder, who named them after the fallow deer then found here.

Only three of the islands are inhabited: Šipan, Lopud and Koločep, while Jakljan is devoted to farming. Characteristics common to the islands are the woods of maritime pines and cypresses in the uncultivated areas and beautiful beaches and bays frequented by pleasure boats. The islands have long been popular with the aristocracy of Dubrovnik, who built villas here. Some islands had monasteries which were suppressed with the arrival of French troops in 1808. Many of the churches date from the pre-Romanesque period, but few, however, are still intact.

Koločep
This is the nearest island to Dubrovnik and for this reason has been a summer retreat since the 16th century for its

The island of Lokrum in front of Dubrovnik, a protected nature reserve

Sunj beach on the southeast coast of Lopud, one of the Elaphite islands

citizens. Most of the island is covered in maritime pines and subtropical undergrowth.

The churches of **St Anthony** and **St Nicholas** have pre-Romanesque origins, while the **Parish Church** dates from the 15th century.

Lopud

The island, measuring 4.6 sq km (1.7 sq miles), has a fertile valley sheltered from the cold winds by two ranges of hills. Most of the inhabitants live in **Lopud**, a village in a bay. The two forts, now in ruins, date from the 16th century and the Franciscan monastery is from 1483. The monastery church, **St Mary of Spilica** (Gospa od Spilica), contains a polyptych by Pietro di Giovanni (1520), a triptych by Nikola Božidarević, a painting by Leandro da Bassano, a triptych by Gerolamo di Santacroce and a carved choir from the 15th century.

Sunj, in the southeast, draws visitors because of its sandy beach, but the church is also worth visiting for its many works of art, including a painting by Palma il Giovane and a polyptych (1452) by Matko Junčić.

Šipan

This is the largest of the Elaphite Islands (15.5 sq km/ 6 sq miles) and there are two towns. In **Šipanska Luka** stands the pre-Romanesque church of St Michael and the ruins of a Benedictine monastery. In **Suđurađ** there is a castle and the ruins of a bishop's palace.

Cavtat ③⑤

Map F6.
🏠 1,900. 🚌 (020) 478 065.
🚢 from Dubrovnik.
🏛 Tiha 3, (020) 478 025, 479 025.
📅 Summer in Cavtat, Gospa od Cavtata (5 Aug).

Cavtat is the Croatian name for Civitas Vetus, the site of the Roman town of Epidaurum, destroyed by the Avars in the 7th century (occasional excavations have revealed the remains of a theatre, several tombs and parts of a road). The beauty of the area, the beaches, the luxuriant vegetation and the interesting monuments attract many visitors to the present-day village.

The **Baltazar Bogišić Collection**, assembled and donated by the scholar and jurist of the 19th century, is housed in the 16th-century

Count's Palace. The works of the painter Vlaho Bukovac are especially fine.

At the end of the seafront is the church of **St Blaise** (Sv. Vlaho) and a Franciscan monastery, both from the end of the 15th century. On the hilltop stands the **Račić Mausoleum** built by Ivan Meštrović (see p157) in 1922.

Konavle ③⑥

Map F6.
🏛 Tiha 3, Cavtat,
(020) 478 025, 479 025.

The area southeast of Cavtat occupies a narrow piece of land between the sea and the mountains of Bosnia-Herzegovina. Its name derives from the channels (konavle) which collected the water to supply the aqueduct – of which some traces remain – for the Roman town of Epidaurum.

The hilly areas are covered in vineyards and olive groves. The small villages maintain the old customs and traditional costumes are still worn by the inhabitants. Konavle was heavily damaged by bombing in 1991 and the houses are still being rebuilt. This area is also renowned for its excellent cuisine and there are numerous restaurants.

Traditional dress of Konavle, still used for festivals

One of the best known is **Konavoski Dvori**, housed in a watermill near the waterfalls of the River Ljuta.

The pretty seafront and port of Cavtat

ZAGREB

The capital of Croatia, Zagreb is also the heart of the political, economic and cultural life of the country. Surrounded by woods and parks, the city lies between the slopes of Mount Medvednica to the north and the River Sava to the south. Located at the centre of continental Croatia, this Central European city constitutes a meeting point between eastern and western Europe.

The political scientist Max Weber once declared that the quality of life in a city could be measured by the number of its cultural institutions. Zagreb has 20 museums, 16 theatres, 350 libraries, a university, and lively programmes of artistic and cultural events. This is not just because Zagreb is the capital (it has only been the capital since 1991), but is also due to the leading cultural and political role that Zagreb has played over the centuries.

Zagreb was originally two separate medieval towns. Two settlements were built on two adjacent hilltops: Kaptol, the centre of religious power, and a bishopric from 1094, and Gradec (now part of Gornji Grad). In 1242, with the proclamation of a "Golden Bull", Gradec was given the title of royal free city by the Croat-

History of Croatia by Ivan Meštrović, Meštrović Gallery

Hungarian King Bela IV. This granted various economic and administrative privileges to the inhabitants. From the 16th century onwards Gradec was also where the Ban – the governor of Croatia delegated by the Hungarian kingdom – and the Croat parliament carried out their business and where Croat nobles met to govern this turbulent territory. The two towns were both fortified with ramparts, towers, moats and gates, and were separated by the river Medveščak. The river was often the site of violent clashes between Gradec and Kaptol, and that time is vividly recalled by the street called the Bridge of Blood (Krvavi Most).

In 1880, a terrible earthquake struck the city and many of the major monuments date from after this time.

The colourful Dolac market with fruit and vegetable stalls

◁ View of the centre of Zagreb from Kralja Tomislava square

Exploring Zagreb

The city is divided into two large sectors; the
old town (Gornji Grad or Upper Town), which
includes the two districts of Gradec and Kaptol,
situated in the hills, and the modern area (Donji
Grad or Lower Town) on the plain. The large square
dedicated to the Croat governor Jelačić (Trg bana
Jelačića) is where the upper and lower towns meet.
The old town is home to the main centres of
religious, political and administrative power. The
more modern part developed after 1830 around a
U-shaped series of parks and open spaces (known
as the "horseshoe"). The major museums, including
the Ethnographic Museum, Mimara Museum, Gallery
of Old Masters and Gallery of Modern Art, are all
located here, as well as the National Theatre. To the
south of a series of gardens with sculptures lies the
Botanical Garden. Around Jelačić Square there are
plenty of cafés with summer terraces.

LOCATOR MAP

0 metres   200

0 yards   200

SIGHTS AT A GLANCE

Museums and Galleries
Archaeological Museum ㉕
City Museum ❻
Croatian Historical Museum ⑫
Ethnographic Museum ⑳
Gallery of Modern Art ㉔
Gallery of Old Masters
  pp164–5 ㉓
Meštrović Gallery ❽
Mimara Museum ⑲
Museum of Arts
  and Crafts ⑱
National Museum of
  Naive Art ⑬
Natural History Museum ❼

Churches
Cathedral of St Stephen ❶
Church of St Catherine ⑯

Church of SS Cyril
  and Methodius ⑭
Church of St Francis ❸
Church of St Mark ❾
Church of St Mary ❹

Palaces and other Buildings
Archbishop's Palace ❷
Art Pavilion ㉒
Ban's Palace ⑪
Croatian National Theatre ⑰
Parliament Building ❿
Stone Gate ❺
Tower of Lotrščak ⑮

Parks and Gardens
Botanical Garden ㉑
Maksimir Park ㉖
Mirogoj Cemetery ㉗

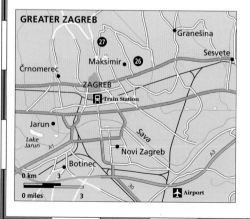

GREATER ZAGREB

Granešina
Sesvete
Črnomerec
Maksimir ㉖
㉗
ZAGREB
Train Station
Jarun
Lake Jarun
Sava
Novi Zagreb
Botinec
A1
30
A3
0 km   3
0 miles   3
✈ Airport

TUSKANAC
STRELJAČ
DEŽMANOVA
ILICA
P
MEDULIĆEVA
FRANKOPANSKA
DALMATINSKA
PRILAZ GJURE DEŽELIĆA
TRG
MARŠALA TIT.
⑱
⑰
KLAIĆEVA
ROOSEVELTOV
TRG
⑲
PERKOVĆEVA
⑳
TRG BRAĆE
MAŽURANIĆ
VUKOTINOVIĆEVA
MARULIĆEV
TRG
SAVSKA
VODNIKOVA
CRNATKOVA

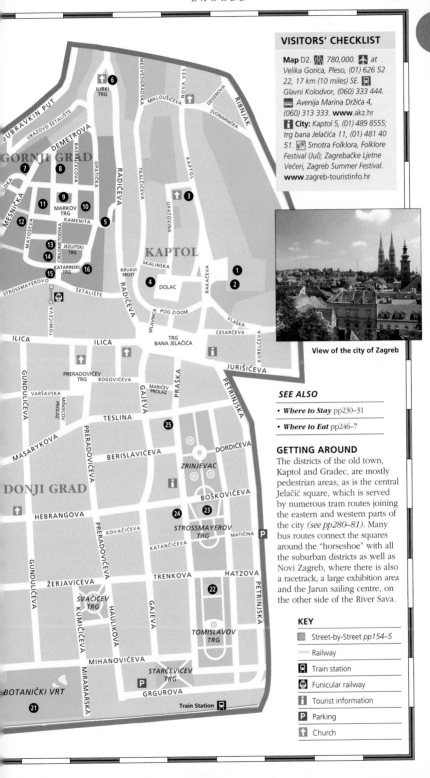

VISITORS' CHECKLIST

Map D2. 780,000. at Velika Gorica, Pleso, (01) 626 52 22, 17 km (10 miles) SE. Glavni Kolodvor, (060) 333 444. Avenija Marina Držića 4, (060) 313 333. www.akz.hr City: Kaptol 5, (01) 489 8555; trg bana Jelačića 11, (01) 481 40 51. Smotra Folklora, Folklore Festival (Jul); Zagrebačke Ljetne Večeri, Zagreb Summer Festival. www.zagreb-touristinfo.hr

View of the city of Zagreb

SEE ALSO

- *Where to Stay* pp230–31
- *Where to Eat* pp246–7

GETTING AROUND

The districts of the old town, Kaptol and Gradec, are mostly pedestrian areas, as is the central Jelačić square, which is served by numerous tram routes joining the eastern and western parts of the city *(see pp280–81)*. Many bus routes connect the squares around the "horseshoe" with all the suburban districts as well as Novi Zagreb, where there is also a racetrack, a large exhibition area and the Jarun sailing centre, on the other side of the River Sava.

KEY

	Street-by-Street pp154–5
	Railway
	Train station
	Funicular railway
	Tourist information
	Parking
	Church

Cathedral of St Stephen ❶
Katedrala Sv. Stjepana

Kaptol. **Tel** (01) 481 47 27.
◯ 10am–5pm Mon–Fri, 1–5pm Sun.

Dedicated to the Assumption and the saints Stephen and Ladislaus, this is the most famous monument in the city. Its present appearance dates from renovations carried out by Friedrich von Schmidt and Hermann Bollé after the earthquake of 1880, which destroyed the dome, the bell tower and some of the walls. The rebuilding, which retained the medieval plan of the cathedral, was just the latest in a series of alterations the building had undergone in its long history. The building was already in existence in 1094 when King Ladislaus transferred the bishopric here from Sisak. Destroyed by the

Decorative detail of one of the spires of St Stephen

Mongols in 1242, the cathedral was rebuilt by Bishop Timotej a few years later. In the centuries that followed, the side aisles were added and the church was decorated with statues and reliefs.

The new Neo-Gothic façade (1880) is flanked by two twin spires. The façade has a large ornate doorway with sculpted decorations, a rose window and three high windows, the whole crowned by a tympanum.

The interior has three aisles and a polygonal apse. During a late 19th-century reorganization, the Baroque and Rococo altars were transferred to other churches in the diocese, and as a result only a few Gothic and Renaissance works remain. These works include a statue of St Paul (13th century), wooden statues of the saints Peter and Paul from the 15th century, a triptych entitled *Golgotha* (1495) by Albrecht Dürer and a 14th-century *Crucifixion* by Giovanni da Udine. The cathedral also contains the tombs and votive chapels of bishops and important personalities in Croatian history, such as Petar Zrinski, Krsto Frankopan and the blessed Cardinal Alojzije Stepinac, whose tomb behind the main altar is by Ivan Meštrović.

Of great interest are the frescoes from the Giotto-esque school in the sacristy: the oldest (12th century) in inland Croatia. In the basement of the bishop's sacristy, the **Cathedral Treasury** preserves a rich collection

The central nave in the Neo-Gothic Cathedral of St Stephen

of religious objects. These include illuminated manuscripts, finely crafted church ornaments from the 11th to the 20th centuries, and objects of veneration such as the Cloak of King Ladislaus (11th century), a bishop's veil from the 14th century and the so-called Sepulchre of God. This last was made by the embroiderers of the village of Vugrovec, where Bishop Petar Petraetić founded an embroidery school in around 1650. Among the oldest works are a 10th-century ivory diptych and a bronze Crucifix from the 11th–12th centuries.

Archbishop's Palace ❷
Nadbiskupska Palača

Kaptol. ◯ to the public.

The enormous Baroque buildings comprising the Archbishop's Palace enclose the other three sides of the cathedral square. The building incorporates three of the five round towers and one square tower, which were part of the fortifications built from 1469 as defence against Turkish attacks. The present palace dates from 1730, when several buildings were linked and united by an imposing Baroque façade.

Inside the complex is the Romanesque chapel of

The tall spires of the Cathedral of St Stephen

St Stephen Protomartyr (13th century). This is the oldest building in Zagreb to have survived in its original form: the frescoes are from the same period.

In the square in front of the palace stands a fountain with a column crowned by a statue of Mary with four Angels, the work of the Viennese artist Anton Dominik Fernkorn (1813–78) in around 1850.

The moats that once surrounded the walls have been filled in and turned into the **Ribnjak Public Gardens**, with various statues including one called *Modesty* by Antun Augustinčić (1900–79). The defences were partially demolished in the 19th century, however. At No 18 Ulica Kaptol, opposite the cathedral, is the **Northeast Tower**, which is now a residence. At No 15 stands the **Northwest Tower** (Prišlinova Kula), now part of a 15th-century building.

The Archbishop's Palace by the Cathedral of St Stephen

Church of St Francis ❸

Sv. Franjo

Ulica Kaptol 9. **Tel** *(01) 489 83 33.* ☐ *5–8pm daily.*

Founded, according to legend, after St Francis' return from the East, this church in fact dates from the 16th century. After the earthquake of 1880, the church was rebuilt in the Neo-Gothic style. It was at

Stained-glass windows by Ivo Dulčić in the church of St Francis

this time that the Baroque altars were removed. Some of the side altars are Neo-Gothic, while on the main altar there is a fine painting of St Francis by Celestin Medović (1857–1920). The brightly coloured stained-glass windows were designed by Ivo Dulčić in the 1960s.

In the adjacent 17th-century **Monastery**, where the saint supposedly stayed, is the much-visited chapel of St Francis (1683), with ornate stucco decorations and Baroque paintings.

Church of St Mary ❹

Sv. Marija

Dolac 2. **Tel** *(01) 481 49 59.* ☐ *for mass.*

Opatovina Ulica is a narrow street where some of the houses were built using parts of the late-15th century fortifications. The street leads into the ancient district of Dolac, at the end of which stands the church of St Mary, which dates from the 14th century. It was rearranged in 1740 when several Baroque altars were built by Franjo Rottman, but its present appearance dates

back to rebuilding after the earthquake in 1880.

Near the church stands a statue by Vanja Radauš of the legendary wanderer and minstrel Petrica Kerempuh, playing to the figure of a hanged man.

The large, picturesque **Dolac Market**, which was first held in 1930, takes place around the church. This is a characteristic district of the city where Baroque houses face narrow streets and lanes. A historic pharmacy at No 19 Ulica Kaptol and an ancient house at No 7.

Stone Gate ❺

Kamenita Vrata

Kamenita.

In the walls around Gradec, the part of Upper Town built on a neighbouring hill to Kaptol, there were once five gates. Stone Gate is now the only one of these remaining. It was built in the 13th century, and stands beside a square tower from 1266. In 1731 a fire destroyed all the nearby houses, but a painting of Mary with Child on the gate was left undamaged. A chapel was established around this painting and a Baroque wrought-iron grille now protects the work, attributed to a local master from the 16th century.

On the west façade of the church is a statue of a woman, the work of the sculptor Ivan Kerdić in 1929. On the other side of the gate, on the corner of Kamenita and Habdelićeva, stands an 18th-century building. On the ground floor of this building is a **Pharmacy** (Alighieri ljekarna) which has been in existence since 1350 and which, from 1399 onwards, belonged to Nicolò Alighieri, the great-grandson of the great Italian writer Dante.

The monument to Petrica Kerempuh, Dolac

Street-by-Street: the Upper Town (Gornji Grad)

In the Upper Town there are various institutions which have played a significant part in the history of the city and of Croatia. They now house the political and cultural centres of the country: the presidency of the Republic, Parliament, the State Audit Court and several government ministries. All of these buildings were restored, repaired or rebuilt after the terrible earthquake of 1880. Some of the ancient noble palaces have been converted into museums. There are also three interesting churches: the ancient church of St Mark, the Baroque church of St Catherine built by the Jesuits, and the church of Saints Cyril and Methodius. The daily signal to close the city gates was rung from the medieval tower of Lotrščak (Turris Latruncolorum).

Pietà by Ivan Meštrović

Natural History Museum
Created from three collections, the museum houses most of the finds from Krapina, which date human presence in Croatia back to the Palaeolithic era 7

Ban's Palace
The building dates from the 17th century and was built after the city became the seat of the Ban (governor of Croatia) in 1621. It now houses the presidency of the Republic 11

Croatian Historical Museum
This museum, housed in the splendid Vojković-Oršić palace, has works of art and documents collected since 1960 12

★ National Museum of Naive Art
Over 1,500 works of Naive art by the founders and followers of the Hlebine school are held here 13

Church of SS Cyril and Methodius
Built by Orthodox Christians in the first half of the 19th century, the church, designed by Bartol Felbinger, has a fine iconostasis 14

Tower of Lotrščak
At noon every day a cannon is fired from this tower, which dates from the 12th century 15

KEY

- - - - Suggested route

★ **Meštrović Gallery**
*The great Croatian
sculptor Ivan
Meštrović lived in this
18th-century building
from 1922 to 1941.
About ten years before
his death he donated
his home and all the
works of art in it to
the state* **8**

LOCATOR MAP

Parliament Building
*This building dates from 1910, when
the provincial administration offices
were enlarged. The independence
of Croatia was proclaimed from
the central window of the
building in 1918* **10**

★ **Church of St Mark**
*The coloured tiles on the roof of this fine
Gothic church form the coats of arms of
Croatia, Dalmatia, Slavonia and Zagreb* **9**

| 0 metres | 50 |
| 0 yards | 50 |

**The Gallery of
Contemporary Art**
in the Kulmer Palace
puts on exhibitions
by Croatian and
foreign artists.

The Klovićevi Dvori,
an important temporary
exhibition site, has been
housed since 1982 in a
17th-century Jesuit
monastery.

Church of St Catherine
*Built on the site of an ancient
Dominican church, this is the
city's most fascinating
Baroque building* **16**

STAR FEATURES

★ Church of St Mark

★ Meštrović Gallery

★ National Museum
of Naive Art

City Museum ❻
Muzej grada Zagreba

Opatička ulica 20. *Tel (01) 485 13 64.* ☐ *10am–6pm Tue–Fri; 10am–1pm Sat & Sun.* ✏ *by appt.*

Three historic buildings (the convent of the nuns of St Clare from around 1650, a 12th-century tower, and a granary from the 17th century, now converted into a school) have been linked to form the City Museum. Its 12 collections, consisting of 74,000 pieces, illustrate the history and culture of Zagreb from its origins to the present day.

The exhibits include paintings, maps and views of the city, standards, flags, military uniforms, coats of arms and fragments of sculpture from civil and religious monuments, and also archaeological finds. Many of the exhibits were donated by the city's famous townsmen and women, including the actress Tilla Durieux, the musician Rudolf Matz, the composer Ivan Zajc, the soprano Milka Trnina and architect Viktor Kovačić.

Along the street is the 19th-century **Ilirska Dvorana Palace,** which houses part of the Croatian Academy of Arts and Sciences, and the **Paravić Palace** (19th century), with fine wrought-iron gates, now the Institute of Historical Studies.

Some of the statues on display in the City Museum

Sculptures in the garden of the Meštrović Gallery

Natural History Museum ❼
Prirodoslovni Muzej

Demetrova 1. *Tel (01) 485 17 00.* ☐ *10am–5pm Tue–Fri, 10am–1pm Sat & Sun.* **www**.hpm.hr

The 18th-century Amadeo Palace, a theatre from 1797 to 1834, has been the Natural History Museum since 1868, when collections from the Department of Natural Science at the National Museum were transferred here. At the end of the 19th century there were three museums of natural history: Mineralogy and Petrography, Geology and Palaeontology, and Zoology. These three museums merged in 1986 to form the present museum.

The over 2,500,000 exhibits include minerals from all over the world and the palaeontology collections include some of the material found in Krapina. The zoological collection documents every species of animal found in Croatia as well as many exotic species.

A mineral in the Museum of Natural History

Meštrović Gallery ❽
Atelje Meštrović

Mletačka 8. *Tel (01) 485 11 23.* ☐ *10am–6pm Tue–Fri, 10am–2pm Sat & Sun.* ✏

The gallery building dates from the 17th century; the sculptor Ivan Meštrović himself modernized it to live in from 1922 to 1942. It now houses a collection of his work. It belongs to the Meštrović Foundation, which also owns the Gallery and the Kaštelet in Split, as well as the mausoleum in Otavice *(see p110).* There are almost 300 works on display, including exhibits in the courtyard – copies of *History of Croatia, Deposition* and *Woman in Agony.* The drawings, models, and sculptures in wood, stone and bronze testify to the great expressive ability and the technical skills of the great sculptor. His personal archives are also here, as well as photographic records and works by other artists associated with the master.

Ivan Meštrović

Regarded as one of the most important sculptors of the 20th century, Ivan Meštrović was born in 1883 in Vrpolje, on the Pannonian Plain, where his parents had gone for the harvest from their native town of Otavice in the Dalmatian hinterland. As a young boy he delighted in making clay figures and his work was noticed by the town mayor and by Lujo Marun, an archaeologist, who sent him to Zagreb when he was 17 to study sculpture. Thanks to the Viennese industrialist Koenig, he was able to attend the Academy of Fine Arts in Vienna, where he designed works for later production. Here he met and became friends with

Portrait of Ivan Meštrović

the great French sculptor, Auguste Rodin. In 1907 he moved to Paris and his first exhibition established his reputation. He worked in various cities, including Split – where he created many of the works now on show in the Meštrović gallery there – and Zagreb. Here he also took up politics: during World War II he was imprisoned by the Ustaše and freed on the intervention of the Vatican. He then sculpted the *Pietà Romana*, now in the Vatican Museum. After the war he taught at universities in the US, where he died in 1962. He was buried in the mausoleum in Otavice *(see p110)* that he designed for himself and his family.

Meštrović, intent on his work

Detail of the *Resurrection of Lazarus* (1944)

Woman on the Shore *is a splendid female figure in marble (1926) which seems to twist around on itself. The form of the body is vigorous and yet the hands are delicate and slender.*

THE SCULPTOR AT WORK

The speed at which Meštrović executed his works was proverbial, although the preparation time was lengthy. To satisfy demand, he duplicated his works in wood, marble and bronze. Three copies exist of the statue of the Bishop of Nin, in Nin, Split and Koprivnica.

Maternity *is a wooden sculpture from 1942 which demonstrates the artist's great expressive talent. The figure of the child is almost insignificant, leaving the face of the mother to play the main role.*

History of Croatia *is a work from 1932 of which there are three versions; one in bronze is in the Meštrović Galley in Zagreb. The woman's thoughtful gaze looks to the future, symbolizing expectations and hopes.*

The church of St Mark, with its colourful glazed tile roof

Church of St Mark **9**
Sv. Marko

Markov trg. **Tel** *(01) 485 16 11.*
◯ *8am–8pm daily.*

Today this is the Upper Town's parish church. St Mark's was first mentioned in 1256 when King Bela IV granted the town of Gradec permission to hold a market fair in front of the church. The fair lasted for two weeks and was held to celebrate the saint's day.

The church has undergone various alterations over the centuries. All that is left from the original construction is a Romanesque window and a splendid Gothic doorway, created by the sculptor Ivan Parler between 1364 and 1377. The 15 niches on the door contain statues of Jesus, Mary, St Mark and the 12 apostles. Some of these were replaced by wooden copies in the Baroque era.

On various occasions fires and earthquakes have been responsible for changes in the church's appearance. Its present look dates from 1882, when the coloured glazed tiles on the roof were added. The tiles bear the coats of arms of Croatia, Dalmatia, Slavonia and the city of Zagreb. The church interior has been refurbished with several statues by the sculptor Ivan Meštrović. On the high altar is a large *Christ on the Cross*, a *Pietà* stands on the altar of the Holy Cross and a bronze statue of *Mary with Child* adorns an altar dedicated to the Virgin Mary. The modern frescoes depicting Croat kings in action were painted by Jozo Kljaković.

Parliament Building **10**
Sabor

Markov trg. ▮ *(01) 456 92 22.*
◯ *by appt.*

Built in Neo-Classical style in 1908 after several 17th- and 18th-century Baroque buildings were razed, this building holds an important place in the story of Croatia. Historic proclamations have been issued from the balcony: the seceding of the nation from the Austro-Hungarian kingdom (29 October 1918) and independence from Yugoslavia after a referendum in 1991. Today the Sabor is still the centre of 21st-century Croat politics.

Mary with Child by Meštrović, St Mark's

Viceroy's Palace **11**
Banski Dvori

Markov trg. ▮ *(01) 456 92 22.*
◯ *by appt.*

The parliament chamber, the central archives, the law courts, the President of the Republic's residence and government offices are all housed in this building in front of St Mark's. The palace is similar in design to the parliament building and is made up of two long 18th-century structures. In the 19th century two two-storey wings were added.

Croatian Historical Museum **12**
Hrvatski Povijesni Muzej

Matoševa ulica 9. **Tel** *(01) 485 19 00.* ◯ *10am–5pm Tue–Fri,10am–1pm Sat & Sun.* ◼ *public hols.* ▨ ▮ ▯

A museum has been housed here since 1960, but it only became the Croatian Historical Museum in 1991 when several collections were merged. The museum illustrates the history of Croatia from the Middle Ages to the present day by means of all kinds of mementoes. These include documents and paintings of political, military and cultural events, as well as items such as firearms, flags and medals. There is also a well-stocked specialist library.

The museum is housed in the Baroque Vojković-Oršić Palace, which dates from the second half of the 18th century. The decorated ballroom is still preserved.

The Parliament Building (Sabor), built in Neo-Classical style in 1908

My Homeland by Ivan Rabuzin (1961), National Museum of Naive Art

National Museum of Naive Art ⓭

Hrvatski Muzej Naivne Umjetnosti

Ćirilometodska ulica 3. *Tel* (01) 485 19 11. ◯ 10am–6pm Tue–Fri, 10am–1pm Sat & Sun. ◉ public hols. 🖼️ 📷 www.hmnu.org

Since 1994, this 19th-century building with its beautiful Neo-Baroque façade has housed works from an exhibition of Naive painters which opened in Zagreb in 1952. The paintings are characterized by the use of vivid colour and a strong feeling for narrative. There are paintings by the founders of the Naive trend, Ivan Generalić and Mirko Virius, as well as by the Hlebine school (*see p21*), where works by Ivan Večenaj and Mijo Kovačić stand out, and primitive artists from other regions (Ivan Lacković, Ivan Rabuzin, Stjepan Stolnik and Matija Skurjeni). Among the sculptures are several by Lavoslav Torti.

Church of SS Cyril and Methodius ⓮

Sv. Ćiril i Metod

Ćirilometodska ulica. *Tel* (01) 485 17 73.

First built in around 1830 in Neo-Classical style by the architect Bartol Felbinger (1785–1871), the church was rebuilt after the earthquake of 1880 in a Neo-Byzantine style designed by Hermann Bollé.

The interior has a large iconostasis painted by the Ukrainian Epaminondas Bučevski, and four large paintings by Ivan Tišov.

The adjacent Greek-Catholic seminary was built in 1774 and enlarged at the beginning of the 20th century.

Tower of Lotrščak ⓯

Kula Lotrščak

Strossmayerovo Šetalište. *Tel* (01) 485 17 68. ◯ Apr–Oct: 11am–7pm Tue–Fri, 2–7pm Sat & Sun. 🖼️

Since the middle of the 19th century, the inhabitants of Zagreb have set their clocks at noon by the cannons fired from this tower. dating from the 13th century, it is one of the oldest buildings in the city.

At one time this square tower had a bell, which announced the closing of the city gates each evening. Its name comes from the latin *campana latruncolorum* – bell of thieves – anyone left outside at night ran the risk of being robbed.

The tower originally stood alongside the southern side of the walls of Gradec. Even at that time, the walls, nearly 2 m (6 ft) thick, were built with chains inside them as an anti-earthquake measure.

The tower now houses a gallery. It is worth climbing to the top for spectacular views over the city.

Church of St Catherine ⓰

Sv. Katarina

Katarinin trg. *Tel* (01) 485 19 50. ◯ 8am–8pm daily.

The Jesuits built this church in around 1630 on the site of a Dominican building. The church is considered to be one of the most beautiful religious buildings in Zagreb. The white façade has a doorway and four niches with statues and six prominent pilasters. Above is a niche with a statue of Mary.

The single-nave church is home to numerous Baroque works of art. Of particular interest are the stucco reliefs (1721–3) by Antonio Quadrio, the *Scenes of the Life of St Catherine* by the Slovenian artist Franc Jelovšek (1700–64) in the medallion on the ceiling, a beautiful *Altar of St Ignatius* by the Venetian sculptor Francesco Robba (1698–1757) and, on the main altar (1762), *St Catherine among the Alexandrian Philosophers* by Kristof Andrej Jelovšek (1729–76).

In the nearby square called Jezuitski trg, there is a fountain with a statue of a *Fisherman with a Serpent* by Simeon Roksandić (1908). Facing this is a Jesuit monastery (17th century) and a large building from the same period which was the Jesuit seminary and later, a boarding school for boys of noble parentage.

The rich Baroque interior of the church of St Catherine

The Neo-Baroque building housing the Croatian National Theatre

Croatian National Theatre ⑰
Hrvatsko Narodno Kazalište

Trg Maršala Tita 15. **Tel** *(01) 482 85 32.* ⬤ *for performances only.* ⬤ *Mon, 1 Jan, Easter, 1 May, 1 Nov, 25–26 Dec.* **www**.hnk.hr

The Croatian National Theatre stands in the square marking the beginning of a U-shaped series of parks and squares forming a "green horseshoe", the design of the engineer Milan Lenuci (1849– 1924). The theatre, one of a number of imposing buildings in the square, was completed in 1895 and is a blend of Neo-Baroque and Rococo. It was designed by the Viennese architects Hermann Helmer and Ferdinand Fellner. The roof has two small domes at the front and a higher dome further back. The exterior is ornamented with two orders of columns running along its entire length.

A 19th-century clock, Museum of Arts and Crafts

The interior is richly decorated with works by Croatian and Viennese artists. Five stage backcloths include one called *The Croatian Renewal*, a splendid work by Vlaho Bukovac.

In the area in front of the theatre stands a masterpiece by Ivan Meštrović, *The Well of Life:* a group of bronze figures huddled around a well.

Museum of Arts and Crafts ⑱
Muzej Za Umjetnost i Obrt

Trg Maršala Tita 10. **Tel** *(01) 488 21 11.* ⬤ *10am–7pm Tue–Fri, 10am–1pm Sat & Sun.* ⬤ *by appt.* ⬤ ⬤ ⬤ **www**.muo.hr

This museum was first established in 1880 to house collections of artworks by craftsmen and artists. The building was designed by Hermann Bollé and was built between 1882 and 1892. More than 160,000 works of applied arts from the Gothic period to the present provide an overview of Croatia's cultural history and its close ties to the rest of Europe.

The collections include jewellery, fabrics (the famous embroidery from Varaždin, and 15th- and 16th-century tapestries from Tournai, Antwerp and Brussels), wooden sculptures, musical instruments, Austrian furniture, French ivory, 16th-century Italian paintings, and chandeliers from Murano, Germany and Bohemia (the section covering the era from the Biedermeier to the Viennese Secession style is particularly interesting). The ceramic collection has works from all the leading European manufacturers. The adjacent library has 50,000 books on arts and crafts.

Mimara Museum ⑲
Muzej Mimara

Rooseveltov trg 5. **Tel** *(01) 482 81 00.* ⬤ *10am–5pm Tue, Wed, Fri & Sat, 10am–7pm Thu, 10am–2pm Sun.* ⬤ *Mon.* ⬤

In 1972, Ante Topić Mimara, a businessman who was also a collector, painter and restorer, donated his extensive collections to the city of Zagreb, and the Mimara Museum was set up for their display. The museum is housed in an enormous Neo-Renaissance building built in 1895 by the German architects Ludwig and Hülsner. It was formerly a grammar school.

The works are displayed chronologically from the prehistoric era to the present day. The archaeological section is particularly fascinating, with important finds from ancient Egypt, Mesopotamia, Persia, Pre-Columbian America, as well as the Middle and Far East (Japan, Cambodia, Indonesia and India are represented).

The icon collection not only contains Russian pieces, but also has icons from Palestine, Antioch and Asia Minor dating from the 6th to the 13th centuries. There are ancient Persian, Turkish and Moroccan carpets, and about 300 exhibits cover over 3,500 years of the development of Chinese art, from the Shang to the Qing dynasties.

The 550 glassware exhibits come from Europe, as well as Persia, Turkey and Morocco. About 1,000 objects and

***The Bather* by Renoir (1868) in the Mimara Museum**

pieces of furniture give a good overall picture of European craftsmanship from the Middle Ages to the 19th century.

There is also a wide-ranging collection of 200 sculptures, which date from ancient Greece to the time of the Impressionists. They include works by the Italian sculptors Giambologna, the Della Robbias and Verrocchio, and the Frenchmen Jean-Antoine Houdon and Auguste Rodin. Italian painting is represented by, among others, Veronese, Paolo Veneziano, Pietro Lorenzetti, Raphael, Canaletto, Giorgione and Caravaggio.

Dutch Baroque painting is represented by Rembrandt, Jacob Van Ruisdael and Jan Van Goyen. Flemish masters here include Rogier van der Weyden, Hieronymus Bosch, Van Dyck and Rubens. Diego Velázquez, Bartolomé Esteban Murillo and Francisco Goya represent the Spanish painters.

The museum also has paintings by the English artists John Constable and J M W Turner and the French painters Edouard Manet, Pierre-Auguste Renoir and Camille Pissarro.

Ethnographic Museum ⑳
Etnografski Muzej

Mažuranićev trg 14.
Tel (01) 482 62 20.
◯ 10am–6pm Tue–Thu, 10am–1pm Fri–Sun. 🏛 public hols. 🎫

This is the most important museum of its kind in Croatia. It was founded in 1919 and set up in this harmonious domed building, constructed in 1902 in the Secession style by the architect Vjekoslav Bastl, for exhibitions held by the Chamber of Commerce. The statues decorating the central part of the façade are by the sculptor Rudolf Valdec and the frescoes on the dome inside were painted by Oton Iveković. Only a small

Traditional Croatian costumes on display, Ethnographic Museum

proportion (2,800 pieces) of the 80,000 exhibits which the museum possesses are on display. Croatian culture is illustrated through exhibits of gold and silver jewellery, musical instruments, splendid embroidery, furnishings, kitchen utensils, tools, beautiful traditional women's costumes embroidered in gold and men's ceremonial dress. Reconstructions of farmhouses and rooms illustrate the customs and way of life of Croat farmers and fishermen. There is also a fascinating collection of dolls dressed in traditional costumes, called the Ljeposav Perinić collection.

The valuable collection of pieces from non-European civilizations, including Latin

Putto by Verrocchio, Mimara Museum

America, Central Africa, the Far East and Australia, was assembled from donations made by scholars and explorers, among them Dragutin Lerman and brothers Mirko and Stevo Seljan.

Botanical Garden ㉑
Botanički Vrt

Marulićev trg 9. 🚶 (01) 484 40 02. ◯ Mar–Sep: 9am–2.30pm Mon & Tue, 9am–7pm Wed–Sun.

Part of the "green horseshoe" designed by Milan Lenuci is a large, English-style garden created in 1890 by Antun Heinz, a professor of botany, and entrusted to the faculty of Mathematics and Natural Sciences at Zagreb university.

The garden, covering an area of 50,000 sq m (540,000 sq ft), is an oasis of tranquillity in which to escape the bustle of the city, and for this reason it is a popular place in which to stroll. There are about 10,000 plant species here, including around 1,800 tropical plants from all over the world, with Asia particularly well represented.

Paths link the conifer woods, artificial ponds, the university pavilions and glasshouses. A wonderful display is provided by the different varieties of trees, shrubs and flowers which are grown here. Aquatic plants are cultivated in special ponds.

One of the many ponds in the Botanical Gardens

The Art Pavilion, venue for major exhibitions

Art Pavilion ②
Umjetnički Paviljon

Trg Kralja Tomislava 22.
Tel (01) 484 10 70.
◯ 11am–7pm Mon–Sat; 10am–1pm Sun. ♿
www.umjetnicki-paviljon.hr

In 1896 the Art Pavilion represented Croatia at the international exhibition in Budapest. It was set up on this site in 1898 by Ferdinand Fellner and Hermann Helmer. Since then it has been used for art exhibitions. A work by Ivan Meštrović, a monument to the Renaissance painter Andrija Medulić, stands in front of the pavilion.

The pavilion faces onto a square, Trg Kralja Tomislava, dedicated to the first Croatian king, Tomislav. An equestrian statue by the sculptor Robert Frangeš-Mihanović stands here in commemoration.

Gallery of Old Masters ②
Galerija Starih Majstora

See pp164–5.

Gallery of Modern Art ②
Moderna Galerija

Andrije Hebranga 1.
Tel (01) 492 23 68. ◯ 10am–6pm Tue–Sat; 10am–1pm Sun. ● 1 Jan, Easter, 25, 26 Dec. ♿

Since 1973, Vraniczany Palace (1882) has housed works by the most eminent Croat painters and sculptors of the 19th and 20th centuries. The institution itself dates from 1902 when the first works of Ivan Meštrović, Mirko Rački and F Bilak were acquired. Later purchases and donations added to the gallery's extensive collections which now boast 9,500 paintings, sculptures, watercolours, drawings and prints.

At the entrance, the large painting, *Gundulić – Osman's Dream,* 1894 by Vlaho Bukovac, immediately establishes the standard of the collection. The gallery also has works by Ljubo Babić,

Head of Plautilla, Archaeological Museum

Miljenko Stančić, V Karas, M Mašić, Emanuel Vidović, C Medović, MC Crnčić, B Csikos-Sessia, Ivan Meštrović, Robert Frangeš-Mihanović, Josip Račić, Miroslav Kraljević, V Becić, O Hermann and Edo Murtić.

Archaeological Museum ②
Arheološki Muzej

Trg Nikole Šubića Zrinskog 19.
Tel (01) 487 31 01. ◯ 10am–5pm Tue–Fri, 10am–1pm Sat–Sun. ♿ 📷 by appt. ◻ **www**.amz.hr

A large 19th-century building, the Vraniczany-Hafner Palace, has housed the Archaeological Museum since 1945. The institution itself, however, was founded in 1846. The imposing rusticated façade has columns marking the entrance. Around 400,000 pieces from all over Croatia, and particularly the area around Zagreb, are on display here. The museum has five main sections: prehistoric, Egyptian, ancient and medieval, and a part devoted to coins and medals.

The first section covers the period from the Neolithic to the late Iron Age and includes

Gundulić – Osman's Dream by Vlaho Bukovac, founder of modern Croat painting, Gallery of Modern Art

An avenue in Maksimir Park, home of the Zoo

the famous *Vučedol Dove*, a pouring vessel shaped like a bird. Despite the rustic materials used, it nonetheless reveals the technical skills that the pre-Illyrian civilizations had acquired.

Another important exhibit is the bandage used to bind the Mummy of Zagreb. This bandage has mysterious origins and bears text in the Etruscan language, which has not yet been completely deciphered.

The ancient collection is the most important of all, and includes splendid painted Greek vases, inscribed stones and, in the Roman section, sculptures and metal objects from the numerous towns which were built during the Imperial Age. From Salona *(see pp116–7)* came the *Head of Plautilla,* one of the most valuable exhibits here. It is now an emblem of the museum.

The medieval collection begins with the "Great Migrations of the Peoples", documented by an inscription dating from 888 (the oldest in Croatia), which mentions Duke Branimir, an ancient prince of Croatia *(see p36)*.

The coin section is divided into Greek, Celtic, Roman (Republic and Imperial), Byzantine and modern.

The library next door houses 45,000 volumes, some of which are extremely rare.

Maksimir Park 26
Maksimirski Perivoj

Maksimirska Cesta 125.
🔲 *daily.*

The largest park in the city (covering over 3 sq km/ 1 sq mile), is considered one of Croatia's living monuments.

It is named after Bishop Maksimilijan Vrhovac, who initiated the project in 1794. The park was finally completed in 1843.

The park is landscaped in the English style with wide lawns and flower beds, small woods and lakes. Near one of the lakes is the **Zoo** (Zoološki vrt), with hundreds of different animal species. Among the follies scattered around the park is one called **Vidikovac** (Belvedere).

Sword hilt decoration, Archaeological Museum

Mirogoj Cemetery 27
Groblje Mirogoj

Mirogoj. 🔲 *7.30am–6pm daily, summer: 7.30am–8pm daily.*

At the foot of Mount Medvednica, 4 km (2 miles) from the centre of the city, is the Mirogoj Cemetery, built in 1876 by Hermann Bollé. This great architect had already demonstrated his ability and talent with the building of the new city district. The cemetery covers an area of 28,000 sq m (6.91 acres) and the tombs of the most illustrious figures in the political, cultural and artistic life of Croatia lie here.

An imposing façade covered in ivy forms the entrance to the Catholic and Orthodox chapels. From here branch two long Neo-Renaissance arcades which house the burial rooms of the most important families.

A long tree-lined avenue divides the area into two sections which in turn are divided into squares of trees and bushes. Among the areas of greenery stand funeral monuments by leading Croatian sculptors and engravers. There are works by Ivan Meštrović, Jozo Kljaković, Ivan Rendić, Antun Filipović, Antun Augustinčić, Edo Murtić, Markus Sutej, Dozo Dražić, Ivan Kerdić and Robert Frangeš-Mihanović.

As well as the tombs of notable personalities there is also a monument dedicated to the memory of the soldiers who died during World War I, by Juri Turkalj and V Radauš, and a monument dedicated to the Jews who died in World War II, by Antun Augustinčić. On one of the cemetery lawns there is a monument dedicated to the German soldiers killed in the war.

The well-preserved cemetery is a real open-air museum and is often visited by the local inhabitants, who regularly put fresh flowers and candles on the tombs of great Croats of the past.

Arcade in the Mirogoj Cemetery, one of the most beautiful in Europe

Gallery of Old Masters ㉓
Galerija Starih Majstora

In 1876 Josip Juraj Strossmayer, the rich and powerful Bishop of Đakovo and one of the leading proponents of a pan-Slav movement, had this gallery built to house the Academy of Arts and Sciences and later the Gallery of Old Masters, to which he donated his own impressive collection of about 600 works of art.

The Neo-Renaissance building has a large internal porticoed courtyard. Ten rooms on the upper floor house around a hundred works from the major European schools from the 14th to the 19th century. Opposite the entrance is a large statue of Bishop Strossmayer sculpted by Ivan Meštrović in 1926.

Virgin with Child and St Francis and St Bernard
This small painting is one of the few works by Bartolomeo Caporali (c.1420–1505) to be found outside Perugia in Italy.

Susanna and the Elders
The three figures depicted in the painting stand out against the landscape in the background. The faces of the two old men are very expressive; it is as though they are revived by gazing at the beautiful Susanna. The artist, Majstor Izgubljenogsina, demonstrates great technical skill and vivid use of colour.

Second floor

GALLERY GUIDE
The gallery is on the second floor of the building. Exhibits include works by important Italian, German, Flemish and French masters, representing schools and artistic trends from the 14th to the 19th century. Before visiting the gallery, note, in the entrance hall, the Baška Tablet, one of the oldest documents of Croat culture (11th century), written in Glagolitic script.

Bridge with Three Arches on the Cannaregio Canal
This painting, by Francesco Guardi (1712–93), is one of numerous views painted by the Venetian artist. The subject is one of the lesser known corners of his native city.

Virgin Mary with Jesus, John and an Angel

This tondo by Jacopo del Sellaio uses exuberant colour. The Tuscan artist belonged to the circle of Filippo Lippi and Sandro Botticelli.

VISITORS' CHECKLIST

Trg Nikole Šubića Zrinskog 11.
Tel (01) 489 51 17.
🕐 10am–1pm & 5–7pm Tue;
10am–1pm Wed–Sun.

Adam and Eve

This lively painting is by Mariotto Albertinelli (1474–1515), a Florentine painter who worked in Perugino's circle. It shows Adam and Eve being expelled from Earthly Paradise.

KEY

- ☐ Italian School 14th–16th century
- ☐ Italian School 16th–18th century
- ☐ Flemish and Dutch Masters and European School 15th–16th century
- ☐ Flemish and Dutch School 16th–17th century
- ☐ French Masters 18th–19th century

★ St Nicholas and St Benedict

The work reveals the expressive skill of the great Venetian master, Giovanni Bellini (1430–1516). The figures of the saints occupy simple niches.

★ St Sebastian

This delicate image of the saint by Vittore Carpaccio (1465–1525) was probably part of a polyptych. In this painting with its vivid colouring, the Venetian master expresses the drama of the martyrdom through the smile of the young man at the moment of his death.

Main entrance

STAR PAINTINGS

- ★ St Nicholas and St Benedict
- ★ St Sebastian

ALTARE PRIVILEGIATUM
IN
PERPETVVM.

CENTRAL CROATIA

*C*entral Croatia is bordered to the west by the vine-covered hills *of Samobor, which continue on towards Karlovac and Ogulin, and to the south by the Bosnia-Herzegovina border as far as Jasenovac. To the northeast is a stretch of fertile valley formed by the Sava river, which goes from Zagreb to the Lonjsko Polje Nature Park. These wetlands, south of Sisak, are home to all kinds of birds.*

This region of Croatia has long been a meeting point for different civilizations. Until the 12th century BC, this area was inhabited by the Illyrians, who were joined by Celts in the 4th century BC. The first Illyrian cities became Roman towns after the 1st century AD. The most important was Siscia (now called Sisak), which was destroyed by the Avars but repopulated by Slavic tribes called Sisak.

Head of Mitra, 2nd century AD, Sisak

The southern border with Bosnia, which dates back to 271 AD, was confirmed at the time of the division between the Western and Eastern Churches in 1054, and later re-confirmed when the Turks occupied the Balkans. To stop the continuous Turkish raids, in 1578 the Austrian Emperor established a *Vojna Krajina* (Military Frontier) in areas which had mostly been abandoned by the Croats, who had fled to the coastal cities for refuge. To help guard the borders, Serbian refugees were brought in, along with minorities of Vlachs, Albanians, Montenegrin and German-speaking groups. Villages sprang up which were inhabited by Catholics, Muslims and people of the Orthodox faith. These diverse communities lived together without any serious tension until the mid-19th century, when feelings of nationalism swept across Europe. The most recent war, fought in the name of nationalism, not only created widespread destruction but also "ethnic cleansing", resulting in the exodus of thousands of Serbs.

This part of Croatia is the area least visited by tourists, although it offers magnificent scenery with rivers and wood-covered hills and good Croatian cuisine. There is plenty to see, with ancient castles, churches, museums and nature reserves.

Horses grazing in the Lonjsko Polje Nature Park

◁ *The Assumption,* a fresco by Franc Jelovšek in the Franciscan church of St Anastasia, Samobor

Exploring Central Croatia

Three distinct areas make up this part of the country:
the lowlands around the capital, Zagreb, with numerous
18th-century buildings constructed on the sites of
ancient castles; the hilly area between Samobor and
Karlovac, renowned for its wine production; and the
strip of border with Bosnia-Herzegovina, south of Sisak.
The landscape of Central Croatia is varied, with areas of
rolling plains alternating with vine-covered hills. Higher
areas are covered in thick woods and there is also an
area of wetlands that comprise Lonjsko Polje Nature
Park. In the cities and larger towns there are Baroque
churches, monasteries, castles, fortresses and
museums. Most suffered damage in the recent
war, but some have now been repaired.

**Roman piece,
Civic Museum, Sisak**

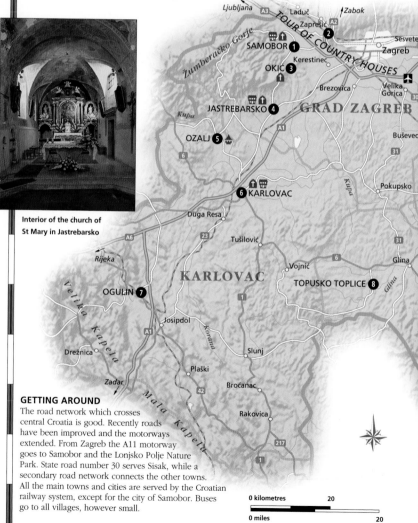

**Interior of the church of
St Mary in Jastrebarsko**

GETTING AROUND

The road network which crosses
central Croatia is good. Recently roads
have been improved and the motorways
extended. From Zagreb the A11 motorway
goes to Samobor and the Lonjsko Polje Nature
Park. State road number 30 serves Sisak, while a
secondary road network connects the other towns.
All the main towns and cities are served by the Croatian
railway system, except for the city of Samobor. Buses
go to all villages, however small.

0 kilometres   20

0 miles   20

SIGHTS AT A GLANCE

Garić ⑮
Jasenovac ⑪
Jastrebarsko ④
Karlovac ⑥
Kostajnica ⑩
Kutina ⑭
Lonjsko Polje Nature Park ⑬
Novska ⑫
Ogulin ⑦
Okić ③

Ozalj ⑤
Samobor ①
Sisak ⑨
Topusko Toplice ⑧

Tour
Tour of Country Houses
pp172–3 ②

LOCATOR MAP

SEE ALSO

• *Where to Stay* p231–2

• *Where to Eat* p247–8

The River Sava near Sisak

The vine-covered hills around Okić

KEY

▬▬	Motorway
▬▬	Major road
═══	Minor road
⊷⊷	Main railway
▬▬	County border
▬▬	International border

The main altar in the church of St Anastasia, Samobor

Samobor **①**

Map C2. 🏛 *35,000.*
🚌 *(01) 336 66 34.* 🛈 *Trg kralja Tomislava 5, (01) 336 00 44.*
🎭 *Carnival (Feb); Day of the city (26–28 Jul).*

Samobor is built below the ruins of what was once a large fort (Stari Grad). In 1242 it was granted the status of a royal free town, and became an important trading centre. Today it is one of the capitals of Croatian gastronomy.

In the central area (Taborec) there are some old wooden houses and Baroque buildings as well as the Gothic church of **St Michael** (Sv. Mihovil), which was remodelled in the Baroque period. Dating from the same time is the church of **St Anastasia** (Sv. Anastazija) and a Franciscan monastery: the *Assumption* behind the main altar was frescoed by Franc Jelovšek in 1752, while the altar on the left was decorated by Valentin Metzinger (1734). The adjacent monastery is laid out around a beautiful quadrangular cloister and has Baroque frescoes in the refectory and library.

The history of the city and local area is well documented in the **Civic Museum** (Muzej Grada Samobora), housed in the 18th-century Livadić Palace. The section dedicated to the history of Croatian mountaineering is especially interesting.

🛈 **St Anastasia**
Ulica Sv. Anastazija. **Tel** *(01) 336 38 61.* ☐ *by appt.*

🏛 **Civic Museum**
Livadićeva 7. **Tel** *(01) 336 10 14.* ☐ *9am–3pm Tue–Fri; 9am–1pm Sat, Sun.* 🖼 📷 🚫 🛈 *English, German.*

Tour of Country Houses **②**

See pp172–73.

Okić **③**

Map C2.
🛈 **County:** *Remetinečka 75, Zagreb, (01) 652 11 17.*

On the isolated hilltop above Okić stand the ruins of a fortified town. These consist of the remains of a wall with round towers, an entrance gate and a Gothic chapel. The town, mentioned in documents from 1183, belonged to the counts of Okić, Zrinski, Frankopan and Erdödy. It was destroyed by the Turks and the town was eventually abandoned in 1616.

In the village around the foot of the hill is the church of **St Mary** (Sv. Marija). It was rebuilt in 1893 incorporating a decorated doorway from 1691. Inside are some Baroque altars, a splendid pulpit and a font. In front of the church is an octagonal bell tower with a vestibule.

A painting by Metzinger in the church of St Mary in Jastrebarsko

Jastrebarsko **④**

Map C2. 🏛 *17,000.* 🚉 *from Zagreb.* 🚌 *from Zagreb.*
🛈 **County:** *Remetinečka 75, Zagreb, (01) 652 11 17;* **Town Hall:** *Braće Kazić 1, (01) 628 11 15.*
www.jastrebarsko.com

At the foot of the Plešivica mountain chain, between Samobor and Karlovac, stands Jastrebarsko. The town appears in documents of 1249. It assumed greater importance in 1257 when it was declared a royal free town by Bela IV and became a trading centre for timber, livestock and the wine which is still produced locally.

In the 15th century the town was a feudal holding of the Erdödy family, who built an imposing **castle** on a square ground-plan with round towers at the corners and an internal porticoed courtyard. Two centuries later it was altered and turned into a residential building which is now the town's **Civic Museum** (Gradski Muzej).

The ruins of the fortified town of Okić, perched on a hilltop

For hotels and restaurants in this region see pp231–2 and pp247–8

The Baroque church of **St Nicholas** (Sv. Nikola; 1772–75) contains a fresco by Rašica and the tomb of Petar Erdödy (1567). In the church of **St Mary** (Sv. Marija; 1740), originally Dominican and later Franciscan, the altars are all Baroque. The painting on the altar dedicated to Mary is by Valentin Metzinger and dates from 1735.

Ozalj ❺

Map C2. 🏘 *1,200.* 🚉 *(047) 731 158.* 🚌 *Karlovac, (047) 614 701, Ozalj, (047) 731 107.* ℹ️ *Kurilovac 1, (047) 731 196.* 🎭 *Day of the city (30 Apr); Summer evenings in Ozalj (15–20 Aug).*

A castle (Stari Grad) which belonged to royalty once stood on this rocky spur. It was built in the 13th century to monitor the roads and the traffic on the river Kupa which flows below it. The castle was strengthened by the Babonić counts and was also the property of the Frankopan family and, in the late 16th century, of Juraj Zrinski. After the Ottoman threat had passed, a village grew up around the castle which had become a residential manor.

Parts of the fortress remain visible: two encircling walls with five semicircular towers. Next to these are some more recent buildings: the granary

Coat of arms, Civic Museum, Karlovac

Ozalj castle, once owned by the Frankopans and Juraj Zrinski

(palas) (16th century) and a Gothic family chapel. The main building, on several levels, was renovated in 1928 by the Thurn und Taxis family who had inherited it. For a time the building was abandoned but in 1971 it became a **Museum**. Exhibits explain the history of the fort and local area and there are some Glagolitic inscriptions.

🏰 **Castle and Museum**
Ulica Zrinski Frankopana.
ℹ️ *(047) 731 170.* ⏰ *9am–3pm Mon–Fri; 11am–5pm Sat, Sun.* 🎟️ 📷

Karlovac ❻

Map C2.
🏘 *71,000.* 🚉 *(060) 333 444.* 🚌 *(047) 600 740.* ℹ️ **Local:** *Ulica Petar Zrinskog 3, (047) 615 115;* **Regional:** *A Vraniczanya 6, (047) 615 320.* www.karlovac-touristinfo.hr 🎭 *Carnival (Feb); Summer in Karlovac (Jun); International folk festival (Aug).*

Today Karlovac is an industrial city and an important junction for roads to Slovenia. It originated as a bulwark against Turkish raids, but was actually founded in 1579 by the Archduke of Austria, Charles of Habsburg, from whom the town gets its name.

The town was planned by the Italian N Angelini as a city-fort at the confluence of the rivers Korana and Kupa. The layout was based on a six-pointed star with bastions and moats which have now been transformed into public gardens. The interior contained 24 buildings, all similar, all of which are still preserved today – although they are used for different purposes.

The heart of the city is Strossmayer Square with the Baroque Frankopan Palace which houses the **Civic Museum** (Gradski Muzej). The archaeological and ethnographic collections document the city's history.

Clock tower of the church of the Holy Trinity in Karlovac

In the square Trg Bana Jelačića is a Franciscan monastery, with a **Museum of Sacred Art** in the cloisters.

The town is also the site of the Catholic church of the **Holy Trinity** (Sv. Trojstvo), mainly from 1683–92 with an 18th-century clock tower (1795). The church has an elaborate black marble altar made by Michele Cussa in 1698. The Orthodox church of St Nicholas (Sv. Nikola) dates from 1786.

To the east the city now extends as far as **Dubovac Castle**, a medieval construction with three towers, now a hotel.

🏛 **Civic Museum**
Strossmayerov trg 7. **Tel** *(047) 615 980.* ⏰ *Apr–Oct: 7am–3pm Tue & Thu; 7am–3pm, 5–7pm Wed–Fri; Nov–Feb: 7am–3pm Tue–Fri, 10am–noon Sat & Sun.* 🎟️ 📷 *by appt.*

🏛 **Museum of Sacred Art**
Trg bana Jelačića 7. **Tel** *(047) 615 950/1.* 🔧 *for restoration.*

🔒 **Holy Trinity**
Trg bana Jelačića 7.
Tel *(047) 615 950/1.* ⏰ *for mass. Other times by appt.*

Tour of Country Houses ❷

To the south and west of Zagreb are several small towns which are easily reached from the A1 motorway, where there are numerous buildings of great architectural interest. Several of them are found along the road which goes from Zaprešić to the Zagorje hills. They were built by members of the Croatian aristocracy after the threat of Turkish invasion had passed and are mainly 18th- and 19th-century reconstructions of older houses. Almost all of the buildings were expropriated after World War II when the Croatian state was set up, and put to different uses. The interiors are not open to the public.

Lužnica ④
Built in the 18th century, this large building has two storeys and a U-shaped ground-plan. The central part is flanked by two round towers with conical roofs. The centre of the long façade culminates in a high tympanum and there are three arched windows on the upper floor above a splendid doorway.

Januševec ⑤
This building, 6 km (4 miles) from Zaprešić, is one of the most beautiful examples of Neo-Classical architecture in Croatia. It was built around 1830 and has three storeys and a rectangular ground-plan centred around a central hall lit by a lantern in the roof. In the centre of the Palladian façade is a three-arched portico with four columns above, crowned by a large tympanum.

0 kilometres   3

0 miles   3

Bregana   E70

Samobor   309

JASTREBARSKO

Laduč ⑥
This castle, 7 km (4 miles) west of Zaprešić, was constructed by the architect K Waidman in 1882 for Baron Vladimir Vranyczani. The pastel colour of the large two-storey building blends harmoniously with the deep green lawns in front. In the centre of the façade is a three-arched portico with an arched loggia above. Today the building houses a nursery school.

Novi Dvori ③

This Neo-Romanesque building near Zaprešić stands on the site of an older structure which was once the country residence of the Ban, Josip Jelačić (1801–59). The house, surrounded by a large park, was partly restored in 1991. The façade has a high stepped tympanum and in front of the entrance is an arched portico with a terrace above. The family tomb stands in the grounds.

TIPS FOR DRIVERS

Departure point: Brezovica.
Length of tour: 40 km
(25 miles) one way.
Information: All the houses included in this tour can be seen from the outside. Some may be partially open for visitors.
🛈 Zagreb Tourist Office: Trg bana Jelačića 11, (01) 481 40 51, 481 40 52. *Stopping-off points:* Hotel Restoran Babylon, Betonska cesta 5 **Tel** (01) 337 15 00, is an award-winning restaurant near Samobor. In Samobor, cheaper restaurants include the Samoborska Pivnica beerhall.

Kerestinec ②

This villa, southwest of Zagreb, was built in 1575 over older buildings by the Erdödy family. It is famous as a place where many intellectuals were imprisoned in World War II. The square building stands in a lovely park and has four round corner towers, a fine doorway and an internal arcaded courtyard. Today it is used as a barracks.

KEY

▰▰▰ Tour route

▬▬▬ Motorway

‑ ‑ ‑ Other roads

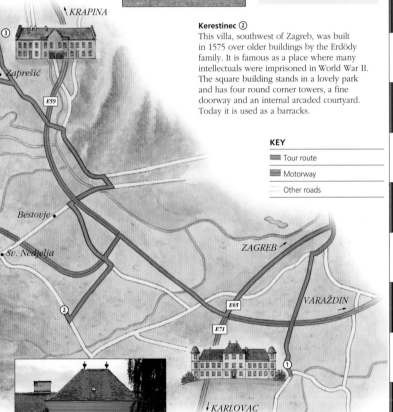

Brezovica ①

The Drašković family built a house here in the 16th century. It was converted into a Baroque palace two centuries later and for some time has been a luxury hotel. The two-storey building has a U-shaped ground-plan and the façade has two round corner towers and a raised central section.

The 15th-century castle of the Frankopan counts in Ogulin

Ogulin ❼

Map C2. 🏘 *11,000.* 🚋 *(047) 525 001.* 🛈 *Ulica B. Frankopana 2, (047) 532 278.* **www**.ogulin.hr

When Marshal Tito was imprisoned here in 1927 and 1933 *(see p42)* this town became well-known throughout Croatia. The prison was part of a castle built by the Frankopan counts in the 15th century. The castle walls enclosed a large building with two tall towers at the ends, a Gothic chapel and several houses which were built when Ogulin became a staging post on the *Vojna Krajina* (Military Frontier, *see p39*) in 1627. Part of the structure is given over to the **Regional Museum** which has sections on archaeology, folklore and mountaineering.

A short distance from the fortified town is the Old Castle (Zulumgrad) situated near the Đula abyss: a chasm formed by the Dobra river.

Topusko Toplice ❽

Map D2.
🏘 *4,400.* 🚌 *from Zagreb.* 🛈 *Trg bana Jelačića 4, (044) 885 203.* 🎿 *A summer of sport (30 May–15 Sep).*

The presence of a Cistercian abbey made this a centre for spreading Christianity in the Banovina area (a region of green valleys south of Sisak, between the Sava and Glina rivers). The abbey was founded in 1204 by King Andrew II and a village grew

up around it in the Middle Ages. The complex was destroyed but the foundations are now being excavated. The church, of which parts of the façade survive, surrounded by a dense wood, is also being uncovered. Incisions, difficult to decipher, have been discovered on the base of some of the columns.

The nearby hot water springs (up to 78°C/ 172°F) were used in Roman times and in the first half of the 19th century a thermal spa was established which was frequented by the Emperor Franz Joseph and other court dignitaries. Today the spa treats rheumatic and neurological problems, and the after-effects of incapacitating injuries.

Sisak ❾

Map D2. 🏘 *61,000.* 🚋 *(044) 524 724.* 🚌 *(060) 330 060.* 🛈 *Rimska ulica, (044) 522 655.*

The city of Sisak stands at the point where the rivers Kupa and Odra flow into the Sava and has always played an important role in Croatian history. Its name has changed a number of times over the course of its 1,000 years of existence. It originated as the Illyrian Segestica, becoming Siscia with the Celts, and Colonia Flavia Siscia in the Imperial Roman period. Rome conquered the town after a

Hercules (1st century AD), Sisak museum

bloody battle in which Emperor Augustus was wounded. After the conquest of the Balkans, the emperor nominated it the capital of the Pannonia Savia province, making it an important trading centre.

It was destroyed by Attila in 441, and in the 6th century it was raided by the Avars and Slavs. The town was finally rebuilt by the Croats and became Sisak. It was from here that Prince Ljudevit began the conquest of Croatia in the 8th century. Sisak was destroyed again by the Hungarians in the 10th century, and was also abandoned by the bishop, who transferred the see to Zagreb, but built a fort here. In 1593 this fort was the site of a battle which resulted in the first Turkish defeat in the Balkans.

The town rose again nearby and began to enjoy a long period of prosperity, thanks to the tolls on river traffic. It still has some Baroque buildings, including the old and new town halls.

A park surrounds the **fortress** (Stari Grad) on the River Kupa, south of the city. The fortress was built in the 13th century and reinforced at the time of the Turkish invasions. It has a triangular ground-plan, with three large round brick towers (1544–55), connected by a high wall with openings for firearms. In the park is a beautiful traditional farmhouse. The **Civic Museum** (Gradski Muzej) has material from the Roman settlement.

⚓ **Fortress**
Brkljača Erdelja. 🛈 *(044) 811 811.* 🛠 *for restoration.*

🏛 **Civic Museum**
Kralja Tomislava 8. **Tel** *(044) 811 811.* ⏰ *9am–5pm Tue–Fri; 10am–1pm Sat.* 📷 🚫

Environs
About 20 km (12 miles) southwest is **Gora** which, in the Middle Ages, was the centre of a Županija (county) of the same name. The county seat was a castle which

Fortress of Sisak next to the Kupa river, built in the 13th century

appears in documents in 1242, but which was destroyed by the Turks in 1578. The Gothic church of **St Mary** (Sv. Marija) was also badly damaged but survived and was restored in the 18th century in the Baroque style. The church has chapels on all corners and resembles a castle. Inside are traces of the original paintings, and a fine marble altar and pulpit.

Kostajnica ⑩

Map D2. 🏛 *2,700.*
🚉 *from Zagreb, Sisak.*
🚌 *from Zagreb, Sisak.*
ℹ️ *Vladimira Nazora, (044) 672 366.*

Standing on the left bank of the River Una which, for much of its length, marks the border between Croatia and Bosnia-Herzegovina, this village still bears the signs of damage from the recent war. On an island, near a destroyed bridge, is a castle built in the Middle Ages but frequently razed. Only three towers connected by a high wall remain in the wake of the last war. The church and monastery of **St Anthony of Padua**, built after the Turks left at the end of the 17th century, have been restored but are without furnishings (some of the Baroque altars were famous for their beauty).

Environs

Around 14 km (9 miles) to the southwest is **Zrin**, where the ruins of a castle built in the 14th century by the Babonić family stand on a hill. In 1347 it passed to the Bribir princes of Šubić. A

The tulip-shaped monument by Bogdanović in Jasenovac cemetery

branch of the family took the name of Zrinski after the village around the castle. It was occupied by the Turks from 1577 until the end of the 17th century when they destroyed it.

The Zrinskis played an important role in Croatia's history: as fierce defenders against the Turks; then as the authors of the failed attempt to free the territory from Habsburg rule *(see p177)*.

Jasenovac ⑪

Map E2. 🏛 *1,200.* 🚉 *from Sisak.*
🚌 *from Sisak.* ℹ️ *Trg kralja Petra Svačića 3, (044) 672 366.*

This town is notorious as the place where, during World War II, tens of thousands of prisoners of war, Jews, Gypsies, Serbs and Croats, perished in the concentration camp which was located here. In memory of this terrible genocide, a large

tulip-shaped monument, designed by the artist Bogdan Bogdanović, has been erected in the centre of the cemetery.

The church of St Luke in Novska

Novska ⑫

Map E2. 🏛 *8,000.*
🚉 *from Zagreb, Sisak, (044) 600 060.* 🚌 *from Zagreb, Sisak.*
ℹ️ *Trg Luke Ilića Oriovčanina 2, (044) 601 305.*

The town of Novska is the starting point for visiting the Lonjsko Polje Nature Park *(see p176)* and for excursions to the Psunj mountains.

The church of **St Luke** (Sv. Luka) has Gothic origins but was rebuilt in the Baroque style. It has a fine altar and a painting by the modern painter Z Šulentić.

In the **Bauer Gallery** there are many works by Naive and contemporary artists.

Novska's economy is based on industry and trade and rail and road links are good.

The castle of medieval origins in Kostajnica, on the banks of the Una

Nesting storks in the Lonjsko Polje Nature Park

Lonjsko Polje Nature Park ⑬

Map D2. **Park office (Jasenovac)**
🛈 *(044) 672 080. Entrance at Čigoć*
🛈 *(044) 715 115.* ⏰ *8am–4pm daily.* 🖳 **www.pp-lonjsko-polje.hr**

The wide bend in the River Sava between Sisak and Nova Gradiška has been a special ornithological reserve since 1963. It became a nature reserve in 1987 to protect an area of 506 sq km (195 sq miles). This vast area was regularly flooded by the river and its tributaries (Lonja, Ilova, Pakra and Čazma) during the thaw, and in the summer and early autumn the waters would recede. Since the 1960s parts of the wetlands have been drained and even though the area is now just a fraction of its original size (it now covers 6.5 sq km/2.51 sq miles), the park is still one of the most fascinating marshes in Europe.

Woods of oak, poplar, ash and willow trees grow along the banks of the river and on the higher ground, while the dry fields are used as grazing for sheep in the summer months. Wild boar live here, as well as deer, and there are also black Turopolje pigs and Posavina horses, both of which are protected species.

The park is an important stopping place for black storks, which arrive in spring and leave in autumn after nesting, for numerous species of heron, for egrets and a variety of birds of prey, including the rare harrier and white-tailed eagles.

Kutina ⑭

Map D2. 🏠 *15,000.* 🚂 *(044) 682 381.* 🚌 *(044) 682 605.* ℹ️ *Hrvatskih branitelja 2, (044) 681 004.*

Kutina, in the Moslavina region, was built over the ruins of a Roman *castrum* and numerous finds have been discovered. The town is linked to two castles; Kutinjac Grad, documented in 1256, and the fortress of Plodvin, however only ruins and parts of the walls remain.

Kutina flourished again in the 17th century, developing on the plain south of the fortress. It is here that the church of **Our Lady of the Snow** (Snježna Marija) was built by Count Karl Erdödy in around 1770. The church is surrounded by a covered portico and is decorated inside with stucco and *trompe-l'oeil* paintings by Josip Görner. The sculpture and the inlaid wooden furnishings which enclose the altar of the Holy Sepulchre are a unique example of Baroque composition.

Erdödy Castle, rebuilt in 1895, houses the **Museum of Moslavina** (Muzej Moslavine) which tells the history and folklore of Moslavina, through documents, objects and traditional costumes.

🏛 **Museum of Moslavina**
Trg kralja Tomislava 13. *Tel (044) 683 548.* ⏰ *8am–1pm Mon–Fri.*

Interior of the church of Our Lady of the Snow in Kutina

Environs
Around 50 km (31 miles) northwest of Kutina is **Ivanić-Grad** and the nearby towns of **Klostar Ivanić** and **Križ**. In Ivanić- Grad there are workshops making pretty flax and linen products, keeping local traditions alive.

In Klostar Ivanić there is a Franciscan monastery founded in 1508 and the church of St Mary (Sv. Marija), with collections of silver, paintings and richly illustrated music codices.

In Kriz, the parish church of the Cross was founded by the Knights Templar in the 11th century. The church has a decorative Baroque interior and a magnificent 1787 organ.

Some remains of the old fortifications around Garić

Garić ⑮

Map D2. 🏠 *76 (Podgarić).*
🛈 **Regional**: *Trg Eugena Kvaternika 4, Bjelovar, (043) 243 944.*

On a hill in the Moslavačka chain (Moslavačka Gora) near Podgarić stand the ruins of the fortified town of Garić, noted as a *castrum* in 1256. In 1277, it was granted by the king to Timotej, Bishop of Zagreb, who entrusted its defence to the counts of Gardun, and later to the counts of Celje. Nearby, below Garić, the Pauline order founded the monastery of St Mary in 1295. In 1544 the town and the monastery were destroyed by the Turks.

The fortified town was protected by high walls and was an irregular shape. There was a moat with towers, and further towers inside the walls.

The Zrinski and Frankopan Dynasties

Dujmo, count of Krk, died in 1163 and his descendants took the name of Frankopan *(Frangere Panem)* after Venice confirmed the family's rule over Krk. They were allied with Venice until 1480 when they were forced to surrender the island. However, they still had vast estates given to them by the Hungarian kings. The Šubić family became counts of Bribir when they were granted the town by King Andrew II in 1290, and counts of Zrinski in 1347 when they were obliged to move to Zrin *(see p175)*. The execution of the Ban of Croatia, Petar Zrinski, and his brother-in-law Franjo Krsto Frankopan in 1671 ended the two most powerful Croatian dynasties. The Habsburgs confiscated their property and the Zrinski line died out. A branch of the Frankopan family still survives in Friuli, Italy.

Franjo Krsto Frankopan *(1645?–1671), great grandson of Krsto Frankopan and Mario Frangipane's heir (the Roman branch of the family), was publicly executed in Wiener Neustadt in 1671, for his part in a plot against the Empire.*

Krsto Frankopan, *(1480?–1527), son of Bernard, Ban of Croatia, and Louise of Aragon, was Emperor Maximilian's general in the war against Venice in the early 16th century. He was imprisoned in Venice and died fighting for the independence of Hungary, of which Croatia was part.*

Franjo Krsto Frankopan awaiting execution

Petar Zrinski

EXECUTION OF THE REBELS

On 30 April 1671, in the town square in Wiener Neustadt, the Ban of Croatia, Petar Zrinski, and his brother-in-law, Marquis Krsto Frankopan, were beheaded on charges of high treason on the orders of Emperor Leopold I. The two brothers-in-law had attempted to form a coalition of the Croatian feudal lords in order to limit Austro-Hungarian influence.

Nikola Zrinski *fought against the Turks and was a defender of Christianity. He died in the Battle of Siget in 1566, after he refused the sultan's offer to make him Governor of Croatia if he abandoned the Emperor.*

Petar Zrinski *was the Ban (governor) from 1664, and the leader of the movement which sought to limit Habsburg activity in Croatia. The attempted revolt was foiled by betrayals and the promise of a possible agreement. The two leaders went to Vienna to negotiate with the Emperor. When they reached the capital they were imprisoned, and a few months later were beheaded.*

SLAVONIA AND BARANJA

The easternmost part of northern Croatia, between Hungary, Serbia and Bosnia-Herzegovina, is one of the most fertile areas of Europe, known as "the granary" of Croatia. The landscape of Slavonia and Baranja is characterized by expanses of wheat and maize fields and hills covered with vineyards or ancient woods. The main city, Osijek, is famous for its fortified centre.

First inhabited by the Illyrians, present-day Slavonia and Baranja came into contact with the Roman world in the 2nd century BC. It took the Romans more than 200 years to subdue the inhabitants of this region, which they referred to as Pannonia. From 402 Pannonia was invaded, first by the Goths, then the Huns, Visigoths, Burgundians, Gepids, Longobards, Sarmatians and finally the Avars. When the Slavs arrived, very little remained of Roman rule, and the land, ever since then called Slavonia, was practically uninhabited.

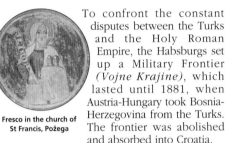

Fresco in the church of St Francis, Požega

In 925 the Kingdom of the Croat Sovereigns was set up and this lasted until 1097, when King Koloman conquered Slavonia and created the Hungarian-Croat kingdom. Following the Battle of Mohács in 1526, Slavonia became part of the Ottoman Empire, and remained so until 1689.

To confront the constant disputes between the Turks and the Holy Roman Empire, the Habsburgs set up a Military Frontier *(Vojne Krajine)*, which lasted until 1881, when Austria-Hungary took Bosnia-Herzegovina from the Turks. The frontier was abolished and absorbed into Croatia.

When war broke out in 1991, the presence of Serb villages was a pretext for the Serbian occupation of Slavonia. In 1995, under the auspices of the United Nations, control of Slavonia reverted back to the Croatians. Although war damage is still visible along the border, particularly in Vukovar, great efforts are being made with rebuilding and Slavonia is once again well worth visiting for its historical treasures. It is also an area of great natural beauty and includes the nature reserve of Kopački Rit, a wetlands sanctuary for wildfowl.

Local people in the typical traditional costumes of the region

◁ The tall spires of the Neo-Gothic cathedral in Osijek *(see p188)*, with the River Drava in the background

Exploring Slavonia and Baranja

Slavonia, the region between the rivers Sava, Drava
and Danube, is made up of a vast rolling alluvial plain
with chains of hills at its edges which are covered in
woods and vineyards. At one time the rivers turned the
area into an enormous swamp for many months of the
year. Baranja is a triangular area of land in the far
northeast, bordered at the extreme tip by the rivers
Drava and Danube and the Hungarian border.

The plains are covered in fields of maize and the
hills are given over to viticulture. In the southern
corner, the Drava river regularly
overflows from spring to
autumn to create a broad
area of marshland, now the
Kopački Rit Nature Park.
The park is an important
wildlife sanctuary, a refuge
for hundreds of different
species of bird, including
the rare black stork.

On the right bank of the Drava
river is Slavonia's main city, Osijek.
It has wide avenues, parks, and 19th-
century, Viennese-style buildings, as
well as a Neo-Gothic cathedral.

**The Baroque belfry of
St Roch in Virovitica**

SIGHTS AT A GLANCE

The countryside around Slavonski Brod

GETTING AROUND

For many years Osijek was a rail, road and river junction of some importance. Since the recent war, rail and river traffic has become less significant. However, Osijek is still the centre of the road system in the area and, thanks to a good network, the city can easily be reached from Slavonia and Baranja using state road number 2 heading south from Varaždin, or the same number 2 road north from Vukovar and the E73 from Hungary. There is also an efficient public bus service. About 7 km (4 miles) from Osijek there is a domestic airport with daily connections to Zagreb. Osijek itself has an excellent tram service which makes it easy to get around the city.

LOCATOR MAP

SEE ALSO

• **Where to Stay** pp232–3

• **Where to Eat** p248–9

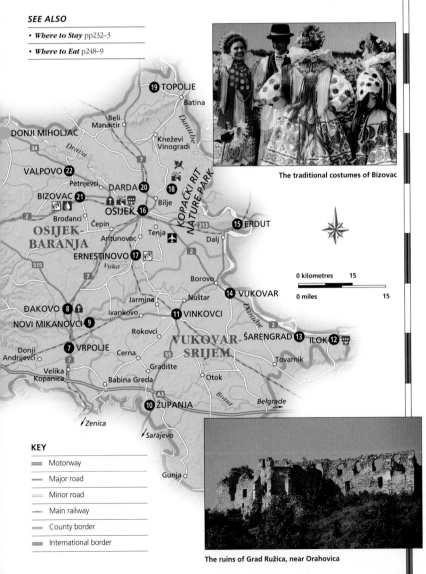

The traditional costumes of Bizovac

⑲ TOPOLJE
Batina

Beli Manastir
DONJI MIHOLJAC
Kneževi Vinogradi

Drava
34
7

VALPOVO ㉒
Petnjevci
DARDA ⑳
BIZOVAC ㉑
Bilje
2
Brodanci
OSIJEK ⑯
KOPAČKI RIT NATURE PARK
Čepin

OSIJEK-
BARANJA
Antunovac
Tenja
213
ERDUT ⑮
Dalj
515
ERNESTINOVO ⑰
Vuka
2

Borovo
7
VUKOVAR ⑭
Jarmina
Nuštar
ĐAKOVO ⑧
Ivankovo
VINKOVCI ⑪ ⑪
NOVI MIKANOVCI ⑨
Rokovci

VUKOVAR-
ŠARENGRAD ⑬ ILOK ⑫
SRIJEM
Donji Andrijevci
VRPOLJE ⑦ ⑦
Cerna
55
Tovarnik
Velika Kopanica
Gradište
Otok
Babina Greda
Bosut

A3
⑩ ŽUPANJA
Belgrade

Zenica

Sarajevo

0 kilometres 15

0 miles 15

KEY

═══ Motorway

─── Major road

⋯⋯ Minor road

╌╌╌ Main railway

═══ County border

▬▬▬ International border

Gunja

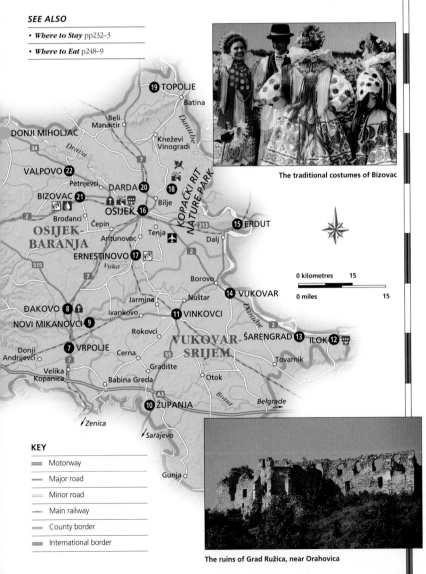

The ruins of Grad Ružica, near Orahovica

Daruvar ❶

Map E2. 🏛 *10,000.* ✈ *Osijek, 91 km (56 miles); Zagreb, 150 km (93 miles).* 🚃 🚌 🛈 *Julijev Park 1, (043) 623 000.* 🍷 *Wine exhibition (May).*

This place was known by the name of Aquae Balissae in the time of the Roman Empire for the quality of its hot water spring, the source of which is at the foot of the Papuk mountains.

The town developed from three medieval settlements. In 1760 the area was given to a Hungarian count, Antun Janković, who built a Baroque manor and the first **spa**. Today, Daruvar (meaning "city of the crane") has a hotel and a **Medical Centre** (Daruvarske Toplice), offering the spa waters.

There are two 18th-century churches in the town, one Catholic and one Orthodox. Daruvar is also a centre for the Czech people in Croatia, who maintain the Czech language and customs.

🛁 **Spa**
Julijev Park. **Tel** *(043) 331 215.*

Lipik ❷

Map E2. 🏛 *11,300.* ✈ *Osijek, 93 km (58 miles); Zagreb, 93 km (58 miles).* 🚃 🚌 *from Pakrac.* 🛈 *Ulica Marije Terezije 27, (034) 421 001.* 🍷 *Day of the city (4 Nov).*

The area (Aquae Balissae) was known in Roman times for its waters. In the early 19th century the hot water spring, rich in fluorine, sodium and calcium, was rediscovered and Lipik became one of the most famous spas in Croatia. It was especially popular between the two World Wars. Lipik was seriously damaged in the 1991 war, but a new **spa** has been built and the hotels and medical centres restored. Lipik is also known as a centre for breeding the famous Lipizzaner horses. The breed originated in the 16th century in Lipizza in Slovenia.

🛁 **Spa (Toplice)**
Marije Terezije 5. **Tel** *(034) 421 322.*

Baroque building in Požega's main square

Nova Gradiška ❸

Map E2. 🏛 *14,800.* ✈ *Osijek, 93 km (58 miles); Zagreb, 155 km (96 miles).* 🚃 *(035) 361 610* 🚌 *(035) 361 219* 🛈 *Slavonskih graničara 15, (035) 361 494.*

In 1725 this town was founded as Fredrichsdorf by the Viennese, who planned to build a fortress here. The town, situated at the foot of Mount Psunj, is built on a fertile plain. An agricultural market is regularly held in the main square, which is lined with Baroque buildings.

The Neo-Classical church of St Stephen of Hungary (Sv. Stjepan Kralj) is now the **Immaculate Conception**. The Baroque **Sanctuary of St Theresa** (Sv. Terezija) dates from 1756.

🛈 **Immaculate Conception**
Aloizija Stepinca 1. **Tel** *(035) 362 203.* 🕐 *8am–6pm daily.*

The Baroque Sanctuary of St Theresa in Nova Gradiška

Požega ❹

Map E2. 🏛 *21,000.* ✈ *Osijek, 67 km (42 miles); Zagreb, 175 km (109 miles).* 🚃 *(034) 273 911* 🚌 *(034) 273 133* 🛈 **Local:** *Trg Sv. Trojstva 1, (034) 274 900.* **Regional:** *Županijska 7, (034) 272 505/668.* 🍷 *Feast of St Gregory (12 Mar), Music Festival Zlatne zice Slavonije (Sep).*

The Romans first founded this town, a halfway settlement between the towns now called Sisak and Osijek, with the name of Incerum. In the 11th century it was one of the centres from which the heretical movement of the Bogomili spread; after their repression in the 12th century the city was granted to the Templars by King Bela IV.

In 1227 the Franciscans founded a monastery, the church of which was used as a mosque during the Turkish occupation. In the 18th and 19th centuries the town was called the "Athens of Slavonia" for the cultural events held to commemorate the expulsion of the Turks in 1691. The city took on a new look during this period: in the main square, Trg Sv. Trojstva, buildings with stucco and Baroque porticoes were built.

In the square stands a column, a memorial to plague victims made in 1749 by Gabrijel Granić. To one side of the square is the renovated 18th-century church of **St Francis** (Sv. Franjo). The monastery alongside still houses a community of Franciscan monks.

Interesting examples of Baroque architecture in the town include the Jesuit College (1711) and Gymnasium (1726), opened by the Jesuits who, in 1763, also founded the Požega Academy. Dating from 1763, the church of **St Theresa** (Sv. Terezija Avilska) became a cathedral in 1997. The frescoed walls are by Celestin Medović and Oton Iveković.

The church of **St Lawrence** (Sv. Lovro, 14th century) was renovated in Baroque style in the early 18th century. It still has some 14th-century frescoes. There are also tombstones testifying to the city's glory; one is for the poet Antun Kanižlić (1699–1777). In the square between the church of St Francis and the Jesuit College is a statue of Luka Ibrišimović, a Franciscan who distinguished himself in the battles against the Turks.

14th-century fresco in the church of St Lawrence, Požega

The **Civic Museum** (Gradski Muzej) contains an assortment of archaeological finds, Romanesque reliefs and Baroque paintings.

Every year on 12 March Požega holds an event called Grgurevo, to commemorate a local victory over the Turks won in 1688.

🏛 **Civic Museum**
Matice Hrvatske 1. *Tel (034) 272 130.* ☐ *8am–3pm, Mon–Fri.*

⛪ **St Theresa**
Trg Sv. Terezije 13. *Tel (034) 274 321.* ☐ *8am–noon, 3–6pm daily.*

Kutjevo ❺

Map F2. 🏘 *7,400.* 🚉 *Osijek 62 km (38 miles).* 🚌 *Našice, 27 km (17 miles).* ℹ️ *Republike Hrvatske 77, (034) 255 092/3.* 🎭 *Feast of St Gregory (12 Mar).*

An important wine-producing centre, the town is famous for a winery founded by the Cistercians. In 1232, the order built a monastery here and encouraged the cultivation of vines. After Turkish rule, at the end of the 17th century, Jesuits took over the monastery and wine-making resumed. The Cistercian cellars are still intact and wine is still an important industry. The Jesuits also built the church of **St Mary** (Sv. Marija) in 1732, which houses a painting of the Madonna with Child by A Cebej (1759).

Slavonski Brod ❻

Map F3. 🏘 *70,000.* 🚉 *Osijek, 47 km (29 miles); Zagreb, 197 km (122 miles).* 🚌 *(060) 333 444.* 🚏 *Trg Hrvatskog proljeća, (035) 444 300.* ℹ️ **Local:** *Trg Pobjede 28, (035) 447 721.* **Regional:** *Petra Krešimira IV 1, (035) 408 393.* 🎭 *Brodsko kolo: folk festival (mid-Jun).* **www**.tzgsb.hr

Built on the site of the Roman town Marsonia, this town was placed so as to monitor the traffic on the river Sava, the border with

Baroque altar in Holy Trinity church in Slavonski Brod

Bosnia-Herzegovina. The town belonged to the counts Berislavić-Grabarski from the Middle Ages to 1526 when it was conquered by the Turks, who occupied it until 1691.

To defend the border, in 1741 the Viennese government built a fort with barracks, residences for governors and religious buildings. Damaged during World War II and again in the war in 1991, the buildings are under repair: some are used as schools and others house museums and galleries.

The town has grown beyond the original ramparts. Along the banks of the Sava is a **Franciscan Monastery**, dating from 1725, recently renovated, and the Baroque church of the **Holy Trinity** (Sv. Trojstvo) with many statues, paintings and magnificent altars.

The **Regional Civic Museum** (Muzej Brodskog Posavlja) contains historic documents and archaeological finds from the region.

The well-known Croatian writer, Ivana Brlić-Mažuranić (1874–1938), spent much of her life in this town. She wrote fairytales for children: among her most famous works are *Fisherman Palunco, Jagor* and *The Forest of Stribor*. The town is also known for its folklore festival (Brodsko kolo) which is held every year in June.

🏛 **Regional Civic Museum**
Ulica Ante Starčevica 40. *Tel (035) 447 415.* ☐ *8am–4pm Mon–Sat, 10am–1pm Sun.* ● *25 Dec, 1 Jan.* 🎫

The cloisters in the Franciscan monastery, Slavonski Brod

View of the 19th-century red-brick Cathedral of St Peter in Đakovo

Vrpolje ❼

Map F3. 🏠 *2,200.*
✈ *Osijek, 39 km (24 miles).* 🚌 *from Osijek.* 🛈 **Regional:** *Petra Krešimira IV, 1, Slavonski Brod (035) 408 393.*

A small country town, Vrpolje is known as the birthplace of the sculptor Ivan Meštrović (1883–1962) *(see p157).* Many of the artist's works, donated to the town he held in great affection, can be seen here. In the small parish church of **St Ivan** (Sveti Ivan Krstitelj, 1774) is his statue of St John the Baptist, a relief and a crucifix, while outside is a striking *Bust of a Woman.* The **Gallery** (Spomen Galerija) has 30 of his works on display: casts, bronzes and wooden sculptures.

Bust of a Woman by Meštrović, Vrpolje

Đakovo ❽

Map F2. 🏠 *25,000.* ✈ *Osijek, 36 km (22 miles).* 🚆 *(031) 811 360.* 🚌 *(031) 811 390.* 🛈 *Kralja Tomislava 3, (031) 812 319.* **Tel** *(031) 811 233.* 🎎 *Đakovo embroidery, Đakovački Vezovi (first week in Jul).* **www**.tz-djakovo.hr

In medieval times this town was known by the name of Civitas Dyaco, and later as Castrum Dyaco. Late in the 13th century it became a bishopric, and its influence extended over most of Slavonia and Bosnia.

Conquered and destroyed by the Turks in 1536, it became a Muslim centre and a mosque was built. After Turkish rule, the city was renovated. Only the mosque, at the end of the central avenue, was retained. It was converted into the parish church of All Saints (Svi Sveti) in the 18th century.

The central square is dominated by the **Cathedral of St Peter** (Sv. Petar), built between 1866 and 1882 by Bishop Josip Juraj Strossmayer; the project was the work of the Viennese architects Karl Rösner and Friedrich von Schmidt. The imposing façade is flanked by two 84-m (275-ft) belfries. The interior has frescoes by Maksimilijan and Ljudevit Seitz, sculptures by Ignazio Donegani and Tomas Vodcka and decorations by Giuseppe Voltolini from the 19th century. The crypt houses the tombs of the bishops Strossmayer and Ivan de Zela. Next to the church is the 18th-century Bishop's Palace, which has an ornate Baroque doorway.

The Festival of Embroidery of Đakovo (Đakovački Vezovi) is held at the beginning of July with displays of traditional local costumes, folk dancing and wine tasting.

🏛 **Cathedral of St Peter**
Strossmayerov trg. **Tel** *(031) 802 225.* ⏰ *6am–noon, 3–8pm daily.*

Novi Mikanovci ❾

Map F2. 🏠 *200.* ✈ *Osijek, 50 km (31 miles).* 🚆 *Stari Mikanovci, 3 km (2 miles).* 🛈 *(032) 203 137.*

The village is famous for the small Romanesque church of **St Bartholomew** (Sveti Bartol), from the first half of the 13th century, a rare example of architecture from before Turkish rule. The church stands in a cemetery and is called the "Tower of Pisa of Slavonia" because of its leaning bell tower, which appears to be held up by the façade. At the cemetery entrance is a colourful statue of St Bartholomew.

Županja ❿

Map F3. 🏠 *12,000.* ✈ *Osijek, 67 km (41 miles).* 🚆 *(032) 831 183.* 🛈 *Josipa Jurja Strossmayera 1, (032) 832 711.* 🎎 *Folklore Festival, Šokačko Sijelo (Feb).*

On the border with Bosnia-Herzegovina, Županja lies along a wide bend in the Sava River. The area has been inhabited since ancient times; Bronze Age finds have been discovered in a necropolis. One of the first Croat settlements was set up here. After Turkish rule it became one of the military staging posts on the *Vojne Krajine* (Military Frontier) *(see p39)* and a trading centre.

The **Frontier House** is a wooden building originally from the early 19th century, used by tax collectors. Burnt

Embroidered head-dress in the Ethnographic Museum, Županja

down during the recent bombings and now rebuilt, it houses the **Ethnographic Museum** (Zavičajni Muzej "Stjepan Gruber").

🏛 **Ethnographic Museum**
Savska 3. *Tel (032) 837 101.*
◯ *9am–1pm Mon–Fri; during exhibitions Sat & Sun 10am–noon.*

Vinkovci ⑪

Map F2. 🏘 *36,000.* ✈ *Osijek, 43 km (27 miles).* 🚊 *(060) 333 444.*
🚌 *(032) 308 937.* ⓘ **Local:** *Trg bana Josipa Šokčevića 3, (032) 334 653;* **Regional:** *Glagoljaška 27, (032) 344 034.* 🎭 *Autumn in Vinkovci, Vinkovačke Jeseni (Sep).*

Founded by the Romans with the name of Aurelia Cibalae, this was the birthplace of the Emperors Valens and Valentinian, and a bishop's see from the 4th century. In the Middle Ages it was called Zenthelye, because of the presence of the (now abandoned) church of **St Elias** (Sv. Ilija). The church dates from the 12th century, and is one of the oldest monuments in Slavonia.

The **Civic Museum** (Gradski Muzej), situated in the former 18th-century Austrian barracks in the main square, holds finds from the Roman necropolis and has a folklore collection. Large Roman sarcophagi are displayed in front of the museum.

Exhibit in the Civic Museum, Vinkovci

Facing the garden is the church of SS Eusebius and Pollio (Sv. Euzebije i Polion) from 1775, and the Town Hall, both under repair.

Each September a festival of music and popular traditions is held in the town and groups from all over the country take part. The streets are decorated, stallholders sell local produce, and musicians and jugglers perform.

🏛 **Civic Museum**
Trg bana Šokčevica. *Tel (032) 332 504.* ◯ *10am–1pm, 5–7pm Tue–Fri; 10am–1pm Sat–Sun.* 📷 📷

The church of St Ivan, next to the fortified walls in Ilok

Ilok ⑫

Map G2. 🏘 *6,800.* ✈ *Osijek, 62 km (38 miles).* 🚊 *Vukovar, 39 km (24 miles).* ⓘ **Local:** *Trg Nikole Iločkog 2, (032) 590 020.* **Regional:** *Glagoljaška 27, Vinkovci, (032) 344 034.* 🎭 *Grape harvest festival (Sep–Oct).*

Overlooking a wide loop in the River Danube, Ilok is the easternmost city in Croatia and the centre of the region of Srijem, famous since Roman times for its wine production. In the late Roman era the city grew in importance and took the name of Cuccium. In the Middle Ages it was a *castrum* with high walls, towers and fortified buildings. The defences were reinforced in 1365, and the town was given to Nikola Kont, whose family later acquired the title of Counts of Ilok.

Around the middle of the 15th century, the church and monastery of **St Ivan Kapistran** (Sv. Ivan Kapistran) were built inside the fort. St Ivan Kapistran was a Franciscan who was famous for uniting Christian forces against the Turks and who was buried here in 1456. When Ilok became a major Turkish administrative and military centre in the 16th century, mosques and baths were added to the fortress.

Both the church and the monastery have recently been renovated and between them, long stretches of the ancient walls can still be seen. Parts of one of the Turkish baths are still visible.

In 1683, after his role in winning the battle of Vienna, Commander Livio Odescalchi was given the town of Ilok by the Austrian Emperor. In this idyllic setting he built a U-shaped mansion, **Odescalchi Manor**. Today, the mansion houses the Odescalchi Collection, a restaurant, public offices and the **Civic Museum** (Gradski Muzej) with archaeological and ethnographic collections. The wines of Ilok are still produced here in the cellars, among them a dry white wine called Traminac.

🏰 **Church and Monastery of St Ivan Kapistran**
Fra Bernardina Lejakovića 13.
Tel (032) 746 021. ◯ *by appt or before mass.*

🏛 **Odescalchi Manor and Civic Museum**
Tel (032) 529 088.
◯ *7am–3pm, Mon–Fri, for wine tastings only.* **Civic Museum** 📷 *for restoration.*

The mansion built by Commander Livio Odescalchi in Ilok

Tabernacle in the Franciscan monastery in Šarengrad

Šarengrad ⑬

Map G2. 🏘 100. ✈ Osijek, 53 km (33 miles). 🚆 Vukovar, 30 km (19 miles). ℹ **Local:** (032) 746 076; **Regional:** Vinkovci, (032) 344 034.

A medieval fort once controlled the heavy traffic along the river Danube at this spot. In the 15th century, Count Ivan Maroivički added a **Franciscan Monastery**. The fort, however, was destroyed during the war with the Turks and the area remained uninhabited until their departure late in the 17th century.

With the return of the inhabitants, the monks set up a school and collected archaeological items for a museum.

During the break-up of former Yugoslavia between 1991 and 1995, the area was heavily bombed. The church and monastery have since been restored and the statue of St Anthony of Padua has been put back in position. From the hill there are good views of the Danube.

Vukovar ⑭

Map G2. 🏘 45,000. ✈ Osijek, 23 km (14 miles). 🚆 Vinkovačka cesta. 🚌 from Vinkovci. ℹ **Local:** Vukovar, (032) 442 889; **Regional:** Vinkovci, (032) 334 034.

This Baroque city was once known for its churches, elegant 18th-century buildings, numerous museums and art galleries. However, Vukovar has come to symbolize the war which raged in Slavonia in 1991, when it was bombed by the Serbs and the JNA (Yugoslav People's Army). The historic Baroque nucleus was almost totally destroyed. Plans for repair in collaboration with UNESCO are under way but hampered by the lack of international funds.

Vukovar has a very long history, as evidenced by the famous "Dove of Vučedol" from 2000 BC. This vessel was found 5 km (3 miles) from Vukovar and is now in the Archaeological Museum in Zagreb (see pp162–3).

The city, at the confluence of the Danube and the river Vuka, was known by the name of Vakovo in the Middle Ages. Later it was given to various families: the Horvat, the Gorjanski and the Talovci. Conquered by the Turks, Vukovar became a military garrison and a key trading centre. After liberation from the Turks in 1687, it resumed its role as an advance post of the Christian Catholic world against the Muslim and Orthodox religions.

In 1736, it was given to the Eltz counts, who called the town Vukovar. As the inhabitants were Catholics or of the Orthodox faith, churches were built for both religions, including a Franciscan monastery (1727).

In 1751, the Eltz family built a huge Baroque mansion. It was nationalized after World War II and then housed the **Civic Museum** (Gradski Muzej). The palace was badly damaged in 1991 and the contents of the museum, along with the Bauer Collection and the Franciscan monastery treasury, were seized and taken to museums in Belgrade and Novi Sad. In December 2001 the collections were returned, and are gradually being restored. The Catholic church of SS Philip and James (Sv. Filip i Jakov) and the Orthodox church of

The Dove of Vučedol, symbol of Vukovar

St Nicholas (Sv. Nikola) were also badly damaged in 1991.

🏛 **Civic Museum**
L Ribara u. 2. **Tel** (032) 441 270.
◻ 8am–4pm Mon–Sat.

Erdut ⑮

Map G2. 🏘 1,500. ✈ Osijek, 37 km (23 miles). 🚌 from Osijek. ℹ **Regional:** Sunčana ulica 39, Bizovac, (031) 675 897; Županijska 2, Osijek, (031) 203 755.

The town of Erdut gained a place in history when, on 13 November 1995, an agreement between Croatia and Yugoslavia was drawn up here, setting out the return of Slavonia and Baranja to Croatia after almost four years of Serb occupation.

The town occupies an important strategic position overlooking the Danube, and a fortification was erected in Roman times. In the medieval period a **Castle** was built. It was damaged by the Turks, but then rebuilt by them. The castle was also used by the Habsburgs. Two towers, one circular and one square, survive from the old castle.

The large **Cseh Mansion**, where the 1995 agreement was drawn up, is now under repair. It was built in the 19th century by the Cseh family, lords of the manor in the area from the early 18th century.

The circular tower of the medieval castle, Erdut

Osijek ⑯

See pp190–93.

A naive outdoor sculpture, Ernestinovo

Ernestinovo ⑰

Map F2. 👥 *200.* ✈ *Osijek, 20 km (12 miles).* 🚌 *from Osijek.* ℹ **County:** *Sunčana ulica 39, Bizovac, (031) 675 112; Županijska 2, Osijek, (031) 214 852.* 🎭 *Open-air exhibition of sculpture (Aug).*

For many years, well-known sculptors have been meeting in Ernestinovo to present their work in a summer show. This small village is now famous for its open-air exhibitions. The first exhibition was organized in 1976 by the sculptor Petar Smajić. It took place in exile from 1991 to 1996 and returned to Ernestinovo the following year. Many works of art are displayed and offered for sale in the village galleries. Ernestinovo was badly damaged during the recent war, but the village is now being rebuilt.

Kopački Rit Nature Park ⑱

See pp194–5.

Topolje ⑲

Map F2. 👥 *200.* ✈ *Osijek, 46 km (28 miles).* 🚉 *Beli Manastir, 16 km (10 miles).* 🚌 *from Osijek.* ℹ **Regional:** *Sunčana ulica 39, Bizovac, (031) 675 112.*

In 1687, after the victory in Vienna over the Turks, Prince Eugene of Savoy, commander of the Imperial forces, decided to build a church to commemorate the victory in the countryside surrounding Topolje. The location has particular charm as the church is set among trees standing alone among a patchwork of fields of maize and tobacco. The church was sacked, however, and nearly completely destroyed in the conflicts following the break-up of former Yugoslavia. The building is now undergoing extensive restoration although the splendid furnishings have sadly been lost.

Here, as in Darda, there are several Hungarian communities, who, together with the Croats, are gradually returning after their exile during the Yugoslav occupation. The Hungarian-style houses with their overhanging roofs add a distinctive character to the area. In the autumn, long strings of chilli peppers can be seen hanging out to dry in the sun.

Environs

Around 10 km (6 miles) east of Topolje is the town of **Batina**. In Roman times this was the site of a fortress on the banks of the River Danube and was known by the name of Ad Militarae. Until the war of 1991, which depopulated this small town set among hills and vineyards, there was a bridge connecting Baranja with Hungary and Vojvodina, but since its destruction, both river and road traffic have stopped.

On one of the small hills, a

Hungarian-style houses with chilli peppers hanging to dry, Topolje

tall monument in white stone with a female figure in bronze representing Victory commemorates the fallen of World War II. It is the work of one of the great Croatian artists of the 20th century, Antun Augustinčić.

Mansion of the Esterházy barons, now the Town Hall of Darda

Darda ⑳

Map F2. 👥 *6,700.* ✈ *Osijek, 15km (9 miles).* 🚌 *from Osijek.* ℹ **Regional:** *Sunčana ulica 39, Bizovac, (031) 675 112.*

An elegant mansion built by the Esterházy barons in the second half of the 18th century, now renovated and used as the Town Hall, is the only evidence of Darda's history. Darda was once a fortified city, represented on 17th-century maps as a large fortress, connected to Osijek by the 8-km (5-mile) bridge of Solimano. Built in 1566 to cross marshland, the bridge was destroyed in 1664 by Nikola Zrinski *(see p177)* to block the Turkish army. On that occasion the city was subsequently devastated.

In the recent war in the 1990s, two 18th-century churches were destroyed: the Catholic church of St John the Baptist (Sv. Ivan Krstitelj) and the Orthodox church of St Michael (Sv. Mihajlo).

Environs

Bilje, 4 km (2 miles) south of Darda, is the site of the information office for the Kopački Rit Nature Park *(see pp194–5)*. It is housed in a palace built by Prince Eugene of Savoy, who was granted the small town of Bilje after the victory in Vienna over the Turks (1687).

Osijek ⑯

The capital of Slavonia sits in the middle of a fertile plain. It is a centre of industry, a university town, and a lively Central European city with wide roads linking three districts: the Fort (Tvrđa), Lower Town (Donji grad) and Upper Town (Gornji grad). The city developed in 1786 when the three areas merged. Due to its position on the River Drava, Osijek has always played a strategic role. In 1806 Emperor Francis I declared it a Royal Free Town (this document is now in the Museum of Slavonia). In 1991, after the declaration of independence by Croatia, the city was bombed for over a year by Yugoslav forces and much of the old centre (Upper Town) was damaged. Liberated in 1995, in 1998 Osijek became part of the Croat state again.

View of the main square in the heart of Tvrđa

Exploring Osijek

The fort (Tvrđa) is the fortified centre of Osijek. It was constructed in the early 18th century after liberation from the Turks. Fortunately, Tvrđa did not suffer serious damage during the war in the 1990s. As a result it has preserved its Baroque architecture, which is characterized by simple, austere lines, unusual at this time. This lack of ornamentation was due to the fact that the buildings were intended for use by soldiers and office workers.

Facing Trg Sv. Trojstva, the central square of Tvrđa, named after the Holy Trinity, are various Baroque buildings, including the Building of the Guard, with an 18th-century clock tower, and the General Headquarters of Slavonia, which is now part of the university, recognizable by its monumental Baroque entrance.

The heart of city life is the main square in the Upper Town, Trg Ante Starčevića.

With its shops, bars and restaurants, this is Osijek's modern face, dating back to the second half of the 19th century and the early 20th century. Facing the square is the County building, built in the early 20th century in the Renaissance style.

🏛 Museum of Slavonia
Muzej Slavonije

Trg Sv. Trojstva 6, Tvrđa. **Tel** (031) 208 501. ⬜ 10am–2pm Mon–Fri; 10am–1pm Sat & Sun. 🎫 📷 🚫 📷

On the eastern side is the old Town Hall which has housed the Museum of Slavonia since 1946. Geological, prehistoric, Greek, Illyrian and Roman objects are on display here. One section is dedicated to ancient Roman Mursa with statues, tombstones, architectural pieces and a coin collection.

Other sections are dedicated to folklore with exhibits of richly decorated costumes. Today these clothes provide models for a flourishing handicrafts industry making golden silk fabrics.

🔒 Church of the Holy Cross
Sv. Križ

Franjevačka ulica, Tvrđa. **Tel** (031) 208 177. ⬜ 8am–noon, 3–8pm.

Northeast of the main square, on the site of a sacred medieval building, stands the church of the Holy Cross, built by the Franciscans between 1709 and 1720. Next to this is the monastery (1699–1767) which housed the first printing press in Slavonia (1735), and from the mid-18th century also housed schools of philosophy and theology. In the church is a statue of the Virgin from the 15th century and some liturgical furnishings.

🔒 Church of St Michael
Sv. Mihovil

Trg Jurja Križanića, Tvrđa. **Tel** (031) 208 990. ⬜ before mass.

Standing a little way back from the square is the church of St Michael, which was built by the Jesuits. The façade is flanked by two bell towers, and the monastery has a splendid doorway (1719). Below street level the foundations of the 16th-century Kasim-paša mosque are still visible.

War memorial in Kralja Držislava park

⛲ Europe Avenue
Europska Avenija

This is the main road of Osijek, linking the Fort (Tvrđa) to the Upper Town (Gornji grad). It crosses some of the city's parks, one of which is Kralja Držislava park, site of a striking bronze memorial to the fallen of the 78th Infantry Regiment (*Soldier in the Throes of Death*), by Robert Frangeš-

Interior of the Neo-Gothic church of SS Peter and Paul

Mihanović (1898), which is regarded as the first modern sculpture in Croatia.

🏛 Gallery of Fine Arts
Galerija Likovnih Umjetnosti
Europska Avenija 9. *Tel* (031) 213 587. ☐ *10am–6pm Tue–Fri; 10am–1pm Sat & Sun.* 📷 📷 *by appt.* 🚫

The Gallery of Fine Arts, founded in 1954, is housed in an elegant 19th-century house. There are collections of paintings from the 18th and 19th centuries, as well as works by contemporary Croatian artists. There is also a section dedicated to the "Osijek School".

⛪ Church and Monastery of St James
Sv. Jakov
Kapucinska ulica 41, Gornji grad. *Tel* (031) 201 182. ☐ *8am–noon, 3–8pm.*

The oldest building in the city is the church of St James (1702–27), with a Capuchin monastery. In the sacristy are mid-18th-century paintings about the life of St Francis.

⛪ Church of SS Peter and Paul
Sv. Petar i Pavao
Trg Marina Držića, Gornji grad. *Tel* (031) 310 020. ☐ *noon–3pm, 5–5.30pm.*

This imposing Neo-Gothic church is dedicated to St Peter and St Paul. The church is known as "Katedrala" (cathedral) to the locals because of its size: the façade has towers 90 m (295 ft) high. It was designed by Franz Langenberg and built in the late 19th century. The 40 stained-glass windows and some of the sculptures are by the Viennese artist Eduard Hauser. Most of the windows were bomb-damaged but are now being restored.

VISITORS' CHECKLIST

Map F2. 🏘 107,000. ✈ 5 km (3 miles) Sv. Leopolda Mandića, (031) 215 650. 🚌 Bartula Kašića, (060) 334 466. 🚉 Trg Ružičke, (031) 205 155. 🛈 **Local:** Županijska 2, (031) 203 755; **Regional:** Sunčana ulica. 39, Bizovac, (031) 675 897. 🎭 City day (2 Dec), Summer Nights of Osijek. www.osijek.hr

🎭 Croatian National Theatre
Hrvatsko Narodno Kazalište
Županijska ulica 9, Gornji grad. *Tel* (031) 220 700.

The Croatian National Theatre was built in the Moorish style in the early 19th century. Opera and drama productions are put on from September to May.

Interior of the Croatian National Theatre

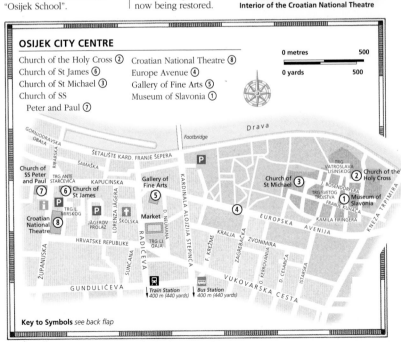

OSIJEK CITY CENTRE

Church of the Holy Cross ②
Church of St James ⑥
Church of St Michael ③
Church of SS Peter and Paul ⑦
Croatian National Theatre ⑧
Europe Avenue ④
Gallery of Fine Arts ⑤
Museum of Slavonia ①

0 metres 500
0 yards 500

Key to Symbols *see back flap*

Street-by-Street: the Fort (Tvrđa)

The fortified centre of Osijek (Tvrđa) was built on the site of the Roman settlement of Mursa, which, in 131 AD, became the capital of Lower Pannonia with the name of Colonia Aelia Mursa. Destroyed by the Avars and rebuilt by the Croats, it

Parchment with the title of "Royal Free Town"

remained a military and administrative centre until it was attacked and burnt by the Turks in 1526. Making the most of the strategic position, the Turks rebuilt the Fort and, under Suleyman II, also constructed a bridge across the Drava. After the expulsion of the Turks in 1687, the Austrian Emperor destroyed the mosques and other reminders of Turkish rule. He then built a fortified series of buildings more like a city than a fort. Tvrđa now houses the Town Hall, the university faculties, and the Museum of Slavonia. The only remaining part of the ramparts is towards the river Drava and includes the "Water Gate" (Vodena Vrata).

★ Church of St Michael
Constructed by Jesuits in the first half of the 18th century, the church has a Baroque façade flanked by two towers.

TRG J. KRIŽANIĆA

FRANJE

KAMILA FIRINGERA

PINTEROVIĆ

KUHAČA

TRG SVETOG TROJSTVO

MARKOVIĆA

BOŠKOVIĆA

KAMILA FIRINGERA

Building of the Guard
On the western side of the square stands the Building of the Guard, with a clock tower from the 18th century and fine porticoes.

KEY

— — — Suggested route

Croatian Academy of Science and Arts

STAR SIGHTS

★ Church of St Michael

★ Museum of Slavonia

Plague Column
The centre of the square is dominated by the "column of the plague", erected in 1729 in thanks for the ending of an outbreak of the disease.

Church and Monastery of the Holy Cross
The church, erected by Franciscans between 1709 and 1720, is next to the monastery which housed the first printing press in Slavonia.

View of Osijek and the River Drava
Splendid views of the city can be enjoyed from the banks of the Drava. It was once important for river trading, but trade is now practically non-existent.

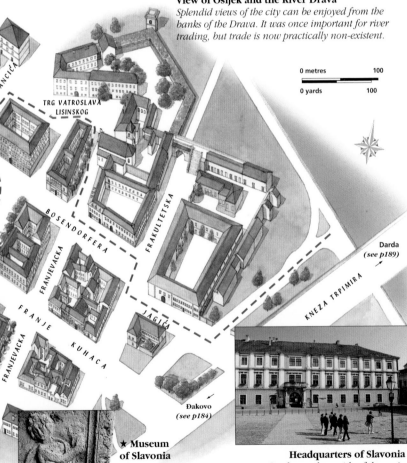

0 metres   100
0 yards   100

ATANCIĆA

TRG VATROSLAVA LISINSKOG

BOSENDORFERA

FRANJEVACKA

FRAKULTETSKA

FRANJE

KUHACA

FRANJEVACKA

JAGIĆA

Darda (see p189)

KNEZA TRPIMIRA

Đakovo (see p184)

★ Museum of Slavonia
This museum contains interesting collections of geological, prehistoric, Greek, Illyrian and Roman material.

Headquarters of Slavonia
On the northern side of the main square of Tvrđa is the former Headquarters of Slavonia, now the University Rectorate, easily recognized by the imposing façade.

Kopački Rit Nature Park ⑱
Park Prirode Kopački Rit

This triangular piece of land is bordered by the final stretch of the river Drava before it meets the Danube. The landscape changes with the seasons and becomes flooded when the Danube overflows. The area covers 170 sq km (65 sq miles) and can turn into an immense wetland marsh. At other times it is a vast grassland plain with pools and ponds. There are also dry areas which support enormous willows and tall oak trees. A nature reserve since 1967, it has a rich and varied fauna and for many months of the year provides a sanctuary for hundreds of different species of bird, both migratory and domestic. A high embankment on the western side stops the further spread of the flood waters. On top is a road which allows cars to cross this part of the park.

White Storks
One of the park's symbols, the white stork is especially visible in the breeding season.

Park Entrance
The main entrance to the Kopački Rit Park is in the village of Bilje (see p189).

OSIJEK

0 kilometres 2

0 miles 2

Black Storks are rare; only a few dozen pairs of the bird inhabit the park.

Sakadaš Canal

Sarvaška Pond

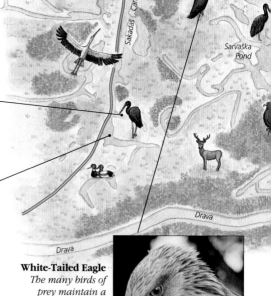

Drava

Drava

Lakes
Forty different species of fish live in the lakes and ponds which form in the park.

White-Tailed Eagle
The many birds of prey maintain a balance among the bird population. The white-tailed eagle is the rarest eagle in Europe.

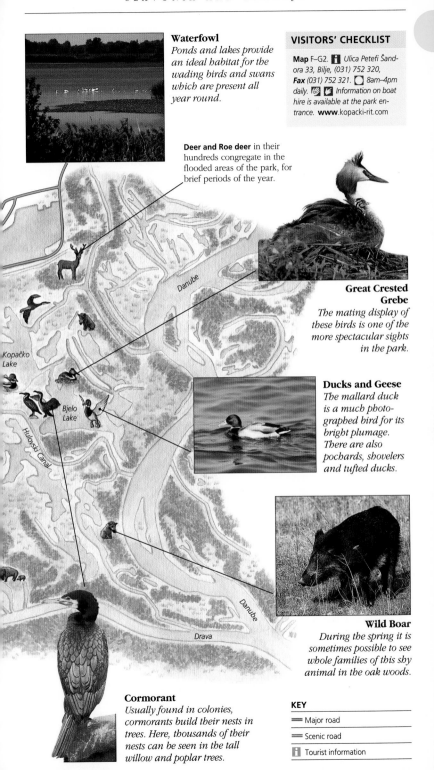

Waterfowl
Ponds and lakes provide an ideal habitat for the wading birds and swans which are present all year round.

Deer and Roe deer in their hundreds congregate in the flooded areas of the park, for brief periods of the year.

Danube

Great Crested Grebe
The mating display of these birds is one of the more spectacular sights in the park.

Kopačko Lake

Bjelo Lake

Hulovski Canal

Ducks and Geese
The mallard duck is a much photo-graphed bird for its bright plumage. There are also pochards, shovelers and tufted ducks.

Danube

Drava

Wild Boar
During the spring it is sometimes possible to see whole families of this shy animal in the oak woods.

Cormorant
Usually found in colonies, cormorants build their nests in trees. Here, thousands of their nests can be seen in the tall willow and poplar trees.

KEY

═══ Major road

═══ Scenic road

🛈 Tourist information

The thermal spa in the village of Bizovac

Bizovac ㉑

Map F2.
🏛 5,000. ✈ Osijek, 20 km (12 miles). 🚉 from Osijek. 🚌 from Osijek. 🛈 **Regional:** Sunčana ulica 39, (031) 675 112.

During the search for petroleum in the middle of the 20th century, a hot water spring was discovered here. The water of the spring reaches a temperature of 90°C (194°F) and is rich in minerals. A few years later, the thermal spa of **Bizovačke Toplice** was built. The spa proved to be extremely successful and it is now an enormous complex including a hotel, two large swimming pools, and cabins for mud baths. Every day hundreds of guests come here to undergo thermal treatments which are helpful in treating rheumatic and respiratory illnesses, and in healing injuries.

The small centre of Bizovac is also well known in Slavonia for its exquisite gold and silver embroidery. The work is carried out by the young women of the area, usually for a commission.

🄴 **Bizovačke Toplice**
Suncana 39. **Tel** (031) 685 100.
www.bizovacke-toplice.hr

Environs
Around 9 km (5 miles) south of Bizovac is the village of **Brodanci**, famous for the Olympics of Ancient Sports, held here in August every year. During the competition, athletes take part in some of the sports once practised by the peasants

of Slavonia, such as tug-of-war, boulder-throwing, bare-back riding and other strenuous challenges and competitions.

A lively popular festival has developed around the event; musicians perform in the streets and there are displays of old crafts. Local handicrafts can be bought and regional food can be sampled.

Valpovo ㉒

Map F2. 🏛 8,200.
✈ Osijek, 30 km (18 miles). 🚌 (031) 651 185. 🛈 Ulica Matije Gupca 32, (031) 656 207. 🎦 Summer in Valpovo: dancing, folk music and theatrical shows (summer).

The centre of Valpovo stands on the remains of the fort of Lovallia, one of many fortified settlements which the Romans established on the Pannonian plain. In the Middle Ages, a castle was erected to keep a look-out over the nearby Drava river. The castle was later granted to the Morović, Gorjanski and Norman families. After the Turkish conquest in 1526, the castle was used as a garrison.

In 1687, after the expulsion of the Turks, the area was handed over to the Hilleprand Prandau family. At the beginning of the 19th century they demolished parts of the castle in order to construct the large building which today houses the **Valpovo Museum** (Muzej Valpovštine). The museum contains period furniture and interesting archaeological finds. The complex stands in a large

The imposing castle at Valpovo, now a museum

park and a moat surrounds the medieval walls, the tower, the new building and the church. A town developed around the fort, and with it the splendid Baroque church of the **Immaculate Conception** (Začeće Marijino) of 1722.

🏛 **Valpovo Museum**
Dvorac Prandan-Norman.
Tel (031) 650 490.
⬤ for restoration. The old castle, park and tower can be visited.

Majláth, a mock-medieval manor in the town of Donji Miholjac

Donji Miholjac ㉓

Map F2. 🏛 7,000. ✈ Osijek, 45 km (28 miles). 🚉 Valpovo, 20 km (12 miles); Našice, 30 km (18 miles). 🚌 (031) 631 207. 🛈 Kolodorska 2, (031) 633 103. 🎦 Miholjačko Sijelo: festival in costume (summer).

On the banks of the Drava river, this small town lies on the Hungarian border. All traces of the past have been erased, except for the church of **St Michael** (Sv. Mihovil). The mock-medieval **Majláth Manor** was built at the beginning of the 20th century by the Majláth family. It has pinnacles and a tall tower on the façade. The manor is now the town hall.

🎪 **Majláth Manor**
Vukovarska 1. **Tel** Tourist Office (031) 633 103. ⬤ by appt. 🎦

Environs
About 25 km (15 miles) west is the village of **Čađavica**. Traces from ancient Croatian settlements have been discovered near here. The Romanesque church of St Peter was used by the Turks as a mosque and was renovated in the 18th century.

Našice

Map F2. 8,300. Osijek, 42 km (26 miles). (060) 333 444. (060) 313 333. Pejačevićev trg 4, (031) 614 951.

A small plateau is the setting for the town of Našice, which is surrounded by vineyards and woods. Built on the site of an ancient settlement, it was referred to in the first half of the 13th century under the name of Nekche, as property of the Templar Knights. After the dissolution of this order in 1312, it passed to the Gorjanski nobles and, later, through marriage, to the counts of Ilok, before falling into the hands of the Turkish forces in 1532.

After the expulsion of the Turks, Našice's fortunes changed. The Franciscans returned and restored the church of **St Anthony of Padua** (Sv. Antun Padovanski). They also rebuilt their monastery, which had been founded here at the start of the 14th century. Both needed repairing after war damage suffered in 1991.

A short distance away is a large manor house, built at the beginning of the 19th century in Neo-Classical style by the Pejačević family, where the musician Dora Pejačević (1885–1923) lived. Situated in a large park, the two-storey building has recently been restored.

The church of St Anthony of Padua in Našice

This building is now the **Civic Museum**.

🏛 **Civic Museum**
Pejačevićev trg 5. **Tel** (031) 613 414. 8am–3pm Mon–Fri; 9am–noon Sat.

Orahovica

Map F2. 4,300. Osijek, 62 km (38 miles). (033) 646 079. (033) 673 231. F. Gavkačića 6, (033) 673 351. Spring in Orahovica: folklore event (Jun).

The town of Orahovica is well known in Croatia for its wines. It was a feudal estate in 1228, and later a Turkish garrison, acquiring its present-day look in the 18th century.

On one of the hills around the town stand the ruins of **Rosetta** (Ružica Grad), one of the largest of Croatia's medieval forts. The walls were 9m (29 ft) thick and enclosed military buildings, a church, and the governor's residence. The complex was so large it was often referred to as a city.

The Turks burnt down the fort, then partially restored it and used it as a military garrison. Liberated in 1690, the fort was once again used for defence, and a village, inhabited by Serbs, developed around its base.

Environs
Along the road to Kutjevo, 5 km (3 miles) south of Orahovica, near the village of Duzluk, is the Orthodox **Monastery of St Nicholas** (Manastir Sv. Nikola), which has ancient frescoes and illuminated manuscripts. Some 30 km (18 miles) from Orahovica, following the road to Virovitica, then turning left for Ceraljie, is **Voćin**, a small village where the destruction caused by the war in 1991 is still evident. The village lies at the foot of a large castle built in the second half of the 13th

century by the Aba counts. Today, the houses in Voćin are in ruins. All that remains of the church of **St Mary** (Sv. Maria), which was built by King John Corvinus in the first half of the 15th century, is part of the apse wall.

The ornate altar in the Baroque church of St Roch, Virovitica

Virovitica

Map E2. 16,000. Osijek, 89 km (55 miles). Ulica Stjepana Radića, (033) 730 121. Trg Fra. B. Gerbera 1, (033) 721 113. Trg Kralja Tomislava 1, (033) 721 241. Day of the City (16 Aug).

Documents from the end of the first millennium give the town its Hungarian name of Wereuche. It was declared a free town by King Bela IV in 1234 and it developed into an agricultural and trading centre. Later occupied by the Turks, it remained under their rule until 1684. When it later flourished, all Ottoman traces were destroyed.

The Baroque church of **St Roch** (Sv. Rok), decorated by the sculptor Holzinger and the painter Göbler, dates from the 18th century. On the site of the ancient Wasserburg Castle stands the imposing **Pejačević Manor** (1800–4), now the **Civic Museum** (Gradski Muzej) with archaeological and folklore collections and an art gallery.

🏛 **Civic Museum**
Palazzo Pejačević, Trg Bana Jelačića. **Tel** (033) 722 127. 9am–2pm Mon, Wed, Fri; 9am–7pm Tue, Thu; 9am–noon Sat.

THE NORTHERN COUNTIES

T*he landscape in this part of Croatia is made up of a variety of elements: the rolling hills of Zagorje with their therapeutic spring waters and thermal spas; the county of Prekmura, which is famous for its wines; the cities of Varaždin and Čakovec, which developed around ancient castles; Koprivnica, surrounded by lush countryside and vineyards, and Bjelovar and Križevci with their palaces.*

The principal towns in the area have ancient origins and two, Varaždin and Križevci, were also at various times the seat of the Sabor, the Croatian Parliament. Bjelovar is the most recent and largest city-fortress in the country. Even before the 1991 war which affected the south of this area, the wars of the second half of the 18th century had already destroyed all evidence of the Middle Ages and Turkish occupation.

However, there are many religious buildings in the area, including a number of Catholic Franciscan and Pauline monasteries in places once inhabited by Orthodox communities. Religious life is still very active here and church buildings are cherished.

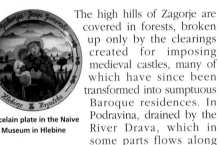

Porcelain plate in the Naive Museum in Hlebine

The high hills of Zagorje are covered in forests, broken up only by the clearings created for imposing medieval castles, many of which have since been transformed into sumptuous Baroque residences. In Podravina, drained by the River Drava, which in some parts flows along the Hungarian border, the hills are lower and are characterized by vineyards and sparse woodland.

This part of Croatia has preserved all kinds of ancient customs and traditions, a source of inspiration for the Naive art movement. The home of Naive art is Hlebine, where artists such as Ivan Generalić encouraged and fostered the talent of local amateur painters.

Typical countryside between Belec and Marija Bistrica

◁ Café life in the pretty Baroque town of Varaždin

Exploring the Northern Counties

This is an area of good, fertile agricultural land and the lush countryside produces an abundance of maize, tobacco and sunflowers. The hillsides are covered in vineyards as far as the eye can see and yield wines, good whites in particular, which can be bought along the Wine Road, from wineries or in the village shops. Despite these attractions, the region does not see a great deal of international tourism. This is particularly true of Međimurje, the valley crossed by the River Mura, granted to Croatia after World War I. Part of the population here is of Hungarian origin and the people have preserved their Hungarian customs and traditions.

A side chapel of St Mary of the Snows, Marija Bistrica

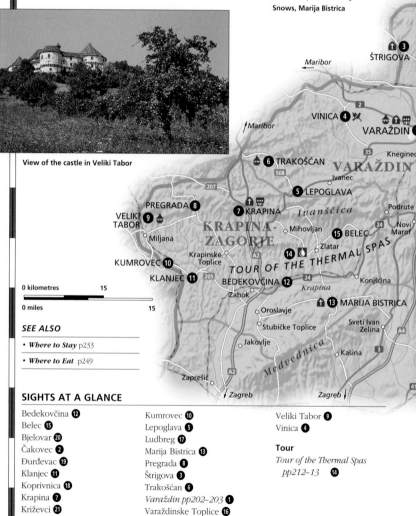

View of the castle in Veliki Tabor

SEE ALSO

- *Where to Stay* p233
- *Where to Eat* p249

SIGHTS AT A GLANCE

GETTING AROUND

New motorways connecting Zagreb to Maribor in
Slovenia, and passing through Krapina and Hungary
(and serving Varaždin), have been built. Cars still use
state roads which run more or less parallel to the
two motorways. State road 2 goes from the Slovenian
border, northwest of Varaždin, and continues on
towards Osijek. A railway line runs alongside state
road 3 and at Varaždin interconnects with railway
lines from Zagreb, Slovenia and Hungary. There are
also train connections to Slovenia and Hungary from
Čakovec and Koprivnica stations.

LOCATOR MAP

A Naive painting from the Hlebine Gallery

KEY

▬▬	Two lane motorway, toll-free
▬▬	Major road
▭▭	Minor road
⌁⌁	Main railway
▬▬	County border
▬▬	International border

Varaždin Castle in winter

Varaždin ①

Door detail, church of the Assumption

Traces of occupation from the Neolithic age, the La Tene civilization and the Roman period have been found around Varaždin castle. Despite this, the first mention of the town is found in a document from 1181, when King Bela III confirmed the rights of the Zagreb Curia to the thermal spas in the area. In 1209, it was declared a free town by King Andrew II and it began to develop as a trading centre. In the late 14th century it passed into the hands of the counts of Celjski, followed by the counts of Frankopan, Brandenburg and Erdödy. In 1446, it was destroyed in a fire and in 1527 the Turks attacked. In 1776 another fire destroyed the houses, but the Baroque buildings, for which the town is famous, were fortunately spared.

Aerial view of the Castle, today home to the Civic Museum

🏛 Castle and Civic Museum
Stari Grad & Gradski Muzej
Strossmayerovo šetalište 7. *Tel (042) 212 918.* ☐ *summer: 10am–6pm Tue–Sun; winter: 10am–5pm Tue–Fri; 10am–1pm Sat & Sun.* 🖼 🗍 📷
This castle was built by the Zrinskis (the rectangular tower is from this period) over the ruins of an observation tower and, in the 15th century, two round towers were added. The castle was rebuilt in 1560 by the Italian architect Domenico dell'Allio, who created a Renaissance structure on two floors with arcades and corridors facing courtyards.

The castle's present look dates from the time of the Erdödy counts, who added the bastions and a moat. It is now the Civic Museum which has collections of weapons, porcelain, furniture, handicrafts, and a pharmacy from the 18th century. Remains of the wall and the Lisak tower, to the east of the castle, are the only evidence remaining of the ancient walls.

🏛 Gallery of Old and Modern Masters
Galerija Starih i Novih Majstora
Stančićev trg 3. *Tel (042) 214 172.* ☐ *10am–6pm Tue–Fri; 10am–1pm Sat & Sun.* 🖼 🗍 *by appt.* 📷
The gallery has a large collection of works from all over Europe, particularly landscapes by Flemish and Italian artists, and portraits by German and Dutch painters.

🏛 Tomislav Square
Trg Kralja Tomislava
Town Hall (Gradska Vijećnica):
Trg kralja Tomislava 1. *Tel (042) 210 985.* ☐ *by appt.*
Drašković Palace (Dvor Drašković):
Trg kralja Tomislava 3. *Tel (042) 210 985.* ☐ *to the public.*
This square is the heart of the town. Facing the square is the **Town Hall** (Gradska Vijećnica), the oldest building in Varaždin. Built in the Gothic style in the 15th century, it has since been altered and a clock tower added. It has been the Town Hall since 1523, when Prince George of Brandenburg gave

it to the city. It is guarded in summer by the Purgars, who wear richly decorated blue uniforms and bearskin hats.

To the east of the square stands **Drašković Palace** (Dvor Drašković), built in the late 17th century with a Rococo façade. The Croat Parliament met here in 1756–76. Opposite stands the Renaissance Ritz House, one of the oldest in the town, as evidenced by the date (1540) engraved on the doorway.

🏛 Cathedral of the Assumption
Uznesenja Marijina
Pavlinska ulica. *Tel (042) 210 688.* ☐ *8am–12.30pm, 4–6pm daily.*
The church of the Assumption became a cathedral in 1997. Both the church and the annexed monastery were built in the first half of the 17th century by the Jesuits. Later, the Pauline order moved in.

The cathedral's tall façade is enlivened by pillars. The interior is a triumph of the Baroque. The main altar occupies the width of the central nave and has gilded columns, stuccoes and engravings. At the centre of the altar is an *Assumption of the Virgin,* reminiscent of Titian's work in Venice. Evenings of Baroque music concerts are held here.

The rich Baroque altar in the Cathedral of the Assumption

🏛 Church of St John the Baptist
Sv. Ivan Krstitelj
Franjevački trg 8. *Tel (042) 213 166.* ☐ *7am–noon, 5.30–7.30pm daily.*
The church was built in 1650 in the Baroque style on the site of a 13th-century church. The façade has a Renaissance

The bell tower of St John the Baptist in Tomislav Square

doorway with a tympanum and two statues of St Francis of Assisi and St Anthony of Padua. The interior has eight side chapels and an ornate gilded pulpit from the late 17th century. The bell tower is 54 m (177 ft) high.

In front of the church is one of the copies of the *Monument of Bishop Gregory of Nin* by Ivan Meštrović. The adjacent pharmacy has many works of art, among them some allegorical frescoes by Ivan Ranger *(see p206)*.

🏛 Herzer Palace
Dvor Herzer

Franjevački trg 6. *Tel (042) 210 474.* ● for restoration.
Entomological Museum: *Tel (042) 210 474.* ◯ *10am–6pm Tue–Fri; 10am–1pm Sat & Sun.* 🈂 🗹 🔀
Built at the end of the 19th century (the founders' coat of arms is on the door), the palace has housed the well-organized **Entomological Museum** (Entomoloski Odjel) since 1954. The museum was founded thanks to the entomologist Franjo Košćec (1882–1968), who, in 1959, donated his natural history collection to the city. From 1962 to 1980, his work was carried on by his daughter Ružica, a biologist. As well as thousands of insects, the museum also has a herbarium. Periodically the museum organizes exhibitions on the effects insects have on the land and its inhabitants.

🔒 Church of the Holy Trinity
Sv. Trojstvo

Kapucinski trg. *Tel (042) 213 550.* ◯ *6.30am–noon, 5.30–7.30pm daily.*
The church dates from the early 18th century and houses numerous Baroque paintings, furnishings by local masters, and an organ with figures of angels playing instruments.

The neighbouring monastery, which dates from the same period, is famous for its library which contains many parchments, incunabula and manuscripts, and some of the oldest documents written in ancient Croatian *(kajkavski)*.

🏛 National Theatre
Narodno Kazalište

Ulica Augusta Cesarca 1. *Tel (042) 214 688.* ◯ *for performances only.*
Built by Hermann Helmer in 1873, this is one of the main cultural centres in the city. During the summer and autumn, theatre-goers from all over Europe come to attend the performances.

VISITORS' CHECKLIST

Map D1. 👥 *49,000.* 🚉 *Frane Supila, (042) 210 444.* 🚌 *Kralja Zvonimira 1, (042) 210 555.* ℹ️ **Local:** *Ivana Padovca 3, (042) 210 987;* **Regional:** *Stanka Vraza 4, (042) 394 100.*
www.tourism-varazdin.hr
🎭 *Baroque evenings, Varaždin, (Sep–Oct); Gastrolov (Oct).*

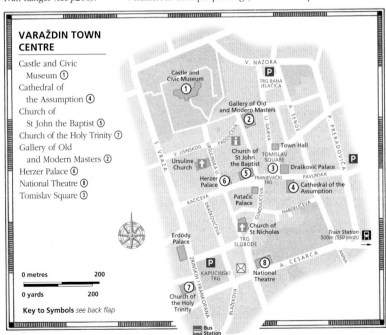

VARAŽDIN TOWN CENTRE

Castle and Civic Museum ①
Cathedral of the Assumption ④
Church of St John the Baptist ⑤
Church of the Holy Trinity ⑦
Gallery of Old and Modern Masters ②
Herzer Palace ⑥
National Theatre ⑧
Tomislav Square ③

0 metres 200
0 yards 200

Key to Symbols *see back flap*

Vineyards in the countryside around Čakovec

Čakovec ❷

Map D1. 🏘 *16,000.* 🚌 *(040) 384 333.* 🚃 *Masarykova ulica, (040) 313 947.* ℹ️ **Local:** *Kralja Tomislava 1, (040) 313 319, 310 969;* **Regional:** *R. Boškovića 2, (040) 390 191.* 🎭 *Croatian music (Carnival); Founding of the city festival (29 May).* **www**.tourism-cakovec.hr

In the second half of the 13th century, on a site once inhabited by Romans, Count Demetrius Chaky, a magistrate at the court of King Bela IV, built a tower here which was called Chaktornya. In the following century, the main defensive structure in Medimurje was built around the tower. In 1547 Emperor Ferdinand gave it to the Ban (governor) of Croatia, Nikola Zrinski *(see p177)*, together with a large estate, as a reward for the victory against the Turks and to settle a debt.

Nikola Zrinski died heroically while fighting against the Ottomans in defending Siget, and became a national hero. On 29 May 1579, one of his successors, a member of the Zrinski family of Siget, guaranteed tax privileges to whoever went to live in the city that was developing around the fort. This date is considered the founding of the city and is celebrated with a festival. Bastions and a moat were added in this period as defence against cannon fire. Inside the walls, a four-storey palace was built around a square courtyard.

In 1671 Petar Zrinski led a plot to separate Croatia from the Kingdom of Hungary. The plot was discovered and Zrinski and his co-conspirator Franjo Krsto Frankopan were beheaded on 30 April 1671. Čakovec then came under the direct rule of the Emperor.

The Renaissance "**Old Castle**", of which only the first floor remains, and the Baroque "**New Castle**" with a rectangular plan, face each other inside the medieval walls. For a long time the Old Castle was used as a prison. It is now being restored and is to be used in future for cultural activities. The church has been reopened for worship.

The **Medimurje Civic Museum** of Čakovec has on display exhibits of prehistoric material, many Roman finds, and ethnographic collections. There is also an exhibition dedicated to the local composer, J Slavenski (1896–1955), who was known for his love of the traditional music of the region.

Čakovec is the main administrative centre of the Medimurje, a frontier region which borders Slovenia and Hungary. The land in the western part of the region is hilly with broad valleys, and is renowned for its wines, while the fertile plains of the eastern part produce cereal crops.

🏛 **Medimurje Civic Museum**
Trg Republike 5. **Tel** *(040) 313 285.*
⬜ *10am–3pm Tue–Fri; 10am–1pm Sat–Sun.* 📷 🎫

Environs
In a small village 2 km (1 mile) from Čakovec stands the church of **St Helen** (Sv. Helena). What little remains of its original Gothic form has

The Old and New castles of Čakovec

been integrated into an overall Baroque appearance. The church is all that survives of the monastery founded by the Paulines in 1376. It has been rebuilt at various times, firstly after a Protestant revolt, then because of a fire and finally after an earthquake.

Fresco on the door of the church of St Jerome, Štrigova

Inside the church are the tombstones of the powerful Zrinski family, the lords of Čakovec: that of Nikola Zrinski and his wife Catherine Frankopan, and also that of Petar Zrinski.

The church also contains several tombs of members of the Knežević family, who became the successors to the Zrinskis.

One of the frescoes decorating the church of St Helen, Čakovec

Štrigova ❸

Map D1.
👥 *600.* 🚗 *from Čakovec.* 🚌 *from Čakovec.* ℹ️ **Regional:** *R Boškovića 2, (040) 390 191.*

Numerous finds of Roman origin have been discovered here, leading historians to believe that this village was built on the site of the Roman city of Stridon, the birthplace of St Jerome.

The counts of Strigovcak lived here, but their castle was destroyed during a raid by the Turks. Nearby, the Bannfy counts also built a castle, which was transformed

into a palace in the 17th century. At one time the palace was famous for its rich furnishings, its art collections, and for the fact that the Hungarian king, Matthias Corvinus, was often a guest here.

The church of **St Jerome** (Sv. Jerolim) stands on a hill at the edge of the village. Restoration has uncovered the frescoes above the doorway and in the niches on the façade, which is flanked by two harmonious bell towers and culminates in a curvilinear tympanum.

In the church are numerous *trompe-l'œil* paintings by the Tyrolean artist Ivan Ranger *(see p206),* depicting *Angels,* the *Evangelists* and the *Life of St Jerome.* There are also statues representing the fathers of the Church.

Vinica ❹

Map D1. 👥 *1,200.* 🚌 *from Varaždin.* ℹ️ **Local:** *Vinička 5, (042) 722 233.* **Regional:** *(042) 394 000.*

This small town lies at the foot of vine-covered hills. It was first mentioned in documents in 1353 as the site of a medieval fortress. At one time it was known for the large palace built by the Patačić counts on the site of their old castle. The palace

The frescoed façade of the church of St Jerome, Štrigova

is now in ruins, as is that of the Drašković counts, which was situated in the centre of a large park.

In the late 19th century, Count Marko Bombelles created **Opeka Park,** 2 km (1 mile) south of Vinica. This large arboretum was at that time the only one of its kind in Croatia. Here Bombelles planted exotic trees and plants from around the world, including the Americas, Japan, Tibet and the Caucasus, over an area of flat and hilly ground.

Next to this wonderful park, declared a protected nature reserve in 1961, a School of Horticulture has been set up. This school has several glasshouses and a large garden of flowering plants.

🌺 **Opeka Park**
⏰ *at all times.*

Colourful floral display in Opeka Park, near Vinica

Choir stalls in the church of St Mary, frescoed by the artist Ivan Ranger

Lepoglava ❺

Map D1. 🏠 38,000.
🚉 (042) 791 193. 🚌 for Ivanec.
🛈 **Local:** Ulica Hrvatskih Pavlina,
(042) 791 090;
Regional: Varaždin, (042) 394 000.
🎭 Lace exhibition (Sep).

This town is famous for the intricate lace which is made here, thanks to its Lace School, which was founded some centuries ago.

The town is also notorious in Croatia as being the site of a historic prison. At various times, Marshal Tito and Archbishop Stepinac, head of the church in Croatia in World War II, among others, were imprisoned here.

The prison building was formerly a Pauline monastery, built on the orders of the Count of Celje at the end of the 14th century. It was embellished and enlarged in the second half of the following century by King Matthias Corvinus. It was used as a school of theology, grammar and philosophy, as well as a secondary school open to lay pupils.

In 1854, after the dissolution of the Pauline order, the monks' cells became prison cells. Behind the large, ancient cloisters a more modern prison was built, but it is no longer in use and is awaiting repair.

However, restoration has been completed on the beautiful Gothic church of **St Mary** (Sv. Marija), which was rebuilt in the Baroque style in the late 17th century. The church has a single nave and polygonal choir. The façade has prominent pilasters enclosing niches, and two tympana. Inside is 18th-century stuccowork by Antonio Giulio Quaglio alongside magnificent works by the fresco painter Ivan Ranger (of note is his *Apocalypse* in the choir stalls). Ranger's largest cycle of

Typical lace from Lepoglava

frescoes can be found here. Also of interest is the pulpit and the altar of St Anne by the Pauline monk and sculptor Aleksije Köninger.

🔒 **Church of St Mary**
Trg 1. hrvatskog sveučilišta 3.
Tel (042) 791 128.
◻ by appt.

Trakošćan ❻

Map D1. 🏠 30.
🚌 for Bednja. 🛈 **Regional:**
Varaždin, (042) 796 281.
www.trakoscan.net

The pretty surroundings of the **Castle of Trakošćan**, and its excellent state of conservation, make this one of the most visited tourist sights in Zagorje. The castle was built to guard the road which descends from Ptuj towards the valley of the River Sava. The castle was listed in 1434 as one of the properties granted by Sigismund of Austria to the Count of Celje. It was used for defence purposes until the

IVAN RANGER (JOHANNES BAPTISTE RANGER)

Born in Axams, today a suburb of Innsbruck in Austria, in 1700, Ivan Ranger joined the Pauline order at a very early age. Not much is known of his years as an apprentice, but it is certain that he lived for a time in Italy, where he encountered the Baroque style in Venice, Rome, Bologna and Mantua. At the age of 30 he was invited to Lepoglava, then the headquarters of the order, to which he remained loyal until his death in 1753. He also worked in nearby towns and in Slovenia (at the monastery of Olimje and the castle-monastery of Sveti Jernej in Rogatec). In line with Pauline principles, he created a school of fresco painters. With these artists he produced colourful fresco cycles which were full of expression (the *trompe-l'œil* paintings also reveal great technical skill). His themes were always religious, and he was much imitated.

Fresco painted by the Pauline monk Ivan Ranger

The Castle of Trakošćan, now a museum

end of Turkish rule. In 1568 it became the property of the Drašković counts.

During the second half of the 19th century, it was transformed into a splendid Neo-Gothic residence by Djuro Drašković. He also added an artificial lake, a park and gardens, while at the same time preserving some of the military aspects of the castle. It stands on a wooded hilltop and is surrounded by a high wall with a tower, which encircles the imposing palace.

In 1953, 25 of the rooms were turned into a **Museum** where furniture, armoury, vestments and paintings, as well as a rare series of portraits of the Drašković family, are on display.

🏰 **Castle and Museum**
Tel (042) 796 422, 796 495.
⬜ *Jun–Sep: 9am–6pm daily;*
Oct–May: 9am–3pm daily. 📷 🎫

Krapina ❼

Map D1.
🏛 *4,500.* 🚉 *Frana Galovića, (049) 371 012.* 🚌 *A. Starčevića, (049) 315 018.* ℹ *Magistratska 11, (049) 371 330.* 🎭 *Week of music and Kajkaviana culture (Sep).*

The town is well-known in the scientific field because the remains of Krapina man, *Homo krapinensis*, who lived in the Palaeolithic age, were found nearby. The Neanderthal skeleton, discovered in 1899 in a hillside cave, is now in the Archaeological Museum in

Zagreb. However, some of his possessions, such as utensils and weapons, have remained in Krapina, and are exhibited in the small **Museum of Evolution**.

Krapina is first documented in 1193 as the site of a castle, now destroyed, built to guard the river of the same name. After the danger of Turkish attack had passed, it was conceded to the Keglević counts and became an important administrative town.

It also became a religious centre. In the mid-17th century, a Franciscan monastery and the Baroque church of **St Catherine** were built. The sacristy and some of the monastery rooms are decorated with vivid frescoes by Ivan Ranger.

Bust of Ljudevit Gaj, Krapina

In one of the town squares is a monument to Ljudevit Gaj, born in Krapina in 1809. During the first half of the 19th century he was a prominent figure in the movement which promoted the revival of Croatian politics and culture.

🏛 **Museum of Evolution**
Šetalište V Sluge. *Tel (049) 371 491, 371 161.* ⬜ *Jun–Sep: 8am–6pm daily; Oct–May: 8am–3pm daily.* 📷 🎫 *by appt.*

Environs
A short way northeast of Krapina is the sanctuary of the **Madonna of Jerusalem** in Trški Vrh, regarded as one of the most magnificent examples of Baroque art in Croatia. Built in 1750–61, on a square plan, the façade has a bell tower with an onion dome. Inside is an arched portico with rounded corners and four chapels similar to the tower. The walls, vaults, ceilings and dome of the church are covered with a cycle of frescoes of biblical subjects and scenes from Mary's life by the Styrian artist, Anton Lerchinger. The ornate main altar (with a statue of the Virgin brought from Jerusalem in 1669) is by sculptor Filip Jacob Straub of Graz, while the pulpit and the other three altars are the work of Anton Mersi, a gilder and sculptor.

Fresco in the Baroque church of the Madonna of Jerusalem in Trški Vrh

Pregrada ❽

Map C1. 🏛 *400.* ℹ *Local: Trg Gospe Kunagorske 3, (049) 377 050;* **Regional:** *Zagrebacka 6, Krapinske Toplice, (049) 233 653.* 🎭 *Carnival (Feb), Branje grojzdja, grape harvest (Sep).*

The village church has ancient origins but now presents a 19th-century appearance, made distinctive by the façade flanked by two pointed bell towers. Inside, as well as the tombs of members of the Keglević and Gorup families, there is also a very large organ, which was at one time in Zagreb Cathedral.

On the site of a medieval castle, in the Hrvatsko Zagorje woods, along the Wine Road, stands **Gorica Castle**, once owned by the Keglević family and the feudal manor of the area. Two round towers frame the structure of the elaborate façade. Other buildings behind the towers are now used as a winery.

Environs

On a vineyard-covered hill, 7 km (4 miles) west of Pregrada, in **Vinagora**, stands an unusual sanctuary of ancient origins. This place of worship became the parish church in 1780. The church of St Mary of the Visitation (Sv. Marija od Pohoda) contains some Gothic statues and rich furnishings. The church is surrounded by walls which encircle the hill.

Two round towers guard the sanctuary entrance, which also once had a drawbridge. These towers are now used as chapels.

Inside the church of St Mary of the Visitation, Vinagora

Veliki Tabor ❾

Map C1. 🚌 *from Krapina or Zagreb for Desinić.* ℹ **Regional:** *Zagrebačka 6, Krapinske Toplice, (049) 233 653.* 🎭 *hunting tournament with falcons (Oct).* **www**.veliki-tabor.hr

One of the most famous and best preserved castles in Croatia, Veliki Tabor stands on a bare hilltop, making it visible from a great distance. It was royal property in the 14th century at the time of King Matthias Corvinus I (the fact that it was royal property justified its imposing appearance). It was granted to the family of the Ratkaj counts, who in the 16th century altered and softened its rather austere rooms, transforming it into a sumptuous residential palace.

Walls with four semicircular towers encircle the main body of the castle, which is built on a pentagonal ground plan. Two floors with porticoes face the central courtyard. The bastions (no longer extant), made Veliki Tabor a fortress to be feared. The castle is now a museum.

🏛 **Castle**
Desinić. **Tel** *(049) 343 052.* **Fax** *(049) 343 055.* 🕐 *10am–5pm Mon–Sun.* 🎫

Environs

Miljana, just to the southwest of Veliki Tabor, is home to one of the most picturesque Baroque castles in Croatia. Construction began in the 17th century but was not completed until the mid-19th century. This time span resulted in a variety of styles; there are striking Rococo frescoes in some rooms.

Kumrovec ❿

Map C1.
🏛 *300.* 🚉 *(049) 553 129.* 🚌 *from Zagreb.* ℹ *(049) 502 044.* 🎭 *Marriage of Zagorje (Sep).*

This was the birthplace of Marshal Tito, born Josip Broz in 1892. His house, which dates from 1860, was turned into a museum in 1953. On display are the furniture and household goods which belonged to his family.

In the square in front of the house is a monument to Tito, the work of Antun Augustinčić in 1948. Along with other village houses, Tito's birthplace is now part of a folk museum, the **Ethnological Museum – Staro Selo**, which means "old village". The houses are furnished with utensils and household goods of the time. Reconstructed workshops

The Castle of Veliki Tabor, one of the best-preserved castles in Croatia

◁ Vineyards around Kumrovec, in the hilly region of Zagorje

Birthplace of Marshal Tito, part of the Staro Selo museum in Kumrovec

have been set up to demonstrate crafts such as hemp- and flax-weaving.

🏛 Ethnological Museum – Staro Selo
Tel (049) 553 107. ☐ Jun–Sep: 9am–6pm daily; Oct–May: 9am–3pm daily. 🖼 🎫

Klanjec ⑪

Map C1.
🏘 600. 🚉 (049) 550 404.
🚌 from Zagreb, Krapina, Zabok.
🛈 Trg A. Mihanovića 3, (049) 550 235. 🎭 Carnival (Feb).

The sculptor Antun Augustinčić (1900–79) was born here, and the **Antun Augustinčić Museum and Gallery** has displays of his work. The artist was the co-founder of Zemlja (Union of Artists of the World), based on ideas of politically committed art.

Also of interest are the Franciscan monastery and the annexed church of St Mary, both built in the 17th century by the powerful Erdödy family, whose tombs lie here.

In the main square is a monument by Robert Frangeš-Mihanović, dedicated to the poet Antun Mihanović, who wrote the Croatian national anthem.

Another memorial dedicated to Antun Mihanović is the 9-m (29-ft) memorial stone which stands in Zelenjak, 3 km (2 miles) north of Klanjec, in the direction of Tuheljske Toplice.

Statue of Antun Mihanović, Klanjec

🏛 Antun Augustinčić Museum and Gallery
Trg A. Mihanovića 10. *Tel* (049) 550 343. ☐ 9am–4pm Mon–Sat.

Bedekovčina ⑫

Map D1.
🏘 3,500. 🚉 Trg A Starčevića 12, (049) 213 106. 🚌 from Zagreb.
🛈 **Regional:** Zagrebacka 6, Krapinske Toplice, (049) 233 653. 🍷 Wine fair (Jun).

This town is home to a particularly attractive castle and palace, one of many buildings erected over the ruins of ancient castles in the Zagorje hills. The majority of these were destroyed during the wars against the Turks. This particular castle was built in the early 18th century, and now houses public offices. The castle is built on a quadrangular plan, on two levels and with a sloping roof. Coats of arms are emblazoned above the two entrance doors.

Marija Bistrica ⑬

Map D1. 🏘 1,000. 🚉 Zlatar Bistrica, 5 km (3 miles). 🚌 from Zagreb. 🛈 Zagrebacka, (049) 468 380. 🎭 Bistrica week (Jul).

This small village on the northern side of the Medvednica mountain is home to the **Sanctuary of St Mary of the Snows** (Sv. Marija Snježna), one of the best-known pilgrimage sites in Croatia. There has been a church on this site since 1334. In the mid-16th century, when a Turkish invasion seemed imminent, a wooden statue of the *Black Madonna with Child* was hidden in the church. Some decades later, it was miraculously rediscovered, to great joy and emotion. It still inspires tremendous devotion today.

The church has been enlarged several times and was the first to be declared a sanctuary of Croatia by Parliament (1715). It was rebuilt in 1883 by the architect Hermann Bollé. He adopted an eclectic approach, combining Romanesque, Gothic and Baroque styles. The church also has a large frescoed portico.

The sanctuary possesses a rich store of beautiful religious pieces: gold and silver items, furnishings and sacred vestments adorned with gold embroidery. Some objects are now on exhibit in the Diocesan Museum in Zagreb.

⛪ Sanctuary of St Mary of the Snows
Trg pape Ivana Pavla II 24. *Tel* (049) 469 156. ☐ 8–11am daily.

Sanctuary of St Mary of the Snows in Marija Bistrica, a place of pilgrimage

Tour of the Thermal Spas ⑭

Between Varaždin and Zagreb are five thermal spas (*toplice*), dating from different eras. Set in a pleasant hilly landscape of vineyards and woods, the spas are popular with Croatians and visitors from German-speaking regions. As well as being attracted by the well-equipped thermal spas, visitors are also drawn by the cities and towns nearby. In addition there are numerous castles, sanctuaries, churches and museums, making this a very pleasant area to stay in.

Decorative detail from the Roman baths, Varaždinske Toplice

Krapinske Toplice ③

This thermal spa was built in the second half of the 19th century near a hot water spring rich in calcium, magnesium and carbonate. The hospital treats rheumatic, cardio-vascular and neurological illnesses with bathing in the pools (four outdoor and one indoor) and mud treatments.

Sutinske Toplice ④

Located 8 km (5 miles) northwest of Zlatar, at an altitude of 170 m (557 ft), this site has been famous since the 13th century for its curative waters, which are slightly radioactive and rich in minerals, particularly calcium and magnesium. Mud baths are particularly effective for the treatment of a variety of ailments. Outdoor pools only.

Belec

24

Mihovljan

35

KRAPINA

Donja Šemnica

④ 29

24

Zlatar

③

Zlatar Bistrica

E59

205

24

Bedekovčina

Zabok

307

↓ZAGREB ①

Stubičke Toplice ①

This spa is at the foot of Mount Medvednica, 3 km (2 miles) from Donja Stubica. The spa dates from 1776. There is a hotel with a pool, and a hospital specializing in the treatment of degenerative diseases of the joints and spine. The hot spa waters emerge at 69°C (156°F).

Tuheljske Toplice ②

This spa town is 46 km (28 miles) from Zagreb. At the hotel with its eight pools, rheumatic, respiratory, urological and gynaecological illnesses are treated.

0 kilometres	10
0 miles	10

For hotels and restaurants in this region see p233 and p249

Varaždinske Toplice ⑤

The spa resort in Varaždin is one of the oldest in Croatia. The first baths were set up at the end of the 18th century and the first public spa was opened to the public in 1829. The thermal waters are used to treat rheumatic and orthopaedic conditions.

KEY

▬ Tour route

▬ Motorway

▭ Other roads

ℹ️ Tourist information

The decorated interior of the church of St Mary of the Snows, Belec

Belec ⑮

Map D1.
🚶 500. 🚌 from Zabok.
ℹ️ Magistratska 11, Krapina, (049) 371 330.

Among the hills of Zagorje is the village of Belec, much loved by art historians, because on its outskirts is the small church of **St George**, one of the few Romanesque buildings preserved in inland Croatia. The bell tower takes up nearly all of the façade (it resembles a defensive tower rather than a campanile). On the right is a small portico with two thin columns. This leads to the interior, where there is an ornate Gothic altar and interesting frescoes dating from the year of its construction.

Lower down the hillside is the church of **St Mary of the Snows** (Sv. Marija Snježna), constructed by the Keglević family in 1674. This church is considered a masterpiece of Croatian Baroque, because of its sumptuously decorated and ornamented interior. The monk and artist Ivan Ranger *(see p206)* painted some of his *trompe-l'œil* masterpieces here, including *Scenes from the Old Testament* and *Episodes of the Virgin Mary's Life*. The church also has a magnificent main altar, surrounded by cherubs and saints.

🔒 **Church of St Mary of the Snows**
Tel (049) 460 040. ⭕ by appt.

Varaždinske Toplice ⑯

Map D1. 🚶 2,000. 🚊 from Zagreb and Novi Marof. 🚌 from Zagreb.
ℹ️ Trg Slobode 16, (042) 630 000.

The waters that gush from a sulphurous spring at the foot of the hill south of Varaždin were known to the Jasi, an Illyrian tribe, in the 3rd century BC. The town was known as Aquae Jasae by the Romans, and the spa rapidly developed, as shown by the numerous archaeological finds discovered here. The baths were used until the area was invaded by the Goths. Later, a landslide buried the baths in mud and for centuries they were forgotten.

In the 12th century, under the rule of the bishop of Zagreb, a village was founded with the name of Toplissa and the inhabitants began to use the hot water from the spring once more. During the construction of the present-day resort, the Roman town was rediscovered.

Varaždinske Toplice also boasts a medieval district which includes a castle, part of which houses an **Archaeological Museum**. Inside a small fortress is the parish church with an organ from 1766 and two carved altars made by Francesco Robba.

In a nearby park is Seoska Kuća, an 18th-century rural house with furniture and objects from the same era.

The sanctuary dedicated to the Trinity, Ludbreg

Ludbreg ⑰

Map D1.
🏛 *3,300.* 🚉 *from Koprivnica.*
🚌 *from Zagreb.* 🛈 *Trg Sv. Trojstva 14, (042) 810 690.* 🎭 *Celebration of Miraculous Blood (1st Sun in Sep).*

Many traces from the Roman era, such as walls and baths, have been found in this area. In researching these finds, some historians have identified Ludbreg as being the Roman site of Jovia.

The town later became one of the first bishop's sees in inland Croatia. In 1414, during a mass, a priest saw the wine in the chalice turn to blood and the town chapel where this miracle took place became a destination for pilgrims. In 1513 Pope Leo X declared Ludbreg the only **Sanctuary of the Trinity** (Sv. Trojstvo) in Croatia.

The church, originally Gothic, was altered in 1829, and now features a Baroque altar and frescoes by M Racki (1937). The portico is typical of churches of pilgrimage and dates from 1779.

In 1739, Parliament voted to build a large chapel dedicated to the Precious Blood of Christ here, in order to preserve the miraculous chalice in an appropriate place. The chapel was not finally consecrated until 1994.

A manor house in Baroque and Classical style, built by the Battayany family in 1745, today houses workshops belonging to the Croatian Restoration Institute.

Koprivnica ⑱

Map D1. 🏛 *24,000.*
🚉 *Kolodvorska 10, (048) 621 017.*
🚌 *Zagrebačka ulica, (048) 621 282.*
🛈 *Bana Jelačića 7, (048) 621 433.*
www.tz-koprivnicko-krizevacka.hr
🎭 *Podravski Motivi, Naive art exhibition (first week of Jul).*

Koprivnica (originally Kukaproncza), was founded by the powerful Ernust family, and was a key trading centre for the Podravina area as well as a royal city from 1356. It was burnt down by the Turks in the 16th century, destroying one of Croatia's first free towns.

Slowly rebuilt in the 17th century, the town took on a Baroque appearance with a wide avenue flanked by the main public and private buildings. At one end stands the 19th-century County Hall of Koprivnica and Križevci. There are many Serbian immigrants here, hence the Orthodox Church of the Holy Spirit (Sveti Duh), dating from the late 18th century.

A significant event for the city was the establishment in 1685 of a **Franciscan Monastery** and the church of St Anthony of Padua. The monastery was a source of culture and learning for the whole region and it has resumed this role in recent times.

Nearby is the **Civic Museum** (Gradski Muzej) with archaeological, historical and cultural collections, and the **Koprivnica Gallery** with a collection of Naive works linked to the Hlebine school *(see p21)*. Next door, in a former old brewery, is the beer hall Kraluš *(see p247)*, much loved by the locals.

🏛 **Civic Museum**
Trg Leandera Brozovića 1.
Tel *(048) 642 538.* ⏰ *8am–2.30pm Mon–Fri; 10am–1pm Sat.*

🏛 **Koprivnica Gallery**
Zrinski trg 9/1. **Tel** *(048) 622 564.*
⏰ *8.30am–3.30pm Mon–Fri, 9.30am–1pm Sat.* 🎟

Environs
Hlebine, 13 km (8 miles) east of Koprivnica, owes its fame to the peasant painters fostered by the artist Krsto Hegedušić. In the 1930s this group founded the so-called "Hlebine school" *(see p21)* of Naive art: the core of a trend in painting which represented the landscape and people of this region in a simple and original way. Their work is exhibited in both the **Hlebine Gallery** and the Koprivnica Gallery.

🏛 **Hlebine Gallery**
Trg Ivana Generalića 15. **Tel** *(048) 836 075.* ⏰ *10am–4pm Mon–Fri, 10am–2pm Sat.* 🎟

A work of Naive art of the Hlebine school in the Koprivnica Gallery

The medieval castle in Đurđevac, today housing a gallery

Đurđevac ⑲

Map E1. 🏘 7,000.
🚉 Kolodvorska 21, (048) 813 089.
🚌 (048) 812 002. 🛈 Stjepana
Radića 1, (048) 812 046.
🎉 Đurđevo, City Day (23 Apr);
Legend of the Picoki, culture and
folklore show (last week of Jun).

Although the town's name
derives from an ancient
religious building dedicated
to St George (Sv. Jurai), the
town is now known for the
Castle (Starigrad), whose
ancient name is mentioned as
Wasserburg, meaning castle
on the water. In the Middle
Ages the structure was much
larger (excavations reveal a
rectangular plan with a
drawbridge and tower). All
that remains now is a roughly
octagonal building with an
internal courtyard. A gallery
occupies the upper floor and
there is a restaurant on the
ground floor.

Bjelovar ⑳

Map D1. 🏘 27,000.
🚉 Masarykova ulica, (043) 241 263.
🚌 Masarykova ulica, (043) 241 269.
🛈 **Local:** Trg Eugena Kvaternika 4,
(043) 243 944; **Regional:** Trg
Eugena Kvaternika 4, (043) 243 944.
🎉 Terezijana, cultural display (Jun).

In the Middle Ages this town
was called Wellewar. It
acquired greater status in
1756, when Maria Theresa of
Austria built a fort here. It
became a military town, and
was built on an octagonal
layout, centred around two
intersecting roads. These are
now home to the church of

St Theresa, schools, the
Orthodox church of the Holy
Spirit and the barracks. The
Civic Museum (Gradski
Muzej) has a rich collection,
donated by Count Barešić.

🏛 **Civic Museum**
Trg Eugena Kvaternika 1. **Tel** (043)
244 207. ◻ 9am–2pm, 5–7pm
Tue–Fri; 8am–noon Mon & Sat.

The iconostasis in the Church of
the Holy Trinity, Križevci

Križevci ㉑

Map D1.
🏘 12,000. 🚉 (048) 716 193.
🚌 (048) 681 149.
🛈 Nemčićev trg 6, (048) 681 199.
www.tz-koprivnicko-krizevacka.hr
🎉 Križevačko Veliko Spravišče,
cultural and gastronomic event
(first week in Jun).

References to this town are
found in acts from the
early 12th century. In 1252 it
was declared a royal free
town, and at various times it
was chosen as the meeting
place for the Croatian
parliament. During a meeting
in 1397 certain nobles

considered traitors to King
Sigismund were massacred –
one was the Prince palatine,
Stjepan Lacković. The town
was later fortified but after
Turkish rule, only the towers'
foundations and pieces of
the wall remained.

The oldest building is the
medieval **Church of the
Holy Cross** (Sv. Križ), but only
the side doorway dates from
this period. The church was
restructured in the Baroque
style in the second half of the
18th century. The altar of the
Holy Cross was sculpted by
Francesco Robba in 1756 for
Zagreb cathedral.

The Franciscan **Church
of the Holy Trinity** (Sv.
Trojstvo) has an iconostasis,
frescoes by Celestin Medović
and Ivan Tišov from the early
19th century, and a
magnificent main altar, the
work of 18th-century artist
Sante Pardoni.

The attached monastery
became the **Bishop's Palace**
(Biskupski Dvor). It houses
paintings, icons, manuscripts
and holy objects, and a votive
column dedicated to St Florian.
The **Civic Museum** (Gradski
Muzej) has archaeological and
art collections.

🏛 **Church of the Holy Cross**
Ivana Dijankovečkog 1. **Tel** (048)
711 210. ◻ by appt.
🏰 **Bishop's Palace**
Tel (048) 712 171. ◻ by appt.
🏛 **Civic Museum**
Šenoina 2. **Tel** (048) 711 210.
◻ 8am–3pm Tue–Fri; 10am–noon
Sat & Sun. 📷

Altar by Francesco Robba in the
church of the Holy Cross, Križevci

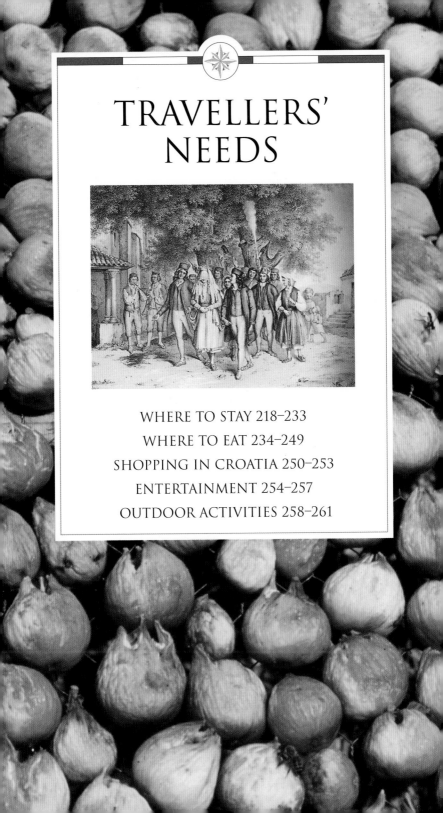

TRAVELLERS'
NEEDS

WHERE TO STAY

Croatia has for some time been quite a popular holiday destination and with Germans, Austrians and Italians in particular. Over the years facilities have improved and there are now more accommodation options available to visitors. Although the tourist industry suffered badly during the war of the 1990s, the damage has largely been repaired and resorts are able to offer a wide range of places to stay. There are plenty of modern hotels, apartments and holiday

Hotel sign at Bežanec, near Pregrada

villages, especially along the coast. Simpler but perfectly acceptable facilities can be found on camping sites or when renting private rooms. Numerous tour operators and travel agencies offer package holidays to different resorts in Croatia, but it is not difficult to make your own travel arrangements. Accommodation is best booked in advance, and planning ahead is a good idea in the peak summer months of June, July and August, as hotels and camping sites get very busy.

The Hotel Palace-Bellevue in Opatija *(see p223)*, on the Istrian coast

HOTELS

Tourism boomed in Croatia in the 1970s and 1980s and most of the hotels, particularly those in the resorts along the coast, date from this period. Facilities are generally of a modern type although decor and furnishings can seem rather monotonous. This type of accommodation may not offer the charm of old-fashioned hotels elsewhere in Europe but service is usually good, rooms are clean and spacious and all the basic facilities (most rooms will have an en-suite bathroom) are provided.

Grander, turn-of-the-century hotels, built during the 19th and 20th centuries, are really only found in Zagreb, the capital, and in Opatija, in the Kvarner gulf. Opatija became a popular seaside resort at the time of the Austro-Hungarian

Empire, when the Habsburgs were regular visitors, and it still has several hotels dating from this time. They offer a style and somewhat faded elegance not found in the more modern multistorey buildings along the coast.

Zagreb is also home to larger luxury hotels including several belonging to well-known international hotel chains, such as Sheraton. The facilities and services offered by these hotels are of a very high standard which is reflected in the prices.

PRIVATE ROOMS

A good value alternative to staying in a hotel is to look for accommodation in private lodgings *(privatne sobe)*. This is not only cheaper, but it also gives you a chance to get to know the local people and understand their culture and way of life. Rooms offered in private accommodation are gradually being classified into three standards (the category of the room will also be reflected in the price).

The first and best category is three-star and this includes all rooms with a private bathroom. The two-star

Typical large resort-style hotel on the Croatian coast

◁ A harvest of figs drying in the sun

The elegant lobby of the Hotel Esplanade in Zagreb *(see p228)*

category indicates rooms where the bathroom is shared with one other room. Lastly, the one-star category indicates the most basic level.

Private lodgings can be booked through the various agencies which can be found in all the tourist resorts. A tourist tax and commission are charged and in summer landlords may require stays of a minimum of four nights.

A cheaper way of finding rooms is by contacting local families directly. A good place to start is at your point of arrival or meeting places such as bus stations, ferry landing stages and at main cafés. These places are often frequented by landladies with rooms for rent. It is always a good idea to check the location and price before committing yourself.

Another way of finding accommodation without official help is by looking for the signs offering rooms – *sobe* in Croatian, *Zimmer* in German or *camere* in Italian – hanging outside the door. It is a good idea to begin looking fairly early in the day. If you find somewhere you like, you can ask to be shown the room and, if you are happy with what you see, you can arrange the terms and the price of your stay. It may even be possible to negotiate the price, especially out of season.

In general this kind of accommodation is offered on a room-only basis, though many rooms have a kitchen corner. Some families offer half-board or even full-board.

SELF-CATERING

Some of the larger hotel complexes on the coast offer self-catering apartments as well as hotel rooms. These can be an excellent solution for families or groups of friends travelling together, as prices are reasonable and you still have access to hotel facilities such as pools and restaurants.

GRADING

Croatia is moving towards adopting the star system common in other European countries, from one star for simple accommodation to five stars for a luxury hotel. However, you will still see the old Croatian classification by letter. According to this system, hotels are divided into five categories. The highest category is "L", the equivalent of a five-star. This

Sign indicating rooms for rent

indicates hotels offering a high standard and a wide range of services and facilities. This type of hotel will usually have one or more restaurants, a night club, sports facilities, a swimming pool, and on the coast, perhaps a private beach. There are not very many "L" category hotels in Croatia and most of them are in Zagreb.

Hotels belonging to category "A" (roughly four-star) offer facilities and services similar to the "L" category but the furnishings are somewhat simpler and more standardized.

Most of the hotels in Croatia fall within the "B" category, which indicates hotels offering a good standard of comfort, roughly equivalent to a three-star. Hotels in the "C" and "D" categories are cheaper but are generally more spartan in their furnishings and offer fewer services. Bathrooms are usually shared.

It is common practice in Croatia for hotels to offer half-board *(polupansion)*, with the price including bed and breakfast, as well as another meal (usually an evening meal). Prices for half-board are very reasonable; often not much more than you would pay for just the room. However, hotel restaurant food is often based on rather standardized "international" cooking, and may lack local character.

Zagreb hotel entrance – more upmarket than most seaside hotels

Sign indicating a camping site, or *Autocamp* nearby

CAMPING SITES

There are plenty of camping sites in Croatia. These range from small, often privately run camping sites to the large *Autocamps*, which offer services and facilities such as restaurants and shops. Almost all Croatian camp sites are located in woods by the sea, so you can keep cool under shady trees on hot summer days. The majority of camping sites are located in Istria and the Kvarner area, and in Dalmatia.

All camping sites are open in the summer months of June, July, August and until the middle of September. However, it is best to check with the camping site itself if you are planning to stay in camping sites during May and late September, as the opening periods can vary from year to year.

Some of the loveliest camping sites, situated as they are in hidden-away spots, are those run by the naturist organization FKK *(see p267)*, which are for naturists only.

Camping outside designated areas is prohibited in Croatia so do not be tempted to stop overnight in the woods or forests, on the beaches or in any areas not specifically reserved for campers.

YOUTH HOSTELS

An economical alternative for young people is to stay in one of the hostels run by the **HFHS** (the **Croatian Youth Hostel Association**).

There are six youth hostels in Croatia. Rates vary according to the season and a Youth Hostelling Card (available from the YHA in your home country) will entitle you to a discount.

PRICES

The hotels and camping sites in the main tourist resorts, such as the coastal areas, the Plitvice lakes and the capital Zagreb, usually charge higher prices compared with similar hotels in other places in Croatia. Prices rise in the high season, particularly in the month of August, at least in the seaside resorts, regardless of a hotel's star rating. However, even these higher prices are still reasonable and visitors to Croatia will find that prices are about 10 per cent to 20 per cent lower compared with other parts of Europe for accommodation of a similar standard.

Prices in Zagreb stay the same all year round.

BOOKINGS

Tourism in Croatia is very much a "do-it-yourself" affair. If you prefer not to opt for an all-in package holiday *(see p274)*, you can plan your excursions as you go along. Excluding the peak of the high season (August), rooms can usually be found without booking in advance.

The Croatian National Tourist Office *(see p267)* can supply information ahead of your trip. Local tourist offices (there is one in every town) will help you find a room or you can apply to a hotel directly to find out if there are rooms available.

The foyer of the Hotel Dubrovnik in Zagreb

DISABLED TRAVELLERS

Care for the disabled in Croatia is good, for the grim reason that the numbers of disabled people have risen as a result of the recent war. However, despite renewed sympathy and consideration, it is taking time to improve disabled access to buildings such as hotels and restaurants. Many hotels can be unsuitable for persons with restricted mobility. This can often be the case with hotels built on steep slopes which are well provided with steps but not ramps or lifts. For further information, contact Savez Organizacija Invalida Hrvatske, the Association of Disabled Organizations of Croatia or RADAR in the UK *(see p267)*.

Outdoor pool – a common facility despite the proximity of the sea

Aerial view of the Sveti Andrija lighthouse near Dubrovnik

LIGHTHOUSES

A delightful and unusual accommodation option in Croatia is the chance to stay in one of the lighthouses which stand on strategic points on the islands and the promontories along the coast. The views can be breathtaking and the setting tranquil, far from the bustle of the tourist resorts.

At the moment it is possible to stay in 11 lighthouses. **Savudrija** is 9 km (5 miles) from Umag, and is the oldest lighthouse in the Adriatic and is built in an ideal spot for windsurfers.

Rt Zub is on the Lanterna peninsula, 13 km (8 miles) from Poreč and Novigrad. Even though it is in a relatively isolated position, it is within reach of a number of tourist resorts.

Sveti Ivan na pučini is situated on an island which is part of the archipelago off Rovinj, which is 3.5 km (2 miles) away, ideal for those who love fishing or diving.

The **Porer** lighthouse, on the island of the same name, is 20 km (12 miles) from Pula. It offers truly spectacular views and is in a particularly isolated position. **Veli Rat** stands among pine trees on the northwestern promontory on the island of Dugi Otok,

35 km (22 miles) from Zadar, while at the entrance to the port of Makarska, near one of the most beautiful beaches in the Adriatic, stands the **Sveti Petar** lighthouse.

The lighthouse of **Sušac** was built in 1878 on the island of the same name, 40 km (25 miles) from Hvar. It stands 100 m (328 ft) above sea level and offers a wonderful view of the open sea. There are numerous paths on the island and it is possible to scuba dive near the rocks at the southern end of the island.

The lighthouse of **Palagruža** is situated 68 km (42 miles) from Split, between the Italian and Croatian coasts, while on the island of Lastovo, 80 km (50 miles) from Split, is the **Struga** lighthouse, dating from 1839. This is a great location for those who love fishing.

The **Sveti Andrija** lighthouse stands on the island of the same name and is 10 km (6 miles) from Dubrovnik. Finally, there is **Prišnjak** lighthouse on the island of Murter, surrounded by a thick pine wood.

The lighthouses contain one or two apartments, able to accommodate four or more people. For more information, contact **Adriatica.net**, who are based in Zagreb.

DIRECTORY

ASSOCIATIONS OF TRAVEL AGENCIES

UHPA Association of Croatian Travel Agencies
Crnčićeva 42, Zagreb.
Tel (01) 230 31 45,
230 49 92.
Fax (01) 230 31 45,
230 49 92.
www.uhpa.hr
www.croatia-travel.org

UNPAH Union of Independent Croatian Travel Agencies
Jurišićeva 1, Zagreb.
Tel (01) 6678 141.
Fax (01) 6678 141.

Studentska Turistička Agencija Zagreb (Students' Tourist Agency)
Ribnjak 36, Zagreb.
Tel (01) 4886 340.

CAMPING SITES

Kamping Udruženje Hrvatske (Croatian Camping Union)
Pionirska 1, Poreč.
Tel (052) 451 324, 451 292.
www.camping.hr

YOUTH HOSTELS

Youth Hostel Association England & Wales
Trevelyan House, Dimple Road, Matlock, Derbyshire DE4 3YH.
Tel 0870 770 8868.
www.yha.org.uk

HFHS Croatian Youth Hostel Association
Savska 5, Zagreb.
Tel (01) 482 92 96.
Fax (01) 482 92 94.
www.hfhs.hr

LIGHTHOUSES

Adriatica.net
Slavonska avenija 26/9, Zagreb.
Tel (01) 2415 611.
Fax (01) 2452 909.
www.adriatica.net
Bookings can be made on-line.

Choosing a Hotel

Hotels have been selected across a wide price range for facilities, good value and location. Most hotels consider July–August to be the high season. Prices will often be much lower outside this period – sometimes reduced by as much as a third. The hotels are listed by area and map references refer to the inside back cover.

ISTRIA AND THE KVARNER AREA

BRIJUNI ISLANDS Karmen

Veliki Brijuni. **Tel** *(052) 525 400* **Fax** *(052) 212 110* **Rooms** *53*   **Map** *A3*

The Brijuni islands are beautiful, not too developed and very quiet. This hotel has a pretty waterside location and is surrounded with the fragrant pines that cover the island. Sea view rooms are obviously desirable but there's a supplement to pay. One of three similar hotels on the island. **www.brijuni.hr/en**

CRES Kimen

Riva Creškin Kapetana, Cres. **Tel** *(051) 571 161* **Fax** *(051) 571 163* **Rooms** *212*   **Map** *B3*

A large resort-style hotel, Kimen is good for families as it has its own good beach and plenty of other sports activities and facilities available. The rooms are on the small side and basic but you'll probably spend most of your time outside them – good value overall. It is a 15 minute walk to town. **www.cresanka.hr**

CRIKVENICA Hotel Esplanade

Strossmayerovo šetalište 52. **Tel** *(051) 785 006* **Fax** *(051) 785 090* **Rooms** *64*   **Map** *B2*

Despite having a pretty old-fashioned building at the front, most of the hotel is modern and low-slung, and more functional than charismatic. Still it has a forest setting and is almost on the beach, so it would be good for families. Try to get a room with a balcony and a sea view. **www.jadran-crikvenica.hr**

CRIKVENICA Kaštel

Frankopanska 22. **Tel** *(051) 241 044* **Fax** *(051) 241 490* **Rooms** *73*   **Map** *B2*

Located in a 14th-century building that was once a monastery and then a castle, this hotel therefore has an imposing exterior. Right by the river and close to the beach the hotel is conveniently situated. Unfortunately the interior leaves a little to be desired, unless 70s décor is your thing. **www.jadran-crikvenica.hr**

KRK Marina

Obala hrvatske mornarice 17, Krk. **Tel** *(051) 221 128* **Fax** *(051) 221 357* **Rooms** *18*   **Map** *B3*

A small charming hotel in the old centre of town right on the pretty harbourfront. The staff try hard to please and there's an agreeable restaurant terrace in front of the hotel perfect for people watching. The rooms are on the small side with no air conditioning, but are pretty good value for money given the location.

KRK Koralj

Vlade Tomašića, Krk. **Tel** *(051) 221 044* **Fax** *(051) 221 063* **Rooms** *190*   **Map** *B3*

This is a large hotel located close to a beautiful bay. There's plenty of facilities to hand and it's therefore a good hotel for families: pools, gym and sauna etc. As a result of a fairly recent renovation, the rooms are simple, modern and comfortable. The catering is a bit industrial but it often is in these places. **www.zlatni-otok.hr**

LOŠINJ Alhambra

Mali Lošinj. **Tel** *(051) 232 022* **Fax** *(051) 232 042* **Rooms** *40*   **Map** *B3*

Hotel Alhambra is a substantial and attractive country villa in pretty Čikat Bay. Surrounded by cypresses and pines, the hotel stands just feet away from the water. Rooms are a decent size and attractively furnished, if a little plain. A sea-view room costs marginally more but is still good value. **www.jadranka.hr**

LOŠINJ Bellevue

Čikat, Mali Lošinj. **Tel** *(051) 231 222* **Fax** *(051) 231 268* **Rooms** *226*   **Map** *B3*

A large and modern hotel thankfully cloaked by the beautiful pine woods of Čikat, close to the sea and 1.5 km (1 mile) from town. Comfortable and well-equipped, it has a better than usual range of entertainments, sports facilities and activities. The rooms are OK too. **www.jadranka.hr**

LOŠINJ Punta

Veli Lošinj. **Tel** *(051) 662 000* **Fax** *(051) 236 301* **Rooms** *231*   **Map** *B3*

Large resort hotel in Veli Lošinj, the smaller sister town to Mali Lošinj. Sitting just around the bay from town and built on the rocks leading to the sea, this establishment has a beautiful location. Usual range of sports facilities and activities including diving and spa and beauty treatments. **www.jadranka.hr**

Key to Symbols *see back cover flap*

LOŠINJ Apoksiomen

Riva Lošinjskih kapetana I, Mali Lošinj. **Tel** *(051) 520 820* **Fax** *(051) 520 830* **Rooms** *25*   **Map** *B3*

This is a lovely boutique hotel set on the harbourfront. It doesn't have every facility going (but it does have wireless Internet) and the rooms are good but nothing special. However, it has an understated sense of style, attention to detail and some great views over the water. There's even a non-smoking floor. **www.apoksiomen.com**

LOŠINJ Villa Favorita

Sunčana Uvala bb. **Tel** *(051) 520 640* **Fax** *(051) 232 853* **Rooms** *8*   **Map** *B3*

Small, 4-star boutique hotel in a delightful setting surrounded by fragrant pines and a mere stone's throw from beautiful clear water. This elegant 19th-century mansion has well-appointed sea-view rooms, a nice garden, a basic sauna and a small swimming pool. **www.villafavorita.hr**

LOVRAN Bristol

Šetalište Maršala Tita 27. **Tel** *(051) 292 022* **Fax** *(051) 292 049* **Rooms** *101*   **Map** *B2*

Attractive late 19th-century wedding cake of a building on the promenade, this hotel has excellent sea views. The best rooms have large windows, high ceilings and a balcony. Despite no air conditioning this is still good value for money. The hotel beach is a little disappointing – stone platforms – but not unusual for Croatia. **www.liburnia.hr**

MOTOVUN Hotel Kaštel

Trg Andrea Antico 7. **Tel** *(052) 681 607* **Fax** *(052) 681 652* **Rooms** *28*   **Map** *A2*

Restored 18th-century town house at the top of a spectacular hill with great views over Istria's interior. The "olde-worlde" steep and winding cobbled streets will do wonders for your fitness. It's the only hotel in town but good value; it also has a fine restaurant serving local specialities – truffles and wines. **www.hotel-kastel-motovun.hr**

OPATIJA Galeb

Maršala Tita 160. **Tel** *(051) 271 177* **Fax** *(051) 271 349* **Rooms** *24*   **Map** *B2*

A lovely little hotel in the centre of town and on the waterfront offering good value for money. There are nice, clean and good-sized rooms with balconies and sea views (those without come a little cheaper). The staff are very friendly and the restaurant and bar come in handy if you want to take it easy locally. Recommended. **www.hotel-galeb.hr**

OPATIJA Istra

Maršala Tita 145. **Tel** *(051) 271 299* **Fax** *(051) 271 826* **Rooms** *115*   **Map** *B2*

Fairly modern medium-sized hotel standing right on the *lungomare* – the promenade that follows the shoreline. The interior is a little drab and dated, but it has a good range of facilities for its price. Centrally located in Opatija and therefore good for wining and dining; only 5 minutes from the main town beach. **www.liburnia.hr**

OPATIJA Palace-Bellevue

Maršala Tita 144–6. **Tel** *(051) 271 811* **Fax** *(051) 271 964* **Rooms** *211*   **Map** *B2*

Actually a combination of two impressive late 19th-century piles next to the town beach, this hotel harks back to the days of the Austro-Hungarian imperial resort. The grand rooms are a little tired around the edges but the basic architecture – marble columns and chandeliers is wonderful. Good for nostalgia buffs. **www.liburnia.hr**

OPATIJA Villa Ariston

Maršala Tita 179. **Tel** *(051)271 379* **Fax** *(051)271 494* **Rooms** *8*   **Map** *B2*

Managing to be both grand in architecture yet small in the number of rooms, this exclusive boutique hotel is set in a beautiful 1924 villa. Standing just a stone's throw from the rocky coastline there's a splendid view. Statuary dots the grounds and adds to the romantic mood. There's also an excellent restaurant. **www.villa-ariston.hr**

OPATIJA Hotel Milenij

Maršala Tita 109. **Tel** *(051) 278 003* **Fax** *(051) 278 021* **Rooms** *125*   **Map** *B2*

Luxury hotel (almost boutique) set in impressive seafront villa-style buildings with classic interiors and nice furniture. A full complement of pools, sauna and beauty therapies add to your relaxation. Good quality catering too. Some rooms have much better views than others though, so be sure to have a look first. **www.ugohoteli.hr**

OPATIJA Hotel Mozart

Maršala Tita 138. **Tel** *(051) 718 260* **Fax** *(051) 271 739* **Rooms** *28*   **Map** *B2*

Five-star hotel located in the centre of town on the main drag close to the waterfront. A substantial five-storey building, its pastel-shading and elegant architecture render it a 19th-century classical idiom. The rooms are nice – with dark wooden floors, good furniture and fresh flowers. Private beach. **www.hotel-mozart.hr**

OPATIJA Admiral

Maršala Tita 139. **Tel** *(051) 271 533* **Fax** *(051) 271 708* **Rooms** *180*   **Map** *B2*

A great ziggurat built on the seafront with fitness studio, beauty parlour, massage, all sorts of saunas, disco and marina. Unlike a lot of the large hotels these facilities are well-maintained. Some may be put off by the modernity and size, but the Admiral Hotel keeps everything nicely shipshape – and so it should at the price. **www.liburnia.hr**

PLITVICE Grabovac

Plitvička Jezera. **Tel** *(053) 751 999* **Fax** *(053) 751 892* **Rooms** *31*   **Map** *C3*

A modern, plain looking building that actually shapes up more as a motel than a hotel. There's a self-service restaurant (and an à la carte one). The rooms are simple and basic. This is away from the main resort complex and 12 km (7 miles) north of the park. Cheap and reasonably cheerful. **www.np-plitvice.com**

PLITVICE Plitvice

Plitvička Jezera. **Tel** *(053) 751 100* **Fax** *(053) 751 165* **Rooms** *52*   **Map** *C3*

Set in the delightful Plitvice Lakes Park, this is probably the best of the four park-run hotels. While the communal areas lack character, the rooms are clean and simple. You can always use the facilities at the main complex if you feel the need for a sauna, sports centre, disco or swim (although you can swim in the lakes). **www.np-plitvice.com**

POREČ Hotel Neptun

Obala Maršala Tita 15. **Tel** *(052) 400 800* **Fax** *(052) 431 351* **Rooms** *143*   **Map** *A2*

Its location at the heart of this ancient town, on the promontory looking out to sea over the harbour, will delight some but this hotel is susceptible to a little noise. It's the best bet in town though, so go for front rooms with harbour views. There's a free boat service to the island of St Nicholas for keen swimmers. **www.riviera.hr**

POREČ Hotel Hostin

Rade Koncara 4. **Tel** *(052) 408 800* **Fax** *(052) 408 857* **Rooms** *41*   **Map** *A2*

Not the prettiest of hotels this is typical Croatian hotel complex architecture – a modern construction, glaringly white-washed. Short on character but near a safe beach and stacked with facilities such as Internet and satellite tv, gym, swimming pool and sauna. Good for families and very close to town. **www.hostin.hr**

POREČ Tamaris

Lanterna. **Tel** *(052) 401 000* **Fax** *(052) 443 500* **Rooms** *345*   **Map** *A2*

A large resort-hotel complex set about 10 km (6 miles) from Poreč. It has a secluded setting (well, as quiet as a possible 700 people can be) and there's oodles of activities for those who want them. The pebble beach is nearby with pine trees providing the shade. Good for families. **www.riviera.hr**

POREČ Parentium

Zelena Laguna. **Tel** *(052) 411 500* **Fax** *(052) 451 536* **Rooms** *340*   **Map** *A2*

Large resort-hotel set on its own peninsula amid shady pines. There's a marina round one side of the promontory and some good beaches round the other. The hotel provides the usual array of facilities and there's plenty for children to do. The rooms are clean but be aware that the pine trees hide some sea views. **www.plavalaguna.hr**

PULA Hotel Omir

Serda Dobrića 6. **Tel** *(052) 218 186* **Fax** *(052) 213 944* **Rooms** *18*   **Map** *A3*

This is a tidy two-star hotel in the heart of the city. A friendly family-run establishment, it has a certain individual air – it has its own pizza restaurant and a petshop – with good deals for pampering guests' pets. The rooms are functional but fairly inexpensive; and at least they are air-conditioned. **www.hotel-omir.com**

PULA Hotel Riviera

Splitska 1. **Tel** *(052) 211 166* **Fax** *(052) 540 285* **Rooms** *65*   **Map** *A3*

With an imposing, classically-columned façade in the Austro-Hungarian style, this city hotel looks grander than a one-star establishment. It has plain but clean rooms and, although it's no longer a first-division hotel, it's still a good bet for the centre of town. **www.arenaturist.hr**

PULA Hotel Scaletta

Flavijevska 36. **Tel** *(052) 541 599* **Fax** *(052) 540 285* **Rooms** *12*   **Map** *A3*

Plain but tastefully decorated family-run boutique hotel. Located near to the main sights in the centre of town this hotel offers excellent value for money. Well-known restaurant offers the traditional food of the area and has a terrace for fine dining indoors or out (try the yummy scampi ravioli with truffles). **www.hotel-scaletta.com**

PULA Hotel Histria

Verudela. **Tel** *(052) 590 000* **Fax** *(052) 214 175* **Rooms** *240*   **Map** *A3*

This is a large, comfortable and well-equipped resort hotel located 4 km (2 miles) outside the city, opposite Marina Veruda. The rooms are large and there are some excellent sea views, so make sure you get one. Half-board in big resort hotels like this may be economical but is only recommended if you enjoy mass catering. **www.arenaturist.hr**

PULA Hotel Valsabbion

Pješćana Uvala 1X/26. **Tel** *(052) 218 033* **Fax** *(052) 383 333* **Rooms** *10*   **Map** *A3*

A very good establishment (slickly marketed) that does things right. Past guests include John Malkovich, Placido Domingo, Naomi Campbell – and we know how particular they can be. This is a smart, intimate, family-run boutique hotel in a seaside villa, 6 kms (4 miles) south of Pula. Their restaurant is one of Croatia's best. **www.valsabbion.net**

RAB Imperial

Palit bb. **Tel** *(051) 724 522* **Fax** *(051) 724 126* **Rooms** *134*   **Map** *B3*

Newly renovated, this large hotel is located close to the heart of Rab town in a quiet leafy park with some tennis courts nearby. It has large, simple but nicely furnished rooms, some with balconies and there's a choice of park or sea views – the latter, as usual, cost a few kuna more. **www.imperial.hr**

RAB Padova

Banjol bb. **Tel** *(051) 724 184* **Fax** *(051) 724 117* **Rooms** *175*   **Map** *B3*

A large and modern hotel located across the bay from Rab's Old Town, this has good sports facilities, indoor and outdoor pools, and new sauna and beauty treatments. Excellent views across the bay to Rab. Note that not all rooms have air conditioning. **www.imperial.hr**

Key to Price Guide *see p222* **Key to Symbols** *see back cover flap*

RABAC Hotel Mimosa

52221 Rabac. **Tel** *(052) 872 024* **Fax** *(052) 872 097* **Rooms** *217* **Map** *B3*

Large, low-slung block of a hotel, one of three that dominate the seafront. For people who like resort hotels, it's full of facilities and activities, the restaurants are easily accessible and everything you need is on your doorstep. Those who don't should look elsewhere. Miniclubs for kids, watersports, tennis etc. **www.maslinicarabac.com**

RABAC Villa Annette

Raška 24. **Tel** *(052) 884 222* **Fax** *(052) 884 225* **Rooms** *30* **Map** *B3*

In a wonderful position on a hill overlooking the bay of Rabac, this hotel is about a 15-minute's walk from the sea. A modern building, it is nevertheless the opposite of the huge resort hotels. The rooms are tastefully decorated, bright and comfortable, and there's a stylish swimming pool on the terrace. Good restaurant too. **www.villaannette.hr**

RIJEKA Jadran

Šetalište XIII divizie 46. **Tel** *(051) 216 600* **Fax** *(051) 216 458* **Rooms** *69* **Map** *B3*

Situated on the Rijeka-Split coastal road, this monolithic building has the sea lapping at its foundations. The refurbished rooms are large, well-furnished and most have big windows and expansive views out over the sea (rooms overlooking the road are cheaper). Internet available in rooms. **www.jadran-hoteli.hr**

RIJEKA Bonavia

Dolac 4 **Tel** *(051) 357 100* **Fax** *(051) 335 969* **Rooms** *121* **Map** *B3*

Despite being 125 years old this looks a modern hotel. Set in the centre of town it is upmarket and business oriented. The rooms are very nice and some have sea views. Service is top knotch and the hotel can arrange all sorts of tours and excursions. Internet in every room and a good variety of decent restaurants and bars. **www.bonavia.hr**

ROVINJ Montauro

A Smareglia. **Tel** *(052) 803 000* **Fax** *(052) 813 287* **Rooms** *285* **Map** *A3*

Located about a ten minutes walk from the old town and surrounded by pines, Montauro is a somewhat dated hotel just minutes from the local beach. It is very handy for a whole string of even better beaches backed by woodland. Facilities are a little limited but you can use the swimming pool at the next door hotel. **www.maistra.hr**

ROVINJ Hotel Adriatic

P Budicin bb. **Tel** *(052) 815 088* **Fax** *(052) 813 573* **Rooms** *27* **Map** *A3*

Located at the very heart of Rovinj, it has a superb position on the one of the prettiest waterfronts in Croatia. Large, sea-view rooms (most of them – do check first). This is the oldest hotel in town (1912), but still the best choice in Rovinj if you like being near the hustle and bustle of the harbour. **www.maistra.hr**

ROVINJ Valdaliso

Monsena. **Tel** *(052) 805 500* **Fax** *(052) 811 541* **Rooms** *120* **Map** *A3*

A short distance around the bay from Rovinj, this hotel provides great access to good pebble beaches and bathing rocks. The rooms are decent if uninspiring. Wide range of activities – sports, diving and even a painting class. Good for families. There's also two annexes to the hotel and a large campsite, so it can get busy. **www.rovinjturist.hr**

ROVINJ Hotel Angelo D'Oro

V Svalba 38–42. **Tel** *(052) 840 502* **Fax** *(052) 840 111* **Rooms** *23* **Map**

Boutique hotel recently created in a lovingly restored 17th-century palace – the period detailing really adds atmosphere. There's a pleasant suntrap of a patio and a shady loggia or balcony to look out over the red-tiled roofs to sea. Enjoy the gourmet restaurant and good service – and it should be good at this price. **www.rovinj.at**

ROVINJ Park

I M Ronjigova. **Tel** *(052) 811 077* **Fax** *(052) 816 977* **Rooms** *202* **Map** *A3*

This is a very popular hotel just across the bay from the old town of Rovinj (about a 20-minute walk). The rooms are fair to good and those with sea views get a beautiful vista. Plenty of facilities on offer, good for families. Those on a budget may have to look for less facilities or further away from town. **www.maistra.hr**

UMAG Adriatic

Jadranska. **Tel** *(052) 741 644* **Fax** *(052) 741 470* **Rooms** *145* **Map** *A2*

An unprepossessing looking building, it is at least situated right on the coast with some excellent sea views. The rooms are looking a little tired and there is no air conditioning. Having said that it is only ten minutes walk to town and it does have plenty of sports facilities. Good for those on a budget. **www.istraturist.hr**

UMAG Sol Aurora

Katoro. **Tel** *(052) 717 000* **Fax** *(052) 717 999* **Rooms** *306* **Map** *A2*

This large resort-style hotel has been newly refurbished and is now one of the best of the large hotel complexes around Umag. Set 2.5 km (1.5 miles) from the town centre, and right on the coast – views may be obscured by pine trees so be warned. Rooms are plain but clean. Plenty of activities for everyone. **www.istraturist.hr**

VRSAR Hotel Panorama

Vrsar. **Tel** *(052) 441 346* **Fax** *(052) 441 050* **Rooms** *151* **Map** *A2?3*

One of those large, modern resort hotels popular in Croatia where function comes before beauty. Set a couple of hundred metres/yards from the sea this still has wonderful sea views. Plus points for families are its great outdoor swimming pools – one seawater – and inexpensive price. Recently renovated. **www.maistra.hr**

VRSAR Belvedere
🏠🏊🍴📶📺　🌑🌑🌑

Vrsar. **Tel** *(052) 441 118* **Fax** *(052) 441 730* **Rooms** *134*　　**Map** *A3*

This is a large holiday resort that has all the usual facilities and is good for families. The rooms are functional, clean and modern. In a beautiful location looking out to the islands, this complex offers value for money if you enjoy such large holiday resorts. Note – there's also 176 apartments that offer far better value. **www.maistra.hr**

VRSAR Pineta
🏠🏊🍴📶📺　🌑🌑🌑🌑

Vrsar. **Tel** *(052) 441 131* **Fax** *(052) 441 150* **Rooms** *95*　　**Map** *A3*

A luxurious hotel with delightful sea views, this gets the best of both worlds as it is both close to town and on the sea. There's an indoor pool and guests can use the next door Belvedere's outdoor pool. If activities are your thing, there's plenty to keep you busy, if not just lounge by the pool or on the fine gravel beach. **www.maistra.hr**

DALMATIA

BRAC Hotel Kaktus
🏠🏊🍴📶📺　🌑🌑🌑

Put Vele Luke 4, Supetar. **Tel** *(021) 631 133* **Fax** *(021) 631 344* **Rooms** *120*　　**Map** *D5*

Part of a huge modern super-complex this is bright, modern and the best-equipped three-star hotel in town. It has sea-view rooms and is in Supetar which, with its harbour and riva, has slightly more authentic charm and fewer daytripping tourists than Bol. Offers plenty of activities. **www.watermanresorts.com**

BRAC Hotel Kaštil
🏠📶📺　🌑🌑🌑

F Radica bb, Bol. **Tel** *(021) 635 995* **Fax** *(021) 635 997* **Rooms** *32*　　**Map** *D5*

Excellent choice for a medium-sized three-star hotel with personality. Built in traditional white stone (it was once a Baroque fortress) and set peacefully by the town harbour, all rooms and the terrace restaurant look out across the sea. It's away from the package tours, too, although the restaurant does get busy in the evening. **www.kastil.hr**

BRAC Elaphusa
🏠🏊🍴📶📺　🌑🌑🌑🌑

Bračka Cesta 13, Bol. **Tel** *(021) 306 200* **Fax** *(021) 635 447* **Rooms** *300*　　**Map** *D5*

Situated in a typical island pine wood, not far from the famous Bol beach and ten minutes from town, this hotel has been recently renovated. Half the rooms have air conditioning and most have balconies (sea views cost extra but beware the pine trees). Facilities galore including sports activities and beauty treatments. **www.bluesunhotels.com**

BRAC Hotel Riu Borak
🏠🏊🍴📶📺　🌑🌑🌑🌑

Bračka Cesta 13, Bol. **Tel** *(021)306 202* **Fax** *(021)306 215* **Rooms** *136*　　**Map** *D5*

Best large four-star resort hotel in Bol set amid the cypresses and pines with a few other large hotels. This has been newly renovated and has all the usual facilities. The best thing about it is that it is right beside Croatia's most famous beach, Zlatni Rat (hence the high price). Crowded in high season. **www.bluesunhotels.com**

CAVTAT Hotel Cavtat
🏠📶📺　🌑🌑🌑

Tiha bb. **Tel** *(020) 478 246* **Fax** *(020) 478 651* **Rooms** *94*　　**Map** *F6*

Modern, low-rise hotel secluded by trees, not far from the town centre and overlooking the beach. This hotel provides solid, if rather functional, three-star value in the lovely town of Cavtat (consider staying here rather than Dubrovnik as you can still get a boat over to the big city and Cavtat is so much more genteel). **www.iberostar.com**

CAVTAT Hotel Supetar
🏠📶📺　🌑🌑🌑

Obala Dr A. Starcevića 27. **Tel** *(020) 479 833* **Fax** *(020) 479 858* **Rooms** *28*　　**Map** *F6*

In an old stone house on the waterfront with sea views and a "beach" nearby (a concrete platform with sun loungers), the Supetar is hard to beat for charm, setting and value for money, although the interior is a little drab. Don't worry about the beach, the nearby pine-covered peninsula has beautiful swimming places. **www.hoteli-croatia.hr/supetar**

CAVTAT Croatia
🏠🏊🍴📶📺　🌑🌑🌑🌑

Frankopanska. **Tel** *(020) 475 555* **Fax** *(020) 478 213* **Rooms** *158*　　**Map** *F6*

Like a Bond-villain's hideout this supersized hotel clings to the side of a wooded hill, all but hidden from sight until you're right on top of it. The rooms are nice and well-furnished and it has its own private bathing ledges off the rocks into the open sea. Not as many facilities as you'd expect, but it feels quite exclusive. **www.hoteli-croatia.hr**

DUBROVNIK Adriatic
🏊🍴　🌑🌑🌑

Masarykov put 9. **Tel** *(020) 433 520* **Fax** *(020) 433 530* **Rooms** *8*　　**Map** *F6*

Set in a modern yet dated building, this hotel has fewer facilities than some places but with an appropriately lower price. Please note, it's not for those with walking difficulties as there's quite a few steps around. The rooms are a little tired but the hotel remains popular for its location, sea views and price. **www.hotelimaestral.com**

DUBROVNIK Hotel Sumratin
🏠　🌑🌑🌑

Šetalište Kralja Zvonimira 27. **Tel** *(020) 436 333* **Fax** *(020) 436 006* **Rooms** *44*　　**Map** *F6*

Out of town on the Lapad Peninsular, this three-storey 1922 villa has a pleasant garden, is located near the beach and is handily placed for restaurants and bars. It has been renovated recently, though its dated interior and basic facilities are still not quite enough to transcend its two-star status. **www.hotels-sumratin.com.**

Key to Price Guide *see p222* **Key to Symbols** *see back cover flap*

DUBROVNIK Zagreb ⬛🍽📺 ⓚⓚⓚ
Šetalište Kralja Zvonimira 56. **Tel** *(020) 436 146* **Fax** *(020) 436 006* **Rooms** *18* **Map** *F6*

A small but comfortable hotel set in a pretty late 19th-century villa, surrounded by a pleasant palm tree-filled garden 4 km (2 miles) from Dubrovnik Old Town, in Lapad. The staff are helpful and friendly. The bathrooms can be a little small. There's a regular bus that runs into town.

DUBROVNIK Excelsior ⬛🍽📺 ⓚⓚⓚⓚⓚ
Frana Supila 12. **Tel** *(020) 353 353* **Fax** *(020) 311 425* **Rooms** *160* **Map** *F6*

Top of the market luxury hotel situated to the east of the city, up the hill. Built into the cliffs it reaches right down to the water. The rooms are nice and the views are fantastic; there's good restaurants and a lovely terrace. Facilities and service are sometimes not quite what you'd expect given the price – it is *very* expensive. **www.hoteli-excelsior.hr**

DUBROVNIK Hotel Stari Grad 📺 ⓚⓚⓚⓚ
Od Sigurate 4. **Tel** *(020) 322 244* **Fax** *(020) 321 256* **Rooms** *8* **Map** *F6*

A tiny boutique hotel, rare for its location in the Old Town and furnished like an aristocrat's mansion – chandeliers, rugs, mirrors and paintings etc. The hotel's star feature is the panoramic view from the roof terrace where you can have your breakfast. Light sleepers note, the Old Town is not the quietest of places. **www.hotelstarigrad.com**

DUBROVNIK Hotel Pucic Palace ⬛📺 ⓚⓚⓚⓚⓚ
od Puca 1. **Tel** *(020) 324 826* **Fax** *(020) 324 826* **Rooms** *17* **Map** *F6*

Opened in 2003, this five-star boutique hotel is set in an 18th-century palace overlooking the old town's market square (Gundulic). Fashionable, luxurious rooms with antique furniture and dark wooden beams are the norm, and very expensive; this is where high society stays – good restaurants and a winebar too. **www.thepucicpalace.com**

DUBROVNIK Hotel Vis ⬛🍽📺 ⓚⓚⓚⓚ
Masarykov put 4. **Tel** *(020) 433 540* **Fax** *(020) 437 333* **Rooms** *136* **Map** *F6*

Overlooking Lapad Bay, this wide, white modern complex has all the comforts and regular hotel facilities, with views out to the open sea (make sure you have one). Clean, modern enough and the service is good too. It might be a bit short of character but it works well on its own level. **www.hotelimaestral.com**

DUBROVNIK Villa Dubrovnik ⬛📺 ⓚⓚⓚⓚⓚ
Vlaha Bukovca 6. **Tel** *(020) 422 933* **Fax** *(020) 423 465* **Rooms** *40* **Map** *F6*

Across the bay facing the Old Town and nestled in the cliffs, this hotel has a superb location – rooms have balconies and sea views. The restaurant is on a terrace over the sea for romantic sunset meals. The hotel staff are helpful and there's a boat service to Dubrovnik. Best not to take the half-board option if you can. **www.villa-dubrovnik.hr**

DUGI OTOK Hotel Lavanda ⬛🍽📺 ⓚⓚ
23286, Bozava, Dugi Otok. **Tel** *(023) 291 291* **Fax** *(023) 377 682* **Rooms** *80* **Map** *C4*

Small hotel complex in a good location in Bozava, only a few steps from the waters of a tranquil cove. All rooms have been recently refurbished and have balconies with sea views. The hotel has a lot of the usual facilities – pool, sauna, massage; access to tennis, bowling, table tennis and diving etc. **www.hoteli-bozava.hr**

HVAR Amfora ⬛🍽📺 ⓚⓚⓚⓚⓚ
Hvar. **Tel** *(021) 750 300* **Fax** *(021) 750 301* **Rooms** *330* **Map** *D5*

Large hotel (it includes 100 apartments) on the beachfront not far from Hvar town. It is modern and stylish inside and has made a real effort to furnish the rooms nicely. There's two pleasant restaurants with sea views (one with live music in the evenings). There's good tennis facilities and a diving school too. **www.suncanihvar.hr**

HVAR Hotel Podstine ⬛📺 ⓚⓚⓚⓚⓚ
Podstine bb, Hvar. **Tel** *(021) 740 400* **Fax** *(021) 740 499* **Rooms** *40* **Map** *D5*

Just under 2 km (1 mile) south-west of Hvar town centre, this hotel is set apart in a quiet cove, surrounded by shade-giving trees and with its own private beach and soothing outdoor seaside terraces. The rooms are simple – all of which have views out over the sea and most have balconies. **www.podstine.com**

HVAR Hotel Riva ⬛📺 ⓚⓚⓚⓚⓚ
Obala Sv. Nlikole 71, Hvar. **Tel** *(021) 750 100* **Fax** *(021) 741 147* **Rooms** *57* **Map** *D5*

Once the modest Slavija Hotel, a major renovation has seen it emerge as an upmarket luxury boutique establishment. The rooms have been completely revamped – flat-screen TVs and designer furniture. It has a superb location in the centre of town and near to the lively Carpe Diem bar/club – so don't expect complete quiet. **www.suncanihvar.hr**

HVAR Palace ⬛📺 ⓚⓚⓚⓚⓚ
Hvar. **Tel** *(021) 741 966* **Fax** *(021) 742 420* **Rooms** *63* **Map** *D5*

The oldest hotel in Hvar at the heart of the Old Town and overlooking Hvar bay. There's an elegant rooftop terrace over an archaic and pretty loggia. The rest is more modern but the décor is getting a bit tired. It doesn't have all the facilities of the big modern hotels (eg air conditioning), but there's talk of a refurb. **www.suncanihvar.hr**

KORČULA Bon Repos ⬛📺 ⓚⓚⓚ
Korčula. **Tel** *(020) 711 102* **Fax** *(020) 711 122* **Rooms** *278* **Map** *E6*

Large hotel built in classic 70s architecture and close to the sea. Surrounded by pines and cypresses, the hotel has a water taxi to town in the high season or it's a pleasant 15 minute walk around the bay. The rooms are clean and simple but meal times can be a bit of a scrum when busy. Plenty of facilities.

KORČULA Korčula

Korčula. **Tel** *(020) 711 078* **Fax** *(020) 711 746* **Rooms** *24*

Map *E6*

A small and traditional looking hotel in the centre of town with a great waterfront terrace. Built in light-coloured Korčula stone, this has an old-fashioned feel about it, but some rooms are a bit tired. The hotel's not perfect by any means but the location is unbeatable and people watching from the terrace in the evening is a must.

KORČULA Liburna

Korčula. **Tel** *(020) 726 006* **Fax** *(020) 711 746* **Rooms** *83*

Map *E6*

In a quiet and secluded position about a five-minute walk around the bay from Korčula town, the hotel has a great location looking out to sea. Built in the 80s it has a 70s look about it but is OK. The rooms are good-sized, basic but with air conditioning. Not the best hotel for small children – small hotel beach, but there's better just along the coast.

MAKARSKA Hotel Meteor

21300, Makarska. **Tel** *(021) 602 600* **Fax** *(021) 611 419* **Rooms** *270*

Map *E5*

One of the most comfortable hotels in the area with the facilities to match. Set in shady woodlands on a beachfront west of the town centre, all rooms have sea-view balconies (although you have to crane your neck for those on the side). The food lets it down a bit, so plan to eat out. Seawater pool. **www.hoteli-makarska.hr**

MAKARSKA Biokovo

Obala Kralja Tomislava. **Tel** *(021) 615 244* **Fax** *(021) 615 081* **Rooms** *60*

Map *E5*

Centrally located hotel that stands on the seafront with a palm-lined road separating the building from the delightful bay. Well equipped rooms, plenty of beauty treatments and a nearby sports centre. Scores highly for its location in town – those seeking solitude may wish to look elsewhere (outside Makarska even). **www.hotelbiokovo.hr**

OREBIC Hotel Bellevue

Obala pomoraca 36. **Tel** *(020) 713 148* **Fax** *(020) 714 310* **Rooms** *152*

Map *E6*

Close to the older part of town and situated a stone's throw from a pleasant pebble beach, the amount of facilities on offer belies its two-star status. Most rooms have sea views and some have balconies. Good value and not too far from one of Dalmatia's best beaches – Trstenica – which is almost sandy. **www.orebic-htp.hr**

OREBIC Hotel Rathaneum

Petra Kresmira 1V 107. **Tel** *(020) 713 022* **Fax** *(020) 714 310* **Rooms** *175*

Map *E6*

Outside of town on a woodland beach, the main advantage of this fairly large hotel is its secluded location. The usual raft of facilities and activities is provided – otherwise everything is acceptable rather than memorable. Like a lot of these hotels it has only recently come out of state ownership (service can be inconsistent). **www.orebic-htp.hr**

PAG Pagus

Ante Starčevića 1, Pag. **Tel** *(023) 611 309* **Fax** *(023) 611 101* **Rooms** *70*

Map *C4*

A modern low hotel stretching along its own private pebble beach close to the town of Pag (there's an older building without air conditioning). The rooms are large and those on the front have lovely sea views. There's the opportunity for plenty of watersports. All in all, one of the better hotels in the area. **www.coning.hr/hotelpagus**

POMENA Hotel Odisej

Pomena bb, Mljet. **Tel** *(020) 362 111* **Fax** *(020) 744 042* **Rooms** *157*

Map *E6*

The picturesque harbour of Pomena is in the heart of the Mljet National Park, meaning that this place is located miles off the beaten track on a remote lip of land surrounded by water and unspoilt forest. You can really get away from it all and relax or enjoy the cycling and watersports galore. Worth a detour to stay there. **www.hotelodisej.hr**

PRIMOŠTEN Zora

Velika Raduća. **Tel** *(022) 581 022* **Fax** *(022) 571 161* **Rooms** *385*

Map *D5*

Nestling into a thick blanket of pines and cypresses this large resort-style complex has an excellent location on a narrow isthmus facing Primošten. Nice rooms with balconies, there's lots of facilities in the peaceful and shady forest. It's a pleasant walk into town and the hotel is good for families. **www.dalmacija.net/primosten/zora_eng.htm**

SALI Hotel Sali

Sali bb. 23281, Sali. **Tel** *(023) 377 049* **Fax** *(023) 377 078* **Rooms** *48*

Map *C4*

Top value for money here. This hotel provides basic no-frills accommodation (although there is air conditioning) but in a really beautiful location. The food's good in the restaurant attached and being in a lovely cool forest by the sea is the icing on the cake. **www.hotel-Sali.hr**

ŠIBENIK Hotel Jadran

Obala Dr Franje Tudmana 52. **Tel** *(022) 242 009* **Fax** *(022) 212 480* **Rooms** *57*

Map *D5*

If you prefer to stay in town, this is the only place. It's a modern building which looks a little out of place among the old stone buildings of Šibenik, but it's relatively sympathetically styled. The hotel is very good value for money and has an attractive harbourside location. **www.rivijera.hr**

ŠIBENIK Hotel Jakov

Hotelsko nasilje Solaris bb. **Tel** *(022) 361 800* **Rooms** *238*

Map *D5*

Large, modern complex 6 km (4 miles) outside of town but right on a beautiful beach. There's also bucketloads of facilities: seawater swimming pool; volleyball, mini-football, basketball and tennis courts; mini golf and children's playground. Expect full occupancy in high season. **www.solaris.hr**

Key to Price Guide *see p222* **Key to Symbols** *see back cover flap*

ŠIBENIK Jure

Hotelsko naselije Solaris bb. **Tel** *(022) 362 951* **Fax** *(022) 362 942* **Rooms** *256*   **Map** *D5*

One of several hotels all owned by the same company and in the same area, about 6 km (4 miles) from Šibenik Old Town. Close to the pebble beach and surrounded by pine trees, the location is pleasant enough. The décor of the hotel complex is a little industrial and functional but the rooms are OK. There's a bus to town. **www.solaris.hr**

SPLIT Hotel Consul

Tršćanska 34. **Tel** *(021) 340 130* **Fax** *(021) 340 133* **Rooms** *19*   **Map** *D5*

A small family-run establishment about a five- or ten-minute walk from the centre of town, this hotel scores highly because of its location – close to the Marjan Peninsula and the historical centre. The exterior of the hotel is nothing special but the rooms are pretty good. The restaurant is not bad too. **www.hotel-consul.net**

SPLIT Hotel Jadran

Sustipanski put 23. **Tel** *(021) 398 622* **Fax** *(021) 398 586* **Rooms** *31*   **Map** *D5*

Modern hotel, 20 minutes walk from the bustle of central Split and set on the coast with most rooms looking out to sea. Superb sports facilities e.g. Olympic pool, tennis courts, sailing. A good choice, especially as the pine-covered Marjan Peninsula and some beautiful secluded beaches are a short walk away. **www.hoteljadran.hr**

SPLIT Hotel President

Starcevica 1. **Tel** *(021) 305 222* **Fax** *(021) 305 225* **Rooms** *43*   **Map** *D5*

This is an upmarket hotel with nicely furnished and well-appointed rooms. There's an element of the corporate hotel atmosphere that comes from having business customers, but that's not always a bad thing. It delivers sophisticated service right in the centre of Split, and the prices aren't too high either. **www.hotelpresident.hr**

SPLIT Hotel Globo

Lovretska 18. **Tel** *(021) 481 111* **Fax** *(021) 481 118* **Rooms** *25*   **Map** *D5*

Spacious, refined bedrooms and four-star comforts throughout supplemented by a similarly high quality of service offset the bland exterior and rather ordinary urban setting of the hotel. It's a 15-minute walk into town and further for the beaches, but beaches are not really Split's forte (Marjan peninsula excepted). **www.hotelglobo.hr**

SPLIT Hotel Split

Put Trstenika 19. **Tel** *(021) 303 111* **Fax** *(021) 303 011* **Rooms** *135*   **Map** *D5*

This hotel is about a 25-minute walk from town. With a dated décor and tired interiors the standard rooms are just standard (superior look better). Most rooms have balconies and good sea views. The food is OK and there's a pleasant terrace bar, but the hotel is not half as pretty as it looks on the website. **www.hotelsplit.hr**

STON Vila Koruna

Peljeski put 1, Ston. **Tel** *(020) 754 999* **Fax** *(020) 754 642* **Rooms** *6*   **Map** *E6*

Upmarket family-run boutique villa with only six rooms. Harbour location and restaurant terrace for dining overlooking the sea (the fish are kept in tanks around the edges). In fact, this is really a restaurant with some rooms attached, so there's not far to stagger after a delightful meal. **www.vila-koruna.hr**

STON Hotel Ostrea

20230, Mali Ston, Ston. **Tel** *(020) 754 555* **Fax** *(020) 754 575* **Rooms** *9*   **Map** *E6*

Surprisingly large rooms in this lovely tiny boutique hotel delightfully located in the harbour. Family-run, the standard of service is friendly and professional. Added bonus: two excellent restaurants on your doorstep serving platefuls of the famous oysters and shellfish of the area, with good local wines. **www.ostrea.hr**

TROGIR Villa Sikaa

Obala Kralja Zvonimira 13. **Tel** *(021) 798 240* **Fax** *(021) 885 149* **Rooms** *10*   **Map** *D5*

Small, boutique hotel in a 300-year old building set on the waterfront looking across at the old island town of Trogir. It only has ten rooms, but most of them are large. The hotel has been sympathetically updated inside with decent furniture and fittings and the staff are most helpful. Outstanding value. **www.vila-sikaa-r.com**

TROGIR Hotel Concordia

Bana Berislavica 22. **Tel** *(021) 885 400* **Fax** *(021) 885 401* **Rooms** *14*   **Map** *D5*

Impressive 18th-century stone townhouse converted into an attentive boutique hotel in the centre of Trogir's Old Town. Most of the rooms have sea views but do check beforehand. Some of the accommodation is a little snug but, in general, it offers value and services beyond its modest two-star rating. **www.concordia-hotel.htnet.hr**

TROGIR Trogirski Dvori

Kralja Trpimira 245. **Tel** *(021) 885 444* **Fax** *(021) 881 318* **Rooms** *12*   **Map** *D5*

Small family-run hotel about a ten-minute walk from the centre of town, and two minutes to the nearest beach. There's a tennis court belonging to the hotel but more importantly the restaurant is actually quite good. It serves the usual Dalmatian cuisine and Croatian wines on a pleasant vine-shaded terrace. **www.hotel-trogirskidvori.com**

TROGIR Vila Tina

Arbanija, Trogir. **Tel** *(021) 888 305* **Fax** *(021) 888 401* **Rooms** *24*   **Map** *D5*

Charming, good value place to stay, 5 km (3 miles) east of Trogir. It offers large functional rooms with balconies. Set right on the coast, with easy-access swimming close to hand, the family-run Vila Tina also has a lovely terrace for sipping cool drinks while watching the sun go down. Good restaurant for grilled fish too. **www.vila-tina.hr**

VIS Hotel Tamaris

Obala sv. Jurja 20. **Tel** *(021) 711 350* **Fax** *(021) 711 349* **Rooms** *27* **Map** *D6*

Stately Austro-Hungarian 19th-century villa, with characteristically high ceilings and wooden floors, right in the centre of Vis. Provides a surprising number of activities given its location. The rooms are simply furnished but inexpensive. Getting a room with a harbour-view is a must.

VIS Hotel Paula

Petra Hektorovića, Vis. **Tel** *(021) 711 362* **Rooms** *35* **Map** *D6*

Located in the eastern side of town, amid a nest of cobbled streets and ancient buildings, this is an especially attractive looking hotel. Some of the rooms are better than others so have a look first, but this is a cosy, family-run hotel that does the essentials with a dash of charm. Good restaurant. Good value. **www.paula-hotel.htnet.hr**

VIS Issa

Setaliste Apolonija Zanelle 5, Vis. **Tel** *(021) 711 124* **Fax** *(021) 711 740* **Rooms** *125* **Map** *D6*

Sitting on the edge of Vis bay about 800 m (900 yards) from the centre of Vis, this is a modern hotel with plenty of sports facilities. These include tennis, mini-soccer, volleyball, basketball etc. It's a modern building set close to the water. All the rooms have balconies but check for a sea or park view.

ZADAR Hotel Donat

Majstora Radovana 7. **Tel** *(023) 206 500* **Fax** *(023) 332 065* **Rooms** *240* **Map** *C4*

Large and functional modern complex with better than standard 3-star facilities. Recent renovations have seen the addition of a swimming pool and better sports facilities. However, its selling point remains its economy and position right on the beach on a lovely stretch of coast. **www.falkensteiner.com**

ZADAR Hotel Adriana Select

Majstora Radovana 7. **Tel** *(023) 206 636* **Fax** *(023) 332 065* **Rooms** *48* **Map** *C4*

Part of the same group as the Hotel Donat but a totally different concept. Set in an attractive 19th-century villa, near the beach and upgradingly restored into what they call a lifestyle hotel – they don't have rooms, they have "junior suites". Bit pretentious, but there's a good swimming pool and an excellent restaurant. **www.falkensteiner.com**

ZADAR Hotel President

Vladana Desnice 16. **Tel** *(023) 333 696* **Fax** *(023) 333 595* **Rooms** *27* **Map** *C4*

Smart hotel, verging on plush. The interior is slightly over-the-top – covered in dark cherrywood and thickly draped curtains with plenty of swashes. Nevertheless it exudes calm and quality. As you'd expect there's good service, and a restaurant well worth eating in. The hotel is also close to the beach. **www.hotel-president.hr**

ZAGREB

ZAGREB Hotel Ilica

Ilica 102. **Tel** *(01) 37 77 522* **Fax** *(01) 37 77 722* **Rooms** *23* **Map** *D2*

Near the main square, this small family hotel is top value for money. It has been decorated in an eclectic and individual style. If you want corporate uniformity, don't come here but if you enjoy a bit of character then do consider it. This place gets booked up early and doesn't take credit cards. **www.hotel-ilica.hr**

ZAGREB Hotel Jadran

Vlaška 50. **Tel** *(01) 45 53 777* **Fax** *(01) 46 12 151* **Rooms** *48* **Map** *D2*

This is a conveniently located hotel only minutes from the central square. However the façade looks a little austere and some of the the rooms are a bit dowdy – others though are fine so ask to see the room first. Take rooms at the back to avoid any street noise. **www.hup-Zagreb.hr**

ZAGREB Hotel Sliško

Binićeva 7. **Tel** *(01) 61 84 777* **Fax** *(01) 61 94 223* **Rooms** *18* **Map** *D2*

Modest hotel in mid-town location near the bus station. The rooms are simply furnished in a modern fashion and the hotel offers offers air conditioning and satellite television. The level of facilities is very good for the low prices. Overall it's remarkable value for money. **www.slisko.hr**

ZAGREB Laguna

Kranjčevićeva 29. **Tel** *(01) 382 02 22* **Fax** *(01) 382 00 35* **Rooms** *160* **Map** *D2*

A pleasant and modern hotel located a few minutes taxi drive out of the centre of the city. This means that the hotel offers better facilities at a better price than city-centre hotels. The rooms and common areas are well-furnished and of good quality. Another good value Zagreb hotel. **www.hotel-laguna.hr**

ZAGREB Central

Branimirova 3. **Tel** *(01) 484 11 22* **Fax** *(01) 484 13 04* **Rooms** *79* **Map** *D2*

A modern hotel close to the train and bus station, this is convenient for those on the move and for those doing some sightseeing. The rooms are a bit small but also fairly well furnished. There's an uninspiring bar and Internet capability in some rooms. **www.hotel-central.hr**

Key to Price Guide *see p222* **Key to Symbols** *see back cover flap*

ZAGREB Hotel Vila Tina ▯▯▯▯ ⓝⓝⓝ
Bukovačka cesta 213. **Tel** *(01) 24 45 138* **Fax** *(01) 24 45 204* **Rooms** *25* **Map** *D2*

Relatively modern upmarket hotel in a quiet residential area near to the centre of town. Well-equipped with air conditioning, good indoor swimming pool and beauty centre. It's near the beautiful green open spaces of Maksimir Park. Pretty good value. **www.vilatina.com**

ZAGREB International ▯▯▯▯ ⓝⓝⓝ
Miramarska 24. **Tel** *(01) 610 88 00* **Fax** *(01) 615 94 59* **Rooms** *207* **Map** *D2*

Part of an ultramodern looking complex in the business area of town (but still walking distance to the sights). It is geared mainly towards business travellers, although it does have family rooms. Good room facilities and service. There's a large but ultimately disappointing casino in the complex. **www.hotel-international.hr**

ZAGREB Hotel Palace ▯▯▯ ⓝⓝⓝⓝ
Trg J.J. Strossmayera 10. **Tel** *(01) 489 96 00* **Fax** *(01) 481 13 57* **Rooms** *123* **Map** *D2*

Built in 1891, the Palace is the grand old lady of Zagreb's hotels. Central location near the historical architecture of the city, this hotel oozes old world aristocracy, if a little bit tired. The rooms are decent-sized, smart with wood panels and good furniture. The communal areas are faded and veering towards old-fashioned. **www.palace.hr**

ZAGREB Westin Zagreb ▯▯▯▯▯ ⓝⓝⓝⓝ
Kršnjagova 1. **Tel** *(01) 489 20 00* **Fax** *(01) 489 20 01* **Rooms** *378* **Map** *D2*

Top-knotch luxury hotel within a modern building, this was once known as the Opera Hotel. Now rebranded and refurbished, it provides international levels of service and facilities at a good price. The hotel is located in the very heart of the city near the major cultural and historical attractions. **www.westin.com/Zagreb**

ZAGREB Esplanade ▯▯▯▯▯ ⓝⓝⓝⓝ
Mihanovićeva 1. **Tel** *(01) 456 66 66* **Fax** *(01) 456 60 50* **Rooms** *209* **Map** *D2*

Set in a wonderfully regal building (circa 1925), the Esplanade is a refined establishment with excellent service – probably the best hotel in Zagreb. The rooms are tastefully decorated with luxurious bathrooms and the communal areas are swathed in marble and dripping with chandeliers. Good restaurants and bars too. **www.regenthotels.com**

CENTRAL CROATIA

CAKOVEC Hotel Aurora ▯▯ ⓝⓝ
Franje punčeća 2. **Tel** *(040) 310 700* **Fax** *(040) 3100 787* **Rooms** *10* **Map** *D1*

This grandiose building for a hotel, harbouring only ten bedrooms has most essential and luxury facilities – indoor swimming pool, sauna, sporting opportunities. The rooms are pleasantly spacious and therefore the hotel is probably the best bet for accommodation in Cakovec. **www.gutex.hr**

CAKOVEC Park ▯ ⓝⓝ
Zrinjsko Frankopanska. **Tel** *(040) 311 255* **Fax** *(040) 311 244* **Rooms** *10* **Map** *D1*

A modern looking (well maybe from the 1970s) building about five-minutes walk from the centre of town, this is handily located for sightseeing. The rooms are small but cosy and the communal areas are uninspiring. However, the rooms are inexpensive so a good choice if you are on a budget or Hotel Aurora is fully booked. **www.union-ck.hr**

KARLOVAC Hotel Carstadt ▯▯▯ ⓝ
A. Vraniczanyeva 2. **Tel** *(047) 611 111* **Fax** *(047) 611 111* **Rooms** *37* **Map** *C2*

Excellent central location. The rooms are simple if uninspiring but offer all necessary facilities. There's a decent restaurant on the ground floor (although the terms "casino" and "cocktail bar" are really triumphs of optimism over truthful description). Popular with travelling businessmen, especially at this price. **www.carlstadt.hr**

KARLOVAC Hotel Korana Srakovcic ▯▯▯ ⓝⓝⓝⓝ
Perivoj Josipa Vrbanica 8. **Tel** *(047) 609 090* **Fax** *(047) 609 091* **Rooms** *15* **Map** *C2*

This is, by far, the best hotel in the area – it has a delightful location right on the River Korana. The hotel is in a grand, sophisticated and exclusive villa set apart from the town and there's everything you could want – at a price. Plenty of sports facilities for those who want to tire themselves out. **www.hotelkorana.hr**

SAMOBOR Hotel Livadić ▯ ⓝ
Kralja Tomislava 5. **Tel** *(01) 336 58 50* **Fax** *(01) 336 58 51* **Rooms** *12* **Map** *C2*

Close to the historic picture-postcard centre of Samobor, this little hotel fits in perfectly. Pastel exterior, antique furniture, plush bedding and friendly service all create a wonderful atmosphere. There's also a nice café with a terrace where you can enjoy the treat of the region – a custard slice called a *Samoborske kremsnite*. **www.hotel-livadic.hr**

SAMOBOR Babylon ▯▯ ⓝⓝ
Franje Tuđmana 5, Novaki. **Tel** *(01) 337 15 00* **Fax** *(01) 337 10 44* **Rooms** *23* **Map** *C2*

Located about 3 km (2 miles) from Samobor, this characterful hotel looks quite plain from the outside but is quaintly decorated on the inside in wood and white stone. It has a good restaurant attached, specializing in traditional *peka* (iron pot) cuisine. The hotel is on the road between Zagreb and Sveta Nedelja. **www.babylon.hr**

SAMOBOR Garni Hotel Samobor

Josipa Jelačića 30. **Tel** *(01) 336 69 71* **Fax** *(01) 336 69 71* **Rooms** *12*   **Map** *C2*

A pretty alpine-style building housing this small and friendly hotel nestles into the wooded hills just outside the town of Samobor. The rooms are fairly plain and simple but the communal areas are quirkily decorated. There's a nice terrace bar/restaurant overlooking the hotel tennis courts. Some limited business facilities. **www.hotel-samobor.hr**

SISAK Hotel I

Obrtnička bb. **Tel** *(044) 527 277* **Fax** *(044) 527 278* **Rooms** *16*   **Map** *D2*

With three stars and sixteen rooms this is about as good as it gets in Sisak. It's a modern building that is more like a motel than a proper hotel. It has air conditioning but the rooms are still plain and characterless. It should be OK as an overnight stop for visitors on a driving tour of Central Croatia.

SISAK Panonija

Ivana Kukuljevića Sakćinskog 21. **Tel** *(044) 515 600* **Fax** *(044) 515 601* **Rooms** *84*   **Map** *D2*

Possibly one of the least attractive hotel exteriors there can be, this hotel thankfully is much nicer on the inside. The refurbished rooms are actually quite tastefully furnished. There's a good restaurant in the same building as the hotel. Not great but there's not a lot of choice in Sisak. **www.hotel-panonija.hr**

SLAVONIA AND BARANJA

ĐAKOVO Blaža

A Starčevića 156a. **Tel** *(031) 816 760* **Fax** *(031) 816 764* **Rooms** *23*   **Map** *F2*

Strange-looking hotel 1.5 km (1 mile) from the centre of Dakovo with a surprising number of facilities – a large outdoor swimming pool, access to tennis courts and gym. These have elevated its star rating undeservedly. Rooms are very plain, there is a restaurant but the communal areas are not great. Somewhere to stop for the night only.

DARUVAR Hotel Balise

Trg Kralja Tomislava 22. **Tel** *(043) 440 220* **Fax** *(043) 440 220* **Rooms** *17*   **Map** *E2*

Small, centrally located budget hotel set within a once-grand building but now looking slightly down-at-heel – the front section of the building has been taken over by a bank. The rooms are fairly basic and without pretentions but the hotel offers good value for money.

DARUVAR Termal

Julijer Park 1. **Tel** *(043) 623 000* **Fax** *(043) 331 455* **Rooms** *150*   **Map** *E2*

Large modern hotel (built 1980) located in a leafy park in Daruvar near the thermal springs. Provides the usual Croatian spa experience – a cross between a hospital and a sports club – health treatments and gyms, swimming pools, saunas etc. More intimate accommodation available next-door in Vila Arcadia, run by the same company.

OSIJEK Hotel Central

Trg A Starčevića 6. **Tel** *(031) 283 399* **Fax** *(031) 283 891* **Rooms** *39*   **Map** *F2*

Medium-sized traditional hotel set in the heart of town and catering to a discerning clientele. Rooms are good with modern but classic-styled furniture. The common areas are cosy, characterful and dated, but in the best way – it was originally built in 1889. Enjoy the Viennese coffee-house. **www.hotel-central-os.hr**

OSIJEK Hotel Waldinger

Županijska ulica 8. **Tel** *(031) 250 450* **Fax** *(031) 250 453* **Rooms** *16*   **Map** *F2*

A lovely old-fashioned hotel, near the centre and only 100 metres/yards from the Drava Promenade. It's only got 16 elegant rooms (some with a Jacuzzi) but offers a far more intimate four-star experience than its huge sky-scraper rival, Hotel Osijek. There's a coffee shop in the hotel for some rich pastry consumption. **www.waldinger.hr**

OSIJEK Hotel Osijek

Šamačka. **Tel** *(031) 230 333* **Fax** *(031) 212 135* **Rooms** *147*   **Map** *F2*

Large modern building that has been completely renovated and updated. Now aimed at the business market there's wireless Internet in the rooms, a wide range of catering outlets and other business facilities. The rooms are smart and modern and you can always relax in a Turkish bath once the work is done. **www.hotelosijek.hr**

SPISIC BUKOVICA Hotel Mozart

Kinkovo bb. **Tel** *(033) 801 000* **Fax** *(033) 801 016* **Rooms** *14*   **Map** *E2*

This hotel, with only 14 rooms, has all the comforts of town but is right out in the middle of the countryside. The interior décor has an over-the-top period charm, but that seems appropriate in a country house hotel. Idyllic peace and quiet in pretty rural grounds – you can go horse riding or even hunting. **www.hotelmozart.hr**

VINKOVCI Slavonija

Duga ulica 1. **Tel** *(032) 342 555* **Fax** *(032) 342 550* **Rooms** *86*   **Map** *F2*

A tall modern-looking hotel in the centre of town, overlooking the turgid Bosut river (famed for its slow flow!), this hotel offers the best facilities in town. Not a great boast perhaps but its two restaurants, a café and a hairdressers will keep you well fed and groomed. **www.son-ugo-cor.com**

Key to Price Guide *see p222* **Key to Symbols** *see back cover flap*

VINKOVCI Cibalia

A Starčevića 51. **Tel** *(032) 339 222* **Fax** *(032) 332 920* **Rooms** *23*   **Map** *F2*

Situated a short distance north of the centre of town, this newly-built hotel provides large clean rooms with a decent level of facilities. There is a small restaurant inside. The atmosphere lacks a little in character but the rooms represent good value for the price. Handy for train and bus connections. **www.hotel-cibalia.com**

VUKOVAR Dunav

Trg Republike 1. **Tel** *(032) 441 285* **Fax** *(032) 441 762* **Rooms** *35*   **Map** *G2*

This hotel has an unexciting exterior and fails to create a much better impression with its interior. However, it is situated right on the river so it has pleasant river views. Built in the 1980s it was completely destroyed in the war – it was rebuilt exactly as it was before. Good value for money.

VUKOVAR Hotel Lav

J J Strossmayera 18. **Tel** *(032) 445 100* **Fax** *(032) 445 110* **Rooms** *38*   **Map** *G2*

By far and away the smartest hotel in Vukovar. This is a newly built but impressive building. Four-star facilities and clean and functional rooms (although lacking a little in character) with pretty river views. Good levels of service and wireless Internet access. **www.hotel-lav.hr**

THE NORTHERN COUNTIES

KRAPINSKE TOPLICE Hotel Aquae Vivae

A Mihanovića 2. **Tel** *(049) 202 202* **Fax** *(049) 232 322* **Rooms** *155*   **Map** *D1*

A modern and fully operational spa hotel where guests bump into patients. It has a decent facilities but Croatian spa resorts don't cater for the luxury end of the market. The rooms are built for function not comfort. However, if you're in the area for the water it's the best – indeed the only – place to stay. **www.aquae-vivae.hr**

PREGRADA Hotel Dvorac Bezanec

Valentinovo bb. **Tel** *(049) 376 800* **Fax** *(049) 376 810* **Rooms** *21*   **Map** *C1*

One of the rare 5-star hotels in Croatia, but fantastic value for money. If you've ever wanted to stay in a chateau here's your chance. It's a 17th-century stately home set in lovely rolling green countryside with a great restaurant as well. Tennis courts, bikes and other activities available. **www.bezanec.hr**

STUBIČKE TOPLICE Hotel Matija Gubec

Ulica Viktora 31. **Tel** *(049) 282 501* **Fax** *(049) 282 403* **Rooms** *97*   **Map** *D1*

It's here or nowhere in Stubičke Toplice. Another medium-to-large fairly uninspiring spa hotel. The rooms are plain but you can have plenty of fun in the wealth of pools, waterfalls, whirlpool baths available and the natural water baths are steamy hot. There's also a gym and sauna. **www.hotel-mgubec.com**

TRAKOŠĆAN Hotel Coning

Trakošćan 5. **Tel** *(042) 796 224* **Fax** *(042) 796 205* **Rooms** *80*   **Map** *D1*

Close to the Slovenian border and just over the road from the best castle in Croatia, this hotel is set in beautiful countryside. It's a modern building but sympathetically styled. The hotel looks a bit like a motel but offers plenty of wholesome outdoor activities and a sauna and gym. Good food too. **www.coning.hr**

VARAŽDIN La'Gus

Varaždinberg. **Tel** *(042) 652 940* **Fax** *(042) 652 944* **Rooms** *26*   **Map** *D1*

Because this small hotel is a fifteen-minute drive from Varaždin, it is probably only an option if the hotels in town are booked up or you really like the countryside – a nice vineyard setting. The rooms are pleasant enough and there's a large terrace out the back, but it's not terribly appealing from the road. **www.hotel-lagus.hr/enama.html**

VARAŽDIN Pansion Garestin

Zagrebačka 34. **Tel** *(042) 214 314* **Fax** *(042) 214 314* **Rooms** *10*   **Map** *D1*

This combination of a hotel and restaurant is only a few minutes walk from the Baroque centre of town. An attractive-looking building there's a faux-Baroque exterior on one side with a modern rustic-style on the other. Rooms are plain but it has a restaurant and a large terrace where it serves excellent food.

VARAŽDIN Hotel Turist

Kralja Zvonimira 19. **Tel** *(042) 395 395* **Fax** *(042) 215 028* **Rooms** *104*   **Map** *D1*

This is a large modern hotel in the centre of town, aiming at the business market. It has basic business facilities, bar, restaurant and café (although you'd be better off dining at the Zlatna Guska or Pansion Garestin). The rooms are nice but the rest of the hotel lacks character. As often is the case, the casino is not worth it. **www.hotel-turist.hr**

VARAŽDINSKE TOPLICE Minerva

Kralja Zvonimira 19. **Tel** *(042) 630 438* **Fax** *(042) 630 826* **Rooms** *261*   **Map** *D1*

This large hotel was built in 1981 near the site of the original Roman baths (hence Minerva) next to Hotel Terme and a large rehabilitation hospital. The hotel is modern and equipped with sports facilities good enough for most Olympians. The rooms are not bad but meal times are always going to be a bit characterless. **www.varazdinsketoplice.com**

WHERE TO EAT

The food in Croatia is very varied, from the fresh fish and seafood found in towns along the coast to the Central European dishes, such as goulash, offered in inland Croatia. Croatia has its own gastronomic traditions, but the coastal areas have been greatly influenced by the long years of Venetian rule and inland areas reflect the cuisines of Central Europe, in particular those of Vienna and Hungary. Pasta dishes

Veljko Barbieri, cook and writer

and pizza (with a thin base, in the Italian style) can be found virtually everywhere. Croatian kitchens commonly make the most of a wide range of fresh produce including meat, fish and vegetables. The specialities include the famous sheep's milk cheese *(paški sir)* of Pag and air-dried hams called *pršut*. Prices are generally lower than in other western European countries, making eating out in Croatia a value-for-money experience.

The Boban restaurant in Zagreb *(see p246)*

RESTAURANTS

The Croatian word *restoran* generally means a formal restaurant, run as part of a hotel or large tourist complex. These establishments are characterized by a good level of service but they often offer so-called "international" cuisine. Although the food is usually perfectly good and satisfying, it has no regional flavour and is often rather standardized. Prices for a main meal in a place classed as a restaurant start from 190 kuna (about £16).

Less formal places to try out are the numerous *gostionica* or *konoba* (both are similar to a trattoria or taverna). These are often family-run businesses and they are good places to try good, traditional, local dishes.

One of the drawbacks of these establishments, from a tourist's point of view, is that they often do not display a menu outside indicating the kind of dishes on offer. If you are unsure about a place, it is best to go in and ask to see the menu (or get the owner or waiter to tell you the dishes of the day) and then decide whether to stay or not. Remember you are under no obligation and can feel completely free to leave if the food, the service or the prices on offer are not to your liking.

Most of the *gostionica* and *konoba* fall within the mid-price range and some offer very good value for money. The average cost of a meal is from around 120 to 200 kuna (from about £10–17). This sum would include a starter, a main course (always served with a vegetable) and a

Sign for the Zlatna Guska restaurant *(see p249)*

dessert. Prices vary according to the standard of the place and its location. A *gostionica* or *konoba* along the coast will almost certainly be more expensive than those inland. Sometimes there is an extra charge for bread, but the service charge is usually included in the price of each single dish.

Along the coast, fresh fish is plentiful though not inexpensive. On menus, prices of fish and seafood are generally given by the kilo. A useful rule of thumb is that a good-sized portion of fish or seafood will usually weigh about 250 grams (10 ounces) and so you should be able to predict roughly how much you will be spending. The choice of fish and seafood on offer will vary daily depending on the catch.

Wine is often drunk with restaurant meals in Croatia (for an overview of Croatia's wines see pp238–9), but it is very common for restaurants to serve a drink consisting of a mixture of wine and water

Sign of one of many *gostionica* offering traditional cooking

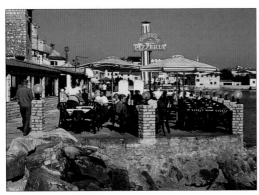

Tables outside a pizzeria on the seafront in Umag

look vegetarian, like *manistra* (vegetable soup), may contain meat stock. However, restaurants, pizzerias and cafés serving Italian-style food will provide various options from pizzas with vegetable toppings to pasta dishes. Otherwise several side orders of vegetables are usually an option and omelettes *(omlet)* may be available in some places. The choice increases in autumn with the fresh mushroom season, especially in the Istria region.

(bevanda), or *gemišt*, which is mineral water and local wine, brought to the table separately for you to mix.

PIZZERIAS AND BISTROS

Pizzas are always a good choice for the visitor travelling on a budget in Croatia. Croatian pizzas are very good and can compete with the best Italian tradition. The prices are always reasonable and are on average 30–40 per cent lower than similar meals in many other parts of Europe.

Another type of restaurant is the bistro, offering a range of straightforward dishes: from *rižot* (risotto) and spaghetti (regarded as *hors d'oeuvres* here), to simple basic dishes such as *ražnjići* (pork kebabs), *čevapčići* (meatballs) and seafood dishes such as fried octopus or squid rings *(lignje)*.

Beer, called *pivo*, is normally drunk with meals in pizzerias and bistros, but soft drinks, mineral water and wine are also available.

PICNICS AND SELF-CATERING

There are many temptingly beautiful places to visit in Croatia. If you are planning an excursion to one of the unspoilt but isolated spots where refreshment facilities will not be available, you can always take a picnic. Food can easily be bought from food shops, supermarkets or from one of the typical open-air markets where you can find a great variety of salami, cheeses, bread and olives, as well as fresh fruit and drinks.

Food prices are very reasonable and shopkeepers usually try to be helpful. It is common practice for staff to prepare rolls or sandwiches at the counter at no extra cost. Sometimes it is also possible to find some simple ready-made dishes such as *burek*. This is a type of savoury pastry, filled with meat *(meso)* or cheese *(sir)*, and baked in the oven. Buy *burek* in bakeries or small "fast food" shops.

Families or groups staying in self-catering apartments should also have no problem stocking up. Many hotel complexes with apartments also have mini-supermarkets.

VEGETARIAN FOOD

There are no dedicated vegetarian restaurants in Croatia and even dishes that

PAYING

Payment by credit card, normal enough in most European restaurants, small or large, is not really general practice in Croatia, except in the larger places and in hotel restaurants. Bills for meals are paid in cash in kuna.

Credit cards are often not accepted in the *gostionica* and *konoba* or in smaller bars or cafés, so make sure that you carry enough cash with you.

OPENING HOURS

Places serving food and drinks have very flexible opening hours, and it is possible to eat at more or less any time of the day, especially in the tourist resorts. However the meal times of the local people do not vary much from other Mediterranean countries. Lunch is generally served from about noon to 2pm and dinner is served from around 8 to 10pm.

The elegant restaurant of the Hotel Esplanade *(see p231)* in Zagreb

The Flavours of Croatia

Croatia can be broadly divided into four main culinary regions: Istrian cuisine is proud of its Italian heritage and features elegant pasta, gnocchi and truffle dishes; Dalmatian cuisine is seafood based and has Venetian echoes; the fertile farmlands of Slavonia have a more Hungarian influence of peppers and spice; while central Croatia retains Austrian predilections – schnitzel, desserts and cakes. However, there are some consistent characteristics – bread is key and is always freshly made either at home or in the local bakery (*pekara*); fish is important all over the country given the length of the coastline and the many lakes and rivers; and grilling is the preferred cooking method.

Wild aparagus

Sardines and other seafood on sale at Split's busy fish market

ISTRIA

With a noticeably Italianate cuisine, food is taken more seriously in Istria than anywhere else outside of Zagreb. Here the truffle, *tartufi*, is venerated. Although freshest in autumn, truffles are used dried all-year-round in risottos and pasta dishes such as *mare monti* (a "surf and turf" combination of

mushrooms and shellfish). Many restaurant kitchens roast food in a *peka* – a lidded pot buried in hot ashes – to retain all the flavour and juices. Look out for *srnetina*, venison stew with gnocchi, or roasted, meadow-fed lamb. Other delights are the soft, Istrian smoked ham (*pršut*) and don't miss the best oysters and mussels in Croatia, farmed in the clean waters of the Limski Channel.

DALMATIA

The Adriatic supplies Croatia with much of its fish. Gilthead bream, red mullet, sole and John Dory are common, as are clams, mussels, oysters, octopus, squid, shrimp and even crab and lobster. The channels created by hundreds of islands are perfect for cultivating excellent quality shellfish. Produce is prepared with olive oil, garlic and herbs, cooked quickly – fried, grilled or boiled – and served

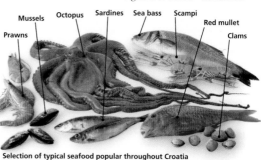

Mussels   **Octopus**   **Sardines**   **Sea bass**   **Scampi**

Prawns   **Red mullet**

Clams

Selection of typical seafood popular throughout Croatia

CROATIAN DISHES AND SPECIALITIES

Many of Croatia's religious and folk holiday festivals are traditionally associated with a particular dish. *Baccala* (salt cod), for example, is eaten on Christmas Eve and Good Friday, *kulen* (spiced salami) is a Harvest Thanksgiving dish and *guska* (goose) served with chestnuts is a St Martin's Day treat.

Pršut – smoked ham

The Turkish occupation, over 200 years ago, has left behind a legacy of grilled meats and kebabs, *sarma* (cabbage leaf stuffed with rice and mince), *burek* (filo pastry tube filled with meat or curd cheese), and *baklava* (pastries filled with nuts and drenched in sweet syrup). Coastal specialities include *brodet* (fish stew with polenta), *crni rizot* (cuttlefish ink risotto) and *lignje* (squid), served lightly fried in breadcrumbs or *na zaru* (grilled whole).

Menestra *A filling soup made of smoked meat, beans, pasta and vegetables – an Istrian version of minestrone.*

Fresh-baked bread and pastries for sale at a Croatian bakery (pekara)

simply. Easy Italian cooking reigns here – risottos, pizza and pasta feature on menus as a result of history, proximity and the sheer number of Italian visitors. Try Dalmatian *pršut*, firmer than the Istrian version, or *janjetina* – lamb fed on lush island grass and herbs; it's great spit-roasted.

CENTRAL & NORTHERN CROATIA

Inland the food is much richer – olive oil is replaced by butter, lard or dripping. Menus are meat-driven with hearty, filling side dishes such as dumplings and noodles – legacies from Austrian rule. Zagreb has a sophisticated gastronomy but outside of the capital, rustic flavours and styles abound and there is a greater use of veal and game. As well as being grilled, meat

is often cooked in a rich stew or spit-roasted *(picenje)* – goose, duck, lamb, wild boar and venison are favourites. But perhaps the most obvious Viennese influence are the rich desserts – pancakes, strudels and ribsticking *strukli*.

Croatian cheese shop, with a variety of hard, soft and goat's cheeses

SLAVONIA & BARANJA

The Austro-Hungarian Empire has also affected Slavonian cooking but with a Hungarian flavour. Large portions of warming dishes insulate the mainly rural population from a cold, wet and often snowy climate. Expect meat or fish in rich sauces, spiced with paprika. The Drava river provides a good supply of freshwater fish like pike and carp. Do try a few slices of Slavonia's famous appetizer, *kulen*. This smoke-cured salami, flavoured with chilli and paprika, is often served with peppers, tomatoes, *tursija* (pickled vegetables) and sometimes curd cheese.

ON THE MENU

Fiš paprikaš: Fiery fish stew from Slavonia often made with carp and spiced with paprika.

Zagrebački odrezat: Veal, ham and cheese fried in bread-crumbs – a super-schnitzel.

Ajvar: A savoury red pepper sauce/relish – everyone has their own secret recipe.

Čevapčići: A Turkish legacy – spicy meat rissoles served with raw onion, flatbread and ajvar.

Blitva sa krumpiron: Popular side dish of chard boiled with potatoes, olive oil and garlic.

Palačinka: One of Croatia's top desserts: jam-filled pancakes, with chocolate and walnuts.

Škampi buzara *Whole scampi is gently simmered in wine, tomatoes, garlic and herbs; finished with breadcrumbs.*

Pašticada *A beef joint and seasonal vegetables are slowly pot-roasted in wine – prunes are also sometimes used.*

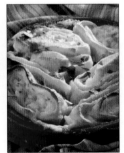

Strukli *This Northern Croatia dish of parcels of curd cheese, boiled and then baked, can be either sweet or savoury.*

What to Drink in Croatia

A wide variety of locally made drinks is available throughout Croatia, from beers to wines to fiery fruit brandies. Croatian beer is usually of the lager type but dark beers can also be found. Foreign brands such as Stella Artois, Tuborg and Kaltenberg are brewed in Croatia under licence, and there are Irish pubs selling Guinness and other Irish beers. Croatia's vineyards yield all kinds of red and white wines, most of which are rarely seen outside the country. Spirits based on grapes are popular as aperitifs rather than after-dinner drinks, as are other fruit brandies made from plums or pears. Brandies flavoured with herbs, walnuts or even honey are also popular. Tap water is safe to drink but if the taste does not appeal there is a wide range of bottled mineral waters, both sparkling and still.

Typical sign for a pub, *pivnica* in Croatian

Traditional utensils for the preparation of strong Turkish coffee

COFFEE AND TEA

Coffee *(kava)* is drunk throughout Croatia. All over the country it is served very strong and black, in little cups, like an *espresso* coffee. If it is too strong you can add a little milk or order a *cappuccino* (freshly ground coffee with frothy hot milk). Strong Turkish coffee is also available in some places. Herbal teas *(čaj)* are sold everywhere. Indian teas can also be found, usually served with lemon, but you can ask for milk.

BEER

Another very popular drink sold in cafés and pubs is beer *(pivo)*, which is always served very cold. Most bottled beers are of the lager-type, but some darker beers can be found. The most well-known brands of lager beer are Ožujsko, made in Zagreb and Karlovačko (Karlovac). Another common brand is Pan. Well-known international beers such

Karlovačko beer

as Stella Artois are also widely available (some brewed under licence in Croatia), but tend to be more expensive.

Ožujsko beer

SPIRITS

A wide variety of spirits is available in Croatia, demonstrating the nation's fondness for strong alcoholic drinks, in particular fruit-based eau-de-vie. One of the most popular spirits is a plum brandy originating in Slavonia called *Šljivovica*. It is found all over the country. *Loza* is a grape-based eau-de-vie

Pelinkovac liqueur   Zrinski brandy

with a high alcohol content, and *Travarica* is a herb-based spirit. *Vinjak* is a brandy, *Pelinkovac* is a herb liqueur, and *Maraskino*, a liqueur from Zadar, is flavoured with maraschino cherries.

Many spirits are drunk as aperitifs. A spirit called *Berme* is produced in Samobor, near Zagreb, and is made according to an ancient, well-guarded recipe. It is drunk as an aperitif, served with ice and a slice of lemon.

Šljivovica eau-de-vie

Some bottles of eau-de-vie with fruit, made at home all over the country

MINERAL WATER, SOFT DRINKS AND FRUIT JUICES

All bars and cafés offer a wide range of fruit juices, as well as internationally known brands of soft drinks and fizzy drinks like cola. Tap water is safe to drink everywhere in Croatia and bottled mineral waters (*mineralna voda*) are also widely available. The two most common brands of mineral water in Croatia are Studena and Jamnica but there are also a great many imported brands available as well.

Mineral water

Orange juice

Pubs and bars with live music: a popular way to socialize

DRINKING CUSTOMS IN CROATIA

Pubs, bars and cafés are not only places to stop at various times of the day for refreshment, but also places to meet friends and socialize. For visitors this can also be a good way of meeting and getting to know local people.

One tradition found in Croatia is that of mixing wine with other drinks such as mineral water or even cola. A *bevanda* is red or white wine with plain water, while *gemišt* is white wine mixed with sparkling mineral water. One of the most popular summer drinks is red wine and fizzy cola, a drink called *bambus*.

Croatians like a drink or two, as is demonstrated by the custom in the Slavonian region of wine drinking with friends. This traditional ritual should only be undertaken by people with a very strong head for alcohol. It begins with the first phase, which is before any wine is consumed, known as the *Dočekuša*. This is then followed by the *Razgovoruša*, during which you chat while sipping at least seven glasses of wine. The final phase is called the *Putnicka*, reserved for the leave-taking, when yet more glasses are emptied before people say their final farewells.

WINES

Croatia is also a land of vineyards, with vines grown on rolling hills inland and in pockets of stony soil on the coast and islands. Production varies in quantity and quality but standards are improving and there are some very decent wines around. From the Kvarner area come the white wine Žlahtina (from Vrbnik on Krk), red Cabernet (from Poreč) and Teran (from Buzet), a light red.

Zlahtina

Dalmatia is known for Pošip and Grk from Korčula (both white wines), Dingač (one of the best Croatian reds) and Postup from the Pelješac peninsula. Plavac (red) comes from Brač and Malmsy from Dubrovnik. Finally, from Slavonia come Kutjevačka Graševina, Kutjevo Chardonnay and Riesling, and Krauthaker Graševina.

Dingač   **Postup**

WHERE TO DRINK

There are various types of establishments which serve drinks and it is useful to know a few of the basic categories. A *kavana* is equivalent to a café, and serves both alcoholic and non-alcoholic drinks, while a *pivnica* serves mainly beer. Irish pubs can also be found, selling Guinness and other Irish beers. Wine is generally drunk in a *konoba*. In the larger towns you can have a snack with your drink in one of the *bife*, the Croatian equivalent of a snack bar. However, there are not really rigid distinctions between the types of drinks served in one or other of these places. Cafés open very early and close late – usually around 11pm or later during the summer months.

Drinks of various kinds (though rarely alcoholic) are also served in pastry shops – *slasticarna*. The close links that Croatia's gastronomic tradition has with Austria, and in particular with Vienna, has influenced the production of delicious cakes and pastries as well as excellent *sladoled* (ice cream). Pastry shops close earlier than cafés in general.

A snack bar with outdoor tables in Fažana, a coastal resort

Choosing a Restaurant

The restaurants here have been selected across a wide price range for facilities, good value and location. They are listed by region, starting with Istria and the Kvarner area. Most restaurants in Croatia do not have separate non-smoking areas. For road map references, see the inside back cover.

PRICE CATEGORIES
For a complete meal with drinks (except wine), including service (a tip is recommended):

Ⓚ Under 100 KUNA
ⓀⓀ 100–200 KUNA
ⓀⓀⓀ 200–300 KUNA
ⓀⓀⓀⓀ 300–400 KUNA
ⓀⓀⓀⓀⓀ Over 400 KUNA

ISTRIA AND THE KVARNER AREA

BUZET Toklarija
Sovinjsko Polje 11, Buzet. **Tel** *(052) 663 031*   **Map** *A2*

In a cottage on a hilltop outside of town, reservations are essential at this fine restaurant. Long menus of food that is "slow cooked" mean a meal that's going to be an event. Attention to detail in the cooking from wood-fired stoves to genuinely local produce make it one of the best restaurants in Croatia.

CRES Gostionica Belona
Šetalište 20 travnja 24, Cres. **Tel** *(051) 571 203*   **Map** *B3*

This restaurant is popular with the locals and particularly lively in the evening. The décor is rustic and so is some of the cooking but it's none the worse for that. Try the seafood or, the island speciality, lamb that has been feeding on the rich herbed island grass and roasted on the spit.

CRES Riva
Obala Creskih Kapetana 13, Cres. **Tel** *(051) 571 107*   **Map** *B3*

Located at the heart of Cres town, this restaurant is doubly blessed. On the one side it faces onto the recently renovated square, while on the other it has a large terrace that overlooks the harbour. As you'd expect the fish is good and fresh – try sea bass, scampi or seafood risotto.

KASTAV Kukuriku
Trg Matka Laginje 1a, Kastav. **Tel** *(051) 691 417*   **Map** *B2*

Providing a gastronomic highlight of the area, Kukuriku prides itself on its creative cooking. Ingredients such as honey, cheese and mushrooms are locally sourced along with the famous lamb. The menu is also seasonal – asparagus in spring and truffles in autumn. Go along with the chef's recommendations.

KRK Konoba Šime
Ulica Antuna Mahnića 1, Krk. **Tel** *(051) 220 042*   **Map** *B3*

This recently renovated restaurant sits right on the main harbour promenade. It is a little dark and medieval inside but has a covered seating area right on the promenade overlooking the sea. They serve simple dishes such as large meaty grilled squid and *blitva* – a garlicky green chard and potato mixture.

KRK Konaba Nono
Krckih Iseljenika 8, Krk. **Tel** *(051) 222 221*   **Map** *B3*

Set in the centre of town this traditional restaurant specializes in local dishes and as well as serving the usual array of seafood – fish, prawns and pasta – has a few more authentic meat dishes. Try the homemade *surlice*, pasta tubes, usually served with a thick goulash sauce enriched with wine.

KRK Marina
Puntica 9, Punat. **Tel** *(051) 854 132*   **Map** *B3*

Used as a harbour since Roman times, Punat bay is a delightful setting for a restaurant. The simple interior is decorated with paintings by a local Naïf painter, while outside there is a simple if not terribly aesthetic terrace. The food is good – fish, of course, and the usual mediterranean fare and locally-made olive oil.

LIMSKI CHANNEL Viking
Limski Kanal 1. **Tel** *(052) 448 223*   **Map** *A3*

The Limski Channel is famous for its shellfish and that's what you should eat here – oysters, the locally-farmed mussels, or scampi served with noodles and porcini mushrooms. The restaurant is traditionally furnished (1970s style) but the location in the winding narrow channel is breathtaking.

LOŠINJ Villa Diana
Baia di Čikat, Čikat13, Mali Lošinj. **Tel** *(051) 232 055*   **Map** *B3*

Part of a small hotel set in secluded Čikat Bay, Villa Diana has a beautiful location with a large waterfront terrace pleasantly shaded by cypress trees. The restaurant offers a wide range of typical Croatian and international dishes. A restaurant genuinely worth seeking out.

Key to Symbols *see back cover flap*

LOŠINJ Lanterna

Sv Marije 71, Mali Lošinj. **Tel** *(051) 233 625*   **Map** B3

Far from the crowds which fill the town, particularly in summer, this small establishment is off the beaten track but it's well worth the effort – head east up the hill from the harbour towards the church. The food is the usual Mediterranean fare of seafood, grilled meats and pasta, but rather well-executed.

MOTOVUN Barbacan

Ulica Barbacan 1, Motovun. **Tel** *(052) 681 791*   **Map** A2

Excellent value restaurant with a romantic candlelit interior, and an outside terrace. The kitchen makes a point of putting truffles in everything – from omelettes to home-made paté to beef. In fact, the only thing without truffles, thankfully, is the rather excellent chocolate pie.

MOTOVUN Restoran Zigante

Livade 7, Motovun. **Tel** *(052) 664 302*   **Map** A2

Restaurants in the interior differ from those on the coast in that they are not fed by a regular stream of tourists regardless of quality – and they are all the better for it. Istria's most famous temple to the truffle (look out for pictures of a record specimen) offers tasting menus and pictures of the international clientele who've dined there. Enjoy!

OPATIJA Madonnina

Pava Tomašića 3, Opatija. **Tel** *(051) 272 579*   **Map** B2

This restaurant is situated opposite the famous, but past its prime, Hotel Kvarner, right on the promenade that stretches the length of Opatija's shoreline. Primarily specializing in thin crust pizzas they also do good seafood pastas. Beer is the recommended beverage here rather than wine.

OPATIJA Amfora

Črnikovica 4, Volosko. **Tel** *(051) 701 222*   **Map** B2

This is a grand and pleasant restaurant that is definitely better than your average seaside *konoba*. A short distance from the centre on the edge of Volosko bay it has a large terrace overlooking the sea. Fish and shellfish is a speciality fresh from their own aquarium. The owner is a well-known Croatian gastro guru.

OPATIJA Bevanda Lido

Zert 8, Lido, Opatija. **Tel** *(051) 712 772*   **Map** B2

Another good Opatija seafood restaurant, this has a choice seaside location on a small peninsula with its own little lido. The terrace is really beautiful and the music is (usually) not too loud. Choose from over 20 starters and all that the sea can offer – known for its excellent lobsters.

OPATIJA Plavi Podrum

Obala Frane Supila 4, Opatija. **Tel** *(051) 701 223*   **Map** B2

There's been a restaurant here for over 100 years and this one is very good. Try the omelette with octopus, scampi or asparagus; or prawns in truffle oil. It specializes in fish, of course, but also takes pride in its meat dishes. The excellent cellar contains local and international wines by the bottle or glass, and there's a first class sommelier.

POREČ Istra

Bože Milanovića 30, Poreč. **Tel** *(052) 434 636*   **Map** A2

A family owned and run affair, this restaurant is popular with the locals. Serving local fare of fish of all kinds but why not try something different – tender braised veal knuckles, or *mučkalica* a stew of beef, peppers, herbs and spices, not unlike a goulash, traditionally served with rice.

POREČ Nono

Zagrebačka 4, Poreč. **Tel** *(052) 453 088*   **Map** A2

Serves probably the best pizza in Croatia, and if not, then certainly the largest. Also does other meat and fish dishes (good steaks and grilled squid) but the crowds gather here mainly for the pizzas. The small size of the restaurant means it's usually full but it is worth the wait.

POREČ Konoba Ulixes

Dekumanus 2, Porec. **Tel** *(052) 451 132*   **Map** A2

Situated in the Old Town of Poreč this small and intimate restaurant is a bit of a gem. Here you can try Istrian truffle dishes without breaking the bank. Good fish and seafood as well. It's rustic and cosy inside but there's also a small sun-trap of a terrace with an olive tree or two.

PULA Vodnjanka

Vitezica 4. **Tel** *(052) 210 655*   **Map** A3

An excellent find, this little restaurant with a few tables outside offers very good value Istrian home cooking (Istrian cooking has a more obvious Italian influence). Not the most sophisticated establishment, this is an informal place where the locals come to relax, drink good, cheap wine and eat honest food.

PULA Milan

Stoja 4, Pula. **Tel** *(052) 210 200*   **Map** A3

This is a good hotel restaurant that has been going since 1967. In that time it has built up a repertoire of 700 wines. It serves some marvellous fish – monkfish, sardines, cuttlefish, red mullet. Try the creamy lobster lasagne (*lazanje sa jastogom*). The décor is restrained, fairly modern, and simple.

PULA Vela Nera

Pješčana Uvala bb, Pula. **Tel** *(052) 219 209*

Map *A3*

Situated a little out of the centre of town, on a little bay to the south, this is a fairly modern restaurant with a good sized terrace. Inside there's a certain nautical feel to things and the menu features local and international cuisine. There's also a wide range of wines from Croatia, Europe and the rest of the world.

PULA Valsabbion

Pješčana Uvala IX/26, Pula. **Tel** *(052) 218 033*

Map *A3*

Voted one of the best restaurants in Croatia by local food critics (and the hotel numbers Sting, Naomi Campbell and Vanessa Mae among its past guests). Excellent cuisine using premium ingredients – fish, oysters, truffles and wild asparagus. Try the foil-baked sea bass in brandy or warm scampi carpaccio.

RAB Konoba Riva

Biskupa Draga 3, Rab. **Tel** *(051) 725 887*

Map *B3*

Good mid-range restaurant with typical *konoba* décor – fishing paraphernalia, wooden beams and a stone-walled interior. There's a nice sea-view terrace, and occasionally live music. They will also deliver to yachts in the marina, which is handy if you want to enjoy fine dining on your own boat.

RAB Kordić

Barbat 176, Rab.

Map *B3*

Set 2 km (1 mile) along the coast (east) from the town of Rab, Barbat has a tradition of fishing. This comes through strongly in the cooking at the Family Kordić restaurant. Try the locally caught spiny crab salad, whole grilled catch of the day or lobsters from the tank – simply grilled or served with a fresh tomato sauce and a glass of crisp, dry wine.

RAB Astoria

Trg Municipium Arba 7, Rab. **Tel** *(051)774 844*

Map *B3*

Ancient Venetian palace with old beams and great stone walls. Situated above the main square, this restaurant has a fine kitchen and terrace with fantastic harbour views. They make a point of growing their own herbs and only using the best local produce. Rab's best dining establishment.

RIJEKA Konoba Korkyra

Slogin Kula 5, Rijeka. **Tel** *(051) 339 528*

Map *B2*

Traditionally a *konoba* is decorated with fishing nets and shells, and this one is no different. The owner is from Korčula and has brought reminders with him in his cooking and wine list. The restaurant serves venison goulash and dumplings, island lamb with vegetables and a menu that changes according to the best seasonal produce.

RIJEKA Municipium

Trg Riječka Revolucije, Rijeka. **Tel** *(051) 213 000*

Map *B2*

One of the best restaurants in Rijeka, Municipium is located in a historic 19th-century building. Try the *škampi buzara* (fish in a rich garlic, tomato and Cognac sauce) or a heartier pašticada (beef stew with home-made gnocchi). Along with a wide range of fish and shellfish, they even have a vegetarian section of the menu – albeit tiny.

RIJEKA Bonavia

Dolac 4, Rijeka. **Tel** *(051) 357 100*

Map *B2*

Set inside the aspirational Grand Hotel Bonavia – motto "5-star service in a 4-star hotel" – this restaurant offers good quality food and service. The hotel-style catering is probably aimed more at business dining than tourists but the restaurant and light and airy conservatory are pleasant enough.

ROVINJ Veli Jože

Svetoga Kriza 1, Rovinj. **Tel** *(052) 816 337*

Map *A3*

This attractive restaurant serves traditional Istrian dishes such as *bakalar* (salt cod) in a white sauce or lamb stew cooked with potatoes; pasta and grilled fish – all washed down with the extremely drinkable, local Malvasia white wine. There's also a good-sized terrace.

ROVINJ Amfora

Obala Aldo Rismondo 23, Rovinj. **Tel** *(052) 816 663*

Map *A3*

A firm favourite with the regulars, this restaurant consistently supplies good food in delightful surroundings and an ideal harbourside location. Standard grilled seafood, pasta and meat dishes skillfully executed. Try the local variation of "surf and turf" – *mare monti* – seafood and mushrooms with pasta.

ROVINJ La Puntuleina

Ulica Svetog Kriza 38, Rovinj. **Tel** *(052) 813 186*

Map *A3*

Set romantically on a balcony over the sea at the edge of the old town this is Rovinj's best. It delivers an Italian/Istrian mix and tasting menus too. Stop off at the bar on the ground floor for a sundowner before heading upstairs with your beloved to the delightful restaurant.

UMAG Badi

Umaska, Lovrečica bb. **Tel** *(052) 756 293*

Map *A2*

This is a fine restaurant in a small village, Lovrečica, 10 minutes drive along the coast from Umag. It has a pleasant terrace and a leafy green setting. No surprises in the menu offerings, but good seafood, pasta, and risottos, with definite Italian characteristics. Try the house specials – baked fish dishes.

Key to Price Guide *see p240* **Key to Symbols** *see back cover flap*

DALMATIA

BRAČ Konoba Marija

Frane Radića 14, near Bol. **Tel** *(021) 524 743*   **Map** *D5*

Worth travelling way off the beaten track to get to this restaurant for the sublime views over the sea to Hvar (and to get away from the daytripping crowds in peak season). Simple but delicious barbecued meat and fish. Enjoy an island adventure as well as a jolly good meal.

BRAČ Ribarska Kućica

Ante Starčevića, Bol. **Tel** *(021) 635 144*   **Map** *D5*

From the terrace there are beautiful views out over the sea with its own secluded beach. There is a wide choice of fish dishes and a fixed price menu after 8pm every evening. Also does pizza, but try rather the gnocchi with *pršut* in a cheese sauce – it's a bit of a rib-sticking dish but perfect if you've tired yourself out swimming.

BRAČ Taverna Riva

Frane Radića 5, Bol. **Tel** *(021) 635 236*   **Map** *D5*

Bol is such a popular place that some restaurants don't bother trying very hard as they'll still be full. Thankfully, this is not one of those – it has a large stone terrace, and serves excellent versions of the usual fish dishes – try *salata od hobotnice* (octopus salad), *pršut* (dalmatian ham), or *rižot od liganja* (squid risotto).

CAVTAT Galija

Vuličevićeva 1. **Tel** *(020) 478 566*   **Map** *F6*

Cavtat's top restaurant – close to the main promenade on the way to the peninsula near the Franciscan monastery. Old-fashioned tavern with lovely terrace under pine trees and by the sea – all tables still have linen and candles. The menu is a little more adventurous than most. Worth booking ahead, especially at weekends.

CAVTAT Kolona

Put Tiha 2, Cavtat. **Tel** *(020) 478 787*   **Map** *F6*

This is a nice restaurant with a cosy and traditional interior. It also has a terrace, surrounded by aromatic greenery with views out over the sea. The food is good – typical seafood specialities – but what really marks this place out is the genuinely friendly service – they've even been known to drive the last diners home.

DUBROVNIK Lokanda Peskarija

Na Ponti. **Tel** *(020) 324 750*   **Map** *F6*

Where the locals go for simple, fresh fish and seafood. Traditional wood-heavy interior, quite cosy and small with a buzzing bar – food is served in "traditional" black pots. Next to the harbour fish market (so be sensible and order the delicious fish). Always busy – so booking ahead is advised. They can put tables outside in summer.

DUBROVNIK Tabasco

Cavtatska 11. **Tel** *(020) 429 595*   **Map** *F6*

This pizzeria is situated just outside the old fortified part of town to the north of the Ploče Gate. It serves decent-sized pizzas and large portions of *panzerotti* (large pasta parcels stuffed with cheese and ham topped with tomato sauce). Also has some pasta dishes and fresh salads. The vibe here is filling and cheap.

DUBROVNIK Orsan

Ivana Zajca 2. **Tel** *(020) 435 933*   **Map** *F6*

Orsan, affiliated to the local yacht club, keeps everything shipshape by serving mainly seafood – fish or lobster is the catch of the day and cooked to your liking, priced by the kilo. It's not fancy but it's simple, fresh and tasty. Also octopus salad (*salata od hobotnice*) and squid ink risotto (*crni rižot*). They do steaks for landlubbers.

DUBROVNIK Rosarij

Zlatarska 4. **Tel** *(020) 321 257*   **Map** *F6*

A lovely little family run restaurant in the old part of Dubrovnik, at the end of the road parallel to Stradun near the Sponza Palace. Good value food and only the freshest fish and seafood. Enjoy the melon and ham, fried squid, cuttlefish ink risotto (*crni rižot od sipa*) and the Croatian version of crème caramel (*rozata*).

DUBROVNIK Levenat

Šetalište Nika i Meda Pucica 15, Lapad. **Tel** *(020) 435 352*   **Map** *F6*

Top place in Lapad with rather formal interior. This small restaurant is set right by the sea in Lapad Bay and has an outdoor terrace with panoramic views – ideal for the regular rosy red sunsets. The food is simple but very good – the usual seafood, grilled meats and traditional pancakes (*palačinke*) filled with chocolate and walnuts.

DUBROVNIK Orhan

Od Tabakarije 1. **Tel** *(020) 414 183*   **Map** *F6*

Unpretentious fish restaurant with other options, hidden away down some steps in a secluded cove just by the Old Town. Not being within the walls of the city is an actual advantage as the day-trippers rarely make it here from the cruise boats. Fine terrace with views of Dubrovnik's mighty sea walls.

DUBROVNIK Jadran

Poljana Paška Miličevića 1. **Tel** *(020) 429 325*
Map F6

Local and international cuisine in an elegant historical setting – it is located in the cloister of the Convent of St Clare, just to the right of the Pile Gate as you enter. With a setting like this it is easy for the food to seem good – usual fish dishes but why not treat yourself to a steak (*biftek*); or, if on a budget, the kebabs (*ražnjići*) are just as tasty.

DUBROVNIK Nautika

Brsalje 3. **Tel** *(020) 442 526*
Map F6

This is probably the most elegant restaurant in the city, and offers a lovely view of the walls and sea just by the Pile Gate. The food is of a similarly high standard and although fairly expensive, the fish dishes are definitely worth trying. The grilled lobsters are excellent as is the fish stew (*brodet*) with polenta. Reserve ahead at weekends.

DUGI OTOK Tamaris

Obala Kralja Tomislava 17, Sali. **Tel** *(023) 377 377*
Map C4

Sali is the main village on the island of Dugi Otok and this restaurant, although it doesn't look anything special from the outside (and not much better from the inside) serves decent food and is popular with the locals (especially the bar and nearby pool room). Usual fish dishes such as grilled scampi and spaghetti with shellfish.

HVAR Jurin Podrum

Srnja kola bb, Stari Grad. **Tel** *(021) 765 804*
Map D5

The restaurant is in a small street off the beaten track. It has a spartan air – simple stone décor that matches the simple but good food. Try the tiny fried whitebait and shellfish in tomato sauce (*buzara*) – great washed down with the cold white local wines. Also serves good local cheeses.

HVAR Eremitaž

Priko, Stari Grad. **Tel** *(021) 765 056*
Map D5

Located in what was once a hospital for sailors in quarantine, this family-run restaurant serves up a wide range of excellent fish specialities. Situated on the quieter side of the bay, the restaurant has a fine shady terrace facing the old part of town over the sea. It's a romantic spot at night looking across the water at the town lights twinkling.

HVAR L'Antica

Stari Grad.
Map D5

Well-known small restaurant in the pretty cobble-stone centre of old Hvar – supposedly the favoured haunt of artists and intellectuals. As much a bar as a restaurant it serves decent cocktails. The food is good too – tuna steaks in caper sauce, monkfish in dill sauce and seafood risottos. Open-air roof terrace.

HVAR Hanibal

Pjaca 12, Hvar. **Tel** *(021) 742 760*
Map D5

Named after the 16th-century Hvar poet Hanibal Lucic, and situated by the Church of St Stephen, this restaurant has a very nice designer interior – old stone and wooden beams. Serves excellent fish cuisine – scampi, lobster, prawns, oven-cooked octopus but also grilled lamb and steaks. Best to book in advance, as it can get quite busy.

HVAR Macondo

Groda, Hvar. **Tel** *(021) 742 850*
Map D5

Fine restaurant set up the hill from the main square (look for the signs) – serves good fish cuisine. Try the marinated anchovies or sublime spaghetti with lobster; finish off with the home-made *prosec* (fortified wine). From the terrace you get a good view of the passers-by. Can get busy at weekends with the glitterati of Hvar.

HVAR Panorama

Smokovnik, Hvar. **Tel** *(021) 742 515*
Map D5

Set in a small Austrian fort with a terrace and a wonderful view of the bay, 2 km (1 mile) from Hvar Town. One of its specialities is lamb roasted in a covered metal pot (*peka*) with other vegetables – cooked like this, the outside of the food caramelizes and the juices combine for a delicious sauce (must be ordered 24 hours in advance).

KORČULA Morski Konjić

Stari Grad 47a, Korčula. **Tel** *(020) 711 642*
Map E6

An intimate *konoba* (sort of fishing-themed restaurant) right on the end of the fortified peninsula. It can get busy so be prepared to queue for the fresh cooked fish dishes and excellent shellfish. It's plain inside – chequered tablecloths and a few nautical items but there's tables outside too. Stocks a wide range of good Croatian wines.

MAKARSKA Jež

Petra Krešmira IV 90. **Tel** *(021) 641 741*
Map E5

Traditional Dalmatian cuisine served in a modern, light and airy environment. The olive oil they use comes from the nearby olive grove. Excellent fish dishes and Croatian wines. Handily located near the Split-Dubrovnik motorway for a proper lunch if you're on the road (although absolutely no drinking if driving – it's the law).

METKOVIĆ Villa Neretva

Kravac 2. **Tel** *(021) 672 200*
Map E5

Located in the heart of the fertile valley of the River Neretva, on the road from Opuzen to Metković, this is one of the best restaurants in Croatia. Traditional but smart inside, with a curved wooden roof, the restaurant serves good fish dishes (both freshwater and sea). The special local cuisine features fish, eels and frogs legs.

Key to Price Guide *see p240* **Key to Symbols** *see back cover flap*

OREBIĆ Amfora

Kneza Domagoja 6. **Tel** *(020) 713 719* **Map** *E6*

Handily located right on the waterfront this is a popular family restaurant. You can tell the food is good as the restaurant is full of locals attacking large portions of splendid seafood. Meat's on the menu, too. You can get a good value feed up here before getting the local ferry to Korčula just round the corner.

PAG Konoba Bodulo

Vangrada 19. **Tel** *(023) 611 989* **Map** *C4*

Fresh and simple food is served in the welcoming shade of a grapevine in this inexpensive family-run restaurant. Typical country dishes of the ubiquitous Dalmatian ham (*pršut*), local cheeses, delicious soupy fish stew (*brodet*), all sorts of grilled meats and pasta dishes.

PELJEŠAC Kapetanova Kuća

Mali Ston. **Tel** *(020) 754 264* **Map** *E6*

This "Captain's Cabin" serves excellent oysters, shellfish and black cuttlefish ink risotto, as well as all the other usual seafood food dishes. Also has a good selection of the excellent wines of the area. Save a big space for their legendary Macaroni Cake made with pasta, nuts and chocolate – it is filling. Idyllic location on the harbour front.

ŠIBENIK Tinel

Trg Pučkih Kapetana 1. **Tel** *(022) 331 815* **Map** *D5*

One of the finest restaurants in town and definitely the best wine list. Situated in a small square just near the Church of St Chrysogonus, this restaurant covers two floors and serves up all the usual Dalmatian classics – seafood, grilled meat, stews, sausages and steaks.

ŠIBENIK Uzorita

Bana Josipa Jelačića 50. **Tel** *(022) 213 660* **Map** *D5*

A bit of a hidden gem – it's a little off the beaten track but it combines a stylish modern interior within a characterful stone vine-clad building. It specialises mainly in seafood (it produces a lot of its own ingredients such as shellfish, olive oil and wines). Be adventurous and try one of the delicious house specialities such as octopus and mussels in aspic.

SPLIT Galija

Tončićeva 12. **Tel** *(021) 347 932* **Map** *D5*

Central Split is not known for its good restaurants – pizza's are the budget order of the day. Try this place for the best, large brick-oven baked pizzas. It's not enormous, so it can get busy. Good *pršut* and prawn, and tuna and olive pizzas with thin and crispy bases. It's located near the fish market, north of the main square (Trg Republike).

SPLIT Ponoćno Sunce

Teutina 15. **Tel** *(021) 361 011* **Map** *D5*

Located near the Croatian National Theatre, this simple and small restaurant is popular with the locals. The service is friendly and the food is good and filling – try the gnocchi with salmon. Vegetarians, traditionally hard done by in Croatia, should take note – this place serves good food, some of it cooked without meat or fish.

SPLIT Stellon

Šetalište Bačvice. **Tel** *(021) 489 200* **Map** *D5*

Set in a concrete and glass pavilion of dubious architectural taste , located above the town beach and resort of Bačvice, this restaurant offers good value pizza, pastas and fried fish dishes. It looks out over the bay. It's not terribly stylish but it's very popular in the evening and a good spot for people watching.

SPLIT Boban

Hektorovićeva 49. **Tel** *(021) 543 300* **Map** *D5*

Well-respected restaurant whose style of décor is modern but a bit cheap and dated (lots of chrome and smoked glass). Nevertheless the food (eg veal steaks with mushrooms) is extremely good and the fish fresh so everyone has a good time. Ask what the catch of the day is. One of the top destinations of the great and glorious Split.

SPLIT Kod Joze

Ulica Sredmanuška 4. **Tel** *(021) 347 397* **Map** *D5*

Tucked away in an old stone house, this traditional tavern can be a little tricky to find, but it's worth doing as it serves fine fish (depending on what has come in that day) and well-cooked traditional meat dishes in generous portions. Cool and shady terrace as well. North of the Golden Gate and popular with the locals.

SPLIT Šumica

Put Firula 6. **Tel** *(021) 389 897* **Map** *D5*

To the east of the city in a chic part of town, this restaurant has a lovely location shaded by cooling pines and overlooking the sea. It's worth the stroll. Eat out on the terrace as the interior is nothing special. Excellent fish and shellfish as well as typical grilled meats and pastas. Enjoy some scampi and dry white wine, while the sun sets.

TROGIR Kamerlengo

Vukovarska 2, Trogir. **Tel** *(021) 884 772* **Map** *D5*

In the heart of the old town this restaurant has a lovely walled patio garden which also houses its wood-burning oven and char-grill. Its speciality is seafood but it also serves anything else that can be roasted, grilled or barbecued. The restaurant is a little hidden down a cobbled side street but you should see the sign.

TROGIR Fontana

🅼🅟 ⓚⓚⓚ

Obrov 1. **Tel** *(021) 884 811* **Map** D5

Although the interior is a trifle drab, the terrace of this hotel restaurant is an excellent choice for dining on this beautiful island-town with a spectacular waterfront vista. Everything from pizzas to local fish specialities and classic Dalmatian beef stew (*pastičada*).

VIS Villa Kaliopa

🅱🅼🅟 ⓚⓚⓚⓚⓚ

V Nazora 32, Vis. **Tel** *(021) 711 755* **Map** D6

A restaurant set in the middle of the walled garden of a 16th-century Garibaldi palace, dotted with statues and unusual plants. Very atmospheric this establishment attracts the well-heeled yachting crowd and romantic couples. The food and wines are excellent, if a little on the expensive side.

ZADAR Konoba Marival

🅱 ⓚⓚ

Don Ive Prodana 3. **Tel** *(023) 213 239* **Map** C4

Cheap and cheerful tavern in the old part of town with an intimate family ambience and where fish are the speciality. The repertoire has few surprises and includes – salted anchovies, fish stew (*brodet*), seafood spaghetti, deep-fried fish, squid; but the restaurant also serves standard meat dishes such as kebabs and stews.

ZADAR Maestral

🅶 ⓚⓚ

Ivana Mažuranića 2. **Tel** *(023) 236 186* **Map** C4

On the waterfront, this place is right in the marina complex, with excellent harbour views from the first floor up. More upmarket than your average beachside restaurant, it does both good meat – especially steaks – and of course locally caught fish. Can be busy at weekends when the shipping traffic increases.

ZAGREB

ZAGREB Mimice

ⓚ

Jurišićeva ulica 21. **Tel** *(01) 481 45 24* **Map** D2

A bit of an institution and deservedly popular with the locals, offering a limited range of simple hot or cold fish dishes. More of a food bar than a restaurant this can be crowded at any time of the day. Fried fish is served informally – the local style is to eat it standing and then get back to work. Try the sardines or anchovies.

ZAGREB Pizzicato

🅶 ⓚ

Gundulićeva ulica 4. **Tel** *(01) 483 15 55* **Map** D2

A busy pizzeria and bar that offers delicious pizzas with a crispy thin base and the usual variety of toppings at very reasonable prices. Located in the Lower Town area of the city. There are some outside tables set in a pleasant courtyard or you can eat indoors, or just have something light to eat and a drink at the bar.

ZAGREB Boban

ⓚⓚ

Gajeva ulica 9. **Tel** *(01) 481 15 49* **Map** D2

A characterful restaurant in a basement with great sweeping brick arches, it serves an Italian inspired menu – pasta a speciality. The food is not bad although the length of the menu shows more ambition than is wise. There's a very popular bar upstairs although it can get smoky – but at least this has a terrace if you need some fresh air.

ZAGREB Gračanka Kamanjo

🅼🅟 ⓚⓚ

Gračanka cesta 48. **Tel** *(01) 461 75 55* **Map** D2

A little way out of the centre of the city, on the way towards Mount Medvednica, this restaurant is popular with the locals and, it claims, actors, sportsmen and politicians. Anyway, the food is good especially the meat and also excellent mushrooms dishes – in season, of course.

ZAGREB Kaptolska Klet

🅶 ⓚⓚ

Kaptol 5. **Tel** *(01) 481 48 38* **Map** D2

This restaurant is in obvious tourist territory situated just in front of the cathedral; but it is nonetheless a beautiful location. It is a large barn of a building with a cosy, old-fashioned interior despite its size. It also has large covered terraces. The food is traditional and good value, if not particularly inspiring.

ZAGREB Ćiho

ⓚⓚ

Pavla Hatza 15. **Tel** *(01) 48 17 060* **Map** D2

Basement restaurant with walls full of bric-a-brac give the place a somewhat wacky ambience. Predominantly a fish restaurant serving specialities from the island of Korčula, the food is very good – especially if you consider the price. The service can seem slow, so just relax end enjoy a bit more of the good house wine.

ZAGREB Vallis Aurea

ⓚⓚ

Tomićeva 4. **Tel** *(01) 48 31 305* **Map** D2

Located near the funicular this place has a pleasantly old-fashioned interior – whitewashed walls and dark wood. Often busy it serves Slavonian food – try the beef stew with prunes (*pastičada*) and the stuffed pastries (*strukli*). Other specialities are smoked pork ribs or trout. Wines are OK too and the staff are helpful.

Key to Price Guide *see p240* **Key to Symbols** *see back cover flap*

ZAGREB Baltazar

Nova Ves 4. **Tel** *(01) 466 68 24*

Map *D2*

An old favourite on the Zagreb scene, just north of the cathedral – and justifiably acclaimed. All the classic dishes, good service plus a wonderful atmosphere created within a traditional arched basement. On sunny days reserve ahead for one of the desirable summer courtyard tables.

ZAGREB Dubravkin Put

Dubravkin Put 2. **Tel** *(01) 483 49 75*

Map *D2*

A good restaurant based just outside the centre in a leafy setting beside a park. The owner gets daily deliveries from Dalmatia, thus guaranteeing the freshness of the produce. As result the seafood is definitely worth trying at this restaurant. There's a pleasant terrace in summer.

ZAGREB Jagerhorn

Ilica 14. **Tel** *(01) 483 3877*

Map *D2*

Up some steps and near the cathedral, this restaurant's peaceful terraces – one covered, one open – belie its central location. The décor manages to blend traditional rustic with over the top kitsch but it is the place *par excellence* for game dishes like grilled venison and wild boar stew.

ZAGREB Okrugljak

Mlinovi 28. **Tel** *(01) 467 4112*

Map *D2*

This large country-style restaurant on the road between Zagreb and Mount Medvednica has a garden for children and large shady terraces. At simple wooden tables you can try the specialities of the house: roasted lamb, duck, or turkey, served with *mlinci* –a traditional Croatian dish of pasta strips that are boiled and then baked.

ZAGREB Pod Gričkim Topom

Zakmardijeve stube 5. **Tel** *(01) 48 33 607*

Map *D2*

Take the funicular to the top and then, in an almost rural setting, you can find this delightful and characterful restaurant. There's a nice terrace and plenty of meat dishes Croatian style, but also tasty grilled fish served with a loose mix of *blitva* – green chard – garlic and potatoes.

ZAGREB Paviljon

Trg Kralja Tomislava 22. **Tel** *(01) 481 30 66*

Map *D2*

A striking building – externally and internally – this pavilion in the park would be worth visiting for the architecture alone. Luckily the food and service is excellent too. Italian-inspired menu – beef carpaccio with grana and rocket; white truffle tagliatelle; and a Dalmatian version of saltimbocca using pork fillets, sage and ham (*pršut*).

ZAGREB Zinfadels

Hotel Esplanade, Mihanoviceva 1. **Tel** *(01) 456 6666*

Map *D2*

Set within an architecturally stunning building, this place for gourmet haute cuisine in Zagreb. It may be an uber-posh hotel dining room but there's no dress code and a pleasantly relaxed ambience. The interiors are elegantly designed, and only let down is the occasional intrusion of piano music – although some may like that sort of thing.

CENTRAL CROATIA

JASTREBARSKO K Lojzeku

Strossmayerov trg 12. **Tel** *(01) 628 11 29*

Map *C2*

A well-respected restaurant with a large and shady terrace. The kitchen tries to give traditional Croatian home-cooking a creative twist – turkey breast with gorgonzola sauce and olives; but it's not always successful. However, it does the standard grills, pastas and fish well. Large choice of wines.

KARLOVAC Žganjer

Turanj-Jelaši 41. **Tel** *(047) 641 304*

Map *C2*

This restaurant is also a motel on the road to Plitvice. Most of the dining is enjoyed outdoors on a covered terrace. The kitchen prides itself on serving Croatian specialities like lamb from the islands, roast suckling pig (but also has ostrich on the menu). If you eat or drink too much you can always sleep it off in one of the rooms.

SAMOBOR Pri Staroj Vuri

Giznik 2. **Tel** *(01) 336 05 48*

Map *C2*

In a cottage in a charming village you can enjoy proper country cooking – try their *Hrvatska pisanica* (steak with mushrooms, onions, tomatoes and red wine sauce), or rib-sticking dumplings with beef or, for dessert, *strukli*. The décor is very Hansel and Gretel – gingham curtains and clocks all over the walls (the name means Ancient Clocks).

SAMOBOR Samoborska Pivnica

Šmidhenova 3. **Tel** *(01) 336 13 33*

Map *C2*

Near the town park this "olde worlde" basement restaurant offers good traditional local specialities at reasonable prices, all day long. The proper translation of *pivnica* is tavern, and this retains an element of the old-fashioned charm associated with that term – although it verges on the twee.

SISAK Cocktail

A Starčevića 27. **Tel** *(044) 549 137*   **Map** *D2*

A restaurant in the centre of Sisak near the town museum, serving traditional and more up-to-date Croatian and Italian cuisine. The establishment is in a modern building with refreshing clean lines (no gingham in sight). The food is pretty good value and there's a good selection of wines.

SLAVONIA AND BARANJA

ĐAKOVO Trnavački Vinodom

A Starečevića 52. **Tel** *(031) 811 891*   **Map** *F2*

A small simple Slavonian restaurant serving simple Slavonian food at very good prices. Try the fried carp or the *ražnjići* (pork kebab) with a glass or two of local Graševina or Traminac wine. The interior is a bit drab but the restaurant is conveniently located near the road for those driving around the country (but no drinking and driving).

ĐAKOVO Croatia Turist

Preradovića 25. **Tel** *(032) 813 391*   **Map** *F2*

This restaurant serves typical Slavonia food – they have their own smoke-house so be sure to try something home-smoked – smoke-cured spicy sausage (*kulen*), locally caught venison and freshwater fish. Try the *kobanac* a typical Hungarian-influenced goulash dish. Wash it all down with the excellent regional white wines.

DARUVAR Terasa

Julijev Park 1. **Tel** *(043) 331 705*   **Map** *E2*

Located near the thermal spas of Croatia, this restaurant has mock-Baroque furnishings, as though it expects the Austro-Hungarian aristocracy come back and take the waters. Its menu is suitably historical too – it serves Croatian, Hungarian, Czech and Italian cuisine. A large terrace unsurprisingly (the name is a clue).

KUTJEVO Schön Blick

Zagrebačka 11, Vetovo. **Tel** *(034) 267 108*   **Map** *F2*

In a rural location and scenically situated next to a lake, 8 km (5 miles) from Kutjevo, this place offers typical country cuisine. You can find the this popular restaurant on the Kutjevo to Velika road. Be sure to try the famous wine – *Kutjevački Risling* – as the local wine industry was started by Cistercian monks.

LIPIK Lipa

Marije Terezije 5. **Tel** *(034) 421 244*   **Map** *E2*

This eatery forms part of a small, candy pink hotel, whose main clientele consists of people travelling to enjoy the medicinal thermal waters of Lipik. The restaurant is a bit bland but it serves good examples of the local hearty, Slavonian cuisine – which is actually not everyone's idea of a healthy diet.

NAŠICE Ribnjak

Stjepana Radića 1, Ribnjak, Našice. **Tel** *(031) 607 006*   **Map** *F2*

This rustic restaurant, also has a very scenic location, 10 km (6 miles) from Našice, on the road from Osijek. This watery region is known for its freshwater fish and this is a good place to try Slavonian fish dishes and specialities such as *fiš paprikaš* – with obvious Hungarian influences.

NOVA GRADIŠKA Slavonski Biser

Nikole Tesle 2–4, Nova Gradiška. **Tel** *(035) 363 259*   **Map** *E2*

Conveniently located for travellers near the train and bus station, this restaurant offers Croatian cooking and the standard range of international dishes. The terrace is unfortunately next to the road but it's not too busy a thoroughfare. It's a large establishment that also operates as a motel

OSIJEK Bastion

Trg Vatroslava Lisinskog 1, Osijek. **Tel** *(031) 207 800*   **Map** *F2*

This is a both a café and a restaurant – so you can also stop by for a coffee and one of the cakes. Its strong point is the distinctive atmosphere created by its setting in an ancient tower in the old fort, close to the beautiful Drava river – from where it gets some of its freshwater fish. Try the *fiš paprikaš* (only on Fridays).

OSIJEK Bijelo Plavi

Martina Divalta 8, Osijek. **Tel** *(031) 571 000*   **Map** *F2*

Located near the town swimming pool and the Gradski Vrt stadium, this restaurant offers typical dishes of the region such as spicy paprika flavoured stews and freshwater fish dishes. With a pleasant interior of dark wooden beams and simple white walls and a good choice of wines, this is a restaurant worth visiting.

SLAVONSKI BROD Slavonski Podrum

Andrije Štampa 1, Slavonski Brod. **Tel** *(035) 444 856*   **Map** *F2*

In a lovely old building with an exterior of black oak beams and white plaster and old wooden benches and tables, the restaurant offers lovely rustic cooking, typical of the area. Try the *kulen* the spicy local sausage, or the roast knuckle of pork or veal. Sometimes has a traditional Slavonian band playing.

Key to Price Guide *see p240* **Key to Symbols** *see back cover flap*

VUKOVAR Tri Vrske

Parobrodska 3. **Tel** *(032) 441 788*

Map *G2*

Riverside restaurant with laidback charm, specialising in regional freshwater fish dishes – choose from spicy fish stew (*fiš paprikaš*), sturgeon (*kečiga*), fried carp (*šaran*), catfish with mushrooms (*som u šampinjonima*). One of the few restaurants here to have survived the war and still going strong.

THE NORTHERN COUNTIES

KOPRIVNICA Kraluš

Zrinski trg, 10. **Tel** *(048) 622 302*

Map *D1*

Traditional 250 year-old beer hall on a square at the centre of town. Although the region is proud of its wines, there's also strong beer culture. This establishment brews its own beers and has special tasting menus designed for specific beers. Try the beer sausage (*pivskih kobasica*) with beans (*podravskog graha*).

KOPRIVNICA Podravska Klet

Starogradska Cesta (4km/2 miles from Koprivnica). **Tel** *(048) 634 069*

Map *D1*

Rustic restaurant with a thatched roof, stained-glass windows and solid wooden tables. There's a lot of good local produce on offer – homemade sausage, creamy cows' cheese, home-prepared cows' tongue and a house special rustic stew (*Gorički gulaš*). Local wines too. Sometimes features traditional live music.

KRAPINSKE TOPLICE Zlatna Lisica

Martinišce 38a. **Tel** *(049) 236 627*

Map *D1*

With a great view overlooking the rolling hills of the surrounding region this is a simple restaurant serving good, honest country food. Try the sausages "by the metre" (*kobasice na metre*), game stews (*gulaš od divljači*) and especially the locally caught roasted boar (*pečena veprovina iz banjica*).

PREGRADA Dvorac Bezanec

Valentinovo. **Tel** *(049) 376 800*

Map *C1*

One of Croatia's top dining experiences in a 17th-century stately home set in the countryside. Large restaurant and even bigger wine list. A real treat, if the budget allows. They call it "regional aristocratic cooking": perch in champagne, venison with cranberries and pancakes with ice-cream and marinated cherries.

STUBIČKE TOPLICE Slamnati Krovovi

Ljube Đalsog 4. **Tel** *(049) 282 569*

Map *D1*

A cute little rustic restaurant with a great big thatched roof and little wooden windows looks like something out of Hansel and Gretel. The cuisine is unsurprisingly traditional country cooking typical of the region. The black sausage, pickled cabbage and *strukli* (pastry parcels filled with cream cheese) are excellent.

TRAKOŠĆAN Coning

Trakošćan 5. **Tel** *(042) 796 224*

Map *D1*

Set by a lake and near to the medieval castle of Trakošćan, this large hotel complex restaurant serves Croatian specialities from the Zagorje hills. The hotel is set in the beautiful countryside below the imposing castle. There's a nice large terrace. Try the pork cutlets in grape juice (*svinjski kotlet u moštu*).

VARAŽDIN Restoran Raj

Gundulićeva 11. **Tel** *(042) 213 146*

Map *D1*

Although the restaurant has stone arches, and medieval chandeliers, it is pleasantly minimalist in a modern way. Serving home-made traditional foods – chicken liver in bacon (*pileća jetrica u slanini*); black pudding (*krvavice*); roast duck (*domaća pečena patka*). The terrace is covered with wisteria which is wonderful when in bloom.

VARAŽDIN Royal

Uska ulica 5. **Tel** *(042) 213 477*

Map *D1*

In the town centre this restaurant offers very good food and Croatian wine and a bar in the basement. The mahogany covered interior is a bit dark but there is a small terrace. Serves all the usual suspects but game is a speciality with venison and wild boar on the menu. They also do fish – freshwater and from the coast.

VARAŽDIN Zlatna Guska

Habdelića 4. **Tel** *(042) 213 393*

Map *D1*

This restaurant in a 17th-century palace has a good reputation (and therefore may get busy – so book ahead). The cavernous stone interior is adorned with pikes, shields and flags. Good steaks – try the *biftek u požaru 1776* (steak flamed in brandy with a mustard and cream sauce).

VELIKI TABOR Grešna Gorica

Taborgradska Klet, Desinić. **Tel** *(049) 343 001*

Map *C1*

This farmhouse on a hill facing the town of Veliki Tabor, near Miljana castle, offers simple Croatian dishes. It has an orchard with tables and a rustic interior. There's a menagerie for the kids with peacocks, chickens, turkeys and deer wandering about – most of whom feature on the menu. Hearty food – grilled/roasted chicken, turkey and venison.

SHOPPING IN CROATIA

Croatia does its best to encourage its visitors to go shopping (indeed it is a significant factor in local economies) and there is a range of traditional and typical crafts, which are excellent souvenirs. The prices are by and large very reasonable too. Shoppers can choose from a variety of products from works of creative handicraft such as handmade lace or hand-painted ceramics to jewellery.

Doll in costume, Osijek

On the island of Pag, exquisite lace is made and in Osijek, where beautiful embroidery is a proud tradition, you can also buy pretty costume dolls. Ties and fountain pens, both of which originated in Croatia, also make good purchases. In some resorts, local artists make a living by selling their watercolours. Visitors can also buy all sorts of delicious Croatian consumables from honey to plum brandy.

Jars of various types of honey, a speciality on the island of Šolta

OPENING HOURS

Shops and department stores are usually open from 8am to 8pm from Monday to Friday (but some stores may open at 7am and close at 9pm) and from 8am to 2 or 3pm on Saturdays. However, it should be remembered that smaller shops often close at lunchtime, usually from noon to 4pm. Shops are generally closed on Sundays and holidays but in the high season in the tourist resorts many shops stay open for business as usual.

PRICES

The prices are fixed in the shops and it is not generally done to haggle over prices. However, in the markets and the street stalls it is acceptable practice, and it can also be fun, to negotiate a good price. The prices are

often displayed in the markets, but it should be remembered that at times the prices displayed are not always the same as those applied to the local people. The spending power of foreign visitors is frequently much greater than that of the local Croats and can occasionally result in pricing variations for locals.

PAYING

In department stores, shopping centres and the major chain stores, it is only possible to pay in local currency or by using one of the main international credit cards. In the smaller shops and in places such as markets, payments should be made in cash, in kuna.

VAT REFUNDS

Tourists in Croatia who spend more than 500 kuna on a single item are entitled to a refund of the Value Added Tax (VAT), which is called PDV in Croatia. When making your purchase, you should ask the sales assistant for the appropriate form (PDV–P), which should be properly filled in and stamped, on the spot.

This document should be handed to the customs authorities on departure from Croatia, thus verifying that the item bought is genuinely destined for export.

A PDV refund in kuna can be obtained within six months,

either at the same shop where the goods were purchased (in which case the tax is refunded immediately), or by posting the verified receipt back to the shop, together with the number of the bank account into which the refund should be paid. In this case the refund is dealt with within 15 days of receipt of the claim.

MARKETS

The street markets of Croatia are colourful, lively places to stroll around.

In Zagreb, the Dolac *(see p153)* is a daily market where food is sold under colourful red umbrellas. There is also an underground area here where other products such as household articles and furnishings are sold.

In Split there is a morning market which is held every

Fruit and vegetables on sale at the Dolac market in Zagreb

day on Pazar, just east of the palace walls. This market sells absolutely everything: fruit, vegetables, flowers, shoes, clothes and a vast assortment of souvenirs. There is a local saying which has it that if you cannot find what you are looking for at this market, it probably does not exist (at least not in Split).

SHOPPING CENTRES

Large shopping centres can also be found in Croatia, mainly in the larger towns and cities. Here you will find a number of shops selling assorted merchandise under one roof, usually including a large department store or supermarket.

In Zagreb the busiest and best-known department store is **Nama**, which is right in the centre of the city. Another useful shop, also in the city centre, is **Importanne**, which also has a pharmacy which is open 24 hours a day and sells cigarettes and newspapers. The **Importanne Galerija** is only open on weekdays.

Another useful store is **Plaza** which is open from Monday to Saturday. The **Rotonda** is also open from Monday to Saturday.

TRADITIONAL HANDICRAFTS

There are plenty of opportunities for the visitor to buy a variety of typical Croatian handicrafts and produce, which make very tempting souvenirs.

The country has a long tradition of skilled production of a rich range of handicrafts and typical produce. Production of these crafts is encouraged and supported by the local authorities, who see it as a good way of preserving the cultural heritage and the ancient traditions and crafts of the country.

In Zagreb, you can buy handicrafts, embroidered articles, dolls in traditional costume, terracotta, ceramics, wooden objects and many other similar items at **Rukotvorine**.

Decorated ceramic objects on display in a shop

In Split you can find a large assortment of souvenirs, including objects clearly inspired by maritime themes. You can also buy good reproductions of objects from the era of Roman rule in the underground area of Diocletian's Palace *(see p120)*.

In Osijek, many shops in the centre of the city sell typical locally made handicrafts. Here you can also find dolls dressed in beautifully made costumes, packages of special lace and in particular fabrics finely embroidered with gold and silver thread.

EMBROIDERY AND LACE

One important typical Croatian craft is the art of embroidery, which is carried out more or less everywhere.

Gold thread embroidery produced in the town of Osijek

A characteristic design is a red geometric pattern stitched onto a white background. This design is used to decorate table linen, pillowcases and blouses.

The lace of Pag is justly famous and widely admired. The origins of the lace date back to the Renaissance period, when it was used to decorate the blouses of the ladies of the island of Pag.

However, it was not until the beginning of the 20th century that this particular handiwork assumed its well-deserved fame, thanks to a beautifully decorated blouse given by a noblewoman to the Archduchess of Austria Marie Josephine. This gift was so greatly appreciated and admired that the archduchess went to Pag in person to order more items of clothing. At that time, the Austrian court set trends for others to follow, and this was enough to guarantee the future success for the production of this lace.

The lace is made on a long cylindrical cushion by lacemakers of great skill and tremendous patience. The lace patterns produced are the lacemaker's interpretation of patterns and designs which have been passed down from generation to generation. In this way, the pieces of lace that are produced can often be very different from one another. However, all the patterns originate with the same geometric structure which forms the base.

Lacemaker working on a piece of Pag lace

Pag lace is surprisingly light but at the same time strong. If at all possible, pieces of the lace should be bought in Pag itself. Not only can you be sure of paying a better price than elsewhere but you will be helping to keep alive a tradition which is over a century old.

Prices vary according to the size of the piece you buy, but if you consider that a table centrepiece measuring 10 cm (4 in) in diameter takes a good 24 hours to make, you will have some idea of the labour involved.

Lace is sold in the shop adjacent to the **Pag Museum** (summer opening hours are from 6 to 9pm), but the best buys to be had may be found on the same road as the museum and along the ulica Tomislava, where every morning you can find women at their work, selling their lace directly to the public.

LUCKY JEWELLERY

There is one item of jewellery which can only be found in Croatia or, more precisely, only in Rijeka. This is the *morčić* or small Moorish figure. The figurine, in the form of a black character wearing a turban, was originally produced as earrings but today you can also find tie-pins and brooches. The *morčić* has become the symbol of the city and, in 1991, it was proclaimed the mascot of Rijeka. A legend dates the origins of the figurine to the

city's unexpected liberation from a Turkish siege during the 16th century. It was shown that a determining factor in the victory was the contribution of the women of Rijeka and it is said that their men decided to give them a gift of special earrings made to represent the invaders who had been forced to flee for their lives.

In fact, it seems more likely that the *morčić* originated in the 17th and 18th centuries as a local reproduction, made from decidedly poor materials, of a figurine set with stones which was very popular with the Venetians. The figurine represented the connections between Venice and the East and the mystery that this part of the world symbolized for them at the time.

The figure soon became a symbol of good luck among

An earring with the *morčić* of Rijeka

the Istrian people and since that time it has become more lavish and elaborate, so much so that its production has become the preserve of goldsmiths. The body of the figure is traditionally glazed ceramic. On request, precious stones may be used to decorate this figure. The best place to buy a *morčić* in Rijeka is the **Mala Galerija**.

CURIOSITIES

Croatia can claim to have invented one of the most well-known of men's accessories, the tie, or cravat. The tie actually originates from a type of scarf worn by Croatian cavalrymen to distinguish them from other soldiers during the bloody 30-year war which devastated Europe in the 17th century.

The French took to referring to this particular way of tying the scarf as *"à la cravate"*, meaning "in the Croatian way". Since that time the tie, or cravat, has become a standard symbol of smart, elegant dressing for hundreds of millions of men in the world.

The production of ties in Croatia today is still of a very high standard, and a tie would make a highly appropriate choice for a souvenir of your visit.

There are some very good clothes shops in the centre of Zagreb where you can buy an assortment of ties, and these

One of many jeweller's shops in Croatia

include **Follow Me, Heruc Galeria** and **Jobis**.

Another little-known fact is that the inventor of the fountain pen was an engineer from Zagreb. In 1906, one Eduard Slavoljub Penkala patented a mechanical pencil and a year later a pen with a reservoir of ink, called the "mechanical pen", which revolutionized the way people wrote.

The inventor opened the first factory for the production of fountain pens in Zagreb in 1911. Within a short space of time it became an enormous success and developed into one of the most important manufacturing centres for writing instruments, producing fountain pens which were exported all over the world. There could not be a more appropriate place to buy this everyday item than Zagreb itself.

Elegant ties on display in a shop in the centre of Zagreb

LOCAL PRODUCE

The gastronomic specialities and local produce of Croatia are as varied as the landscape of Croatia.

Among the country's best-known natural products, one of the most important is lavender. Lavender is sold dried in small bags or as essence in bottles. It can be found more or less all over the country but is particularly linked with the island of Hvar (see pp126–7), where its colour and scent can nearly

Paški sir, the sheep's cheese of Pag, sold on the island

overwhelm the senses when the shrubs are in flower. The scent is particularly pungent when you browse the lavender stalls near the port, where you can buy any number of cosmetic products made with lavender.

The gastronomic specialities of Croatia also make excellent souvenirs. Many places have their own particular speciality. Among many items worthy of mention are the mustard (in traditional containers) made in Samobor, near Zagreb, the honey from Grohote, on the island of Šolta, and cukarini biscuits from Korčula.

Another unmissable delicacy is the delicious truffle found around Buzet, overlooking the Mirna valley in Istria (although these are only available in season).

However, the most highly valued of all delicacies is cheese. Croatia produces a range of its own cheeses, and the most well-known is paški sir, a mature cheese made from sheep's milk, produced on the island of Pag (see pp102–3). It is still made according to traditional methods and the grazing pasture for the sheep, full of aromatic herbs, is said to give it a distinctive flavour.

To buy the cheese on the island just look for signs with the name of the cheese, "paški sir" outside the farmhouses, or go to the well-stocked shop of **Tonći Buljanović**.

DIRECTORY

SHOPPING CENTRES

Importanne
Starcevicev trg, Zagreb.
Tel (01) 457 70 76.
⏱ 9am–9pm Mon–Sat.

Importanne Galerija
Iblerov trg, Zagabria.
Tel (01) 461 95 03.
⏱ 9am–9pm Mon–Sat.

Nama
Ilica near trg Jelačića, Zagreb.

Plaza
Maksimirska 2, Zagreb.
Tel (01) 230 18 17. ⏱ 9am–8pm Mon–Fri; 8am–3pm Sat.

Rotonda
Jurišićeva 19, Zagreb.
Tel (01) 481 77 85. ⏱ 9am–8pm Mon–Fri; 9am–3pm Sat.

SHOPS

Follow Me
Teslvia 5, Zagreb.
Tel (01) 481 93 93.

Heruc Galeria
Ilica 26, Zagreb.
Tel (01) 483 35 69.

Jobis
Gajeva 21, Zagreb.

Mala Galerija
Užarska 12, Rijeka.
Tel (051) 335 403.

Pag Museum
Kralja Zvonimira, Pag.
⏱ summer: 6–9pm.

Rukotvorine
Trg Jelačića 7, Zagreb.

Tonći Buljanović
Prošika 6, Pag.

Seller of essence and lavender bags on the island of Hvar

ENTERTAINMENT IN CROATIA

Although Croatians speak a language which is most likely completely unknown to the average visitor, the country still manages to offer a surprisingly varied range of accessible and engaging entertainment for visitors of all age groups. A choice of opera, ballet, folk music festivals, disco nightclubs, cinemas, casinos, tennis, football and basketball matches should be sufficient to satisfy

Classical ballet,
National Theatre
in Zagreb

anyone. The settings for many of these entertainments are often memorably spectacular, too. Performance details are readily available from weekly or monthly magazines of events and from tourist offices and websites. Tickets are usually easy to come by, and can be bought at venue ticket desks or often in advance from local tourist offices. Read ahead to see what's on and where to go.

![The ornate interior of the National Theatre in Zagreb]

The ornate interior of the National Theatre in Zagreb

INFORMATION AND TICKETS

For information concerning dates, times, prices and booking details of the various festivals, shows, theatre performances and musicals, it is best to get in touch with the relevant local tourist information office in Croatia. All these offices can provide details about the cultural events happening in their part of the country. Another good source of information can be the Internet. The Croatian National Tourist Office's website is www.croatia.hr

Posters announcing forthcoming events are often displayed all over the cities and towns and these are often useful for finding out about the more important or more popular shows.

For information concerning theatre performances, you can also go to the theatre box office itself, where you can usually buy tickets on the spot.

THEATRE AND DANCE

Plays are generally performed in the Croatian language which, unless you speak it, can marginalise the theatre as an evening's entertainment for all but the most ardent thespians. There is, however, an important reason why you should nonetheless check out what's on at the theatre in any town you happen to be in. High-class performances of opera and ballet, for which not knowing the language is not a barrier to enjoyment, are put on by Zagreb's **Croatian National Theatre**, Zadar's **National Theatre**, Rijeka's **Ivan Zajc Theatre** and Split's **National Theatre**.

For a more unusual form of drama which also has the advantage of being accessible to visitors, especially families with younger children, consider a visit to the unique Zagreb puppet theatre, the **Zagrebačko Kasalište Lutaka**.

They put on performances almost every weekend.

Croatia's many traditional festivals not only have particular dishes associated with them, but dances too. The most famous of these is undoubtedly Korcula's sword dance, traditionally enacted in the town centre on the evening of St Theodore's Day, July 29th. Such is the attraction of the *moreska*, as it is known, that this costumed 15th-century dance is now performed outside of that holiday date – every Monday and Thursday at 9pm throughout July and August, sometimes even in June and September as well. Tickets at the event, or in advance from an agency, are not terribly expensive. It is obviously touristy, but still worth seeing as they really do swing those swords around. At every festive occasion in Croatia, there are several famous folk dances you may well come across: the *poskocica*, where couples weave themselves into intricate configurations; the *kolo*, a pan-Slavic circular dance and the *drmes*, a type of speeded-up polka.

Costume drama in Dubrovnik, at the Rector's Palace

Musicians playing traditional Croatian music

MUSIC

Whilst Croatia has nurtured classical composers and does have many aspiring rock bands, unfortunately few people outside of Croatia have ever heard of them. But don't let that put you off.

Croatia does have a rich tradition of folk music and these bands play all along the Adriatic at summer open-air concerts, on holiday festivals and even in hotel lobbies to entertain tourists after dinner.

Unusual instruments to look out for are the *tamburitza*, a sort of Turkish mandolin, and in Slavonia the *citura*, a poignant-sounding type of zither (a horizontal stringed instrument). You will also come across variations on the folk theme, such as *klapa* – five- to ten-part harmony singing, mainly by males – or lively *turbofolk*, where the instruments and beats of modern pop (with dancing, mini-skirted female lead singers) try to inject a bit of new life into old folklore.

For a wide range of musical styles, global, local and avante garde, the **Aquarius Club** in Zagreb is one of the top places in Croatia. Otherwise, be sure not to miss the music and pyro-technics of **Dubrovnik's Summer Festival**, held over five weeks between July and August, and anything at all

going on in the evening at Pula's ancient and stunning **Roman Amphitheatre**.

NIGHT CLUBS

Cafés, bars and pubs all over Croatia often put on live music, especially at weekends. But if, after a few drinks, you want to party on into the night, then the capital or the coast in summer are the places to be. Entrance prices vary within between 50–100 kuna and venues open around 10pm, although most people arrive fashionably late, towards midnight or later.

Winter closing times are 11pm from Sunday to Thursday and midnight on Friday and Saturday, but in the summer clubs go on into the early hours of the morning. Open-air bars on the Adriatic coast will serve until 3am; open-air discos stop at 5am.

Younger Croats simply don't have the cash to go out as often as they would like – but if there's a Croatian band on and it's a weekend they'll be out in force, dressed-up and fully made-up. Weekday parties in the coastal resorts are therefore going to be predominantly for holiday-makers. Where you will find plenty of locals almost anytime are the new multi-purpose entertainment complexes as in Zagreb or Split, where all their café-bars, cinemas, discos etc are usually crowded with youngsters.

Zagreb, Rijeka, Split, Pula and Dubrovnik all have well known discos and nightclubs, though times and conditions change so frequently that they should be checked out locally beforehand.

Zagreb has the ever-popular **Aquarius Club** which although 4 km (over 2 miles) from the city centre has dancing to commercial, techno and Croatian bands on a terrace overlooking Lake Jarun. **Saloon** is more sophisticated, with an older crowd dancing to well-known hits and paparazzi lurking in the wings as local celebrities are liable to pitch up. **Sokol Klub** has live concerts on Sundays, free entrance for women on any day before midnight and is well-established on the disco scene. **Mocvara**, in a disused factory on the banks of the river Sava, is relatively new and currently "in", being home to gigs, exhibitions and performances of an alternative, off-beat kind.

Down a side street in Rijeka is a cult venue which over the last 20 years has seen the

The amphitheatre in Pula, summer venue for spectacular concerts

A late-night bar in Dubrovnik

birth of many new bands. It's called **Club Palach**, after the Czech student who set fire to himself in 1968 to protest at the Soviet invasion, and is easily the top place in town. If you prefer a big, techno party house teeming with teenagers, the **Colosseum** in otherwise staid and stately Opatija is the place to go.

Split has clubs with open-air terraces looking out to sea, the best of which are the two-storey **Shakespeare** and the palm-filled **Tropic Club Ecuador**. **Mississippi** is predominantly techno while **Metropolis** is more mainstream, with occasional live concerts.

Rock Club Uljanik has Pula's liveliest alternative concerts in a vacant building above the shipyards. Out of town are two classics: the Napoleonic **Fort Bourguignon** for techno and rave crowds and **Aquarius**, one of the largest outdoor nightclubs in Croatia.

Dubrovnik is diverse in what it offers: **Labirint** is a more expensive, up-market fusion of food, dancing and spectacle; **Latino Club Fuego** is casual, relaxed and plays a range of music. **Esperanza** is popular and charged-up, with a diet of imported techno and home-grown Croatian bands.

On the islands, Hvar has become a fashionable centre for night life and developed a bit of a reputation as a party island. Early evening activity centres around the harbour, in bar-cum-clubs like **Carpe Diem** where the dancers warm up before heading up the tree-covered hillside to a big old Venetian fort that has

been converted into an open-air nightclub, **Veneranda**. The **F1** club near Trogir town is a big club for dance-music. Less fashionable but just as much fun is the **Faces Club**, on the island of Brac, near Bol.

CASINOS

As you would expect, the capital Zagreb has the most casinos and as with the rest of Croatia they are found in the more upmarket hotels. (There are "casinos" in lesser hotels but they are usually not worth visiting.) Try those at the **Hotel International, Hotel Esplanade** and **Hotel Panorama**. Any casino will have an array of slot machines along with a number of card tables where stakes are relatively low. Normally you can wear just smart casual clothing and walk straight in. However, it might be worth calling ahead before-hand – the most upmarket casinos may ask to see your passport before you can enter.

CINEMA

Going to see a film is easy to do, with most large towns having a cinema. Zagreb has 20 movie-houses including the **Kinoteca** which runs cult, arthouse and experimental films. Tickets only cost about 20 kuna and films are shown in their original languages with Croatian subtitles. You can expect to see the latest Hollywood box-office hits with all the usual comforts. Conditions can be more basic in smaller towns where you may come across rows of wooden chairs, rather like being back at school. Neither will things be so luxurious in the summer open-air cinemas which are more atmospheric: the films too might not be your first choice but the experience is worth trying.

SPECTATOR SPORTS

Tito's post-war Yugoslavia, of which Croatia was a part, consistently put out strong teams in handball, football (soccer), basketball and water polo. Since 1991, when Croatia broke away to become an independent nation, this small country of only 4.5 million people continues to excel in those sports and has added tennis to its sporting repertoire. If you love tennis then go to www.croatiaopen.hr to find out the latest news on the ATP Croatia Open Championships, held at Umag in July.

Croats, just like so many other Europeans, love their football. The 1990's saw now legendary Croatian players

The Hotel Esplanade in Zagreb, home to a casino

like Stimac and Boban rise as international stars as Croatia for the first time became a serious footballing nation: quarter-finalists in the 1996 European Championships and, two years later, third at the World Cup, 1998. Although they haven't scaled those heights since. If you want to see a game during your stay, try either Dinamo Zagreb at the **Maksimir Stadium** on the capital's east side or Hajduk Split at the **Poljud Stadium**, Split. Matches are traditionally held on Sunday afternoons throughout most of the year, with only a short holiday break in the summer.

Like football, the country's top two basketball teams are in Split – KK Split who have

been European Club Champions many times – and Zagreb - with rival contenders, Cibona. Those familiar with the game will know the names of the local stars on the international scene, such as Cosic, Petrovic, Kukoc, Tabak and Rada, and that Croatia was the third best team at the Toronto World Cup in 1994.

If you want to see a basketball game the Cibona team in Zagreb, hosts top quality matches at the **Drazen Petrovic Basketball Centre** every Saturday evening from October to April – tickets are sold on the door.

The Cibona basketball team from Zagreb during a match

DIRECTORY

THEATRES

Croatian National Theatre
Trg Maršala Tita 15,
Zagreb.
Tel (01) 482 85 32.

Ivan Zajc Theatre
Uljarska 1,
Rijeka.
Tel (051) 355 900.

National Theatre
Trg Gaje Bulata 1,
Split.
Tel (021) 344 999.

National Theatre
Široka ulica 8,
Zadar.
Tel (023) 314 552.

Zagrebačko Kasalište Lutaka
Ulica Baruna Trenka 3,
Zagreb.
Tel (01) 369 54 57.

MUSIC

Dubrovnik Summer Festival
Poljana Paska Milicevica 1,
Dubrovnik (ticket office).
Tel (020) 323 40

Roman Amphitheatre
Tourist office: Forum 3,
Pula.
ℹ *(052) 219 197, 212 987.*

NIGHT CLUBS

Aquarius Club
Aleja Matije Ljubeka,
Jarun, Zagreb.
Tel (01) 364 02 31.

Aquarius
Medulin, Pula.

Carpe Diem
Riva Center,
Hvar.

Club Palach
Kruzna 6,
Rijeka.
Tel (051) 215 063.

Colosseum
On the Lido,
Opatija.

Esperanza
Put Republike 30,
Dubrovnik.

Faces Club
near Bol, Brac.

F1
Junction of Magistrala and
Airport Rd, Trogir.

Fort Bourgignon
near Valsaline Bay, Pula.

Labirint
Svetog Dominika 2,
Dubrovnik.
Tel (020) 322 222.

Latino Club Fuego
Brsalije 11,
Near Pile Gate,
Dubrovnik.

Metropolis
Matice Hrvatska 1,
Split.
Tel (021) 305 110.

Mocvara
Trnjanski Nasip,
Zagreb.
Tel (01) 615 96 67.

Mississippi
Osjecka,
Split.
Tel (021) 314 47 88.

Rock Club Uljanik
Dobrilina 2,
Pula.

Saloon
Tuskanac 1a,
Zagreb.
Tel (01) 481 07 33.

Sokol Klub
Trg Marsala Tita 6,
Zagreb.
Tel (01) 482 85 10.

Shakespeare
Cvijetna 1,
Split.
Tel (021) 519 492.

Tropic Club Ecuador
Kupaliste Bacvice 11,
Split.
Tel (021) 323 571.

Veneranda
On the hill behind the
Delphin Hotel, Hvar.

CASINOS

Hotel Esplanade
Mihanovićeva,
Zagreb.
Tel (01) 450 10 00.

Hotel International
Miramarska 24,
Zagreb.
Tel (01) 615 00 25.

Hotel Panorama
Trg Sportova 9,
Zagreb.
Tel (01) 309 26 53.

CINEMA

Kinoteca
Kordunska 1,
Zagreb.
Tel (01) 377 17 53.

SPECTATOR SPORTS

Poljud Stadium
Mediteranskih igara 2,
21000 Split
Tel (021) 381 235
www.hnkhajduk.hr

Maksimir Stadium
Maksimirska 128,
Zagreb.
Tel (01) 48 43 769.

Drazen Petrovic Basketball Centre
Savska cesta 30,
Zagreb.
Tel (01) 48 43 333.

OUTDOOR ACTIVITIES

One of the keys to Croatia's tourist success is that it is blessed with such bountiful natural resources – waterfalls, islands, hills, rivers, lakes, canyons, mountains, pine woods and verdant parks – all soaked in dependable Mediterranean sunshine. To its credit, Croatia has responded well by providing a good infrastructure backed by a multitude of organizations to get visitors

Sailing school along the coast

climbing and rafting, sailing and surfing, hiking and biking throughout its wonderfully diverse topography. There are also less energetic activities to be enjoyed. Croatia has several thermal spa centres that can be a bit utilitarian but are getting better as retreats for unwinding after some activity. Finally, of course, the coastline and myriad islands have a glittering choice of beaches for sun worshippers.

Sailing along the Croatian coast

SAILING

The Croatian coastline has many natural harbours, ports and marinas, making it a real haven for sailors. As a result, the best way to fully appreciate the rugged beauty of Croatia's Adriatic coastline is not by car but by yacht or motorboat. With clean, clear sea; steady, moderate winds; waters in which it is easy to anchor and well-equipped marinas open all year-round, a sailor's life is made easy in Croatia. If possible, avoid July to August, unless you really want to spend the time with every weekend admiral in Europe. May to June or September to October are more peaceful, cost less and what is more the weather is still good.

The **Croatian National Tourist Board** (www.croatia.hr) lists over 140 companies with some 2,700 boats available for hire, typically rented out on a weekly basis from 5pm Saturday to Saturday next at 9am. The most important decision for the holiday maker is whether to go

"bareboat" or "skippered". The former requires that you show a valid licence with at least 2 years' experience on it and register the crew. You are then free to sail off on your own. "Skippered" means that for about another 130 euros per day, plus food, you'll have a local in charge who knows exactly what he's doing. Prices vary depending on the size of boat and time of year. The British company **Nautilus Yachting**, for example, will arrange a week "bareboat" on an 11-metre (36 ft) boat sleeping six for around 2,200 euros, whilst the Croatian company **Club Adriatic** have a few 4-berth 10-metre (33 ft) craft for around 1,800 euros, again for seven days.

Anyone sailing to Croatia in their own boat must report to the nearest Harbour Master's Office on arrival if it is over 3 m (10 ft) in length and has an engine over 4 kW.

From Umag to Dubrovnik, Croatia has 50 marinas with everything a sailor could want: refuelling and repair services, water and electrical

hook-ups, medical assistance and surveillance, cafes, bars and restaurants. Marinas are classified according to the level of service they offer and charge accordingly. The **Adriatic Croatia International Club**, known as **ACI**, runs a chain of 21 marinas to which you can take out a yearly contract for use of all facilities and discounted berth fees. In addition there are plenty of temporary moorings available. Or you could simply overnight in a deserted bay.

Another way to experience the combination of sailing and Croatia's unique coastline is to enroll on a special holiday to learn how to sail. **Adriatica.net** offer holidays for sailors of all different levels of experience, although there are plenty of other similar companies.

Coastal radio stations give weather updates in both Croatian and English. Useful radio stations include Radio

Mooring in the harbour at Makarska

Rijeka UKW channel 24, Radio Split UKW channels 07, 21, 23, 81 and Radio Dubrovnik UKW channels 07 and 04.

WINDSURFING

Most coastal resorts offer windsurfing courses and boards for hire, but serious surfers will enjoy two places in particular: Bol, on the island of Brac, and Viganj on the Peljesac Peninsular, close to Orebic1. Both resorts have many renowned windsurfing clubs, offering kit and courses from beginner to expert. Also, note, both places play annual host to international championship events in July.

The windsurfing season runs from early April to late October and the westerly winds are at their peak in the early afternoon. Conditions

Windsurfing, a very popular sport along the Croatian coast

are ideal in late May/early June and in late July/early August – though the latter, of course, is in the high season.

DIVING

Although Croatia may not be the Caribbean or the Red Sea, it nonetheless has its fair share of interesting dive sites. Nature has fashioned plenty of underwater caves from the porous karstic limestone along the coast, to which you can add the further attractions of sea walls and shoals of fish and, at greater depths, shipwrecks and corals. Losinj Island has all the above features and is probably the most comprehensive dive site

The clear waters off Croatia, rich in marine life and coral

in Croatia. If fish are your interest, try Vis – thanks to its military background the island was never commercially fished and consequently, has the richest marine life. The best underwater caves are around the beautiful Kornati Islands, while interesting shipwrecks can be found near Rovinj (Baron Gautsch,1914 passenger ferry), Dubrovnik (Taranto, 1943 merchant ship) and the Peljesac Peninsular (S57, another merchant casualty of war, from 1944).

There are, however, rules and regulations about who can dive where. To dive at all, you will need to show a current diver's card issued by an internationally recognized diving organisation. For a small fee, this is then given a year-long validation by the **Croatian Diving Federation** or any of its agents – which could be an authorised tourist agency or the nearest diving

club to your hotel. Diving clubs abound in the Adriatic and are useful not only for hiring equipment but also for going on guided tours with English-speaking instructors.

Areas off-limits to divers are around military installations, protected cultural monuments and some, but not all, nature reserves. Diving is forbidden in Krk and Brijuni parks for example but, with a permit, is allowed in the Kornati National Park and the islands of Mljet. Check beforehand if you intend to be adventurous.

FISHING

The Adriatic Sea is one of the richest in Europe and draws all kinds of fishermen. In order to go fishing you will need a licence. These are issued by tourist offices, authorised agencies and diving centres and clubs which have an arrangement with the Ministry of Agriculture and Forestry. The cost of a licence is not terribly great and depends on its duration – you can purchase licences valid for 1 day, 3 days, a week or 30 days. The licences permit fishing with a rod and line or a spear gun and it is possible to fish everywhere except in the protected areas of the marine parks (that is, Kornati, the Brijuni islands, Krk and Mljet). Along with the licence you will receive a list of the areas which are off-limits and indications of the number of each fish species that you are allowed to catch.

Locals showing the wide variety of fish and shellfish in the Croatian sea

HIKING IN THE MOUNTAINS

Croatia is criss-crossed with countless hiking paths and trekking trails – marked by a white dot within a red circle painted onto a tree or rock. Contact the **HPS (Croatian Hiking Association)** for information about the many local walking clubs, maps and the national whereabouts of mountain huts for simple overnight accommodation. The best time of year for hiking is between April and October. However, be aware that the removal of unexploded mines is still taking place in the conflict zones of the 1991–95 war and don't wander off established trails. See the Croatian Mine Action Centre website (www.hcr.hr) for specific information.

Top trails would have to include the Premuzic ridge path, heading for 50 km (31 miles) at around 914 meters (3,000 ft) through the Velebit massif, a short distance east of the central Dalmatian coast, and offering breathtaking views both into continental Croatia and way out to sea; the gorges and beech forests of Paklenica National Park, 40 km (19 miles) northeast of Zadar; Mt Ilija above Orebić for superb mountain coastal scenery; the fortified hill-towns of the Istrian interior; Samobor and the Risnjak National Park in central Croatia and the Zagorje Castles district in the northern counties.

FREE CLIMBING

As with hiking, climbing is also best pursued from April to October – after which there's the prospect of a sudden snowfall or being blasted by the *bura,* a strong cold wind from the northeast. Croats may not be thought of as Alpinists but they have scaled the Himalayas many times, have their own **Croatian Mountaineering Association** and plenty of home mountain ranges in which to practice their sport. Again, the Paklenica National Park is popular, having more than 400 climbing routes to choose from. Cetina Valley near Omiš in central Dalmatia is another prime destination for climbers. Should you want to climb and spend time

Abseiling down a rock face in summer

at the beach as well, consider heading for the peaks on the islands of Brac, Vis, Mjlet, Krk, Hvar, Cres and Losinj plus those on the peninsulars of both Istria and Peljesac.

CYCLING

Cyclists, like hikers, get the full benefit of the outdoor fragrances, riotous bird-song and chance encounters with the locals that their sport brings. Regional tourist boards in Croatia have worked hard to promote a sensible series of designated bike routes. The national parks and nature reserves lead the way with clearly marked bike trails taking you in a circlular tour back to where you began. The Plitvice Lakes provide scenic cycling at its European best. Similarly circuitous routes exist on the islands of Rab, Hvar and Mjlet where out-of-the way beaches and restaurants come into the picture, too. Istria tourist board has also been prominent in looking after cyclists by running rural trails out of and back into Rovinj, Labin and Novigrad. You can find more details at www.istria.com. Hiring bikes can be the best way to get around the island and find secluded bays. Expect to pay around 10–15 euros a day for bike hire.

Hikers on one of the paths in Paklenica National Park

Clay court tennis, a popular sport in Croatia

TENNIS

After football, tennis is Croatia's most popular sport. Almost every town, holiday hotel and camping site will have the necessary facilities – usually plenty of excellent clay courts. Two of the best-equipped clubs are the **Tennis Club Pecine** in Rijeka and the **Tennis Club Smrikve** in Pula. If you enjoy watching tennis, the ATP Croatia Open Championships are held at Umag in July. At any tennic club in Croatia you're likely to be reminded of the achievements of their best known sportsman: Goran Ivanisevic, who won the Men's Singles at Wimbledon (in 2001). He can sometimes be seen knocking up at his local club, Tennis Club Split.

GOLF

With just two courses in the whole of the country, golf has not yet captured the interest of Croatia's sportsmen and women. Visiting golfers are likely to find themselves on a long list with other tourists hoping for a round. If you are still determined to play, there is an 18-hole course at **Dolina Kardinala**, near Karlovac, and a 9-hole course tucked away on **Brijuni Island**, near Pula.

To play at either of the Croatian golf clubs you may need to show a membership card issued by the national federation from your home country. This will show your handicap, which may be required prior to you tee-ing off.

WHITEWATER RAFTING

This most accessible of the extreme sports began in Croatia around the late 1980s, opening up remote canyons and rivers known before only to kayakers and fishermen. The most rewarding places to raft through wild scenery on greenish waters clear down to the riverbed itself – and innocent of vicious rapids or huge waves – are the Dalmatian rivers of Zrmanja, near Zadar and Cetina, near Omis and the rivers Dobra and Kupa, near Karlovac in central Croatia. Agencies like **General Turist** in Zagreb organise trips with guides and all the gear. Otherwise try the website **www.rasah.hr**

RELAXATION

Several spa resorts offer natural thermal springs and treatments. They emphasise the treatment more than the relaxation but have excellent sporting facilities *(see Thermal Spas Tour pp212–13).*

A golfer on a practice course

SURVIVAL
GUIDE

PRACTICAL INFORMATION

Tourism is an important source of revenue and every effort is being made to foster the growth and development of the industry. Since independence in 1991, a number of measures have been introduced to encourage visitors, including simplifying border formalities and introducing tax reductions on items destined for export. Hotels and historic buildings damaged in the war have been rebuilt and there are also pro-

Logo of the Croatian National Tourist Board

grammes in place to improve road and maritime links, both internally and also with neighbouring countries. Public services are also being improved. The country is rapidly reaffirming itself as a popular holiday destination, able to offer tourist facilities of international standard at quite competitive prices. Croatia is not yet a member of the European Union, but many of its regulations and practices already fall in line with EU standards.

The busy embarkation point for the Brijuni islands at Fažana

WHEN TO GO

The busiest, most popular times to visit the Croatian coastline are the summer months of July and August. With its crystal clear seas, combined with thousands of islands and bays for exploration or swimming, the coast is a major attraction. In addition, the summer weather is reliably sunny, another important aspect for many. The island of Hvar, for example, can count on over 200 days of sunshine a year.

In the peak season, hotels and resorts are at their busiest, so if in fact a quieter holiday is preferred it would be better to choose the months of May, June or September, when the weather is still fine but resorts are not quite so crowded.

Another advantage of travelling out of peak season is that much lower prices are

on offer. The countryside, with its countless beauty spots, offers breathtaking scenery all year round but spring and autumn are the best months for hunting or fishing in the many lakes and rivers.

Inland Croatia is also home to a number of thermal spas, and it is possible to combine a few days of therapeutic treatment or relaxation (*see pp212–3*) with visits to cities and towns with their rich historical and artistic heritage.

Unlike nearby Slovenia, Croatia's facilities for winter tourism are not yet well-developed, although there are a few ski slopes, for example in Platak and the Medvednica and Bjelolasica mountains.

Zagreb, the capital, offers numerous attractions the whole year round.

TRAVEL DOCUMENTS

To enter Croatia, visitors need to be in possession of a valid passport. People from countries in the European Union, the US, Canada, Australia and New Zealand do not need a visa to enter Croatia and may stay for up to 90 days.

To check whether you require a visa, visit the website of the Croatian Ministry of Foreign Affairs (www.mvp.hr) for a list of countries whose citizens require visas. Information is in Croat and English. If you do need a visa, seek advice from the Croatian Embassy in your home country.

The Croatian authorities have formed a bilateral agreement with Italy, according to which Italian citizens need only carry an identity card.

All foreign citizens must register with the local police within 48 hours of arrival. Failure to do so may result in a fine or even expulsion from the country. In practice, if you are staying in a hotel, the reception staff will take care of this procedure for you.

People travelling with pets (dogs or cats) must have an International Certificate and all the necessary documents demonstrating that their pets' vaccinations are completely up to date, particularly with regard to rabies.

Bottle of Croatian wine

◁ Winding Magistrala highway running along the Dalmatian coast

CUSTOMS INFORMATION

There are no restrictions on personal effects brought into Croatia by travellers and customs regulations are harmonized with the standards of EU member states. It is also possible to bring into the country or export 200 cigarettes or 50 cigars, 1 litre of spirits, 1 litre of wine, 500 grammes of coffee and 50 millilitres (one bottle) of perfume or essence.

On entering the country, any major, high-value items such as radio equipment, computers, photographic equipment, video cameras, recorders and any other recording equipment and portable televisions must be declared.

If you are arriving by boat you must report your arrival to the Harbour Master's Office and register the number of people on board and all equipment.

There is no limit to the import and export of foreign currency. The limit for the export of local currency is 2,000 kuna.

TOURIST INFORMATION

Every town and city has a tourist offfice, called Turisticki Ured, Turisticki Zajednica, Tourist Information Centar, or, usually in the smaller towns, by the name of Turist Biro. These offices provide information on excursions and transport and will often help visitors to find accommodation in hotels or private rooms (see p218–9).

There are also county and regional tourist offices, managed by the Ministry of Tourism, which are divided according to their administrative territories. These offices can provide information about the whole county.

Another way of finding out about the country is to contact the Croatian National Tourist Board in your own home country before leaving. The Croatian Ministry of Tourism is very aware of the important role the tourist offices play in encouraging

Tourist asking for help and directions

visitors to Croatia and has set up information offices in all the major countries, with the aim of publicizing the attractions that Croatia has to offer. The Internet is also a very useful source of all kinds of relevant information. One particularly helpful website is run by the Croatian National Tourist Board (www.croatia.hr).

OPENING HOURS

Public offices open from 8am to 4pm on weekdays, and most other kinds of office business more or less follow these standard opening times. These hours may vary and can sometimes be extended (or even reduced) for other businesses, for example banks (see p272–3) and post offices (see p270), which are also open on Saturdays. Shops are usually open

early in the morning (see p250), as are cafés, sometimes as early as 6am.

DISABLED TRAVELLERS

In Croatia there is a great awareness of the problems faced by the disabled, emphasized by the country's recent history and the fact that the country now has many more people with disabilities caused by the war for independence. Stations, airports, larger hotels and restaurants above a certain standard and the main public offices in the larger towns are accessible to those in wheelchairs.

However, facilities are not so good at the ports and the disabled may have difficulty getting on and off ferries.

For further information on this subject, contact the **Savez Organizacija Invalida Hrvatske**, the Croatian organization for the disabled, which has its main headquarters in Zagreb. **RADAR** in the UK may also have details.

TRAVELLING WITH CHILDREN

Tourist complexes such as large hotels and resorts, particularly those on the coast and in the larger towns and cities, usually provide facilities for children, such as playgrounds, children's pools and baby-sitting services.

In smaller towns and inland regions less visited by tourists it is usually more difficult to find facilities provided especially for the very young.

Children at play in one of the larger tourist resorts

Enjoying outdoor café life in Varaždin

LANGUAGE

In the national language, which is *hrvatski* or Croatian, Croatia is called Hrvatska. It is not a particularly easy tongue to learn but since most people in Croatia have studied at least one other foreign language, visitors should be able to make themselves understood in most circumstances. Italian, German and English are widely spoken, particularly in the coastal tourist resorts and by those who often have contact with foreign visitors, such as in hotels, restaurants and shops. French is less common. Young Croatians generally speak very good English, so if you need to ask for help in English, seek out a younger person or a student.

FORMS OF GREETING

Croatians tend to be quite reserved with strangers, particularly in the interior regions which see fewer tourists. Attempting a few words of the country in which you are a guest is good manners and will be appreciated. The forms used vary according to the person you are addressing: he or she may be a *gospodin* (a man), a *gospodja* (a married woman) or a *gospodjica* (a young single woman).

Greetings vary for the different times of the day: *dobro jutro* (good morning), *dobar dan* (good afternoon, but also, in a broad sense, good day), *dobra večer* (good evening), *laku noć* (good night). *Bog* (hi) and *Ciao* are informal greetings used by people with whom you have become familiar.

Words that can be used for everyone are *zbogom* or *dovidenja* (goodbye) or *zdravo* (hello). For polite requests use *molim* (please) and *hvala* (thank you). For more vocabulary, see the Phrase Book (pp295–6).

DRESS

Although it is rarely necessary to dress formally, clothes which are neat and tidy will be appreciated. For example, trainers are not suitable for dining in upmarket restaurants.

CUSTOMS

Women, particularly those travelling alone, face no particular risks when travelling in Croatia, though single women will probably attract attention. However, this is more likely to be of a gallant and courteous nature rather than a real nuisance. Making it clear that the attention is unwanted should be sufficient to deter someone.

Visitors should feel free to wear whatever clothing they want, bearing in mind that Croatia is quite a religious country. When visiting churches visitors should try and dress more conservatively than if they were at the beach.

It should also be remembered that certain places, particularly local bars and pubs, are often frequented predominantly by men, and a woman alone in these places may feel a little embarrassed by the attention with which she is observed.

Croatia is a very tolerant country. An example of this is the acceptance of skimpy bikinis, topless bathing or even nudism on the beaches.

Homosexuality is not illegal, although up to now no real gay communities have emerged as they have in other countries.

TIPPING AND BARGAINING

The practice of tipping, usually calculated at ten per cent, is widespread in Croatia, even in restaurants, where a service charge is normally included in the price. When paying in bars or in taxis it is expected that at least the sum will be rounded up. Another customary practice is the tipping of tourist or museum guides after a tour has ended.

In department stores, supermarkets and shops the prices for goods are fixed but elsewhere, particularly in the

Strolling down the street, a safe enough activity everywhere in Croatia

street markets that are held in the town squares, or at stalls along the road, it is possible to haggle over prices.

SMOKING

Smoking is very common in Croatia, and in most public places there is a very lenient attitude towards smoking. No-smoking regulations are applied with a certain flexibility, and only in smarter hotels and restaurants will you find special areas for smokers and non-smokers.

NATURISM

Croatia is a popular country for naturism, where it is practised freely at designated places and resorts which are outstanding for their quality and high standards. Defined by the International Naturist Federation as "a way of living in harmony with nature, characterized by the practice of communal nudity", naturism has a very long tradition in Croatia. In fact, it was back in 1934 that the first vacation resort for naturists was opened in Rajska plaza (Paradise beach), on the island of Rab. Among early visitors were the Duke of Windsor and Mrs Simpson.

Today, naturism is widely practised. There are about 30 naturist centres along the Croatian coast, and some have Blue Flag (clean beach) status. These places are appropriately screened, allowing guests to enjoy the absolute freedom and peace the surrounding nature has to offer in total relaxation.

The beaches that are reserved for naturism are flanked, in some places, by tourist resorts with holiday villages and camping sites.

UK tour operators offering naturist holidays in Croatia include **Dune Leisure** and **Peng Travel**.

ELECTRICITY

The electric current is 220V, 50Hz all over the country. Throughout Croatia, standard European two-pin plugs are used.

TIME

Croatia is one hour ahead of Greenwich Mean Time (GMT) in winter, and two hours ahead in summer.

A secluded beach on the Dalmatian coast

DIRECTORY

CROATIAN NATIONAL TOURIST OFFICE

In Croatia
Iblerov trg 10/IV, Zagreb.
Tel (01) 469 93 33.
Fax (01) 455 78 27.
www.croatia.hr

EMBASSIES AND CONSULATES

American Embassy, Zagreb
Thomas Jefferson 2, Zagreb.
Tel (00 385) 1 661 2200.
Fax (00 385) 1 661 2373.
www.usembassy.hr

Australian Embassy, Zagreb
Centar Kaptol, Nova Ves 11/111 Kat, Zagreb.
Tel (00 385) 1 489 1200.
www.auembassy.hr

British Consulate, Dubrovnik
Buničeva Pol Jana 3 Dubrovnik.
Tel (020) 324 598.

British Consulate, Split
Obala Hrvatskog Narodnog Preporoda 10/III, Split.
Tel (00 385) 21 341 464.
Fax (00 385) 21 362 905.

British Embassy, Zagreb
I. Lučića 4, 10000 Zagreb.
Tel (00 385) 1 600 9100.
Fax (00 385) 1 600 9111.

Canadian Embassy, Zagreb
Prilaz Gjure Dezelica 4, Zagreb.
Tel (00 385) 1 488 1200.
Fax (00 385) 1 488 1230.

Irish Honorary Consulate
Turinina 3, Zagreb.
Tel (00 385) 1 667 4455.
Fax (00 385) 1 241 3901.

SERVICES FOR THE DISABLED

Savez Organizacija Invalida Hrvatske
Savska ceska 3, Zagreb.
Tel (01) 482 93 94.

RADAR
12 City Forum, 250 City Road, London EC1V 8AS.
Tel (020) 7250 3222.

NATURISM

Dune Leisure
Tel (0115) 931 4110.
www.dune.uk.com

Peng Travel
Tel (01708) 471832.
www.pengtravel.co.uk

CROATIA ON THE INTERNET

Banks, Exchange Offices and ATMs
www.zaba.hr
www.hnb.hr
www.amex.hr
www.diners.hr

General Information
www.croatia.net
www.visit-croatia.co.uk
www.croatia.hr

Ministry of Tourism
www.mint.hr

Weather Forecast
www.tel.hr/dhmz

Zagreb Information
www.zagreb-convention.hr

Health and Personal Safety

Croatian public health services meet the standards of those elsewhere in Europe, and in general visitors to Croatia run no serious health risks. There are no endemic diseases. Tap water is drinkable all over the country, and the most common ailments that visitors are likely to suffer are those caused by over-exposure to the sun and insect bites. Travellers in inland regions should be aware that de-mining along former lines of confrontation is not complete. Do not be tempted to stray from known safe routes in these zones. Crime rates are comparatively low, and there is little street crime, although visitors should take the usual precautions in busy places to protect valuables.

VACCINATIONS AND MEDICAL ASSISTANCE

Visitors to Croatia do not require any particular vaccinations unless they are coming from an infected area (check with the health authorities beforehand in the country of departure).

There are hospitals and clinics (bolnica or klinički centar) in all the major towns in Croatia and health centres and pharmacies (ljekarna) in all the smaller towns.

Foreign tourists do not pay for medical services if the Health Care Convention has been signed between Croatia and the country they come from. This applies to most countries in the European Union including the UK, Ireland and Italy. If you come from a country which has not signed the Convention, you have to pay for health services, according to a standardized price list.

It is however advisable to take out an insurance policy to cover medical assistance. The policy should also include repatriation by air-ambulance, as well as the refunding of any medical expenses that are necessary. The insurance company will want to see supporting documents and receipts.

All visitors have a right to emergency medical assistance, but certain medical services must be paid for (the fees are reasonable).

Certain activities, for example diving and rock climbing and in some cases, even hiking or motorcycling, are often not included in travel insurance cover, as they are regarded as dangerous activities. Check the insurance policy details; it may be necessary to pay a surcharge to cover these kinds of sports.

Sign for a private health clinic in the city of Osijek

Klinička bolnica Osijek

PHARMACIES AND MEDICINES

Although it is easy to find all the more common over-the-counter medicines in pharmacies without too much difficulty, it is best to carry an adequate supply of any prescription medicines.

Some medicines are not known by the commercial names given to them in their country of origin, but by the active ingredients contained in them. This may cause difficulty for a pharmacist trying to comply with the request of a foreign visitor. In any event, it is useful if you can produce a legible prescription written by your own doctor as proof that you are authorized to take a particular medicine.

Pharmacies are usually open from 8am to 1pm and from 3 to 7pm.

AILMENTS AND ILLNESS

Most of the problems that visitors suffer from in Croatia are those common to tourists anywhere.

Over-exposure to the sun can cause various problems, from severe burns to sunstroke and dehydration. Sun creams with a high protection factor should be used and it is advisable to wear a hat.

To prevent sunstroke you should drink a lot of liquids and avoid doing very strenuous sports or activities at the hottest time of the day.

A change in diet can cause stomach upsets, which are often a nuisance but can usually be treated quite quickly. In Croatia there is no risk of dysentery or similar illnesses.

On the beaches and near the coast the most common problem is probably irritating insect bites, particularly from mosquitoes, and it is a good idea to take some anti-histamine cream and insect repellent with you.

For hikers and climbers venturing inland there is the possibility of encountering snakes, so take the appropriate serum with you if you are planning such a trip.

People sunbathing on a Dalmatian beach

Travelling by ferry along the coast

DIRECTORY

EMERGENCY SERVICES

Police
Tel 92.

Fire
Tel 93.

Ambulance
Tel 94.

Rescue Service
Tel 112.

Breakdown Service
Tel 987.

Information
Tel 981.

Automobile Club
www.hak.hr

Generally however, most minor ailments and disturbances can usually be avoided with a minimum of care and common sense.

Boat travel is a common means of transport for connections between the coastal towns and cities and obviously the only means of getting to virtually all the islands. Unfortunately many people suffer from seasickness, even when the sea conditions are not particularly rough. People who are susceptible should take some kind of travel sickness pill before embarking. It is advisable to keep to the central areas of the boat where any pitching and rolling is felt less and go on deck where fresh air and a visible horizon may help.

PUBLIC CONVENIENCES

The general standard of hygiene in Croatia is good. There are plenty of public toilets and they are usually clean. There is a charge (2 kuna) for public conveniences in bus and train stations, while those provided for customers in restaurants and cafés are free.

PERSONAL SAFETY

The level of safety on the roads and in public places is good, and the police *(policija)* are deemed responsible for the protection and safety of the country's visitors as well as its citizens. Croatia has a relatively low

crime rate, and violent crime is comparatively rare. If petty theft occurs, it is more likely to happen in crowded bus and railway stations.

It is highly unlikely that the police will create any problems for foreign visitors on holiday in Croatia unless, of course, the law is broken in some way. However, it is advisable to carry your identification documents, such as a passport, with you as the police have the right to ask for identification.

According to an international agreement, if a tourist is held for questioning or detained for whatever reason, he or she has the right to contact a diplomatic representative of his or her country (an embassy or consulate) and receive assistance in appointing a local lawyer, preferably English-speaking *(see p267)*.

Any eventual costs and the lawyer's fee are the responsibility of the accused.

THEFT AND LOSSES

Precautions for avoiding theft and loss of documents and personal belongings are the same as in any other country, so use your common sense. You should avoid leaving objects of value and money unattended, keep an eye on your luggage and bags, particularly in crowded areas, and do not wear showy, expensive jewellery which could attract the wrong kind of attention.

When you travel, it is always a good idea to make a photocopy of your personal documents and keep them in a separate place: in this way it will be much easier to obtain a duplicate. In the event of loss, report the circumstances to the police immediately.

A Croatian policeman with a police car

Communications

A Croatian postbox

The communication systems of the country are of a good standard and the public services, such as the post and telecommunications, function well. The news and information network is well-organized, although most visitors (unless they speak Croatian) will face the obvious obstacle of the language barrier. However, foreign television programmes can be received via satellite and it is also easy to find foreign newspapers and magazines in the newsagents, even if they appear a little later than they would at home.

Using a mobile phone, increasingly common in Croatia

Entrance to the Post Office (HP) in Dubrovnik

POSTAL SERVICES

In January 1999, the national post and telecoms company HPT Hrvatska was divided into HP (postal services) and HT (telecommunications). HP operates a network of post offices, with branches in all towns, and offers a wide range of services, including the sale of stamps and telephone cards, fax facilities and postal services of all kinds. If you are sending ordinary post, such as postcards, stamps *(marke)* can also be bought at newsagents *(tisak)*. Note that unless airmail is specifically requested, postcards and letters will be sent overland.

Letters and cards can be posted at post offices or in the yellow post boxes which are located at roadsides. The costs vary according to the type of correspondence and the destination. The stamp for a card to another European country costs much the same as elsewhere in Europe. Outside Europe costs extra.

Post offices are open from 7am to 7pm from Monday to Friday, and from 7am to 1pm on Saturday. During the summer period the post offices in the tourist resorts extend their opening times until 10pm.

A practical way to receive post while on holiday is to use the poste restante service. Any correspondence sent to the following addresses will be held until it is collected by the addressee. In Zagreb, the address is Poste Restante, 10000 Zagreb, Croatia and in Split, Poste Restante, Main Post Office, 21000 Split, Croatia. Holders of American Express cards and cheques can use a similar service, whereby their post can be addressed to branches of the Atlas travel agency, which has offices in the main towns.

PUBLIC TELEPHONES

Public telephones are found everywhere in Croatia. It is cheaper to telephone from a public phone rather than from your hotel, as hotels generally apply a supplement to any calls which are made. There are 10,000 pay phones in Croatia, operated by telephone cards.

Calls cost less if they are made at particular times of the day within certain time bands. The cost decreases by 25 per cent compared with the full price for calls made between 4 and 7pm and there is a 70 per cent

reduction on calls made during the night and on public holidays.

The telephones use phone cards *(telekarta)*, with cards of 50, 100, 200 and 500 units, which can be bought at tobacconists, newsagents and news kiosks.

MOBILE PHONES

Iin Croatia several companies offer mobile phone services (GSM network): HTmobitel, whose numbers are all preceded by the code 099; Tele 2, with the code 095; T-Mobile, with the code 098; and Vipnet, with the code 091. The HT GSM network covers approximately 98 per cent of the country.

Check with your mobile phone service provider before you leave to see whether they have an agreement of roaming with the Croatian networks.

As elsewhere, do not use mobile phones while driving.

INTERNATIONAL CALLS

Calling Croatia from abroad is very easy: after dialling the international code (00 in the UK), you then dial the international country code (385), followed by the area code without the initial zero (Croatia is divided administratively into counties, each with a corresponding code) and finally the number of the subscriber. To telephone abroad

Croatian telephone card of 100 units

from Croatia, dial the international code (again 00), followed by the international code of the country (for the UK it is 44), then the area code (excluding the initial zero) and finally the subscriber's number. The international codes for other English-speaking countries are as follows: the US and Canada, 1, Australia, 61, New Zealand, 64 and Ireland, 353.

Numbers beginning with the code 060 are information services. These services can be dialled up from anywhere within Croatia, using the same code.

An Internet Café in Dubrovnik, popular with younger people

THE INTERNET AND EMAIL

Internet and email facilities are widely available in Croatia, and it is now easy to find Internet cafés with good speedy connections in most places, even on the islands.

If you have a laptop computer which you want to use, the main internet service provider is T-Com (the telecoms service). The service is subject to a monthly fee, plus a subscription charge.

The lines can be fairly slow, but new optical cables are being introduced.

TELEVISION AND RADIO

The main Croatian radio and television company is Hrvatski Radio i Televizija (HRT). There are two national TV channels: Channel One broadcasts domestic programmes and Channel Two broadcasts foreign programmes. Other television stations are RTL and TV-Nova. Almost all programmes including films and other foreign productions are broadcast in their original language, with Croatian subtitles. The radio has daily news in English and German.

Many hotels have satellite television and hotel guests will have access to a wide range of European stations.

Croatian radio stations broadcast in Croatian only, apart from some traffic reports. On the Second Channel (at RDS-HRT2), reports on road and weather conditions are given in English, German and Italian.

NEWSPAPERS

The main national daily newspapers are called *Vjesnik* and *Jutarnji List* and there is an evening paper, *Večernji List*. The satirical weekly, the *Feral Tribune*, is also widely read. All of these are published in Croatian, but British, Italian and German papers and magazines can often be found at news stands in major resorts and cities.

DIRECTORY

AREA CODES

Bjelovarsko-Bilogorska: 043
Brodsko-Posavska: 035
Dubrovačko-Neretvanska: 020
Istarska: 052
Krapinsko-Zagorska: 049
Ličko-Senjska: 053
Karlovačka: 047
Koprivnicko-Križevačka: 048
Medjimurska: 040
Osječko-Baranjska: 031
Požeško Slavonska: 034
Primorsko-Goranska: 051
Šibensko-Kninska: 022
Sisačko-Moslavačka: 044
Splitsko-Dalmatinska: 021
Varaždinska: 042
Virovitičko-Podravska: 033
Vukovarsko-Srijemska: 032
Zadarska: 023
Zagreb: 01
Zagrebačka: 01

USEFUL NUMBERS

**Information
for International Calls**
Tel 902.

**International
Operator**
Tel 901.

Local Telephone Numbers
Tel 988.

Speaking Clock
Tel 95.

Telegrams
Tel 96.

**Telephone Numbers
in other Counties**
Tel 989.

Wake-up Call
Tel 9100.

**Weather Forecast and
Traffic Conditions**
Tel 060 520 520.

POST OFFICES

Dubrovnik
Dr A Starcevica 2.
Tel (01) 411 265.
Fax (01) 411 265.

Zagreb
Jurisiceva 13.
Tel (01) 48 11 090.

Typical newspaper kiosk in Valpovo

Banking and Currency

The Croatian currency is the kuna, which in May 1994 took the place of the dinar (a descendant of the currency used in former Yugoslavia). Although it has only been in use for just over a decade, the kuna is in fact a very old currency; coins displaying the kuna (meaning marten – the pelts were once used for barter) were known to be in use in Slavonia in 1256. It is not difficult to change money into kuna at bureaux de change and banks throughout the country. Croatia is not yet part of the European Union but the euro is already accepted in many places.

BANKS AND EXCHANGE OFFICES

Money can be changed in banks and authorized bureaux de change or exchange offices. Banks are usually open from Monday to Friday from 8am to 7pm and on Saturday from 8am to 1pm. However, in the smaller towns, some banks may close in the middle of the day from noon to 3pm and on Saturdays a little earlier, at noon.

The exchange offices have much more flexible opening hours and are open until late in the evening in tourist areas. A commission is charged on the exchange which varies from 1 to 1.5 per cent at the exchange offices. These charges are smaller or non-existent if you change money at a bank.

You can also change foreign currency in post offices and tourist agencies. If

One of the many ATMs found in all main towns and cities

at all possible, avoid changing money at hotels or camping sites where the exchange rates are decidedly less favourable.

Do not be tempted to change money at stations and ports or along the roads with people who are not authorized. It may look like a good deal but there is always the risk that you might be given counterfeit banknotes. Finally, if you hold on to your original receipts you can re-convert any unused kuna banknotes back to the original currency at the end of your stay.

This exchange service is, however, only offered by banks.

Note that foreign currency can be imported into and exported freely out of the country.

The Zagrebačka Banka, with offices in Zagreb

ATMs

In the cities and main towns, cash can be withdrawn from Automated Teller Machines (ATM) by using internationally recognized cards. Check that the logo of the card you want to use is on the machine (*bankomat*) before making a withdrawal. ATMs of Zagrebačka banka accept Eurocard/MasterCard and Euronet ATMs accept Diners, American Express and Visa cards.

TRAVELLER'S CHEQUES

Traveller's cheques can only be exchanged in a bank, while American Express card holders can get cash advances through branches of the Atlas travel agency which can be found in all the main cities in the country (Zagreb, Pula, Poreč, Zadar, Opatija, Split).

CREDIT CARDS

The most commonly accepted credit cards are Visa, MasterCard, American Express, Diners and Sport Card International. These can be used in the larger resorts, especially on the coast and in big hotels and restaurants. In the event of the loss or theft of your credit card, it is extremely important to report it immediately so that the card can be blocked. This can be done by phoning the relevant

DIRECTORY

LOST OR STOLEN CREDIT CARDS

American Express
Tel (01) 612 44 22.
www.amex.hr

Diners Club
Tel (01) 480 22 22.
www.diners.hr

Eurocard–MasterCard
Tel (01) 378 96 20.
(Zagrebačka Banka, an intermediary for blocking the card).

Visa
Tel (021) 347 200.
(Splitska Banka)

card's emergency number (which is usually a number providing a 24-hour service, seven days a week).

CURRENCY

The kuna is divided into 100 lipa (the word lipa means a linden tree). The Central Bank issues banknotes of 500, 200, 100, 50, 20, 10 and 5 kuna, featuring Croatian heroes. Coins come in denominations of 5, 2 and 1 kuna, and 50, 20, 10, 5 and 1 lipa. The local abbreviation for kuna is kn, but the international abbreviation is HRK.

The Croatian currency was formerly closely linked to the German mark and until 31 December 2001, prices for accommodation, especially private rooms, were always quoted in marks. However, the mark was replaced by the euro in January 2002. The government tries to keep rates of exchange steady, which helps travellers and also helps to present an overall image of stability to potential foreign investors.

In most towns, particularly along the Adriatic coast, the euro is increasingly accepted in banks and bureaux de change.

Banknotes
The Central Bank issues banknotes of 500, 200, 100, 50, 20, 10 and 5 kuna. Notes bear the portraits of famous Croats such as Stjepan Radić and Josip Jelačić.

5 kuna

20 kuna

50 kuna

100 kuna

200 kuna

Coins
The kuna is divided into 100 lipa. The coin denominations are 5, 2 and 1 kuna and 50, 20, 10, 5, 2 and 1 lipa. The 20 lipa coins are a silver colour and the 10 lipa coin is bronze-coloured.

1 kuna

2 kuna

5 kuna

1 lipa

2 lipa

5 lipa

10 lipa

20 lipa

50 lipa

TRAVEL INFORMATION

Most visitors from the UK arrive in Croatia by direct air connection from Britain, landing at Zagreb, Split or Dubrovnik. During the summer months, numerous charter flights operate and smaller airports in Croatia open. Almost 70 per cent of tourists visiting the country come from Germany, Italy and Austria, relatively near countries which are all well connected by road or sea. These visitors

Road sign indicating customs

often use their own transport, usually car or motorbike, and travel directly by road or by using one of the ferry services. A great deal has been done to develop and improve all means of transport and the country now has good connections to the rest of Europe and the world. It is also possible to get to Croatia by train, for those who prefer this form of transport, although this is a slower method.

ARRIVING BY AIR

The national airline company, **Croatia Airlines**, links Croatia's main airports with the rest of Europe. The major European destinations are Amsterdam, Berlin, Brussels, Düsseldorf, Frankfurt, Istanbul, London, Mostar, Munich, Paris, Prague, Rome, Sarajevo, Skopje, Vienna and Zurich.

Other European airlines offering scheduled services to Croatia include British Airways, Lufthansa, Austrian Airlines, Air France, Lauda Air, SAS and KLM. Flying time from London is 2 hours 10 minutes, from Frankfurt 1 hour 30 minutes.

The no-frills airline Wizzair, a Polish-Hungarian company, flies direct to Split and Zagreb from Luton airport all-year round. Another budget airline Ryanair flies to Ancona on the Italian Adriatic coast, where there are good ferry links with the Dalmatian coast, and to Trieste in northeast Italy, which is very close to the

Istrian border and offers train links to Croatia.

There are no direct flights from Ireland, the US or Canada. Travellers from these countries will need to change at one of the main European hubs such as London, Frankfurt or Rome, and take a connecting flight to Croatia. There is a daily flight to Zagreb from Rome Fiumicino, for example, as well as five flights a week to and from Split, and two flights a week to and from Dubrovnik.

There are also flights to Zagreb from Australia or New Zealand with Malaysia Airlines, with a stopover at Kuala Lumpur.

AIRPORT CONNECTIONS

Croatia has three main airports. Zagreb airport is 17 km (10 miles) from the centre of the city and is connected by a bus service to the central bus station in Držićeva; the journey takes about 25 minutes and runs

from the city to the airport from 6:30am to 8pm and in the opposite direction from 4am to 8pm. The airport at Split is 24 km (15 miles) from the centre of the city and is also connected by a regular bus service. Dubrovnik airport is 18 km (11 miles) from the city and is connected by a regular bus service. The journey time is about 20 minutes.

AIR FARES

Fares on scheduled flights to Croatia vary according to the airline and the time of year. Fares tend to be higher in the summer. From the UK there are regular scheduled flights from Heathrow to Zagreb, with connections to Pula, Split, Rijeka and Dubrovnik, and in summer, direct flights to Dubrovnik from Gatwick and Manchester. There are charter flights to Croatia from a wide range of UK regional airports during the summer months. Contact the Croatian National Tourist Office in your own country for details.

PACKAGE HOLIDAYS

A number of tour operators offer package holidays to Croatia where the price includes flights (usually charter flights) and accommodation. Among the UK tour operators offering package holidays are **Holiday Options, Balkan Holidays, Transun Holidays** and **Thomson Holidays. Saga**

A Croatia Airlines plane in flight

Driving along the Magistrala coastal road

Holidays mainly cater for the 50-plus age group. **Adriatic Holidays** offer sailing holidays including 7- and 14-day trips along the Dalmatian coast, taking in a number of the islands and Dubrovnik.

ARRIVING BY TRAIN

The network on which the Croatian railways is based today was designed in the 19th century, when the country was part of the Austro-Hungarian Empire. The best railway services today are still those offering links with Central Europe.

However, you can travel from London to Zagreb by train, via Paris, Milan and Venice, a trip of around 30 hours. An alternative route goes via Brussels and Ljubljana in Slovenia. **Rail Europe** and **European Rail** can supply information.

Connections from other European cities include the Intercity Munich–Zagreb (9 hours); the Eurocity "Mimara" which covers the Berlin–Leipzig–Munich–Salzburg–Ljubljana–Zagreb route and the Intercity "Croatia" takes the route Vienna–Maribor–Zagreb (6 hours 30 minutes). Vienna–Rijeka takes 8 hours.

There are also rail connections from Italy. From Trieste Centrale, there is one direct train a day to Zagreb, a sleeper. There are also regular trains to Zagreb from Belgrade (four a day) and Budapest (three a day).

The head office of **Croatian Railways (Hrvatske Željeznice)** is in Zagreb.

ARRIVING BY COACH

Croatia is also well connected to other countries by coach. International coaches connect Croatia with the bordering states and also with France, Switzerland, Germany and Slovakia. There are good connections with Austria (there are services from Vienna twice a week to Rijeka, Zadar and Split, and daily connections to Zagreb) and Bosnia. From Dubrovnik

Road sign for the Slovenian border

there are three services a day to Mostar, and two to Sarajevo. From Split there are seven buses a day to Mediugorje, 11 to Mostar and six to Sarajevo. Four buses a day depart from Zagreb to Mostar and six to Sarajevo.

From Germany there are almost daily services from Berlin, Cologne, Dortmund, Frankfurt, Mannheim, Munich, Nuremberg and Stuttgart to Zagreb and the coastal cities, covering the stretch from Rijeka to Split.

Many Italian cities are connected to Zagreb by coach: there is at least one weekly service between the Croatian capital and Bergamo, Bologna, Florence, Milan,

Rome, Turin, Verona and Venice, while there is a daily service from Trieste.

The main bus station in the country is **Autobusni Kolodvor Zagreb** in the capital. The Autoservizio Friuli Venezia Giulia SAF Trieste runs services four times a day in the summer and twice in winter to Pula. From Trieste you can also get to Rijeka and then from there to Split five times a day and and there are daily services to Buzet and Labin. In Istria, these services are run by the Italian company SAITA Autolinee, in collaboration with Croatian companies.

ARRIVING BY CAR OR MOTORBIKE

Travelling to Croatia by car (or by motorbike) is popular with tourists from neighbouring countries. There are six main border crossings between Croatia and Hungary, 23 frontier points between Croatia and Bosnia-Herzegovina, ten frontier points between Croatia and Yugoslavia and 29 frontier points between Croatia and Slovenia.

Traffic coming overland from Italy enters Croatia via border crossings with Slovenia, all classified as international and open 24 hours a day, all year round. Rabuiese-Muggia, towards Savudrja, is the crossing point for Istria; Basovizza-Pesek, for Rijeka and Dalmatia; Fernetti-Villa Opicina, for those going towards Zagreb.

People driving to Croatia need to carry a valid driving licence, the car's log book (if appropriate) and a green card. On entering the country any prior damage to the car which has not yet been repaired must be declared. This procedure is for insurance purposes.

ARRIVING BY SEA

The main international ferry connections are with Italy via the ports of Trieste, Ancona, Pescara and Bari.

The main Croatian maritime company is **Jadrolinija** which runs services between

Ancona and Split (four times a week all year round and daily in the summer). The crossing takes nine hours. Ancona–Zadar runs twice a week, an eight-hour journey, and Bari–Dubrovnik runs twice a week all year (eight hours). In summer there are also connections to and from the islands of Korčula and Hvar (from Split), with services twice a week.

SEM Marina is another Croatian company which runs a daily service between Ancona and Split (nine hours) and Ancona and Zadar.

Adriatica Navigazione is an Italian company running regular, 9-hour ferry services between Ancona and Split, more or less daily in the months of July and August; three times a week in June and September and twice weekly during the rest of the year. It also runs a service called "Linea della Costa Istriana" in the summer months. This links the Italian ports of the upper Adriatic (Grado, Trieste) with destinations in the north of

One of the ships operated by the Jadrolinija company, connecting Croatian ports with the rest of the Adriatic

Croatia such as Rovinj and Brijuni. For information and tickets contact the agencies at the ports of embarkation.

The Croatian company **Lošinjska Plovidba** runs a ferry between Koper in Slovenia and Zadar twice a week in summer (July to September). The crossing takes 14 hours 30 minutes and calls at Pula and at Mali Lošinj. There are also hydrofoil passenger services from Italy run by **Agenzia**

JADROLINIJA

Symbol of the maritime company, Jadrolinija

Marittima Sanmar from mid-June to mid-September. There are departures from Pescara every Monday and Saturday for the islands of Hvar and Brač, and Split, and every Tuesday for Split and the islands of Vis and Korčula. Hydrofoils also run every Friday to the islands of Korčula, Hvar and Split.

The Italian company **SNAV** runs daily catamaran services between Ancona and Split, Ancona and Zadar, and Pescara and Split from mid-June to late September.

DIRECTORY

Croatian National Tourist Office
162–64 Fulham Palace Road, London W6 9ER.
Tel 020-8563 7979.
Fax 020-8563 2616.
www.croatia.hr

AIRLINES

Croatia Airlines
Tel 020 8563 0022 (UK),
(01) 481 96 33 (Cro).
www.croatiaairlines.hr

Wizz Airlines
Tel 00 48 22 351 94 99
www.wizzair.com

PACKAGE HOLIDAYS

Adriatic Holidays
Tel 01865-516577 (UK).
www.adriaticholidays online.com

Balkan Holidays
Tel 0845-130 1114 (UK).
www.balkan holidays.co.uk

Holiday Options
Tel 0870-013 0450 (UK).
www.holidayoptions. co.uk

Saga Holidays
Tel 0800-300 600.
www.saga.co.uk/ travel

Thomson Holidays
Tel 0870-165 0079 (UK).
www.thomson-holidays.com

Transun Holidays
Tel 0870-44 44 747 (UK)
www.transun.co.uk

COACHES

Autobusni Kolodvor Zagreb Information
Tel (060) 313 333 and (060) 340 340 (Cro).
www.akz.hr

RAILWAYS

Croatian Railways
Tel (060) 333 444 (Cro).
www.hznet.hr

European Rail Tavistock Square,
London WC1H 3HR.
Tel 020-7387 0444.
Fax 020-7387 0888.
www.europeanrail.com

Rail Europe
179 Piccadilly,
London W1V 0BA.
Tel 0870-584 8848.

FERRY SERVICES

Adriatica Navigazione
Ancona, Italy.
Tel 071 204 915-6-7-8.
Fax 071 202 296.

Agenzia Marittima Sanmar
Pescara, Italy.
Tel 085 652 47, 451 08 73.
Fax 085 451 08 82.

Jadroagent
Borisa Papandopoula, Split.
Tel (021) 460 556.
Fax (021) 460 848.

Jadrolinija
Riva 16, Rijeka.
Tel (051) 666 100.
Fax (051) 211 485.

Lošinjska Plovidba
Splitska 2/4, Rijeka.
Tel (051) 319 000.
Fax (051) 319 003.

P Amatori
c/o Stazione Marittima, Ancona, Italy.
Tel 071 204 305.
Fax 071 200 211.

SEM Marina
Gat Sv. Duje, Split.
Tel (021) 338 292.
Fax (021) 333 291.

SNAV
Ancona, Italy.
Fax (071) 207 6116.

Getting Around Croatia

The transport system within the country is reasonably efficient, particularly if you are travelling by road or by sea. The connections between the mainland and the islands are excellent, and thanks to an extensive bus network, even the smaller, lesser known towns can be easily reached by bus. Although using air travel to get around the country is not that common, domestic flights link the major towns. Travelling by train is fine only if you have plenty of time, because the rail network is in need of modernization, resulting in very long journey times compared with the time it takes to cover the same distance by road.

DOMESTIC FLIGHTS

There are regular connections between the three major airports in the country, Zagreb, Split and Dubrovnik. There are also connections between these main airports and other secondary airports, such as the airport of Osijek, which is only 3 km (2 miles) from the city and connected by a regular city bus service. There is also a small airport at Zadar which is 15 km (9 miles) from the centre and the bus connection to the city takes about 15 minutes. Rijeka airport is 27 km (17 miles) from the city and, despite its name, is actually situated on the island of Krk, at Omišalj. The airport is connected to Rijeka by a bus service and the journey takes about 35–40 minutes.

The airport of Pula is just 7 km (4 miles) from the centre of the city and there is a bus service to and from Pula with a journey time of about 10 minutes.

Finally, the airport of Brač is a small airport on the island of the same name. It is only open in the summer months.

DRIVING AROUND CROATIA

Cars drive on the right in Croatia and safety belts should be worn in both the front and back seats. Children under 12 must sit in the back.

The speed limits are 50 km/h (30 mph) in towns, 80 km/h (50 mph) outside built-up areas, and 130 km/h (80 mph) on the motorways. Cars towing caravans must not exceed 80 km/h (50 mph).

Road signs are generally more or less identical to those found in the rest of Europe.

On certain stretches of motorway drivers pay a toll: Zagreb–Karlovac, Zapresic– Krapina, Varaždin–Gorican, Zagreb–Oprisavci and Rijeka–Delnice. There is also a toll to pay for the bridge to the island of Krk and the Ucka Tunnel.

As part of a vast programme of improvements to the country's infrastructure, the Croatian road network is currently undergoing extensive development that includes the construction of new motorways.

The most scenic of all the roads is the Magistrala (E65) which winds along the Adriatic coast. Great care should be taken on this road which is quite demanding and busy during the summer.

In the larger towns and cities you can park in the public car parking areas or along the roads. Where indicated, a parking ticket must be clearly displayed inside the windscreen. If you park in a no-parking area, your vehicle can be forcibly removed by officials.

Service stations are open daily from 7am to 7 or 8pm, but in summer the opening times are extended until 10pm. On the main roads in the larger towns and cities and on major international routes you can find service stations open 24 hours a day. All the usual petrol types are available: Eurosuper 95 and Eurosuper 98, normal unleaded and Super 98, as well as Eurodiesel.

The Croatian authorities are extremely tough on drink driving: it is illegal to drive after drinking any amount of alcohol at all.

BREAKDOWN ASSISTANCE AND TRAFFIC INFORMATION

Emergency road services are provided by the local **Automobile Club, HAK**, which can be reached 24 hours a day all year round by simply dialling 987 (preceded by the numbers 01 for calls from a mobile phone). The service provides repairs on the spot or in a garage (subject to transport), the removal of damaged cars and transport up to 100 km (62 miles) distance and is run by the local automobile club and local firms, which operate under the direct control of the automobile club.

HAK also provides information on road and maritime traffic, motorway tolls, any temporary diversions, the prices of petrol, ferry times, possible

AVIS

The logo of AVIS, the car rental company

Town traffic in the charming city of Osijek

alternative routes and general assistance for those travelling by car, 24 hours a day, 365 days a year, on (01) 464 08 00. If you have access to the Internet, the website www.hak.hr is full of useful information and links.

CAR RENTAL

It is straightforward to hire a car in Croatia and car rental agencies can be found in all the main towns and cities, holiday resorts, and at the airports. Besides the well-known large multinational rent-a-car companies such as Avis and Hertz, there are many local independent companies offering competitive prices for similar types of vehicle and insurance cover.

One of the advantages of renting a car through the larger companies, however, is having the option of leaving the car in a different town from the collection point. Not all rental companies are able to offer this flexibility and there is always an extra charge for this service.

BUSES

Buses are used a great deal by the local population and are a valid means of transport for visitors as well, although communication with ticket offices and drivers may be difficult unless you speak a little Croatian. It will help to learn a little basic vocabulary and some useful phrases before setting out to use the buses.

The bus service covers an extensive network across the country with numerous connections and destinations,

Travelling by coach in the city of Dubrovnik

The entrance to the large railway station in Zagreb

although the tickets will be more expensive than on equivalent trains.

Services are divided into "intercity" (direct connections between the larger cities) and the regional services (with connections between the smaller towns and the main cities). Intercity services mean shorter travelling times, but ticket prices are the same.

There are daily connections between the towns and cities of Croatia and night buses cover the longer routes.

For information go to the local bus station *(Autobusni Kolodvor)* and consult the timetable. *Vozi svaki dan* indicates the daily services, while *ne vozi nedjeljom ni praznikom* shows which services do not run on Sundays and public holidays. The main bus station in the country is the **Autobusni Kolodvor Zagreb**, which is in Zagreb.

TRAINS

Except for the area around Zagreb, trains are not widely used for travelling within Croatia: the railway network has not yet been adequately modernized and this is particularly apparent in the very long journey times. However, all the main Croatian towns and cities are linked by rail with the exception of Dubrovnik, where there is no railway station at all.

The hub of the Croatian railway network is the main station in the capital (Zagreb Glavni Kolodvor). There are trains to Rijeka with connections to the Istrian

towns; to Split, with a branch line for Zadar and Šibenik, serving the Dalmatian coast; to Varaždin, to the north; and to Osijek, to the east.

The following journey times can be expected: the minimum time is four hours for Zagreb– Rijeka, seven and a half hours from Zagreb to Split, two hours for Zagreb–Varaždin and four hours for Zagreb– Osijek. Express services operate on some routes. Croatian Railways – **Hrvatske Željeznice** – has its main office in Zagreb.

FERRIES SERVING THE COAST

The ferry services are very good and probably the best option when travelling down the entire coastline, even though it is not the cheapest way to travel.

Fairly large ships which provide good facilities connect the main towns along the Adriatic coast. Accommodation is available in cabins or there are seats inside and on deck (the cheapest). These ferries also transport cars, motorbikes, caravans and campervans.

The routes cover the entire Adriatic coast from Rijeka down to Dubrovnik, with stops in the main towns and also on the larger islands. After Rijeka, stops are made at Zadar, Split, Starigrad on Hvar, Korčula, Sobra on Mljet and Dubrovnik. The full trip lasts one day and usually involves sleeping overnight for the northern part of the journey, while the southern part takes place during the day, in both directions.

ISLAND FERRIES

There is also a wide network of connections between the islands and the mainland. The Croatian ferry network is divided into five districts and services are on ships which can transport both passengers and vehicles.

In the Rijeka district the islands of Cres and Lošinj are connected to the mainland by the Valbiska–Merag and Brestova–Porozina routes.

The island of Rab is connected to the coast by the Jablanac–Mišnjak route and with the island of Krk by the Lopar–Baška route. Finally, the island of Pag is connected to the coast by the Prizna–Zigljen route.

In the district of Zadar there are connections to Preko, on the island of Ugljan, Bribinj and Zaglav, on the island of Dugi Otok and from Biograd to Tkon on the island of Pašman.

In the district of Šibenik, the town is connected to the islands of Zlarin and Prvić.

In the Split district there are connections between Split and the island of Brač (Supetar), the island of Korčula (Vela Luka), the island of Hvar (to Starigrad), the island of Šolta (Rogač), the island of Vis (to the port of the same name) and the island of Lastovo (to Ubli).

There are also connections between Makarska and Sumartin (island of Brač), between Ploce and Trpanj on the Pelješac peninsula, between Orebić and Domince (on the island of Korčula), between Drvenik and Korčula (on the island of the same name) and between Drvenik and Sućuraj (island of Hvar). Finally, in the district of Dubrovnik, the main connection is between Dubrovnik and the island of Mljet (Sobra).

For all the routes mentioned above, services run frequently in the high season (July and August), but services are significantly reduced outside the summer months. On some short routes, such as Jablanac–Misniak and Drvenik–Sućuraj, ferries sail non-stop so as to cope with the long queues which tend to form in the middle of the day.

For those travelling without a car or motorbike, there are some passenger-only services. These catamarans connect Split to the surrounding islands in the months from June to September only. There are also connections to the islands of Brač, Hvar, Vis, Korčula and Lastovo. The crossing times range from 45 minutes to Hvar to two and a half hours to Lastovo, the most distant. These services do not always run daily, particularly to the islands that are furthest away from the mainland.

Finally, a hydrofoil service also covers the routes from Split to Vis (the port on the island of the same name) and back with a daily service in the summer. For further information on hydrofoils, contact **SEM Marina**.

DIRECTORY

AIRPORTS

Brač *Tel* *(021) 648 615.*
Osijek *Tel* *(031) 215 650.*
Pula *Tel* *(052) 530 105.*
Rijeka *Tel* *(051) 842 132.*
Zadar *Tel* *(023) 313 311.*

DRIVING

Automobile Club, HAK
Tel 987 (preceded by 01 from mobile phones).
Tel (01) 464 08 00 (traffic information).

CAR RENTAL

Avis (in partnership with Autotehna)
Tel (01) 483 60 06.
www.avis.hr

Budget
Tel (01) 455 49 36.
www.budget.hr

Hertz
Tel (01) 484 72 22.
www.hertz.hr

BUSES

Autobusni Kolodvor Zagreb
Information
Tel 060 313 333, 060 340 340.

TRAIN TRAVEL

Hrvatske Zeljeznice
Mihanovićeva 12,
HR-10000 Zagreb.
Tel 060 333 444.

FERRIES

Jadrolinija
Riva 16, Rijeka.
Tel (051) 666 100.
Fax (051) 211 485.

Jadrolinija
Zrinjevac 20, Zagreb.
Tel (01) 487 33 07.
Fax (01) 487 31 41.
www.jadrolinija.hr

SEM Marina
Gat sv. Duje, Split.
Tel (021) 338 292.
Fax (021) 333 291.
www.sem-marina.hr

Ferry waiting to depart for the islands

Getting Around Zagreb

The city of Zagreb has developed a good, efficient transport network which, by means of trams, buses and a funicular railway connecting the Lower and Upper Towns, ensures good connections between all the central and suburban districts. Trams run at regular intervals and there are also some night services. Gradec, the old town, has many areas which are pedestrianized and closed to ordinary traffic, making this a pleasant, fume-free zone to stroll around. There is no underground system in Zagreb.

WALKING

Zagreb is a very large city and most visitors will need to use some form of public transport as a means of gettting around. However, the best way to visit the centre, that is the areas of Kaptol and Gradec (together these are known as Gornji Grad or Upper Town), is on foot. Walking is especially rewarding in the old centre of Zagreb with its venerable churches and imposing buildings.

It is a good idea to get a map of the city before setting off. Maps can be obtained from any tourist office. If need be, you can always ask the locals for directions because they are generally helpful to tourists, although the Croatian language may present a barrier to understanding.

TRAMS

The company which runs the capital's public transport is the Zagrebački Električni Tramvaj, known as **ZET**. The network of electric trams is efficient, with frequent services covering a wide area.

A total of 15 tram routes run during the day (starting at around 4am and ending at midnight) and four lines run at night (covering the early hours from midnight to 4am).

The routes operating during the day are: 1 Zapadni kolodvor–Borongaj; 2 Crnomerec–Savisce; 3 Ljubljanica–Zitnjak; 4 Savski most–Dubec; 5 Jarun–Kvaternikov trg; 6 Crnomerec–Sopot; 7 Savski most–Dubrava; 8 Mihaljevac–Zaprude; 9 Ljubljanica–Borongaj; 11 Crnomerec–Dubec; 12 Ljubljanica–Dubrava, 13 Zitnjak–Kvaternikov trg; 14 Mihaljevac–Zaprude; 15 Mihaljevac–Dolje; 17 Precko–Borongaj.

All the lines run frequently during the day at intervals of six to ten minutes between trams, depending on whether it is a weekday or public holiday. On Sundays and other holidays tram numbers 3 and 8 do not run.

The four tram lines which run at night pass every 20 to 40 minutes on the following useful routes: 31 Crnomerec–Savski most, 32 Precko–Borongaj; 33 Dolje–Savisce and 34 Ljubljanica–Dubec.

The main hub for tram stops is Trg bana Jelačica, where seven different routes intersect.

BUSES

There is an intricate network of bus connections with numerous routes branching out to the various termini: Britanski trg, Jandriceva, Jankomir, Savski most, Ljubljanica, trg Mazuranica, Crnomerec, Mandalicina, Zapresic, Kaptol, Petrova, Svetice, Dubrava, Kvaternikov trg, Glavni kolodvor, Zitnjak, Sesvete, Borongaj, Mihalievac and Velica Gorica.

One of many tram lines serving the entire city

TICKETS

Tickets for both buses and trams can be bought in newsagents or kiosks (if need be, also on board, but the price is higher). The basic ticket is for a single journey. It must be punched in the machine as soon as you get on board and is valid for 90 minutes from that time. The tickets cost 6.50 kuna each (or 8 kuna from the driver on the bus). There is also a one-day ticket which costs 18 kuna, a good idea if you intend making various trips during the day (these tickets are valid until 4am on the following day). Monthly season tickets are also available. A useful website is www.zagreb-touristinfo.hr.

Funicular connecting the Lower and Upper Towns of Zagreb

Travelling without a ticket is punishable by a fine. If you are caught, the fine is 150 kuna if it is paid immediately or within eight days, but it can rise to 900 kuna if left unpaid.

FUNICULAR RAILWAY

An interesting method of transport is the *uspinjača*, a steep funicular railway that has been in operation since 1890. This trip is one of the shortest climbs in the world at 66 m (216 ft) long and takes a little less than a minute to climb up from the Lower Town to the Upper Town,

Traffic in Zagreb city centre outside the railway station

arriving close to the Lotrscak tower. Departures are from Tomićeva street right in the centre, and leave every ten minutes from 6.30am to 9pm. The price of a single ticket is 3 kuna.

CABLE CAR

The **Žičara** is a cable car which connects Zagreb with Sljeme, the highest peak of the Mount Medvednica range, in a journey time of 20 minutes. The system has been in operation since 1963 and cabins can carry up to four people. Departures are every 20 minutes past the hour from 8am to 8:30pm daily. Return tickets cost 17 kuna.

TAXIS

In Zagreb, as in any other large city, taxis can be found. All taxis have a meter on board and fares start from 25 kuna as the basic rate and then 7 kuna for every kilometre of your journey. There is an extra charge of 20 per cent for journeys made on Sundays and public holidays and from 10pm to 5am every day, and there is also a charge of 5 kuna for luggage. If a taxi has to wait there is a further charge of 40 kuna an hour.

Yellow taxi sign

There are numerous taxi ranks (identified by a typical blue sign). Croatian speakers can call a taxi by phoning 970, and asking the taxi driver to come and collect you.

CAR RENTAL

In the capital it is also possible to rent a self-drive car by contacting one of the main car rental companies such as **Budget**, **Adria Plus, Kompas Hertz** and **Avis**. Assistance while you are on the road is provided by the Croatian Automobile Club, which can also offer advice on routes (*see p277 and p279*).

DIRECTORY

USEFUL NUMBERS

ZET
Tel (01) 365 15 55.

Žičara Cable Car
Tel (01) 458 03 94.

Taxi
Tel 970.

CAR RENTAL

Adria Plus
Zagreb Airport.
Tel (01) 626 52 15.
Fax (01) 625 60 75.

Avis
c/o Hotel Opera,
Kršnjavoga, Zagreb.
Tel (01) 483 60 06.
Fax (01) 483 62 96.

Budget
c/o Hotel Sheraton,
Kneza Borne 2, Zagreb.
Tel (01) 455 49 36.
Fax (01) 455 49 43.

Kompas Hertz
Vukotinovićeva 4, Zagreb.
Tel (01) 484 67 77.
Fax (01) 488 30 77.

General Index

Acknowledgments

FABIO RATTI EDITORIA would like to thank the following staff at Dorling Kindersley:

Map Coordinator
Dave Pugh.

Senior DTP Manager
Jason Little.

Publishing Manager
Anna Streiffert.

Managing Art Editor
Marisa Renzullo.

Publisher
Douglas Amrine.

Dorling Kindersley would also like to thank all those whose contribution and assistance have made the preparation of this book possible.

Principal Author
Leandro Zoppè was born in Venice and graduated in Political Science from Padua University. At present he lives in Milan where, as a historian, he works as a freelance journalist and writer of tour guides and historical, artistic or naturalistic books.

Contributors
Božidarka Boza Gligorijević, Public Relations Manager for the Croatian National Tourist Board in Milan.

Text Revision
Sanja Rojić (University professor),
Iva Grgic (University professor).

Checking of Practical Information
Lucia Čutura, Viktor Jovanović Marušić, Jane Foster.

Senior Editor, UK Edition
Jacky Jackson.

Proof Reader
Alessandra Lombardi, Stewart J Wild.

Indexer
Helen Peters.

Fact Checker
Katarina Bulic.

Special Thanks
Croatian National Tourist Board, Zagreb, in particular the director Niko Bulić; Croatian National Tourist Board, Milan, in particular the director Klaudio Stojnic and the public relations manager Božidarka Boza Gligorijević; the regional and local tourist boards of Croatia; Vinko Bakija (director of the tourist office, Supetar, island of Brač); Zdravko Banović (tourist office, Split); Daniela Barac (tourist guide in Crikvenica); Nikša Bender (marketing manager of the tourist office of Dubrovnik); Maja Boban (tourist guide of the environs of Zagreb); Ankita Boksic Franchini (tourist office, Split); Tanja Bunjevac (tourist office, Varaždin) Rujana Bušić (tourist guide in Vinkovci); Vanja Dadić (tourist guide in Šibenik); Mirjana Darrer (public relations manager of the tourist office in Dubrovnik); Marchese Doimo Frangipane di Aiello del Friuli; Danijela Duić (tourist guide in Karlovac); Jurica Dužević (director of the tourist office in Stari Grad, island of Hvar); Daniela Fanikutić (tourist office, Poreč); Ennio Forlani (director of the tourist office of Vodnjan); Vesna Gamulin (tourist guide in Dubrovnik); Miljenko Gašparac (guard of the Risnjak National Park); Boris Gržina (front office manager of the Hotel Esplanade in Zagreb); Vesna Habazin and Snježana Hrupelj (tourist guides in the area of the thermal spas); Mladenka Jarac-Rončević (Croatian Consul in Italy); Zoran Jelaska (tourist guide in Split); Vesna Jovičić (tourist guide in Pula); Darko Kovačić (tourist guide in the Lonjsko Polje Nature Park); Darko Kovačić (director of the tourist office, Omiš); Stanka Kraljević (director of the tourist office in the town of Korčula); Vlasta Krklec (Museum of Krapina); Tonći Lalić (tourist guide in Makarska); Damir Macanić (director of the tourist office in Osijek); Damir Mihalić (tourist office, Varaždinske Toplice); Josip Mikolčić (tourist office, Virovitica); Danijela Miletić (tourist office, Zagreb); Smiljan Mitrović (tourist guide in Zadar); Franjo Mrzljak (director of the National Museum of Naive Art, Zagreb); Andro Krstulović Opara (former Croatian Consul in Italy); Ottone Novosel (tourist guide in Križevci); Ankica Pandzic (director of the Museum of Croatian History in Zagreb); Danika Plazibat (Meštrović Gallery, Zagreb); Gordana Perić (tourist office, Zadar); Ante Rendić-Miočević (director of the Archaeological Museum, Zagreb); Mladen Radić (Director of the Museum of Slavonia, Osijek); Ljubica Ramušćak (Civic Museum of Medimurje, Cakovec); Ljiljana Sever (tourist guide in Varaždin); Josipa Šipek (director of Hotel Coning in Trakošćan); Doris Staničić (tourist guide in Osijek); Alka Starac (Archaeological Museum of Istria, Pula); Branka Tropp (director of the tourist office in Varaždin); Đuro Vandura (director of the Gallery of Ancient Masters, Zagreb); Klara Vedriš (Gallery of Modern Art, Zagreb); Vjenceslav Vlahov (tourist guide in Zagreb); Igor Zidić (director of the Gallery of Modern Art, Zagreb); Marko Zoričić (director of the tourist office in Opatija).

Dorling Kindersley wishes to thank Lady Beresford-Peirse of the International Trust for Croatian Monuments for her time and invaluable suggestions.

Photography Permissions
The publisher would like to thank all the museums, the local corporations and associations, hotels, restaurants, shops and other places of interest for their co-operation and their kind permission in allowing their establishments to be photographed.

Additional Photography
Adriano Bacchella, Aldo Pavan, Lucio Rossi, Leandro Zoppé

Picture Credits
Key to positions: t = t;
tl = top left; tlc = top left centre;
tc = top centre; trc = top right centre; tr = top right; cla = centre left above; ca = al centre above; crb = centre right above; cl = centre left; c = centre;
cr = centre right; clb = centre left below; cb = centre below; crb = centre right below; b = below; bl = bottom left; bcl = bottom centre left; bc = bottom centre; bcr = bottom centre right; br = bottom right;
(d) = detail.

While every effort has been made to contact the copyright holders, we apologize for any omissions and will be happy to include them in the following editions of this publication.

The publisher would like to thank the following individuals, associations and photograpic agencies for permission to reproduce their photographs:

DORLING KINDERSLEY ARCHIVES: 12bl, 238cr.

THE CROATIAN NATIONAL TOURIST BOARD ARCHIVES, Milan: 1c, 2–3, 19bl, 20bc, 21tc, 19cl, 23cl, 24tc, 24br, 25tl, 26–27 (all), 28, 32t, 33bc, 34bc, 38tc, 43tc, 46tr, 67t, 98crb, 99tl, 106cla, 107cr, 112br, 113tl, 115cl, 124 (all), 130t, 131tr, 131br, 133 (all), 134cr, 134bl, 135tl, 135c, 136tr, 136bl, 137tl, 137cra, 137br, 138–139, 140c, 143ca, 146c, 146br, 147 (all), 152bl, 158tl, 175bl, 180, 186tl, 194br, 200cl, 201br, 202cl, 212c, 213tr, 219br, 221tl, 234tc, 252tl, 253tc, 255br, 257tr, 258tc, 259cl, 2591br, 261bc, 264tc, 273 (all), 274bl, 276cl, 277cl, 278bl.

MONDADORI ARCHIVES: 9 (frame), 18bcl, 21cr, 30tl, 31tr, 31bc, 37 (all), 38cr, 38bc, 39 (all), 40tl, 40bl, 40br, 41bc, 42tl, 45 (frame), 121tl, 157tc, 157cl, 177ca, 192tl, 194tr, 195cra, 195crb, 195bl, 206br, 217 (frame), 239tlc, 259tc, 263 (frame).

ALAMY IMAGES: Comstock Images: 15c; Jason Wallengren Photography 237tl; Jon Arnold Images/Alan Copson 11cl;

Peter Adams Photography/Peter Adams 10bl; toto 237c.

ALDO PAVAN, AURA AGENCY, Milan: 15tc, 24cl, 46cb, 68br, 97crb, 112cla, 132cl, 132cr, 134tl, 135b, 136cl, 136cr, 137clb, 239cl, 250cl, 254tc, 254cl, 255tl, 256tl.

ANDREA PISTOLESI: 111tr.

ARCHAEOLOGICAL MUSEUM, Zagreb: 31tc, 31br, 164c, 165c, 169c, 190c.

THE ART ARCHIVE: 35br.

CORBIS: Ruggero Vanni: 144b; Reuters/Matko Bijlak 238cl.

DOIMO FRANGIPANE: 177cla, 177cr.

GALLERY OF MODERN ART, Zagreb: 8–9, 162b.

GALLERY OF OLD MASTERS, Zagreb: 164–165 (all).

IMAGE BANK, Milan: 56br, 67br, 86cl, 87tr, 91tl, 145br, 151crb, 160tl.

LONELY PLANET IMAGES: Wayne Walton 13tr.

MEŠTROVIĆ GALLERY, Zagreb: 20tr, 154tl, 157cr, 157bl, 157br.

MARCO LISSONI: 20br, 70cr, 106tl, 114cl, 132tl, 253br, 254br.

MUSEUM OF CROATIAN HISTORY, Zagreb: 40cb, 41tc, 41clb, 42cb, 154cl.

NATIONAL MUSEUM OF NAIVE ART, Zagreb: 21bl, 154bl, 159tl.

PAKLENICA NATIONAL PARK: 18cl, 101c, 101b, 260 (all).

JACKET
Front - ALAMY IMAGES: Mooch Images c; DK IMAGES: Lucio Rossi clb.
Back - ALAMY IMAGES: Jon Arnold Images/Alan Copson tl; Swerve cla; DK IMAGES; Lucio Rossi clb, bl.
Spine - ALAMY IMAGES: Mooch Images t; DK IMAGES: Lucio Rossi b.

All other images copyright © DORLING KINDERSLEY.
For further information: www.dkimages.com

SPECIAL EDITIONS OF DK TRAVEL GUIDES

DK Travel Guides can be purchased in bulk quantities at discounted prices for use in promotions or as premiums. We are also able to offer special editions and personalized jackets, corporate imprints, and excerpts from all of our books, tailored specifically to meet your own needs.

To find out more, please contact:
(in the United States) **SpecialSales@dk.com**
(in the UK) **Sarah.Burgess@dk.com**
(in Canada) DK Special Sales at **general@tourmaline.ca**
(in Australia) **business.development@pearson.com.au**

Phrase Book

Pronounciation

c – "ts" as in rats
č – "chi" as in church
ć – "t" is a soft t
d – "d" is a soft d
g – "g" is a hard g as in get
j – "y" as in yes
š – sh
Ž – shown here as "zh", sounds like the "J" in the French name, Jacques
"aj" – shown here as "igh", sounds like "I" or the "igh" in night.

In Emergency

Help!	**Pomoć!**	pomoch
Stop!	**Stani!**	stahnee
Call a doctor!	**Zovite doktora!**	zoveetey doktorah
Call an ambulance!	**Zovite hitnu pomoć!**	zoveetey heetnoo pomoch
Call the police!	**Zovite policiju!**	zoveetey poleetseeyoo
Call the fire brigade!	**Zovite vatrogasce!**	zoveetey vatrohgastsay
Where is the nearest telephone?	**Gdje je najbliži telefon?**	gdyey yey n-igh-bleezhee telefon
Where is the nearest hospital?	**Gdje je najbliža bolnica?**	gdyey yey n-igh-bleezhah bolnitsa

Communication Essentials

Yes	**da**	dah
No	**ne**	ney
Please	**molim vas**	moleem vas
Thank you	**hvala**	hvahlah
Excuse me	**oprostite**	oprosteety
Hello	**dobar dan**	dobar dan
Goodbye	**dovidenja**	doveedjenya
Good night	**laku noc**	lakoo noch
Morning	**jutro**	yootroh
Afternoon	**popodne**	popodney
Evening	**večer**	vecher
Yesterday	**jučer**	yoocher
Today	**danas**	danas
Tomorrow	**sutra**	sootrah
Here	**tu**	too
There	**tamo**	tahmoh
What?	**što?**	shtoh
When?	**kada?**	kada
Why?	**zašto?**	zashtoh
Where?	**gdje?**	gdyey

Useful Phrases

How are you?	**Kako ste?**	kakoh stey
Very well, thank you	**Dobro, hvala**	dobroh, hvahlah
Pleased to meet you	**Drago mi je!**	dragoh mee yey
See you soon	**Vidimo se**	veedeemoh sey
That's fine	**U redu**	oo redoo
Where is/are...?	**Gdje je/ su?**	gdyey yey/ soo
How far is it to...?	**Koliko je daleko do...?**	kolikoh yey dalekoh doh...
How can I get to...?	**Kako mogu doći do...?**	kakoh mogoo dochee doh...
Do you speak English?	**Govorite li engleski?**	govoreetey lee engleskee
I don't understand	**Ne razumijem**	nay razoomeeyem
Could you speak more slowly please?	**Molim vas, možete li govoriti sporije?**	moleem vas, mozhetey lee govoreetee sporiyey
I'm sorry	**Žao mi je**	zhaoh mee yey

Useful Words

big	**veliko**	veleekoh
small	**malo**	mahloh
hot	**vruć**	vrooch
cold	**hladan**	hlahdan
good	**dobar**	dobar
bad	**loš**	losh
enough	**dosta**	dostah
well	**dobro**	dobroh
open	**otvoreno**	otvohrenoh
closed	**zatvoreno**	zatvohrenoh
left	**lijevo**	leeyevoh
right	**desno**	desnoh
straight on	**ravno**	ravnoh
near	**blizu**	bleezoo
far	**daleko**	dalekoh
up	**gore**	gorey
down	**dolje**	dolyey
early	**rano**	ranoh
late	**kasno**	kasnoh
entrance	**ulaz**	oolaz
exit	**izlaz**	eezlaz
toilet	**WC**	Vey tsey
more	**više**	veeshey
less	**manje**	manyey

Shopping

How much does this cost?	**Koliko ovo košta?**	kolikoh ovoh koshta
I would like...	**Volio bih...**	volioh bee...
Do you have...?	**Imate li...?**	eematey lee...
I'm just looking	**Samo gledam**	Samoh gledam
Do you take credit cards?	**Primate li kreditne kartice?**	preematey lee credeetney carteetsey
What time do you open?	**Kad otvarate?**	kad otvaratey
What time do you close?	**Kad zatvarate?**	kad zatvaratey
This one	**Ovaj**	ov-igh
That one	**Onaj**	on-igh
expensive	**skupo**	skoopoh
cheap	**jeftino**	yefteenoh
size (clothes)	**veličina**	veleechinah
size (shoes)	**broj**	broy
white	**bijelo**	beeyeloh
black	**crno**	tsrnoh
red	**crveno**	tsrvenoh
yellow	**žuto**	zhootoh
green	**zeleno**	zelenoh
blue	**plavo**	plavoh
bakery	**pekara**	pekarah
bank	**banka**	bankah
book shop	**knjižara**	knyeezharah
butcher's	**mesnica**	mesnitsah
cake shop	**slastičarna**	slasteecharnah
chemist's	**apoteka**	apohtekah
fishmonger's	**ribarnica**	reebarnitsah
market	**tržnica**	trzhneetsah
hairdresser's	**frizer**	freezer
newsagent's/ tobacconist	**trafika**	trafeekah
post office	**pošta**	poshtah
shoe shop	**prodavaonica cipela**	prodavaonitsa tseepelah
supermarket	**supermarket**	soopermarket
travel agent	**putnička agencija**	pootneechka agentseeyah

Sightseeing

art gallery	**galerija umjetnina**	galereeyah oomyetneenah
cathedral	**katedrala**	katedralah
church	**crkva**	tsrkvah
garden	**vrt**	vurt
library	**knjižnica**	knyeezhneetsah
museum	**muzej**	moozey
tourist information centre	**turistički ured**	tooreesteechkey oored
town hall	**gradska vijećnica**	gradskah veeyechneetsa
closed for holiday	**zatvoreno zbog praznika**	zatvorenoh zbog praznekah
bus station	**autobusni kolodvor**	aootoboosnee kolodvor
railway station	**željeznički kolodvor**	zhelyeznichkih kolodvor

Staying in a Hotel

Do you have a vacant room?	**Imate li sobu?**	eematey lee soboo
double room	**dvokrevetna soba**	dvokrevetnah sobah
single room	**jednokrevetna soba**	yednokrevetnah sobah
room with a bath	**soba sa kupatilom**	sobah sah koopateelom
shower	**tuš**	toosh

porter	**portir**	**por**tir
key	**ključ**	klyooch
I have a reservation	**Imam**	**ee**mam
	rezervaciju	rezervatseeyoo

Eating Out

Have you got a table for…?	**Imate li stol za…?**	**ee**matey lee stol zah
I want to reserve a table	**Želim** **rezervirati stol**	**Zhel**eem rezerv**ee**ratee stol
The bill please	**Molim vas, račun**	**mol**eem vas, **ra**choon
I am a vegetarian	**Ja sam** **vegeterijanac**	yah sam veget**ee**re**ya**nats
waiter/waitress	**konobar/** **konobarica**	**kon**obar/ kono**bar**itsah
menu	**jelovnik**	**ye**lovneck
wine list	**vinska karta**	**veen**skah kartah
glass	**čaša**	**cha**shah
bottle	**boca**	**bot**sah
knife	**nož**	nozh
fork	**viljuška**	vee**lyoosh**kah
spoon	**žlica**	**zhlee**tsah
breakfast	**doručak**	**do**roochak
lunch	**ručak**	**roo**chak
dinner	**večera**	**vech**erah
main course	**glavno jelo**	**glav**noh **ye**loh
starters	**predjela**	**pred**yelah

Menu Decoder

bijela riba	be**cye**lah **ree**bah	"white" fish
blitva	**bleet**vah	Swiss chard
brudet	**broo**det	fish stew
čevapčići	che**vap**cheechee	meatballs
crni rižot	**tsr**nee **ree**zhot	black risotto (prepared with cuttlefish ink)
desert	des**ert**	dessert
glavno jelo	**glav**noh **ye**loh	main course
grah	grah	beans
gulaš	**goo**lash	goulash
jastog	**yas**tog	lobster
juha	**yoo**hah	soup
kuhano	**koo**hanoh	cooked
maslinovo ulje	**mas**leenovoh **oo**lyey	olive oil
meso na žaru	**mes**oh nah **zhar**oo	barbecued meat
miješano meso	mee**ye**shanoh **mes**oh	mixed grilled meats
na žaru	nah **zhar**oo	barbecued
ocat	**ot**sat	vinegar
palačinke	pala**cheen**kay	pancakes
papar	**pap**ar	pepper
paški sir	**pash**kih seer	sheep's cheese from Pag
pečeno	**pech**enoh	baked
piletina	pee**let**eenah	chicken
plava riba	**plav**ah **ree**bah	"blue" fish
predjelo	**pred**yeloh	starters
prilog	**pree**log	side dish
pršut	**prsh**oot	smoked ham
pržene lignje	**przh**ene **leeg**nyey	fried squid
prženo	**przh**enoh	fried
ramsteak	**ram**steyk	rump steak
ražnjići	**razh**nyeechee	pork kebabs
riba na žaru	**ree**bah nah **zhar**oo	barbecued fish
rižot frutti di mare	**ree**zhot **froot**ee dee **mar**cy	seafood risotto
rižot sa škampima	**ree**zhot sah **shkam**peemah	scampi risotto
salata	**sal**atah	salad
salata od hobotnice	**sal**atah od hobot**neet**sey	octopus salad
sarma	**sar**mah	cabbage leaves
sir	seer	cheese
sladoled	**slad**oled	ice cream
slana srdela	**slan**ah **srd**elah	salted sardines
škampi na buzaru	**shkam**pee nah **boo**zaroo	scampi in tomato and onion
školjke na buzaru	**shkol**kay nah **boo**zaroo	shellfish in tomato and onion

špageti frutti di mare	shp**ag**etee **froot**ee dee **mar**cy	spaghetti with seafood
sol	sol	salt
tjestenina	tjeste**neen**ah	pasta stuffed with meat and rice
ulje	**oo**lyey	oil
varivo	**var**eevoh	boiled vegetables

Drinks

bijelo vino	be**cye**loh **veen**oh	white wine
čaj	ch-igh	tea
crno vino	**tsr**noh **veen**oh	red wine
gazirana mineralna voda	gaz**ee**ranah mee**ner**alnah **vod**ah	sparkling mineral water
kava	**kav**ah	coffee
negazirana mineralna voda	**ney**gaze**ran**ah mee**ner**alnah **vod**ah	still mineral water
pivo	**peev**oh	beer
rakija	**rak**eeyah	spirit
tamno pivo	**tam**noh **peev**oh	stout (dark beer)
travarica	**trav**areetsah	spirit flavoured with herbs
voda	**vod**ah	water

Numbers

0	**nula**	**noo**lah
1	**jedan**	**ye**dan
2	**dva**	dvah
3	**tri**	tree
4	**četiri**	**chet**eeree
5	**pet**	pet
6	**šest**	shest
7	**sedam**	**se**dam
8	**osam**	**os**am
9	**devet**	**dev**et
10	**deset**	**des**et
11	**jedanaest**	**ye**danest
12	**dvanaest**	**dvah**nest
13	**trinaest**	**tree**nest
14	**četrnaest**	**chet**rnest
15	**petnaest**	**pet**nest
16	**šestnaest**	**shest**nest
17	**sedamnaest**	**se**damnest
18	**osamnaest**	**os**amnest
19	**devetnaest**	**dev**etnest
20	**dvadeset**	**dvah**deset
21	**dvadeset i jedan**	**dvah**deset ee **ye**dan
22	**dvadeset i dva**	**dvah**deset ee **dvah**
30	**trideset**	**tree**deset
31	**trideset i jedan**	**tree**deset ee **ye**dan
40	**četrdeset**	**chet**rdeset
50	**pedeset**	**ped**eset
60	**šezdeset**	**shez**deset
70	**sedamdeset**	**se**damdeset
80	**osamdeset**	**os**amdeset
90	**devedeset**	**dev**edeset
100	**sto**	stoh
101	**sto i jedan**	stoh ee **ye**dan
102	**sto i dva**	stoh ee **dvah**
200	**dvjesto**	**dvee**stoh
500	**petsto**	**pet**stoh
700	**sedamsto**	**se**damstoh
900	**devetsto**	**dev**etstoh
1,000	**tisuću**	**tee**soochoo
1,001	**tisuću i jedan**	**tee**soochoo ee **ye**dan

Time

One minute	**jedan minuta**	**ye**dan mee**noo**tah
One hour	**jedan sat**	**ye**dan saht
Half an hour	**pola sata**	**pol**ah sahtah
Monday	**ponedjeljak**	pon**ed**yelyak
Tuesday	**utorak**	**oo**torak
Wednesday	**srijeda**	**sree**jedah
Thursday	**četvrtak**	**chet**vrtak
Friday	**petak**	**pet**ak
Saturday	**subota**	**soo**botah
Sunday	**nedjelja**	**ned**yelyah

Road Map of Croatia

ITALY

SLOVENIA

ZAGRE

CENTRAL CROATIA

ISTRIA

KVARNER AREA

ADRIATIC

SEA

ITALY

Risnjak National Park

Plitvice Lakes National Park

Paklenica National Park

Brijuni National Park

Kornati National Park

Krka National Park

Venice

Limski Channel

Trieste

Umag
Buje
Novigrad
Poreč
Vrsar
Rovinj
Bale
Fažana
Pula
Vodnjan
Barban
Svetvinčenat
Labin
Plomin
Picán
Gračišće
Pazin
Boljum
Motovun
Hum
Roc
Dragu
Buzet
Kastav
Opatija
Lovran
Mošćenice
Porozin
Omišalj
Malinska
Krk
Baška
Cres
Plavnik
Grgur
Lopan
Goli
Rab
Miśnjak
Zeča
Unije
Srakane
Susak
Susak
Veli Lošinj
Mali Lošinj
Ilovik
Silba
Premuda
Ist
Škarda
Olib
Molat
Sestrunj
Božava
Dugi Otok
Sali
Kornat
Piškera
Lavsa
Žut
Žirje
Kaprije
Zlarin
Svetac
Biševo
Vis

Rijeka
Bakar
Kraljevica
Crikvenica
Novi Vinodolski
Senj
Jablanac
Karlobag
Pag
Nin
Zadar
Posedarje
Ugljan
Pašman
Biograd Na Moru
Benkovac
Šibenik
Primošten
Marina

Delnice
Jasenak
Ogulin
Otočac
Gospić
Lički Osik
Doljani
Otri

Karlovac
Duga Resa
Topusko Toplice
Velika Kladusa
Slunj
Glina
Petrinja

Ozalj
Jastrebarsko
Samobor
Okić
Kerestinec
Brezovica
Velika Gorica
Zaprešić
Zagreb
Ladu
Sesvete

Rogaska Slatina
Trakošćan
Vinica
Krapina
Poglava
Veliki Tabor
Vinagora
Pregrada
Lobor
Belec
Kumrovec
Tuhelisk
Krapinske Toplice
Bedekovčina
Klanjec
Stubičke Toplice
Bist
Ma

Ancona
Pescara

SLOVENIA
Sava

0 kilometres 50
0 miles 50